P9-DDV-533

Cooking
Know-How

Be a Better Cook with Hundreds of
Easy Techniques, Step-by-Step Photos,
and Ideas for Over 500 Great Meals

Cooking Know-How

Bruce Weinstein & Mark Scarbrough

Photography by Lucy Schaeffer

JOHN WILEY & SONS, INC.

This book is printed on acid-free paper. ∞

Copyright © 2009 Bruce Weinstein and Mark Scarbrough

Photography Copyright © 2008 Lucy Schaeffer
Book design by Cassandra J. Pappas

Published by John Wiley & Sons, Inc., Hoboken, New Jersey
Published simultaneously in Canada

No part of this publication may be reproduced, stored in a retrieval system, or transmitted in any form or by any means, electronic, mechanical, photocopying, recording, scanning, or otherwise, except as permitted under Section 107 or 108 of the 1976 United States Copyright Act, without either the prior written permission of the Publisher, or authorization through payment of the appropriate per-copy fee to the Copyright Clearance Center, Inc., 222 Rosewood Drive, Danvers, MA 01923, (978) 750-8400, fax (978) 750-4470, or on the web at www.copyright.com. Requests to the Publisher for permission should be addressed to the Permissions Department, John Wiley & Sons, Inc., 111 River Street, Hoboken, NJ 07030, (201) 748-6011, fax (201) 748-6008, or online at http://www.wiley.com/go/permissions.

Limit of Liability/Disclaimer of Warranty: While the publisher and author have used their best efforts in preparing this book, they make no representations or warranties with respect to the accuracy or completeness of the contents of this book and specifically disclaim any implied warranties of merchantability or fitness for a particular purpose. No warranty may be created or extended by sales representatives or written sales materials. The advice and strategies contained herein may not be suitable for your situation. You should consult with a professional where appropriate. Neither the publisher nor author shall be liable for any loss of profit or any other commercial damages, including but not limited to special, incidental, consequential, or other damages.

For general information on our other products and services or for technical support, please contact our Customer Care Department within the United States at (800) 762-2974, outside the United States at (317) 572-3993 or fax (317) 572-4002.

Wiley also publishes its books in a variety of electronic formats. Some content that appears in print may not be available in electronic books. For more information about Wiley products, visit our web site at www.wiley.com.

Library of Congress Cataloging-in-Publication Data
Weinstein, Bruce, 1960-
    Cooking know-how : be a better cook with hundreds of easy techniques, step-by-step photos, and ideas for over 500 great meals / Bruce Weinstein and Mark Scarbrough ; photography by Lucy Schaeffer.
        p. cm.
    Includes index.
    ISBN 978-0-470-18080-8 (cloth)
1. Cookery. 2. Cookery, International. I. Scarbrough, Mark. II. Title.
    TX651.W35 2009
    641.5--dc22   2008044375

Printed in China

10 9 8 7 6 5 4 3 2 1

The Pedigree of Honey
Does not concern the Bee—
A Clover, any time, to him,
Is Aristocracy—

—EMILY DICKINSON (1830–1886)

Contents

Acknowledgments

A published book is the voice of a multitude.

It's hard—no, impossible to underestimate the contribution our editor, Justin Schwartz, has made to this book. Together, we hashed out recipes, concepts, design, photography, and layout. We even worked together on an article for *Fine Cooking*, way back in 2001, an article that got us thinking about this larger project. In the end, Justin's touch is everywhere and this book's the better for it.

And while we're on the subject of John Wiley & Sons' excellent work on the book, we must thank Jacqueline Beach who kept the book on track through production, Suzanne Sunwoo for her work on the cover design, and Cassandra Pappas for the beautiful interior layout. Sara Newberry kept the book hale and healthy with terrific copyediting, as did Lilian Brady with meticulous proofreading, and Gypsy Lovett has worked tirelessly on its publicity.

We've wanted to write this book for years; only a cracker-jack agent like Susan Ginsburg at Writers House could get it done in the face of contractual details and legal not-so-niceties. No wonder Susan has cheered and steered our career through 18 books over the past 12 years, surely something of a record in publishing these days.

We also owe a debt to Emily Saladino, now gone from Writers House and ensconced somewhere in the wind chamber of PR. She effortlessly made sure that two writers were not in a complete tizzy over their contracts. Her shoes are now filled by Bethany Strout, no less a calming voice.

Beth Shepard of Beth Shepard Communications has tirelessly worked to forge our partnerships with the California Milk Advisory Board, the U.S. Potato Board, Smucker's, JIF, and other brands. This work has continually kept our own writing and cooking grounded in the real world of dinner-on-the-table-at-six.

Two weeks? When we found out that the photo shoot would invade our house for that long, we almost fainted. But we've rarely had more fun, mostly because of Lucy Schaeffer, a terrifically talented photographer, and her irresistible assistant, Nishe

Sondhe. And no curried Collie ears, to boot.

A book like this one can only be written on the sturdy backs of others—among them, Harold McGee's *On Food and Cooking: The Science and Lore of the Kitchen*, Jacques Pepin's *La Technique*, Shirley Corriher's *Cookwise: The Secrets of Cooking Revealed*, Julia Child, Simone Beck, and Louisette Bertholle's *Mastering the Art of French Cooking*, Chris Schlesinger and John Willoughby's *How to Cook Meat*, James Peterson's *Fish and Shellfish*, Maya Kaimal's *Savoring the Spice Coast of India*, Ken Hom's *Asian Ingredients: A Guide with Recipes*, Deh-Ta Hsiung and Nina Simonds' *The Food of China*, and the late Sharon Tyler Herbst's *The New Food Lover's Tiptionary*. Our debts are legion.

What's more, a book like this one can't be written without the help of our many testers. Dale Brown of Meadow Vista, California, did the lion's share of the work: She is diligent, patient, and always right. Two voices from Los Altos, California, were invaluable: Daryl Shafran's comments proved profound and stealthily prompted a global rewrite; Amy Kull's careful reading caught many a seemingly picayune problem. Julie Weinstein in San Carlos, California, made sure we didn't mistake a can of chipotles for a canned chipotle. New York City's Katie Kehrig made some last-minute suggestions in both wording and content— and so molded the book in the significant ways only the details afford. And Suzie and Larry Hukill in Oklahoma City, always exceptionally helpful, suggested terrific changes to their parts of the book.

We owe deep gratitude to Kim Roman at Digitas and more importantly, to her client: KitchenAid. Their appliances have created this book (along with an Apple MacBook). Our unfettered bow, too, to Jeffrey Elliot at Zwilling J. A. Henckels for perfect-in-the-hand knives; to Melanie Tennant and Melissa Palmer at All-Clad Metalcrafters for spectacular pots and pans; and to Gretchen Holt and Charlotte Pinelli at OXO International. All this cookware is featured straight from our kitchen in these photos.

We also wish to thank Dave Durian and his WBAL morning team, including the hyper-professional Malarie Pinkard. Who knew one drive-time radio segment a week could produce so many emails?

Much thanks to the knitting group at Sit-N-Knit in Bloomfield, Connecticut, who endured endless rounds of recipe testing— and to owners Barbara and Richard Fabian for allowing us to bring in all the food. Also thanks to Chef Chris Prosperi and Courtney Febbroriello at MetroBis in Simsbury, Connecticut, who provided us with so many meals when we were too tired to cook.

Although we've now left Manhattan for the trees, air, and light in Litchfield county, Connecticut, we'd be nowhere without our friends and families whose love and goodwill inform every recipe. They taste, they comment, they laugh—some even spend the night. Our lives are fuller. Our stomachs, too.

Introduction

GIVE A MAN SOMETHING FOR DINNER AND HE'LL BE HAPPY. Teach him how to make dinner and you'll be even happier.

Nonetheless, knowing how to cook has challenged lots of men. Women, too. What most people learn is a specific recipe: how to make this pasta sauce or that loaf of bread. What about learning how to cook in general? And not just the "how" but the "how come?" *That* requires a technique book.

Unfortunately, most turn inordinately cheffy, a take-cover barrage of chopped chervil, de-inked squid, and 18% gluten pastry flour, all whacked together with knife-fu and a battalion of kitchen underlings. Chefs may well be the masters of culinary technique, but to cook like a chef is not to cook at home. Chefs parboil, partially roast, make a sauce separately, assemble, and finish off at the last minute—all of which is anathema to dinner on Wednesday night.

What's more, most chefs don't read recipes. Nor should they. Carpenters don't watch home-improvement shows. Cooking is art, innovation. So how does a person learn cooking techniques without warming trays, speed racks, and a host of other professional equipment, not to mention the time to make fifteen components for a single dish?

Here's the truth: you don't have to become a chef to cook well at home. In fact, you've been doing it for years. You don't necessarily take down a cookbook to make breakfast because, chances are, you already know what to do.

The good news is that you can be that free in the kitchen the rest of the day, too.

The bad news? It's not just those cheffy techniques that undercut learning how to cook. It's also the sticky-sweet romanticism that clings to food writing in general. "Wander the stalls at your market," we food writers wax, "and find what's in season for dinner tonight." It's become culinary cliché, more food porn than dinner on the table.

Truth be told, most of us can't. Not because we don't want to. But because most cookbooks work, to steal Emily Dickinson's word, "oppositely." Yes, it's superb to cook fresh, to cook in season—all in all, a worthy goal. But dinner is easier if you choose a recipe first, *then* make out a shopping list, gather the ingredients, and line up the equipment.

Still, that notion of cooking fresh from the market sounds pretty good. Just the other day, we spotted some wild ramps at a farm stand near us in Litchfield county, Connecticut. We snapped them up, brought them home, and then wondered how others prepared them. An hour later, cookbooks all over the counters, we gave up. Oops, no fresh rosemary in the house, no shallot marmalade, no pancetta. Had we only known! So we simply sautéed them in olive oil with red pepper flakes. In other words, we used our cooking know-how.

You can, too. Armed with the knowledge of the simple mechanics of a dish, the five or so steps it takes to make it, you can walk into the market, find what's fresh (or on special), bring it home, and have dinner on the table without any worries, any overly romantic pretensions, or any pile of cookbooks on the counter: fresh every time—and your way, too. No de-inked squid or fretty chervil—unless you like those things.

And if you like them, you should use them. We've spent a career giving people choices; our recipes are always followed by loads of variations. If you can make great chocolate gelato, you can make myriad other chocolate variations, all to your taste: chocolate walnut, chocolate marshmallow, double chocolate chunk, and so on. Most people mix it up anyway. Even the two of us, dyed-in-the-wool foodies, don't have the same preferences. One is all butter; the other, olive oil. One has loved fish all his life; the other, only recently. One is pecans; the other, walnuts. You get the picture. We negotiate dinner, making it up as we go along, because we've learned not only what to do but how to do it.

COOKING, JUST COOKING

What you'll find in this book is an alphabetical list of recipe-driven, technique-centered explications that build out into hundreds of dishes. Let's take Vindaloo (page 395). There are five steps: 1) heat the oil, 2) cook the vegetables, 3) stir in the vindaloo paste, 4) sear the meat, and 5) pour in the liquid for braising. Once you've got those down, you can make any vindaloo—shrimp and peppers, lamb and artichokes, chicken and spring vegetables—because you've mastered the techniques of 1) building a spice paste, 2) searing meat, and 3) being patient (otherwise known as braising).

Cooking Know-How is about why you have saucepans, skillets, a Dutch oven, and a roasting pan. This is not a grilling book. Nor a baking one. Yes, there are some sidebars about things like perfect mashed potatoes (page 21); but *Cooking Know-How* is a book of main courses, of general cooking rules, of good techniques.

Which means it's a book of "howevers." Almost every culinary rule can be followed up with a qualifier, a "that said"—because cooking is a matter of taste, personal as well as sensory. It's often been said that there's no "we" in the kitchen; there's just you and your skillet, not a crowd of people making any one dish. Nor should there be. So we give our thoughts, our expertise—but at the cost of "OK, but. . . ." If you do something interesting, different, or just funky, let's all hear about it. Come to www.cookingknow-how.com, write your thoughts, and tell others how you made that vindaloo, those chicken breasts, that fricassee. Your recipes—and all your "howevers"—can and should become part of the body of knowledge that is cooking know-how.

HOW TO USE COOKING KNOW-HOW

This is indeed a technique book, but one with a marked difference: the techniques are focused on and by the recipes. Thus, there's nothing in the book about sautéing per se; rather, there are sautés for chicken breasts (page 39), pork cutlets (page 33), fish fillets (page 134), and shrimp (page 319). Yes, some entries are focused on a single technique—Stir-Frying (page 371), for example. But for the most part, the question was not "how to braise," but "how to make a specific braise" like Cacciatora (page 69).

Following each technique is a chart of specific dishes, 8 or so of our choices—but by no means the end of the story. These charts are little more than ingredient lists, handy but a tad incomplete. For details, explanations, and a host of important information, look foremost at the technique itself. Any specific chart is simply worked out along the lines of the overall technique, the ingredients set into its structure.

That said, you may want to look at those specific recipes first. Choose one, make it, and see how you like it. As you do so, look back at the main explanations of the technique. Read some of the rationale while the onion softens, the chicken breasts cook. Figure out why you're doing what you're doing. Think about how to morph this to your taste. You don't like tarragon? Don't use it. What about thyme, parsley, oregano, or rosemary?

Keep reading. The book builds on itself. There's a discussion of various sweet and savory roots and hard vegetables on page 20, then there's a discussion of the whats and wherefores of basic aromatics like onions, shallots, and scallions on page 40. Gather more information, more ideas—and keep cooking, too. Then finally step away from the book. By now, you know how to make a stir-fry, a biryani, a pasta in cream sauce. So create your own. Get out a sheet of paper and write down your own ingredients that would fit in the chart. Experiment, go nuts, have fun.

But while you're making your own version of these techniques, always hold the ideal—that is, the basic technique itself—in mind. If it says to add ½ cup flour and you add sugar, you'll end up with junk. If it says to use chopped dried fruit and you use, for heaven's sake, a sliced parsnip, you'll end up with a strange dish indeed.

Also, follow basic kitchen rules. Stir, whisk, fold, keep your eye on things. Most importantly, start prepared. Cooking is indeed a journey—but not so much a Zen one, more like a family vacation. If you don't know where you're headed, you might end up at one of those nasty treeless interstate picnic tables. Have the ingredients cut up and on the counter. Have at hand the right utensils, pans and such, as well as sharp knives and a cutting board. Ever wonder why your favorite TV food personality is able to pull off a meal in minutes? He or she isn't fishing in the pantry for a forgotten ingredient or piece of equipment. (Well, that and good video editing—but that's another story.)

EIGHT NOTES BEFORE YOU START

1. Serves how many?

Since we're not giving nutritional information (an impossible task, what with all the possible permutations in each recipe), our serving sizes are a rough guess. We're two big eaters, always ready for a meal; our "serves 6" may well be your "serves 8," especially for soups and stews. Yes, in a quick skillet sauté with four chicken breasts, the dish clearly serves four. But otherwise, look through the ingredients and determine the proportions. There's nothing wrong with leftovers. Lunch from the fridge is comfort indeed.

2. Herbs

Our assumption throughout is mostly for fresh herbs, stated as "prepped" ingredients (in culinary parlance, "already prepared"): 1 tablespoon minced oregano, for example. If the amount needed is for a dried herb, it's so stated. Do we think people always use fresh? Do we ourselves? No. Growing up in the '60s, we never saw a fresh herb; bottles ruled the kitchen from their spice racks. But these days, fresh herbs are widely available and not just in gourmet markets. If in fact you substitute dried for fresh, use about half the stated amount. If you use ground herbs, use a quarter of the stated amount for fresh, half of that for dried. And by the way, those amounts are stated in recipe shorthand: "tsp" for teaspoon and "Tbs" for tablespoon.

3. Read the technique's steps as well as their explications

Not everything that's stated in the steps for a specific technique is again repeated in the explications. For example, if the step says to "season the meat with salt and freshly ground pepper," those instructions are probably not repeated in the text that follows—on the faith that you've indeed salted and peppered said meat.

4. Recipe convention

Thank goodness for Fannie Farmer. She standardized the American recipe: no more "2-cents sugar" or "a large tea cup of flour." Instead, we now use regulation tablespoons and teaspoons. But curses to her, too, because her style has become gospel. This is an unconventional cookbook; some of those time-tested conventions are broken, mostly because we have to. For example, Farmer-standardized recipes almost always list ingredients for any given step in order of volume and/or weight, highest to lowest. We break the rule sometimes because the narrative technique may call for "herbs and salt"—and then in the charted recipe, that works out to "1 teaspoon stemmed thyme and 2 teaspoons salt" and thus not in order of decreasing volume within the step. We think you can take it in stride. If not, may we suggest using the wine for more than cooking?

5. The recipe charts

They're in dialogue with the technique discussions. Sounds high-falutin', but the charts expand, morph, and (rarely) contradict the stated technique, thus furthering the argument for how it all works. Look, there's really no one way to make a fricassee. Instead, there's a basic technique that gets mixed up in practice. Thus, the recipe technique is often restated and refined—and rarely varied—in the recipe chart that follows. However, you shouldn't necessarily run to the charts as the recipes. Think of them as a way to think through the technique as a whole. Everything's a process and in process. So neither the charts nor the techniques form the whole discussion in and of themselves. Those recipes in the charts can and should be varied, particularly in your own kitchen to suit your own tastes.

6. The ingredient amounts

Although the amounts of the fresh ingredients in the techniques are first stated in generalized volumes (for example, 6 to 8 cups roughly chopped vegetables), those amounts in the recipe charts are then stated in supermarket equivalents, the way most of us find fresh ingredients at the store (for example, 3 medium sweet potatoes, peeled and roughly chopped; 2 medium carrots, peeled and sliced; and 6 ounces snow peas, chopped). That first demarcation is the theory; the second one, the grocery list, the way you would shop. Beef, chicken, and other proteins are usually stated in pounds, whether ½ pound or 4 pounds; large vegetables are stated mostly as whole equivalents like 1 large turnip, peeled and sliced, or 2 medium yellow-fleshed potatoes. Smaller vegetables, however, are stated in ounces: 10 ounces cremini mushrooms or 6 ounces snow peas. (Just to be clear, 16 ounces = 1 pound, 8 ounces = ½ pound, and 4 ounces = ¼ pound.) The one exception? Some large vegetables are stated in volume amounts, particularly if the whole of it is not used: for example, 1 cup cored and shredded Napa cabbage. That said, unless otherwise stated, all ingredients in the charts are for the whole ingredient itself: a medium minced scallion is the whole thing, not just the bulb; an apple is unpeeled unless otherwise stated.

7. Sauces

Although this is a book of techniques, there is no recipe for a classic sauce—except for Marinara (technically a sauce, but also a main dish when pasta is added—see page 179). Every other recipe makes whole dishes, sauce included, with few extra steps and very little waste. Always ladle the broth or pan sauce over the protein; don't waste a drop, even in dishes like Mussels (page 201) or Vindaloo (page 395). If the dish looks soupy or saucy, use bowls, not plates. The only exceptions? Don't ladle up a liquid used for steaming, such as that for the Steamed Whole Fish (page 359) or Steam-Roasted Stuffed Duck or Goose (page 365); and throw out the brine used for the Boneless Skinless Chicken Breasts with a Pan Sauce (page 39).

8. High-altitude cooking

These recipes were developed for sea-level cookery. Although we live at one of the highest points in Connecticut, 1,300 feet above sea level hardly qualifies as a cooking dilemma. That said, water loses 1°F off its boiling point every 540 feet above sea level. At our house, water boils a little under 210°F, not at 212°F, a negligible but recordable difference; but in Parker, Colorado, water boils at about 201°F, a more noticeable difference with a dramatic impact on cooking. It's all physics—air pressure lessens at higher altitudes because there's less atmosphere pressing down on you from above—but suffice it to say that you need to braise and sauté meats longer at higher altitudes, perhaps as much as 25% longer at 5,000 feet and above. That's only a few extra minutes for a 15-minute sauté but 30 or 40 minutes for a complicated braise. You'll also need heavy-duty cookware and tight-fitting lids so the liquid doesn't boil away since it's boiling longer before the meat itself comes to the right temperature. Thus, consider increasing the liquid by perhaps 10%. In addition, you must adjust the temperature of the oil when you fry (see page 238). Reduce the required temperature 3°F for every 1,000 feet in elevation. For roasting, simply go by the internal temperature as recorded on an instant-read meat thermometer—the roasted meat itself should adhere basically to the stated timings. For a more complete run-down of the issue, see the USDA's excellent pages on "high-altitude cooking and food safety" at their Web site: www.usda.gov.

WE COOK BECAUSE WE CAN

All of us work in repetitive jobs: the same faces, phone calls, and meetings, not to mention Bob with his bad puns in the next office. Or perhaps we're lucky enough to be retired and away from Bob—or we've chosen to stay home with the kids.

No matter our situation, we face the incessant repetition of the modern age. We need outlets for creativity; we need to stretch our fingers and make something. And cooking is, in its essence, creating.

At the end of the day, that's the best news we cookbook writers have: To cook is both to create and to live. So set yourself free in the kitchen—once you've got some cooking know-how.

A bowl of Persian-inspired Bean Soup

Bean Soup

A doldrums-chaser if there ever was one, this economical soup is also surprisingly easy. Yes, there's the time invested to soak the beans, but the soup really doesn't take much effort beyond that. Once it's at a simmer, there's nothing to do except wait for the beans to get tender. • MAKES 6 TO 8 SERVINGS

• **STEP 1** Set 2 cups dried beans in a very large bowl, cover with lukewarm tap water to a depth of 3 inches, and soak for 8 hours or overnight.

Shopping for and storing dried beans

A North American staple for millennia, beans are dried for long storage, a sure way to get a nutritious meal in winter. Unfortunately, beans, even in their static state, do age, especially in humid climates where their moisture content fluctuates daily. At the market, look for plump, dried beans without withered, rippled skins, a sign they've been sitting on the shelf too long.

At home, toss out any discolored or chipped beans; forgo any with tiny holes, a sign of bugs. Those bought in bulk may need to be picked over for small stones: spread the beans on a lipped baking sheet and pick through them to remove any tiny pebbles.

High temperatures and/or high humidity morph dried beans into little stones nigh impossible to tenderize. Store beans in an air-tight container in a cool, dry place for up to 1 year. Or better yet, freeze them for several years. In any event, keep purchased packages separate. Beans continue to age at home, even under the best of conditions. Separating packets by the date of purchase helps assure even cooking times.

Almost any dried bean you can find in North America will work for this technique: white, kidney, pinto, great northern, or even black-eyed peas. (For split peas, see the box on page 12.) However, all dried beans are not created equal. When you select beans for soup, realize that they have different cooking times, depending on their moisture and starch content. Once soaked, the cooking times for the various varietals fall into this rough schema:

About 1½ hours: black-eyed peas and cowpeas, as well as adzuki, kidney, lima, or navy beans
About 2 hours: black, white, cannellini, anasazi, or great northern beans
About 2½ hours: pinto or cranberry beans
About 3 hours: chickpeas or soy beans

Thus, if you want to work with a mix of various kinds of dried beans in a soup—a three-bean soup, for example—choose those

An unsoaked bean (left) leads to longer cooking times and (worse yet) mushy beans in the soup. The soaked bean (right) has plumped dramatically, its cells rehydrated and ready for the heat.

with similar cooking times. If you cook navy beans with pintos, the navies will be mush, the pintos barely soft. Variety is not worth that compromise.

Soaking dried beans—or not

Dried beans should be rehydrated before being cooked. Soaked, they expand dramatically; give them lots of water in a large bowl. And lukewarm water at that, about like a baby's bath, which gives them a head-start on getting their hulls softened. Any beans that float should be nixed—they're either desiccated or have been picked while immature.

But let's say you're craving bean soup and it's 3:30 pm. (It could happen.) Here are five ways to circumvent the hours-long soaking:

1. **Packaged quick-cooking beans.** A modern convenience, these have been pressure-soaked just to avoid this step. However, their texture is compromised; they are a bit squishy and without much tooth.
2. **Parboiled dried beans.** Put standard dried beans in a large saucepan, cover with hot water to a depth of 2 inches, and bring to a boil over medium-high heat, stirring occasionally. Boil for 2 minutes, then cover and set off the heat for 1 hour. The beans are now ready to be cooked.
3. **Salt the soaking water.** Adding 2 teaspoons salt to every quart (4 cups) water will decrease the *cooking* time by perhaps 30 minutes, the sodium switching out for magnesium in the hulls' cells, thus allowing for quicker softening. However, that additional salt will also result in grainier innards, not the smooth creamy texture prized in beans, so perhaps this compromise is not the best.
4. **Lentils.** Substitute 2 cups brown or green lentils for the dried beans. Do not soak them; add them in step 4 of this technique. They will be tender in about 1 hour.
5. **Canned beans.** This last-minute solution is not a perfect one, as is the wont of shotgun weddings. Stir in 4 cups drained and rinsed canned beans in step 5 below, after the meat and vegetables have cooked about 1 hour; continue simmering for about 15 minutes.

Sociability

Most dried beans are chock full of long-chain sugars (technically, oligosaccharides). We lack an essential digestive enzyme that can break them down, so they arrive intact in our intestines where healthful micro-organisms chow down, producing that familiar gastric discomfort as a by-product. To relieve some of it:

1. Never cook beans in the water used to soak them.
2. Drain the soaked beans and rinse them well.
3. Change the soaking water at least once (unless you've used the parboil method above—in which case convenience trumps sociability).

● **STEP 2** Heat 2 to 3 tablespoons fat in a large Dutch oven or soup pot. Use a large pot for this soup, preferably 5 quarts or more. You will eventually fill it with lots of vegetables, all those soaked beans, 2 quarts liquid, and perhaps some browned meat. Everything needs room for a good swim.

Almost any fat will do, so long as you consider the soup's other ingredients—that is, the vegetables and herbs you'll add with the beans, as well as perhaps a browned lamb shank or a smoked ham hock. Neutral oils like canola and safflower don't compete with the beans' earthy flavor; but either olive or refined peanut oil is a savory and light addition.

Or wander further afield. Unsalted butter yields a gorgeous soup, particularly silky with fat, juicy beans. Untoasted nut oils (walnut, almond, etc.) offer a sophisticated accent rarely prized among the elementary-school set. Even less prized by this group but more so-phisticated is mustard seed oil, an unusually pungent fat favored in Bengali cooking and available at East Indian markets.

No matter what, avoid toasted nut and seed oils: overpowering and unnecessary.

Rinsing soaked beans helps alleviate gastric distress. It also helps keep a bean soup clearer, less cloudy.

• **STEP 3** Add and cook 4 to 5 cups chopped vegetables, stirring often, until somewhat softened or lightly browned. As is usual for stews and soups, choose vegetables that can stand up to long cook-ing: winter squash, celeriac, parsnips, carrots, mushrooms, onions, shallots, bell peppers, celery, roots, tubers like potatoes, and rhi-zomes like sweet potatoes. All should be prepped: seed, skin, and chop winter squash; peel and chop onions; peel and dice celeriac and turnips; or cut carrots and parsnips into ½-inch-thick rings.

Peruvians have been combining beans and potatoes for centuries. Potatoes add lots of vitamin C and potassium; their natural protein, added to that of the beans, makes this soup a real pick-me-up on chilly days. Peeling the potatoes is a matter of preference: take the skins off in a white bean soup for a creamier look; leave them on in a black bean soup for texture.

Steer clear of quick-cooking spring vegetables like peas, green beans, zucchini, or asparagus, as well as softer, leafy greens like escarole and spinach. However, kale and collard greens will stand up to longer cooking. Cut out the center stems and chop the leaves, then stir them into the soup about 30 minutes before you think it will be done. If you would like to add sliced zucchini to, say, minestrone (or in fact any quick-cooking vegetable to a bean soup), stir it or them in during the last 10 minutes of cooking.

One final warning: tomatoes, a lovely complement to beans, are nonetheless high in acid. Because of chemical interactions, they can retard the beans' getting tender, thereby increasing the cooking time if the beans' cell wall structure (the hemicel-lulose) becomes a bit obdurate. There are complex reasons why this may or may not happen—cooking is chemistry, after all—but suffice it to say that this hardening is a distinct possibility. That said, tomatoes—and, indeed, all acids—also help keep the individual beans stable and whole during cooking, mostly because those cellular walls become a little more obdurate and thus less likely to dissolve. So add canned or fresh tomatoes now, but know the consequences: dinner may well be late, a fine thing for two adults and a bottle of wine, but a misstep for little mouths and short attention spans.

• **STEP 4** Add the drained and rinsed beans as well as some herbs and dried spices; stir until aromatic, about 30 seconds. Before adding the beans, drain them in a colander set in the sink and rinse them with tepid water to help get rid of any last-minute bits of those gas-producing sugars that may adhere to their surfaces.

PEA SOUP

There are two ways to make pea soup from dried peas. If you're using dried split peas, skip the first step: do not soak them. With whole dried field peas, green or yellow, soak them as stated in this recipe and use them exactly as indicated. In either case, many prefer their pea soup unadulterated, with no additional vegetables except perhaps an onion and/or a sliced carrot. Finish with lemon juice.

Add two or three herbs with the drained beans: a classic combination like parsley, rosemary, and thyme; or a dried spice combo like curry powder (see page 113) or bottled jerk seasoning. Figure on between 2 tablespoons and even up to ¼ cup minced herbs or maybe as much as 1 tablespoon dried spice mix. However, pare down most dried spices like red pepper flakes, ground cinnamon, and grated nutmeg; beans are incredibly adept at carrying flavors, and most dried spices will become too present and overwhelming in the soup if added in quantities over 1 teaspoon.

Two or three bay leaves are almost always welcome. And don't forget zests: a teaspoon or so of grated orange zest with black beans is a stunning pairing; lemon zest perks up creamy white beans. Or perhaps add some thinly sliced sun-dried tomatoes (if you're not adding chopped tomatoes), chopped pitted olives, or even a splash of Worcestershire sauce. These indeed increase the soup's acidity, but not by as much as, say, several chopped tomatoes.

To make a baked bean soup, add 2 tablespoons or so molasses, a thick condiment high in acid and sugar, both of which again help beans retain their shape in long cooking but which also can retard their cooking slightly. Molasses is the primary reason baked beans can cook for several hours without losing their shape or texture.

• **STEP 5** Add about 8 cups (2 quarts) liquid and, if desired, a browned bone or hock or up to 8 ounces browned bacon, pancetta, or sausage. Bring to a full simmer, cover, reduce the heat to low, and simmer slowly until the beans are tender, from 1 to 3 hours, depending on the bean varietal (see above in step 1). Black beans take to beef broth; white beans, to chicken. But mix and match for new combinations, some lighter, some more substantial: beef broth with white beans, sliced leeks, celery, and a browned lamb shank; vegetable broth with kidney beans, shredded cabbage, and sliced carrots. But always avoid fish broth or clam juice—the flavor is simply overwhelming. And consider adding 4 cups (1 quart) broth and 4 cups (1 quart) water, particularly if any added meat is fatty or rich.

But don't add too much liquid. Most vegetables need a lot of water in the pot so that they don't knock against each other and fall apart during cooking. But beans and legumes need to concentrate their flavors during the cooking time, the various starches thickening the liquid into something like a rich sauce. In other words, less liquid is more—within reason, of course.

The same problem that applied to tomatoes and their acidity now applies to wine. Adding it can increase the cooking time by as much as 25%. If you really want the taste of wine in the soup but don't want to extend the cooking time, consider adding ¼ cup during the last 5 minutes of cooking.

If you're adding meat to the soup—and it's utterly optional—use a smoked or cured meat, some sort of sausage, or a long-cooking cut that's mostly bone like a ham hock. Try adding grilled whole sausages like Italian milds or kielbasa (casings on), or even pan-seared tofu brats. Or try chopped bacon, prosciutto, or pancetta. Smoked or dried meats can be added straight to the pot: Spanish mild chorizo, smoked hocks, a smoked turkey leg, or even cubed smoked tofu. Cured meats should be browned first to help caramelize their sugars and greatly improve their taste—thus, chopped bacon and the like should be cooked until crunchy in a skillet with a little oil over medium heat. For exceptionally long-cooking beans, consider adding a lamb shank, well browned in a skillet with some oil; or even marrow bones roasted on a lipped baking sheet in a preheated 400°F oven until lightly browned.

The meat on well-cooked ham hocks, lamb shanks, and other rich, bone-in cuts is easily shredded with two forks before it's stirred back into the soup.

With everything in the pot, many cooks now begin all sorts of unnecessary, inexplicable culinary contortions to avoid boil-overs and foam. Slow and steady: that's the ticket. Yes, some scum may bubble up: skim the pot once or twice. Setting the lid slightly ajar may also cut down on overspills during the first 30 minutes. But the only real trick is the level of the heat: turn it down so the soup simmers slowly. If it simmers quickly—or God forbid, boils—foam may expand exponentially, resulting in a roiling soup; the beans themselves may also become damaged, their skins floating free, their pulpy innards splitting open.

• **STEP 6** If necessary, remove the meat from the pot, slice into bite-sized bits, return these to the pot, and discard any bones. Stir in about 2 tablespoons acid, then season with salt and freshly ground black pepper to taste. Bacon and pancetta are ready to go in the soup as they are, but whole sausages should be cut into bite-sized rings. Soups are not generally knife-and-fork affairs. Hocks and shanks should have their meat shredded, the bones discarded. Marrow bones? Simply tossed out (after you've sucked out any innards, of course).

The one problem with bean soup? An unwarranted heaviness. Correct it now with a little acid, stirred in with the salt and pepper. Try any unflavored vinegar, lemon or lime juice, or even a little tomato paste (which will also thicken the soup).

Speaking of which, if you want an even thicker soup, transfer ½ cup cooked beans and about ¼ cup of the soup's liquid into a medium bowl. Mash the beans and broth with the back of a wooden spoon, creating a paste. Whisk this paste into the pot with the acid and simmer for 1 minute before serving, stirring constantly.

Recipes for Bean Soups

	Southern Black-Eyed Pea Soup	Black Bean Soup	Persian-Inspired Bean Soup	Lima Bean Soup
1. Soak	2 cups dried black-eyed peas	2 cups dried black beans	2 cups dried pinto beans	2 cups dried lima beans
2. Heat	2 Tbs peanut oil	2 Tbs canola oil	2 Tbs olive oil	2 Tbs olive oil
3. Add and cook	1 medium yellow onion, chopped 1 medium green bell pepper, seeded and roughly chopped 4 medium celery ribs, sliced into ½-inch sections	1 large onion, chopped 2 medium green bell peppers, seeded and roughly chopped 3 garlic cloves, minced	1 large red onion, chopped 2 medium carrots, peeled and sliced into ½-inch rings ½ cup chopped jarred preserved lemon ¼ cup chopped pitted dates	2 medium yellow onions, chopped 2 pounds kale, stemmed and chopped (see explanation in step 3)
4. Stir in	1 Tbs stemmed thyme 1 Tbs minced sage 2 tsp minced rosemary 1 bay leaf (discard before serving) The drained and rinsed beans	3 Tbs minced cilantro 1 Tbs minced oregano 1 Tbs finely grated orange zest ½ tsp red pepper flakes 2 bay leaves (discard before serving) One 4-inch cinnamon stick (discard before serving) The drained and rinsed beans	2 Tbs minced cilantro 2 tsp ground cumin 1 tsp ground cinnamon ¼ tsp ground cloves 2 bay leaves (discard before serving) The drained and rinsed beans	1 Tbs minced oregano ¼ tsp red pepper flakes The drained and rinsed beans
5. Add, cover, and simmer slowly	8 cups (2 quarts) chicken broth 1 smoked ham hock, trimmed	4 cups (1 quart) chicken broth 4 cups (1 quart) beef broth	8 cups (2 quarts) chicken broth 1 lamb shank, well browned in a skillet with 1 Tbs canola oil over medium heat	8 cups (2 quarts) beef broth 1 pound browned Italian sausage, mild or spicy
6. Stir in	The shredded cooked meat from the hock 2 Tbs apple cider vinegar Salt and pepper to taste	2 Tbs orange juice or sherry vinegar Salt and pepper to taste	2 Tbs pomegranate molasses Salt and pepper to taste	The cut-up, cooked sausage 2 Tbs red wine vinegar Salt and pepper to taste

	Cranberry Bean Soup with Country-Style Spare Ribs	Italian-Style White Beans	Minestrone	Spiced Adzuki Bean Soup with Dried Pears
1. Soak	2 cups dried cranberry beans	2 cups dried great northern, anasazi, or cannellini beans	2 cups dried cannellini beans	2 cups dried adzuki beans
2. Heat	2 Tbs canola oil	2 Tbs olive oil	2 Tbs olive oil	2 Tbs canola oil
3. Add and cook	1 large yellow onion, chopped 3 carrots, sliced into rounds 2 celery ribs, thinly sliced 2 garlic cloves, minced	1 large yellow onion, chopped 2 medium carrots, sliced into ½-inch rings 1 medium fennel bulb, trimmed and chopped 1 small head cabbage, cored and shredded[1] 2 garlic cloves, minced	1 medium yellow onion, chopped 2 medium yellow-flesh potatoes, cubed 2 celery ribs, thinly sliced 1 medium carrot, cut into ½-inch rings 3 garlic cloves, minced 3½ cups drained canned diced tomatoes	1 medium yellow onion, chopped 1 medium celeriac, peeled and diced 1 garlic clove, minced 1 cup chopped dried pears
4. Stir in	¼ cup minced parsley 1 Tbs stemmed thyme ¼ tsp red pepper flakes 1 bay leaf (discard before serving) The drained and rinsed beans	2 Tbs minced parsley 2 Tbs minced sage ¼ tsp red pepper flakes The drained and rinsed beans	2 Tbs minced parsley 1 Tbs minced oregano 1 Tbs minced rosemary ¼ tsp red pepper flakes 1 bay leaf (discard before serving) The drained and rinsed beans	¼ tsp ground cloves One 4-inch cinnamon stick (discard before serving) 1 star anise pod (discard before serving)
5. Add, cover, and simmer slowly	4 cups (1 quart) beef broth 4 cups (1 quart) water 1¼ pounds browned boneless country-style pork spare ribs, trimmed	4 cups (1 quart) chicken broth 4 cups (1 quart) water 1 trimmed, browned lamb shank	4 cups (1 quart) chicken broth 4 cups (1 quart) water The rind off a wedge of Parmesan (any inked writing scraped off)	6 cups chicken broth 2 cups water
6. Stir in	The cut-up spare rib meat 2 Tbs lemon juice Salt and pepper to taste	The cut-up lamb meat 2 Tbs tomato paste Salt and pepper to taste	2 Tbs white wine vinegar Salt and pepper to taste (If desired, 4 ounces cooked and drained tubular pasta)	2 Tbs lemon juice Salt and pepper to taste (If desired, drizzle with a little honey to garnish)

[1]To core and cut a cabbage, cut the head in half through its stem. Looking at each of the cut sides of the cabbage, cut out the solid core that juts up from and includes the remnants of that stem. Lay the half cabbage cut side down with the hollowed-out former stem end facing toward you and make thin slices left to right across the cabbage, letting the strips fan out. If desired, these strips, too, can be halved or quartered.

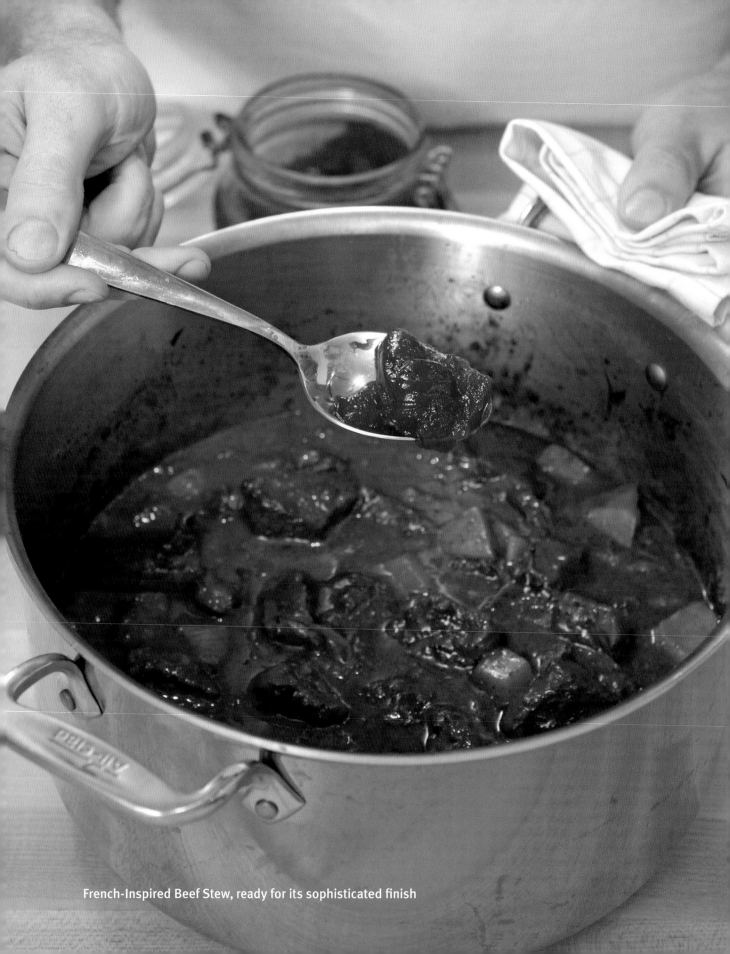

French-Inspired Beef Stew, ready for its sophisticated finish

Here's another chill-chaser. But this technique has an even more astounding array of combinations than Bean Soup (page 9)—from the Belgian Carbonnades Flamandes to French Boeuf Bourguignon, from old-fashioned Sunday pot roast stew to a Shanghai braise with soy sauce and dry sherry. What's more, Beef Stew is surprisingly frugal since it calls for an inexpensive cut of meat, one with lots of collagen and connective tissue. • MAKES 6 TO 8 SERVINGS

• **STEP 1** Heat 2 tablespoons fat in a large soup pot or Dutch oven over medium heat. A good stew requires a good pot, perhaps a sturdy Dutch oven. Yes, it should be quite heavy—and have shiny sides, too, a good radiator of heat. And it should be deep, so the liquid doesn't evaporate too quickly. But most important is a tight-fitting lid. Every wisp of steam must condense and "rain" back into the stew.

Fats in cooking

Very few dishes begin without some sort of fat: the first brush stroke on the canvas, as when a painter limns a scene in a thin wash before filling in the details. Without yet getting into the various smoke points and viscosities (see pages 235–236), here's a quick reference guide to the fat basics in terms of taste, lightest to heaviest:

neutral oils—canola, corn, safflower, sunflower, soy bean, and other vegetable oils, often excellent in spicy dishes or ones with very perfumy ingredients

grapeseed oil—a high-priced neutral-oil alternative, best for high-heat searing

peanut oil—little aroma in refined bottlings; in unrefined, much more

ghee—clarified butter (see page 25)

untoasted nut oils—walnut, almond, hazelnut, and pecan, all available at high-end markets

olive oil—a light, aromatic sweetness

unsalted butter—a very strong taste mitigated by its inherent sourness

duck or goose fat—a slightly heavier, sweeter, and also more bitter taste than other animal fats

lard and schmaltz—rendered pig and chicken fat, the worst varieties being dull and tasteless, the best being earthy and silky

toasted nut and other seed oils—quite heavy and deep, best saved as garnishes except in very flavorful preparations

toasted sesame seed oil—a strong, aromatic burst, often a garnish but sometimes used even at the base of a dish where its aroma is not completely lost

mustard seed oil—a pungent, fragrant ka-pow

Unsalted Butter

Although North Americans prefer salted butter, buying it four times as often as unsalted, the cooking standard remains unsalted butter. It allows you to better control the saltiness of a dish.

rendered bacon fat—an irresistible smokiness that can overwhelm all but the strongest ingredients

Armed with this knowledge, we discover that a beef stew is best at the light end of the scale: canola oil, peanut oil, untoasted walnut oil, if only because of the heavier ingredients to come. Cooking is all about balance: you lighten heavy dishes, enrich light ones. So olive oil might be too perfumy; schmaltz or lard, too heavy; toasted nut oils, too heavy; sesame or almond oil, too darn weird. The only exception? As usual, unsalted butter, if only because of its slightly spoiled sourness that cuts right through a stew and somehow lightens it in taste. (The exact chemical rationale is still a mystery.) Indeed, the best bet here may often be a combination of unsalted butter and one of the lighter oils: 1 tablespoon butter and 1 tablespoon canola oil, for example.

• **STEP 2** Sauté 6 ounces chopped, smoked, and/or cured pork or its substitute until crispy and well frizzled; then transfer to a bowl. A smoked and/or cured pork product—bacon, pancetta, and the like or their substitute—is the beginning of many a stew, braise, and even sauté. This flavor structure, in fact, will be repeated throughout this book. Here, the smoked and/or cured meat is a salty back-taste, something that will both carry the flavors and lighten them, adding greater satisfaction to the dish while cutting through the beef's heavy taste. Divide the choices into these categories:

Smoked

double-smoked bacon—a definite bang, perhaps too strong for many
bacon—avoid flavored or peppered varieties
turkey, beef, or soy bacon—for a pork-less substitute
Canadian bacon—that is, the American variety of Canadian bacon: lean back bacon, taken from the loin, most often smoked, sometimes only lightly so, sometimes not at all
ham hock—here, the meat would first be shredded off the bone

Unsmoked but cured

pancetta—a fatty, hard, Italian salt-cured pork, rich and chewy when cooked
ventrèche—the French version of pancetta, even fattier
peameal bacon—the real Canadian bacon, sweet-pickle cured and often coated in cornmeal, which should be rinsed off
prosciutto—a lean cured pork that will fry up in a couple minutes
duck prosciutto—search for it from high-end suppliers on the Web

Here are two examples: use bacon for a hearty, rich, stew with parsnips, potatoes, and other roots; use pancetta for a lighter stew with tomatoes, butternut squash, and fresh herbs. In general, do not substitute sausage meat; it's far too heavy and loaded with its own spices.

The basic cured meats for many a soup, braise, stew, or sauté: unsmoked pancetta (left) and smoky bacon (right).

- **STEP 3** Brown 2½ pounds cubed beef stew meat in batches; transfer to the same bowl you used in step 2. The meat will be stewed to temperatures far higher than 160°F, even beyond what is commonly considered "well-done," losing almost all the moisture between its cellular layers. Any purported juiciness actually comes from melting collagen and connective tissue. Thus, choose a well-marbled cut with lots of connective tissue (never tenderloin, rib-eyes, or strip steaks: all cuts that lack much connective tissue and are—or should be—eaten rare or medium-rare). Among the cuts to choose from are:

> **Boneless chuck.** Use any number of cuts from the cow's breast: arm, shoulder, or chuck roasts, as well as their various permutations. For a more complete list, see page 267. Avoid brisket, a waste in this economical stew.
>
> **Bottom round.** If you refuse the pleasures of chuck, this moderately fatty cut is a good compromise.
>
> **Top round.** It will yield a leaner stew, with the meat itself tougher, drier, and less appealing to some.
>
> **Beef stew meat.** This last-ditch solution is often made from trimmings and parts of the cow not usually seen in standard cuts.

As a starter for soups, stews, and braises, properly cooked bacon, pancetta, or the like should be well browned but not burned, crisp but not friable.

Or consider a buffalo version of any of these, which will be undoubtedly less fatty. For a richer stew, use venison or elk stew meat, or a combination of beef and a red game meat. The taste will be more pronounced—and so better enhanced later in step 8 with a sweet accent like red currant jelly or a splash of Grand Marnier.

The old saw about browning meat to seal in its juices is just that—an old saw. You brown the meat to enrich the broth, not to flavor the meat. Browning releases juices, a necessary step that allows surface proteins and sugars to be burned onto the meat's exterior and the pot's bottom, all to be later released and dissolved in the simmering broth: coloring it, fortifying it, and even thickening it. Do not gray the meat; brown it.

Work in batches. If the beef is added all at once, it will release too much juice that will then not evaporate quickly enough—and thus, the meat will boil, not brown. Adding the chunks in batches allows their juice to boil off so that they form a deep brown crust, quite dark and a little dry to the touch. In other words, get a good caramelization, about 6 to 7 minutes per batch of six or seven pieces.

- **STEP 4** Add 1 chopped large yellow onion and up to 8 cups roughly chopped root vegetables and/or peeled and seeded winter squash; cook, stirring often, until the onion has softened, about 3 minutes. Look for hard vegetables, tubers, and roots. Sweet, savory, or a mixture—here's the basic schema you should consider:

The biggest mistake in most stews and braises is not letting the meat brown enough. It should develop a rich, dark crust with lots of crunchy bits left in the pot.

Sweet roots and hard vegetables

Peeled and seeded butternut, buttercup, blue hubbard, red kuri, or other so-called "winter" squash including peeled and seeded pumpkins—as well as peeled carrots, rutabaga, and sweet potatoes

Savory roots and hard vegetables

Potatoes (peeled or not), particularly yellow-fleshed varieties or white creamers, and peeled cassava, celeriac, kohlrabi, parsnips, or turnips—as well as thickly sliced celery or peeled Jerusalem artichokes (also called sunchokes)

Steer clear of spring and summer vegetables (asparagus, zucchini, yellow crookneck squash, and green beans) as well as leafy greens or vegetables like broccoli and cauliflower that turn mushy during long simmering. If you really want greens in the soup, consider serving it in bowls over sautéed or braised spinach, mustard, collard, or turnip greens. If you sauté the greens, use the same kind of oil you used in the stew; if you braise them, the same kind of broth.

• **STEP 5** (optional): Stir in an accent vegetable, dried fruit, and/or berry. Here's where the dish truly becomes your own. But any of these additions should be used sparingly—one, maybe two. Indeed, there's no compelling reason to add an accent. A soup of beef, butternut squash, and parsnips is an unadorned, lovely luxury. Still, an accent is often warranted. Here's a quick list, common to unusual:

Mushrooms. They add a rich earthiness and should be in fairly large pieces, perhaps quarters or halves. Because white buttons and creminis are so full of moisture, they should first be sautéed in a large skillet over medium heat with a little unsalted butter or neutral oil until they release all their liquid and it evaporates to a glaze. Their taste will also be concentrated, a better foil to the beef; and their plentiful liquid won't thus water down the stew.

Seeded and chopped bell peppers. One or two will give the stew a homey, American taste.

Roma or plum tomatoes. Several chopped will skewer the flavors toward the Mediterranean. Yes, the skins can be pesky (they can come off and wrinkle in the stew), but it's hardly worth the hassle to parboil and remove them.

Sun-dried tomatoes. If you don't want the attendant liquid tomatoes to leach into the stew, use thinly sliced sun-drieds, perhaps ⅓ cup or so.

Jarred prepared horseradish. This piquant condiment will take a Sunday pot roast to a whole new level. In a soup, a couple tablespoons will do the trick.

Canned chickpeas, drained and rinsed. Adding Middle Eastern flair, these are starchy enough to absorb other flavors well.

Chipotle canned in adobo sauce. Actually a smoked dried jalapeño canned in a fiery sauce; one (seeded and stemmed) will give plenty of heat.

Pitted and halved prunes, raisins, or dried cherries. About ½ cup will offer a sweet richness.

Chopped dried apricots. About ½ cup will be a sour spark to balance carrots and sweet potatoes.

Preserved lemon. This jarred Moroccan condiment, thinly sliced, will offer a perfumy richness, best balanced by lots of dried spices, even garam masala (see page 27).

Blackberries or blueberries. Use between ⅓ and ⅔ cup, always fresh, never frozen. While sweet, they soften the tang of game.

By this point, the bottom of the pot will be lacquered with quite a bit of burned, blackened bits. If you've used mushrooms or tomatoes, some of their liquid may lift it off, but don't worry: it will all come up and thicken the stew in the next step.

• **STEP 6** Whisk 3 tablespoons all-purpose flour into 2½ cups broth or an enhanced broth, then whisk this mixture into the pot along with a few herbs and/or spices. Beef broth is the natural, but don't neglect chicken or vegetable broths, lighter tastes with Spanish and Mediterranean pairings.

In general, broth can also be enhanced or balanced by any number of additives: apple cider to cream, beer to coconut milk. For Beef Stew, use only a clear liquid: no coconut milk, thick cider, cream, or other dairy product. Instead, try wine (red or white), a dry fortified wine (dry Madeira, dry vermouth), port, or beer (never a flavored beer). Consider ½ cup the baseline for these enhancements—1 cup offers more of the flavor; 1½ cups will skew the stew toward much sweeter notes. Instead, a mix of 1 cup dry Marsala and 1½ cups beef broth works far better. One note: if you use beer (one 12-ounce bottle = 1½ cups), whisk the flour into the broth alone. Whisking flour into foamy beer is an exercise in futility.

Because the stew will cook for such a long time, there's no need to release the herbs' oils over the heat; they'll have plenty of time to leach into the mélange. Consider caraway seeds and nutmeg for a German-inspired stew with beer, or try the classic "herbes de Provence" combination of thyme, rosemary, marjoram, and basil with peeled, cubed celeriac and turnips. The important thing is not to underseason the stew; add a little more than you think, particularly of fresh, chopped herbs—up to ¼ cup of these, perhaps 2 teaspoons of a dried-spice mixture like 1 teaspoon ground cumin, ½ teaspoon ground cinnamon, and ½ teaspoon ground ginger. Appealing herbs with beef include sage, marjoram, thyme, oregano, and parsley; dried spices include caraway and celery seeds, smoked paprika, grated nutmeg, or red pepper flakes, as well as ground cinnamon, allspice, mace, or cardamom.

The browned and blackened bits on the pot's sides and bottom should scrape loose after a minute or two.

PERFECT MASHED POTATOES

A rich beef stew needs great mashed potatoes. After years of testing, we've found that the best are made without boiling, steaming, or baking. Instead, place four to six 6- to 8-ounce Russets in a large microwave-safe bowl with a lid; open the steam vent or leave one corner of the lid askew, then microwave on high for 8 or 9 minutes. Do not poke or cut the potatoes; the skin will seal in the steam as it superheats. Remove from the microwave with oven mitts, let stand covered for 2 to 3 minutes, and then smash with a potato masher or beat with an electric mixer, adding milk, butter, sour cream, broth, or Dijon mustard as your whim dictates.

Any beef stew needs a shot of a last-minute finisher to balance the flavors—here, red currant jelly.

• **STEP 7** Once simmering, stir the meat, the cured/smoked pork or its substitute, and any accumulated juices back into the pot; cover, reduce the heat to low, and cook at the slowest simmer until the meat is fork-tender, stirring occasionally, 1½ to 3 hours. Reduce the heat so the sauce is at the lowest simmer imaginable. The meat must get to above 160°F for the collagen to melt. The more slowly it reaches that temperature, the more tender it will be, the fibers staying supple and succulent without drying out and becoming shards.

Some flour may fall out of suspension and stick on the pot's bottom, particularly if the heat is too high. Stir occasionally but efficiently. Reduce the heat even further if you notice any sticking.

No two cuts—even identical cuts—tenderize at the same time: one bottom round may take 2 hours; another 2¼ hours. That said, as a rough estimate, top round will take between 1½ to 2 hours; bottom round, about 2 hours; chuck, about 2½ hours; and stew meat, between 2 and 3 hours. Be patient and keep testing with a fork. The pieces should be meltingly tender but not shreddable.

So what happens if you don't want to watch a pot for that long? Once the meat is back in the simmering soup, pour everything into a large slow cooker, cover, and cook on low until the meat is fork-tender, 8 to 10 hours.

• **STEP 8** If desired, stir in a sweet or sour accent and simmer for 1 minute to blend the flavors; season with salt and freshly ground black pepper to taste. Now's your chance to balance the vegetables and herbs. Taste the stew. What does it need? Something sweet, sour, or vinegary? Try any of these, all classic with beef:

A tablespoon or two of Dijon or another prepared mustard works well against caraway seeds or other savory spices.

A like amount of pomegranate molasses complements lavender, rosemary, and other very nosy herbs.

A tablespoon of vinegar brightens the flavors considerably, particularly if you used a fortified wine like dry Marsala or port.

A few teaspoons of red currant jelly is a typically French finish, a sweet/tart pop.

A couple teaspoons of lemon juice adds a spike, but the flavor is perhaps a touch too bright for some root vegetables; if you're concerned, use orange juice instead—or even an orange-flavored liqueur like Cointreau.

A splash of brandy, cognac, or dry sherry is a sophisticated twist, more sweet than not.

Recipes for Beef Stews

	Carbonnades Flamandes (Belgian Beef Stew)	French-Inspired Beef Stew	Spanish-Inspired Beef Stew	Moroccan-Inspired Beef Stew
1. Heat	2 Tbs unsalted butter	2 Tbs unsalted butter	2 Tbs canola oil	2 Tbs canola oil
2. Crisp and transfer	6 ounces chopped bacon	6 ounces chopped pancetta or ventrèche	6 ounces chopped pancetta	6 ounces chopped lamb sausage
3. Brown and transfer	2½ pounds cut-up bottom round	2½ pounds cut-up beef chuck	2½ pounds cut-up bottom round	2½ pounds cut-up beef stew meat
4. Cook	1 large yellow onion, chopped 4 medium carrots, peeled and roughly chopped 3 medium parsnips, peeled and roughly chopped	1 large yellow onion, chopped 2 large turnips, peeled and roughly chopped 1 medium celeriac, peeled and roughly chopped	1 large yellow onion, chopped 3 medium carrots, peeled and roughly chopped 3 medium yellow-fleshed potatoes, peeled and roughly chopped	1 large yellow onion, chopped 2 medium sweet potatoes, peeled and roughly chopped 3 medium carrots, peeled and roughly chopped
5. (optional) Add	8 ounces thickly sliced mushrooms, sautéed in 1 Tbs unsalted butter	1 cup halved pitted prunes	Omit	½ cup chopped dried apricots
6. Stir in	3 Tbs flour whisked into 1 cup beef broth One 12-ounce bottle of beer 2 tsp stemmed thyme 1 tsp caraway seeds	3 Tbs flour whisked into 1½ cups red wine and 1 cup beef broth 1 Tbs chopped parsley 2 tsp stemmed thyme ⅛ tsp ground allspice 1 bay leaf (discard before serving)	3 Tbs flour whisked into 1½ cups chicken broth and 1 cup white wine 1 Tbs chopped oregano 2 tsp smoked paprika ¼ tsp saffron 2 bay leaves (discard before serving)	3 Tbs flour whisked into 1 cup red wine and 1½ cups beef broth 2 tsp ground cumin 1 tsp ground cinnamon 1 tsp ground coriander ½ tsp ground cardamom
7. Add, cover, and simmer slowly	The browned bottom round and the frizzled bacon About 2 hours	The browned beef chuck and the crispy pancetta About 2½ hours	The browned bottom round and the pancetta About 2 hours	The browned beef stew meat and the lamb sausage About 3 hours
8. Stir in	1 Tbs coarse-grained mustard Salt and pepper to taste	2 tsp red currant jelly Salt and pepper to taste	¼ cup chopped pitted green olives Salt and pepper to taste	Salt and pepper to taste

	German-Inspired Beef Stew	Chinese-Style Beef Stew	Sunday Pot Roast Stew	Venison Stew
1. Heat	2 Tbs unsalted butter	2 Tbs sesame oil	2 Tbs canola oil	1 Tbs unsalted butter 1 Tbs canola oil
2. Crisp and transfer	6 ounces chopped bacon, preferably double-smoked bacon	6 ounces chopped bacon, preferably double-smoked bacon	6 ounces chopped bacon	6 ounces chopped bacon, preferably double-smoked bacon
3. Brown and transfer	2½ pounds cut-up beef chuck	2½ pounds cut-up beef chuck	2½ pounds cut-up beef stew meat	2½ pounds cut-up venison stew meat
4. Cook	2 large yellow onions, chopped 1 medium head cabbage, halved, cored, and roughly chopped	1 large leek, white and pale green parts only, halved lengthwise, washed carefully, and thinly sliced 2 medium yellow-fleshed potatoes, peeled and chopped 2 cups jarred roasted chestnuts 2 Tbs minced peeled fresh ginger	1 large yellow onion, chopped 2 large sweet potatoes, peeled and roughly chopped 1 medium rutabaga, peeled and roughly chopped	1 large yellow onion, chopped 2 medium pumpkins, peeled, seeded, and roughly chopped
5. (optional) Add	2 Tbs prepared jarred horseradish	6 ounces shiitake mushroom caps, stems removed and discarded, the caps sliced (no need to sauté first)	2 seeded and chopped tomatoes 1 small red bell pepper, seeded and chopped	8 ounces thickly sliced mushrooms, sautéed in 1 Tbs unsalted butter 1 cup blackberries
6. Stir in	3 Tbs flour whisked into 1 cup beef broth One 12-ounce bottle of beer, preferably a wheat beer 2 Tbs chopped sage ½ tsp celery seeds	3 Tbs flour whisked into 2 cups beef broth, ¼ cup soy sauce, and ¼ cup shaoxing (see page 374) or dry sherry 1 tsp Szechwan peppercorns One 4-inch cinnamon stick 2 star anise pods (discard pods and cinnamon stick before serving)	3 Tbs flour whisked into 2½ cups beef broth 2 tsp stemmed thyme 1 tsp mild paprika ¼ tsp crushed red pepper flakes	3 Tbs flour whisked into 1½ cups red wine and 1 cup beef broth 2 tsp minced marjoram ¼ tsp grated nutmeg ⅛ tsp ground allspice 1 bay leaf (discard before serving)
7. Add, cover, and simmer slowly	The browned beef chuck and the frizzled bacon About 2½ hours	The browned beef chuck and the frizzled bacon About 2½ hours ·	The browned beef stew meat and the frizzled bacon About 3 hours	The browned venison stew meat and the frizzled bacon About 3 hours
8. Stir in	2 Tbs red wine vinegar Salt and pepper to taste	½ cup chopped cilantro leaves Salt and pepper to taste	Salt and pepper to taste	2 tsp lemon juice Salt and pepper to taste

In some restaurants, biryani is simply a stew ladled over rice. But that's not true biryani—far from it! Biryani is East Indian lasagna: layers of aromatic stew and long-grain rice baked in a casserole—spot-on buffet fare or a company supper. • MAKES 8 SERVINGS

• **STEP 1** Cook 3 cups white or brown basmati rice until tender. Indeed, biryani is aromatic splendor; so a fragrant rice is best, and basmati, an East Indian favorite, is traditional. To cook basmati stovetop, use 4½ cups water for 3 cups white basmati or 6 cups water for 3 cups brown basmati. Bring the water to a simmer in a large saucepan over high heat. Never salt the water, particularly if you're cooking brown rice. Salt toughens the grains, especially the hulls of brown rice. Stir in the rice, cover, reduce the heat to low, and cook until tender, about 20 minutes for white or 35 for brown.

You could also use Texmati (a recent varietal that's less fragrant but more tender), patna (an East Indian varietal very popular in Great Britain), Carolina, jasmine, or even the whole-grain, more toothsome (and somewhat drier) Bhutanese red rice. These are all long-grain varietals; a low amount of amylopectin (see page 23) keeps the grains from clumping. Follow the package instructions to cook 3 cups raw rice.

In some authentic preparations, the kernels are first fried in ghee (that is, clarified butter—see step 2 below). The grains slowly toast, developing a nutty taste; the outer layer of starch is somewhat softened. If you'd like to add this step, melt about 2 tablespoons ghee in a large skillet over medium heat; add the raw rice and cook, stirring constantly, until golden, about 4 minutes. Then boil the rice as directed, shaving 5 or 10 minutes off the cooking time.

One note: this version of biryani is heavy on the rice, in keeping with its traditional roots. If you'd like it a little soupier, consider using only 2 to 2½ cups rice for the casserole. Or moisten each layer of rice in the baking dish (that is, in step 8) with a little chicken, vegetable, or beef broth.

• **STEP 2** While the rice cooks, heat 2 tablespoons ghee, unsalted butter, or a neutral-flavored oil in a large saucepan over medium-low heat. An East Indian staple, ghee is clarified butter: just the liquid fat, no attendant milk solids. High-heat cooking causes those solids to brown and turn bitter. Ghee is a smooth, sweet, carefree alternative, always available in tubs at brick-and-mortar

The first step in clarifying butter is to spoon off any opaque white milk solids ringing the pan.

Then the second step: slowly pour off the clarified fat, leaving almost all of the remaining milk solids behind.

A well-stocked Biryani begins with lots of diced vegetables, small enough so you will get several in each bite.

East Indian markets and their online outlets. However, read the label and beware of imitators that are just hydrogenated oil with food coloring.

Or forgo the purchased and make ghee. Place 4 to 6 tablespoons unsalted butter in a microwave-safe dish and heat on high in 15-second increments until melted, about 1 minute in all. Skim off any foam, then set aside for 5 minutes. After some of the milk solids have settled to the bottom, spoon off and discard those that remain on the top, gently pulling them to the side of the dish with a spoon. Once they're gone, gently and carefully pour off the clarified, yellow fat lying on top—that is, the ghee. You can also melt the butter in a small saucepan over low heat, but the milk solids will take longer to cool and settle, up to 30 minutes.

All that said, this aromatic stew will never cook at high temperatures; the milk solids will brown only slightly, if at all. So for a quick fix, feel free to use plain ol' unsalted butter, a more accessible if slightly less acceptable choice. Or skip the dairy altogether and use a neutral oil like safflower, corn, or vegetable oil. The stew will not be as rich, but the cayenne and other spices will be more present, more nosy.

• **STEP 3** Add 1 chopped large yellow onion, 1 chopped large tomato, several minced garlic cloves, and 1 to 2 tablespoons minced peeled fresh ginger; cook, stirring often, until the tomato pieces begin to break down, about 6 minutes. These aromatics and vegetables make up the unchanging canvas that serves as the background for the spices and protein. Take care not to brown them too deeply; East Indian cooking often eschews the bitter. (Thus, the use of ghee.)

Some biryanis lack tomatoes; others add them, probably in a bow to Western influence. In this streamlined preparation, one tomato adds necessary moisture; its fleshy pulp thickens the stew without hours over the heat.

• **STEP 4** Raise the heat to medium and add about 2 cups diced vegetables; cook, stirring often, until softened, anywhere from 3 to 8 minutes. Once cooked, this stew needs to become a fairly uniform mélange, like the ragú in lasagna, a rich sauce poured between the casserole's layers. There are two complementary techniques to getting that consistency: 1) slow, even cooking and 2) good knife work. Dice everything into ¼-inch cubes or slice it into thin, small pieces. If you're making Biryani out of quick-cooking fish, shellfish, chicken breasts, or tofu, stick with quick-cooking spring and summer vegetables:

asparagus, sliced into ½-inch sections
bell pepper, seeded and diced
broccoli florets, cut into small pieces

cauliflower, florets separated and cut into small pieces

celery, thinly sliced

corn, frozen or fresh, removed from the cob

fennel, trimmed and diced

peas, frozen or fresh, shelled

summer squash, diced

zucchini, halved lengthwise and diced

However, if you're going to use longer-cooking lamb, pork, chicken thighs, or beef, you're free to work with roots, tubers, or winter squash—for example, carrots, potatoes, or acorn squash (that is, the same list used for Beef Stew, page 17). Most of these hard vegetables should be diced into ¼-inch cubes; carrots and parsnips, sliced into thin rings.

For a sweet accent in either case, use an apple or a pear, peeled, seeded, and diced or shredded through the large holes of a box grater. If you add either of these, do not add a sweet dried fruit in step 7; rather, give the stew a somewhat tarter accent like dried apricots or cranberries.

Finally, what about canned chickpeas, drained and rinsed? They add lots of starch but a decidedly authentic touch. Use no more than 1 cup, paired with other vegetables.

• **STEP 5** Stir in 2 tablespoons garam masala and ½ teaspoon freshly ground black pepper; heat until aromatic, about 20 seconds. Garam masala (GAH-rum muh-SAH-luh, "warm spice") is a blend of ground spices, no one standardized recipe. Higher-end spice companies and gourmet markets sell several varieties; East Indian markets, a boggling selection. Unlike vindaloo pastes (see page 395), garam masala

The vegetables are not browned— just softened slightly to sweeten considerably and avoid caramelization.

Stir the meat and vegetables so they're well coated with the garam masala and yogurt.

Build the casserole layer by layer, alternating the long-grain rice and the aromatic stew in the baking dish.

is not hot but rather savory, even a little sweet. Most commercial blends start with ground coriander and cinnamon, then add perhaps ground cloves, nutmeg, cumin, cardamom, fennel and/or bay leaves.

Or create your own garam masala. You'll need 2 tablespoons in all (that is, 6 teaspoons). Start with 2 teaspoons ground coriander; add ½ teaspoon ground cinnamon, ginger, and/or cumin; then fill out some of the volume with turmeric and/or ground fenugreek; and finally add dribs and drabs of other spices, particularly ground ginger, rubbed sage, dried thyme, cayenne, ground cloves, and/or saffron. Here are three blends:

> **For lamb and beef,** mix together 2 tsp ground coriander, 1 tsp ground cinnamon, 1 tsp ground cumin, 1 tsp turmeric, ½ tsp ground cardamom, ¼ tsp ground cloves, and ¼ tsp cayenne.
>
> **For pork, chicken, veal, or tofu,** mix together 2 tsp ground coriander, 1 tsp ground cumin, 1 tsp mild paprika, 1 tsp fennel seeds, ½ tsp ground cinnamon, ¼ tsp ground allspice, and ¼ tsp cayenne.
>
> **For fish and shellfish,** mix together 2 tsp ground coriander, 1 tsp turmeric, 1 tsp mild paprika, ½ tsp ground fenugreek, ½ tsp ground ginger, ½ tsp dry mustard, ¼ tsp grated nutmeg, and ¼ tsp saffron.

• **STEP 6** Add 2 pounds trimmed, cubed meat, chicken, fish fillets, shrimp, scallops, or tofu; ¼ cup plain regular, low-fat, or fat-free yogurt; and 2 tablespoons lime juice. Cover and simmer, stirring occasionally, until tender—if using meat or cubed boneless skinless chicken thighs, about 40 minutes; if using cubed boneless skinless chicken breasts, about 10 minutes; if using fish or most shellfish, 5 minutes; or if using crab or tofu, 2 minutes. The cubes should be smaller than bite-size—about like the vegetables, perhaps ½ inch. Biryani is traditionally eaten with the right hand, the rice and stew scooped together. OK, a spoon's a good idea for most of North Americans; but no knife and fork for sure. Plus, small cubes will cook more quickly. Consider these your choices:

> **lamb,** trimmed, cubed lamb stew meat, leg of lamb, or shoulder
>
> **beef,** trimmed, cubed top round, bottom round, chuck, shoulder, or stew meat
>
> **chicken,** cubed boneless skinless thighs or boneless skinless breasts
>
> **pork,** trimmed, cubed boneless loin, shoulder, or country-style boneless ribs
>
> **veal,** trimmed, cubed stew meat or shoulder
>
> **fish,** cut-up thick, white-fleshed fillets like halibut, cod, or hake
>
> **shrimp,** roughly chopped, peeled and deveined medium shrimp (about 30 per pound)
>
> **scallops,** whole bay or quartered sea scallops
>
> **lobster,** chopped meat from 4 shelled, thawed, frozen tails
>
> **crab,** chopped, shelled meat from several king crab legs; or pasteurized lump crabmeat, picked over for shell and cartilage
>
> **tofu,** firm or dried (see page 147), diced

• **STEP 7** Stir in ½ cup chopped toasted nuts, ½ cup chopped dried fruit, and about 3 tablespoons minced basil, cilantro, or mint; season with salt to taste. To pump up the aromatics, East Indian cooking often finishes a dish with fresh, vibrant tastes—such as these three for Biryani:

1. **Nuts and their imitators.** Toasted and roughly chopped walnuts or pecans add an earthy bite; sliced or slivered almonds should be toasted but needn't be chopped. What about skinned, chopped hazelnuts (see page 217)? Hazelnuts offer a sophisticated, pseudo-Iberian taste, especially delicious if there's saffron in the spice mix. Don't neglect cashews; when toasted, they add a rich sweetness. Do not use salted nuts, such as salted cashews or peanuts.

2. **Dried fruit.** Chop golden or black raisins so they don't plump into squishy little balls. Or try chopped dried apricots, apples, pears, nectarines, or peaches, as well as dried blueberries, cherries, unsweetened cranberries, or blackberries. In all cases, think about how you want to skew the taste. Going for a sour note? Try dried apricots or cranberries. Looking for a sweeter finish against the cayenne? Try golden raisins.

3. **Herbs.** Basil is nosy against fish or chicken; mint, outstanding with lamb or beef. Cilantro? Always appealing.

Taste now and see how much salt the stew needs. Don't forget that the rice has not been salted. Perhaps 1½ teaspoons, maybe more?

• **STEP 8** Preheat the oven to 350°F, layer the casserole in a 9 x13-inch baking dish, cover, and bake 40 minutes for meat or 15 to 20 minutes for fish, shellfish, or tofu. Layer this way:

One-third of the cooked rice, spread evenly in the baking dish
Half the stew, carefully ladled and spread out over the rice
Half the remaining rice, again spread evenly
All the remaining stew
All the remaining rice

After baking, the casserole is best if left to stand for 10 minutes before serving. Biryani is often served by overturning the casserole onto a large, communal platter, but you could just as easily bring the baking dish to the table.

If you don't dump the casserole onto a platter, you can make a crunchy top layer of rice by uncovering the baked casserole, setting it 5 inches from a preheated broiler, and broiling until lightly browned. (The baking dish must be flame-safe!) For an even crunchier top, brush the top with about 3 tablespoons melted ghee or oil before broiling.

A bowl of comfort: Chicken Biryani

Recipes for Biryanis

	Lamb Biryani	Chicken Biryani	Shrimp Biryani	Veal Biryani
1. Cook	3 cups white basmati rice	3 cups white basmati rice	3 cups white basmati rice	3 cups white basmati rice
2. Heat	2 Tbs canola oil	2 Tbs ghee or unsalted butter	2 Tbs canola oil	2 Tbs ghee or unsalted butter
3. Add and soften	1 large yellow onion, chopped 1 large tomato, chopped 2 garlic cloves, minced 2 Tbs minced peeled fresh ginger	1 large yellow onion, chopped 1 large tomato, chopped 2 garlic cloves, minced 2 Tbs minced peeled fresh ginger	1 large yellow onion, chopped 1 large tomato, chopped 2 garlic cloves, minced 1 Tbs minced peeled fresh ginger	1 large yellow onion, chopped 1 large tomato, chopped 1 garlic clove, minced 1 Tbs minced peeled fresh ginger
4. Add and cook	1 medium green bell pepper, seeded and chopped 6 ounces chopped broccoli florets (do not use frozen)	9 ounces chopped cauliflower florets 1 cup fresh shelled or frozen peas	1 medium zucchini, halved lengthwise and thinly sliced 4 pencil-thin asparagus spears, chopped	9 ounces chopped broccoli florets (do not use frozen) 1 large yellow-fleshed potato, peeled and diced
5. Stir in	2 Tbs spice mixture for lamb or garam masala ½ tsp ground black pepper	2 Tbs spice mixture for chicken or garam masala ½ tsp ground black pepper	2 Tbs spice mixture for shellfish, or curry powder (see page 113) plus ¼ tsp cayenne ½ tsp ground black pepper	2 Tbs spice mixture for veal or garam masala ½ tsp ground black pepper
6. Add, cover, and simmer	2 pounds lamb stew meat, cubed ¼ cup plain yogurt 2 Tbs lime juice	2 pounds boneless, skinless chicken thighs, cubed ¼ cup plain yogurt 2 Tbs lime juice	2 pounds medium shrimp, peeled, deveined, and chopped ¼ cup plain yogurt 2 Tbs lime juice	2 pounds veal stew meat, cubed ¼ cup plain yogurt 2 Tbs lime juice
7. Stir in—then season with salt	½ cup toasted sliced or slivered almonds ½ cup chopped golden raisins 3 Tbs minced mint	½ cup chopped toasted cashews ½ cup chopped dried apple 3 Tbs minced basil	½ cup chopped toasted pecans ½ cup chopped dried cranberries 3 Tbs minced basil	½ cup chopped toasted walnuts ½ cup chopped dried peaches 3 Tbs minced mint
8. Preheat the oven; layer, cover, and bake	30 minutes	30 minutes	15 minutes	30 minutes

	Vegetarian Biryani	Crab Biryani	Beef Biryani	Fish Biryani
1. Cook	3 cups brown basmati rice	3 cups white basmati rice	3 cups brown basmati rice	3 cups white basmati rice
2. Heat	2 Tbs canola oil	2 Tbs ghee or unsalted butter	2 Tbs ghee or unsalted butter	2 Tbs canola oil
3. Add and soften	1 large yellow onion, chopped 1 large tomato, chopped 2 garlic cloves, minced 2 Tbs minced peeled fresh ginger	1 large yellow onion, chopped 1 large tomato, chopped 1 garlic clove, minced 1 Tbs minced peeled fresh ginger	1 large yellow onion, chopped 1 large tomato, chopped 3 garlic cloves, minced 2 Tbs minced peeled fresh ginger	1 large yellow onion, chopped 1 large tomato, chopped 1 garlic clove, minced 2 Tbs minced peeled fresh ginger
4. Add and cook	9 ounces chopped cauliflower florets 1 medium zucchini, halved lengthwise and thinly sliced	1 medium fennel bulb, trimmed and diced 1 cup fresh shelled or frozen peas	2 celery ribs, thinly sliced 1 medium carrot, thinly sliced	1 large yellow summer squash, cubed 1 celery rib, thinly sliced ½ cup fresh shelled or frozen peas
5. Stir in	2 Tbs spice mixture for tofu or garam masala ½ tsp ground black pepper	2 Tbs spice mixture for shellfish or garam masala ½ tsp ground black pepper	2 Tbs spice mixture for beef or garam masala ½ tsp ground black pepper	2 Tbs spice mixture for fish or garam masala ½ tsp ground black pepper
6. Add, cover, and simmer	2 pounds firm tofu, cubed ¼ cup plain yogurt 2 Tbs lime juice	2 pounds shelled king crab leg meat, roughly chopped; or up to 2 pounds pasteurized lump crabmeat, picked over for shell and cartilage ¼ cup plain yogurt 2 Tbs lime juice	2 pounds beef stew meat, cubed ¼ cup plain yogurt 2 Tbs lime juice	2 pounds haddock or hake, cubed ¼ cup plain yogurt 2 Tbs lime juice
7. Stir in—then season with salt	½ cup chopped toasted peanuts ½ cup chopped dried pears 3 Tbs minced cilantro	½ cup chopped toasted pecans ½ cup chopped dried cranberries 3 Tbs minced basil	½ cup chopped toasted walnuts ½ cup chopped raisins 3 Tbs minced cilantro	½ cup toasted sliced or slivered almonds ½ cup chopped golden raisins 3 Tbs minced basil
8. Preheat the oven; layer, cover, and bake	15 minutes	15 minutes	30 minutes	15 minutes

Boneless Pork Loin Chops with a Pan Sauce

Look no further for an easy weeknight supper: four chops, one skillet, and just a few other ingredients. Have cooked rice or roasted potatoes on hand—and some steamed or roasted green vegetable like asparagus, broccoli, green beans, or chard. • MAKES 4 SERVINGS

• **STEP 1** **Heat 1 to 2 tablespoons fat in a 12-inch skillet over medium heat.** Because of their relatively mild taste, boneless pork loin chops take to the full range of fats. There are, of course, the classics:

olive oil—best with Italian, Spanish, Greek, or other Mediterranean flavorings
unsalted butter—best with mushrooms, mild curries, creamy root vegetables, or sweeter vegetables like peas and carrots
a neutral oil like canola, safflower, or sunflower—good with chiles and spicy combos

But why stop there? Almond oil has a subtle, nutty taste that pairs well with potatoes and other roots. Peanut oil is a natural with Asian flavors; grapeseed oil will give the chops a very brown crust, thanks to its sky-high smoke point (the point at which the oil can volatilize and ignite). Walnut or hazelnut oils are strong but a fine complement to a fruit-based sauté, like one with shallots and dried cherries or perhaps with onion, garlic, thyme, and sliced peaches. Even toasted nut oils, far stronger in taste, will complement some vegetables. If you're making an Asian-inspired dish with ginger, scallions, snow peas, and/or pears, try sesame oil, an assertive flavor. In the end, any fat will work here—and work better if it's connected to the ingredients to come: leeks or cherries, fennel or radishes.

Never Rinse Meat

Somewhere along the way, it became acceptable, even expected, to rinse meat before cooking. Perhaps this was an attempt to get rid of any sulfurous tang? Whatever the rationale, it's bad. Rinsing inadvertently sprays droplets of potentially contaminated liquid all over the kitchen. Bacteria are and always have been killed by heat, not water. (And besides—if meat smells sulfurous, don't eat it.)

• **STEP 2** **Brown four 4- to 5-ounce boneless pork loin chops; transfer to a plate and tent with aluminum foil to keep warm.** Pork loin chops are cut, obviously enough, from the loin. The best are center-cut chops—that is, rounds of meat from the loin's center with much less fat than other pork chops. In butcher parlance, the loin runs from the pig's shoulder to its hip and has three parts, the center being the leanest; look for chops about ½ inch thick, between 4 and 5 ounces apiece. Thinner and they're in danger of getting tough.

Slip the cutlets into the skillet and leave untouched for 4 to 5 minutes, until one side browns quite well. Then turn with tongs, not a fork. There's a lot written about

Slice your own pork loin chops: buy a pork loin, trim off surface fat, and cut the loin into 1-inch medallions.

using tongs to turn meat, much of it true if misleading, along these lines: "If you use a fork, you'll prick the meat and the juices will run out." Meat is a multi-layered structure of cells; one hole cannot spill "the juices"—otherwise, no one would use a meat thermometer, pricking the meat time and again to get its internal temperature. Yes, we've all seen a little liquid run out of a pricked hole. Thus, a fork spills a fraction of the juice, certainly not "the juices." Still, a fraction counts in almost everything except hand grenades.

Again, leave the turned chops undisturbed 4 to 5 minutes, until well browned. Because they're evenly marbled, the meat cooks quite quickly. There's little to go wrong—other than your impatience. Grayed cutlets are a waste.

By the way, this step is indeed the sauté that gives the dish its technical name: a pork cutlet sauté. To sauté (from the French *sauter,* soh-TAY, "to jump") is a technique whereby food is fried quickly in a fairly small amount of fat (as opposed to say, Pan-Frying, page 235, with its large amount of fat).

Why tent with foil? These chops won't be over the burner very long in step 7 when they're returned to the skillet. They need to retain as much heat as possible.

● **STEP 3** Add and sauté 1 to 2 cups chopped or thinly sliced vegetables, fruits, and/ or nuts. When selecting vegetables, fruits, or nuts, keep in mind that boneless pork cutlets are quite mild, even a little sweet. Capitalize on that with onions, shallots, leeks, zucchini, radishes, tomatoes, apples, pears, chayote, and a host of milder, sweet flavors. If there are bolder tastes in the sauté—sauerkraut, ginger, or mustard greens, for example—ramp up the flavors in the herbs (step 4) and liquid (step 5) to balance any assertiveness.

Chop everything into similarly sized pieces: about ½-inch cubes—or a like size for, say, sliced celery or carrot rounds. No need for a ruler, but remember the rule: the larger a piece, the longer it takes to cook. Save time overall with careful chopping.

Harder vegetables like potatoes and turnips will take a little longer over the heat to get tender—and should perhaps be diced into ¼-inch cubes. You may also need to add an additional tablespoon or so of fat, just to make sure they don't burn.

Timing is a matter of the ingredients. Diced potatoes need 7 or 8 minutes to get brown and soft; diced shallots, only a couple minutes. Tomatoes? That depends—up to 10 minutes to break down into a sauce, only 2 or 3 minutes for a fresher taste. Packaged sauerkraut or canned tomatillos only need to be warmed through.

● **STEP 4** Add 1 or 2 minced garlic cloves and/or some herbs or spices. Think of the process this way: this step complements the one that came before, just as step 6 will later complement step 5. Therefore, garlic isn't obligatory at this stage—it's a nice touch, yes, but sometimes overpowering.

Keep the flavors fairly clean, limiting the herbs to one or two—unless, of course, you're using a bottled spice blend like chili powder or curry powder. Consider 2 teaspoons the outermost limit for a single herb, 1 tablespoon for a blend. Less is more—within reason, to be sure. An eighth teaspoon dried thyme will do no one any good. For a list of herbs and spices that work well with pork, see page 53.

• **STEP 5** Raise the heat to medium-high and add 1 cup liquid; then scrape up any browned bits on the skillet's bottom, bring to a simmer, and reduce the liquid by half. Timing is difficult to predict because different liquids have different viscosities and boiling points. Once at a simmer, plan on 2 to 3 minutes, but watch carefully. Do not let the liquid boil away; the sauce has to go through more cooking in steps 6 and 7.

The usual suspects for the specific liquids here are chicken or vegetable broths, white wine or dry vermouth. Or try a 50/50 split of broth and wine or dry vermouth. Or even a 75/25 split, provided you keep this rule in mind: more broth, more savory; more wine, more sugary.

Fortify any liquid with a splash of brandy, Calvados, Armagnac, or cognac. If the mixture should flame, cover the skillet, take it off the heat, and wait about 20 seconds for the fire to go out.

Finally, consider heavy cream, most often mixed 50/50 or 75/25 with broth, wine, or dry vermouth. Cream can also be mixed with a splash of brandy or any of the liquors listed above, but cream should be a solid component in these pairings. There's no point in adding 2 tablespoons cream—the sauce will turn an unattractive, milky brown.

But there's one warning to go along with the cream. In the next step, you can add an accent to the dish: sweet, salty, or sour. The latter can and probably will curdle the cream. Avoid lemon juice or vinegars if you're making a cream-laced sauce.

• **STEP 6** (optional): Add a small amount of a sweet or salty accent. Build complex layers and take this simple sauté beyond a workaday meal. But go easy: 1 tablespoon is a lot.

Sweet enhancements include
maple syrup
honey
honey mustard
unsalted butter
pomegranate molasses

Reducing Liquids

To "reduce by half" is common cooking parlance. It means that the liquid should boil in the skillet until about half its original volume remains after evaporation. There's no need to get out a measuring cup; simply eye-ball the liquid to determine about when the right reduction has occurred. ("Reduce by half," by the way, is in contrast to another term common in cookbook parlance: "reduced to a glaze"—see page 321).

An easy sauté is made more sophisticated by stirring in one of the three finishers: here (clockwise from top), orange juice (sour), plum chutney (sweet), or grainy mustard (salty).

This apple-and-leek sauce has been reduced by half and is ready for its finisher: some Dijon mustard. The sauce is still fairly wet, since it must continue to simmer as the chops cook through.

Always check the temperature of the chops to make sure they've been thoroughly cooked before serving.

aged balsamic vinegar
fruit chutney
orange marmalade
black or red currant jelly

Among the salty enhancements are
Worcestershire sauce
prepared mustard
tapenade
soy sauce
fish sauce (page 388)
Chinese black bean sauce
hoisin sauce (page 168)—particularly if you're working with Asian flavors
anchovy paste—a very sophisticated finish

Sour sparks (never used in combination with cream) can be
various vinegars—white wine, red wine, white balsamic, and the like, but never flavored
lemon or lime juice
orange juice—or particularly, thawed orange juice concentrate
thawed cranberry juice concentrate
tamarind paste

Of course, you needn't add any. You can keep the dish simpler and "cleaner" by focusing on the vegetables you've sautéed.

• **STEP 7** Reduce the heat to medium, return the meat and any accumulated juices to the skillet, and cook until an instant-read meat thermometer inserted into one of the chops registers 160°F. Season with salt and freshly ground black pepper before serving. The cutlets should now cook to their final temperature, perhaps 3 minutes or so. The only way to tell? With an instant-read meat thermometer, inserted on the diagonal into the center of one of the thickest cuts. The USDA recommends 160°F for medium and 170°F for well-done. Almost all pathogens are killed above 140°F, so 160°F is an excellent goal: the meat remains quite juicy without any resemblance to shoe leather.

Salt and pepper to taste—unless you've already got fish or soy sauce in the mix.

Recipes for Boneless Pork Loin Chops

	Boneless Pork Loin Chops with Zucchini	Boneless Pork Loin Chops with Leeks and Apples	Boneless Pork Loin Chops with Walnuts and Shallots	Boneless Pork Loin Chops with Blackberries and Cream
1. Heat	2 Tbs olive oil	1 Tbs unsalted butter	1 Tbs walnut oil	2 Tbs unsalted butter
2. Brown and remove	Four 4- to 5-ounce boneless center-cut pork loin cutlets	Four 4- to 5-ounce boneless center-cut pork loin cutlets	Four 4- to 5-ounce boneless center-cut pork loin cutlets	Four 4- to 5-ounce boneless center-cut pork loin cutlets
3. Sauté	1 medium onion, diced 2 medium zucchini, diced	2 medium Granny Smith apples, peeled, cored, and thinly sliced 1 large leek, white part only, halved, washed carefully, and thinly sliced	6 ounces shallots, thinly sliced into rings[1] 1 cup chopped walnut pieces	4 ounces shallots, diced 1 cup whole blackberries
4. Add	1 garlic clove, minced 2 tsp finely grated lemon zest	1 garlic clove, minced 1 tsp caraway seeds 1 tsp celery seeds	½ tsp ground cinnamon ¼ tsp grated nutmeg	2 tsp minced sage
5. Pour in and reduce	1 cup chicken broth	1 cup dry white wine	½ cup chicken broth ½ cup cream[2]	¾ cup cream ¼ cup vegetable broth
6. (optional) Add	1 Tbs unsalted butter	2 tsp Dijon mustard	1 Tbs fruit chutney	Omit
7. Return, cook, and season	The pork and accumulated juices Salt and pepper to taste	The pork and accumulated juices Salt and pepper to taste	The pork and accumulated juices Salt and pepper to taste	The pork and accumulated juices Salt and pepper to taste

[1]There are many varieties of shallots, some double-lobed, some single, some fat, some thin—and all fine in this recipe. Thus, the amount for shallots is always stated as its weight, to avoid any confusions among the varieties.

[2]For a discussion of various types of cream, see page 101.

	German-Inspired Boneless Loin Pork Chops	Asian-Inspired Boneless Pork Loin Chops	Boneless Pork Loin Chops, Spicy Italian Style	Curried Boneless Pork Loin Chops
1. Heat	1 Tbs canola oil	1 Tbs sesame oil	2 Tbs olive oil	2 Tbs unsalted butter or ghee
2. Brown and remove	Four 4- to 5-ounce boneless center-cut pork loin cutlets	Four 4- to 5-ounce boneless center-cut pork loin cutlets	Four 4- to 5-ounce boneless center-cut pork loin cutlets	Four 4- to 5-ounce boneless center-cut pork loin cutlets
3. Sauté	2 cups packaged sauerkraut, drained and squeezed dry	2 medium whole scallions, thinly sliced 4 ounces broccoli florets 4 ounces snow peas, thinly sliced	1 large green bell pepper, seeded and diced 2 medium celery ribs, diced Up to 3 jarred hot Italian peppers (peperoncini) or jarred hot cherry peppers, seeded and diced	1 small onion, diced 1 small apple, peeled, cored, and diced 2 celery ribs, thinly sliced ¼ cup chopped golden raisins
4. Add	1 tsp caraway seeds ½ tsp ground cumin ½ tsp dry mustard	1 Tbs minced peeled fresh ginger 1 Tbs chopped cilantro Up to 1 tsp red pepper flakes 2 garlic cloves, minced	3 garlic cloves, minced 2 tsp drained and rinsed capers 2 tsp minced rosemary	2 minced garlic cloves 1 Tbs curry powder (see page 113) ¼ tsp ground cinnamon
5. Pour in and reduce	1 cup beer	¾ cup chicken broth ¼ cup shaoxing (see page 374) or dry sherry	½ cup chicken broth ½ cup dry vermouth	¾ cup dry white wine ¼ cup chicken broth
6 (optional) Add	1 tsp honey	1 Tbs soy sauce 2 tsp rice vinegar	1 tsp anchovy paste or ½ anchovy fillet, minced	1 tsp lemon juice
7. Return, cook, and season	The pork and accumulated juices Salt and pepper to taste	The pork and accumulated juices	The pork and accumulated juices Salt and pepper to taste	The pork and accumulated juices Salt and pepper to taste

Boneless Skinless Chicken Breasts with a Pan Sauce

Here's the best preparation for one of America's favorite dinners. Admittedly, it's a little more time-consuming because the breasts are first soaked in a salt brine to assure their juiciness. Want to avoid that step? Buy kosher boneless skinless chicken breasts, which are already brined. • MAKES 4 SERVINGS

• **STEP 1** (optional): Whisk together a brine of 8 cups (2 quarts) cool water and ¼ cup salt in a large bowl or roasting pan, add four 7- to 8-ounce boneless skinless chicken breasts, cover, and refrigerate 4 hours or up to 12 hours. There are two problems with boneless skinless breasts:

1. Lacking much fat, they can be relatively tasteless.
2. Lacking skin and bone, they're often overcooked, depressingly stringy.

The first problem will be solved by the ingredients in the sauté and sauce that follows in steps 4 through 7; the problem of their texture can be solved now by first submerging them in a brine to assure their juiciness. If desired, add a couple bay leaves and a handful of cracked black peppercorns for more flavor. The salt plumps the meat's cells; you can hardly overcook the chicken. However, you can overbrine it. The meat will then become unappealingly mushy. Consider 12 hours the outside limit.

A salt brine plumps boneless skinless breasts. The pay-off? They can hardly be overcooked.

The best option is to do this step in the morning before you leave for the day. But even if you walk in at 5:00 pm and plop the breasts in the brine for an hour or two while you change and open the mail, they'll be markedly better.

When shopping, look for plump, supple breasts with a pale pink hue; read the package to make sure they haven't already been pumped full of sodium, broth, and chemical cosmetics, often the case with frozen boneless skinless chicken breasts and in most cases, fresh or frozen, when labeled with words to the effect that the meat "contains up to 10% of a solution of. . . ." If so, skip this step. And skip this step if you've bought kosher chicken breasts.

• **STEP 2** Heat 2 tablespoons fat in a 12-inch skillet over medium heat. Remove the breasts from the brine, pat them dry with paper towels, slip into the skillet, and brown well on both sides, turning once; transfer to a plate and tent with aluminum foil. Quite mild, boneless skinless chicken breasts gain nothing from neutral oils like canola and safflower. The whole point is to add flavor.

Consider these your options:

olive oil—best for lighter sautés, Mediterranean flavors, and tomatoes

unsalted butter—a little heavier, best when balanced with sweeter vegetables like squash or peas

untoasted nut oils—a nice touch for sophisticated sautés (but avoid toasted nut oils; they tend to be too heavy)

peanut oil—a good accent to Asian or East Indian flavorings

sesame oil, toasted or not—only used with Asian flavorings like ginger, scallions, and sliced water chestnuts

Once in the skillet, leave the breasts untouched for 4 to 5 minutes. High in proteins and sugars, they need to become deep golden brown. Turn with tongs, then leave undisturbed until well browned, perhaps another 4 minutes. Transfer to a plate, tent with foil, and set aside.

Could you use boneless skinless thighs for this technique? Not really. Yes, they would be cooked through by the end, but they wouldn't be tender, their connective tissue still intact and chewy. Save them for braises and stews like Fricassee (page 139), Tagine (page 379), or a braise designed for them (see page 45).

Don't take a shortcut: the best-tasting breasts are well browned, untouched over the heat for perhaps 4 minutes per side.

• **STEP 3** Add about 1 cup chopped aromatics and cook, stirring often, until softened, about 3 minutes. Because the breasts are low in fat, they can soak up any fat in the skillet quite quickly. If you find it dry, add 1 tablespoon additional fat before continuing.

In Western cooking, nine out of ten dishes begin with one of four basic aromatics, all members of the lily family. All turn markedly sweet over the heat—and thus, they afford the structure to the central tenet of almost all European, North American, Latin American, South American, East-Indian, and Chinese cooking: use sweet as a background to all other tastes. These four aromatics are

1. **Onions**—yellow or red, although Vidalia and other super-sweet varieties might be wasted over the heat.
2. **Leeks**—white and pale green parts only, halved lengthwise and washed carefully to remove muck in the inner chambers, then thinly sliced.
3. **Shallots**—either the tubular French shallot (or "griselle") or the double-lobed variety common to North American supermarkets.
4. **Scallions**—also called "green onions" or "spring onions" (and oddly "shallots" in Australia), a wide variety of bulbless onions, used whole, best minced or diced (but discard any withered or gooey stems).

Why no garlic in the list? Cooking in oil is an evaporative process: oil itself is actually a "dry" medium—despite its being a liquid, there is no water in oil. All those bubbles and pops are the water and other moisture coming out of the various ingredients. Garlic, dried before sale and thus low in moisture, burns quickly and is best added later in the cooking, when there's plenty of protective moisture being released from other vegetables, as in the next step.

• **STEP 4** Add and cook about 2 cups diced or thinly sliced vegetables as well as some chopped garlic and/or one or two minced herbs or dried spices. Boneless skinless chicken breasts are easily overwhelmed. Save sauerkraut or mustard greens for boneless center-cut pork loin chops (see page33); save beets and butternut squash for a dish that takes longer over the heat. Instead, choose quick-cooking, lighter spring vegetables like shelled peas, corn, sliced zucchini or summer squash, broccoli or cauliflower florets, sliced asparagus, snow peas, baby bok choy, sugar snap peas, or sliced radishes. Even tomatoes should be finely diced.

The only exception to the amount of vegetable here are leafy greens. They cook down quite a bit, so consider adding 4 to 6 cups chopped greens, perhaps in two additions, adding the second only as the first wilts.

Before the liquid is added in step 5, the pan should be almost dry with lots of caramelized bits across its bottom.

• **STEP 5** Raise the heat to medium-high and add about 1 cup liquid; then scrape up any browned bits on the pan's bottom, bring to a simmer, and cook until the liquid is reduced by half. Use broth, wine, a dry fortified wine (like dry vermouth, dry sherry, or dry Madeira), or heavy cream—or at best, a combination of any two.

Remember this general culinary rule: wine is sweet, broth is savory, and cream is heavy.

For Asian dishes, consider using a little soy sauce in addition to the broth; for French-influenced preparations, how about ¼ cup apple cider? The point here is to make a quick sauce with all the browned bits on the pan's bottom. And remember this: it's a sauce, not the more fulsome liquid in a braise.

• **STEP 6** Return the meat and any accumulated juices to the skillet, reduce the heat to medium, and cook until the breasts' internal temperature is 165°F; season with salt and freshly ground black pepper to taste. The breasts should now cook to their final temperature, perhaps 4 minutes. The USDA recommends 165°F, a good goal. Use an instant-read meat thermometer inserted into the center of the thickest part of one of the breasts to get the exact temperature.

Add a little ground black pepper, but use salt sparingly if you've brined the breasts. There's no reason to turn the sauce into the Dead Sea.

Sautéed Chicken Breasts with an Asian-Influenced Orange Sauce

Recipes for Boneless Skinless Chicken Breasts

	Easy Chicken Breasts Prima Vera	Chicken Breasts Sautéed with Apricots and Rosemary	Chicken Breasts Sautéed with Swiss Chard	Chicken Breasts Sautéed with Cream and Mushrooms
1. (optional) Brine	8 cups water ¼ cup salt Four 7- to 8-ounce boneless skinless chicken breasts	8 cups water ¼ cup salt Four 7- to 8-ounce boneless skinless chicken breasts	8 cups water ¼ cup salt Four 7- to 8-ounce boneless skinless chicken breasts	8 cups water ¼ cup salt Four 7- to 8-ounce boneless skinless chicken breasts
2. Heat, brown well, and transfer	2 Tbs unsalted butter	2 Tbs olive oil	2 Tbs olive oil	2 Tbs unsalted butter
3. Add and soften	1 large leek, white and pale green parts only, halved, washed carefully, and thinly sliced	4 ounces shallots, halved and sliced into thin rings	1 medium yellow onion, chopped	4 ounces shallots, halved and sliced into thin rings
4. Add and cook	1 medium carrot, sliced into very thin rings 6 pencil-thin asparagus spears, cut into 2-inch lengths ¾ cup fresh shelled or frozen peas[1] 1 Tbs minced parsley 1 tsp stemmed thyme	1 small red bell pepper, seeded and diced 3 ripe apricots, pitted and quartered 1 garlic clove, minced 2 tsp minced rosemary	1 pound Swiss chard, stemmed and roughly chopped 2 garlic cloves, minced ¼ tsp red pepper flakes	8 ounces cremini or white button mushrooms, thinly sliced 1 garlic clove, minced ¼ tsp grated nutmeg
5. Pour in and reduce by half	½ cup dry white wine ½ cup cream	1 cup chicken broth	1 cup dry vermouth	½ cup dry white wine ½ cup cream
6. Return the breasts, cook to 165°F, and season	Salt and pepper to taste	Salt and pepper to taste	Salt and pepper to taste	Salt and pepper to taste

[1]In cooking, there's almost no need to thaw frozen peas. Toss them straight from the freezer into the pan, skillet, or pot, giving them a few extra seconds over the heat. However, they must of course be thawed when eaten raw in salads and such. One pound of peas in their pods or shells yields about 1 cup fresh shelled peas.

	Sautéed Chicken Breasts with an Asian-Influenced Orange Sauce	Portuguese-Inspired Chicken Breast Sauté	Sautéed Chicken Breasts With Apples and Cream	Sautéed Chicken Breasts with Baby Artichokes
1. (optional) Brine	8 cups water ¼ cup salt Four 7- to 8-ounce boneless skinless chicken breasts	8 cups water ¼ cup salt Four 7- to 8-ounce boneless skinless chicken breasts	8 cups water ¼ cup salt Four 7- to 8-ounce boneless skinless chicken breasts	8 cups water ¼ cup salt Four 7- to 8-ounce boneless skinless chicken breasts
2. Heat, brown well, and transfer	2 Tbs peanut oil	2 Tbs olive oil	2 Tbs unsalted butter	2 Tbs olive oil
3. Add and soften	3 medium whole scallions, thinly sliced	1 medium yellow onion, chopped	4 ounces shallots, halved and sliced into thin rings	1 medium yellow onion, chopped
4. Add and cook	1 small red bell pepper, seeded and diced 1 cup sliced canned water chestnuts or bamboo shoots 2 garlic cloves, minced 1 Tbs minced peeled fresh ginger 2 tsp finely grated orange zest	4 plum or Roma tomatoes, seeded and chopped 1 celery rib, thinly sliced 1 garlic clove, minced 1 canned anchovy fillet, minced ½ cup chopped skinned hazelnuts (see page 217) 2 tsp minced parsley 2 tsp minced oregano	2 medium sour apples, peeled, cored, and diced 2 tsp stemmed thyme	One 10-ounce package frozen baby artichoke quarters, thawed and squeezed of excess moisture 3 Tbs chopped pitted black olives 1 Tbs capers, drained and rinsed 2 tsp minced oregano 1 tsp stemmed thyme ⅛ tsp saffron
5. Pour in and reduce by half	½ cup chicken broth ¼ cup orange juice ¼ cup soy sauce	½ cup chicken broth ½ cup dry red wine	½ cup dry white wine ½ cup cream	½ dry white wine ½ chicken broth
6. Return the breasts, cook to 165°F, and season	Salt and pepper to taste	Salt and pepper to taste	Salt and pepper to taste	Salt and pepper to taste

Braised Bone-In Chicken Breasts or Thighs

Fast and flavorful, an elegantly simple braise is the best way to get deep flavor into bone-in chicken. The only difference between the breasts and thighs is how long you cook them. Breasts, with less inter-layer fat, can only go 20 to 25 minutes and should be paired with lighter flavors to match their lighter taste. Thighs can be stewed for longer, yielding a deeper, complex braise, better suited to winter squash and root vegetables. • MAKES 4 SERVINGS

• **STEP 1** Either heat 1 tablespoon fat in a 12-inch high-sided skillet or sauté pan over medium heat, then add 3 ounces chopped, smoked and/or cured pork or its substitute and cook until crisp before transferring to a bowl—or simply heat about 2 tablespoons fat in the skillet or pan, skipping anything smoked or cured at this point. You needn't start with a smoked and/or cured pork product, but it can't hurt! Bacon of any stripe (pork, beef, turkey, or soy) adds smoky, rustic notes; pancetta, by contrast, makes for little, salty bites of sophisticated richness. Dice either into small pieces, perhaps ¼ inch. For a complete list of choices, see page 18.

Whether you use bacon and its ilk, choose as the fat unsalted butter, olive oil, or an untoasted nut oil like almond or walnut—or even a 50/50 combination of butter and oil. Toasted nut oils and sesame oil are simply too assertive. Neutral oils like canola or safflower won't add any flavor—and layering flavors is the trick to making this quick braise taste as if it's bubbled for hours.

• **STEP 2** Brown four 12-ounce bone-in chicken breasts or eight 5-ounce bone-in chicken thighs and transfer to the same bowl you used in step 1. If you've used bacon or other cured pork product and it somehow hasn't rendered (that is, produced) 2 tablespoons fat in the skillet or pan, pour in a little more oil or melt a tablespoon of unsalted butter before adding the chicken. If the pork or its kin has added too much fat, drain it down to about 2 tablespoons—or leave it for an utterly profligate meal.

The chicken's skin on or off? It's a matter of preference—and diet. Lacking the skin, the breasts and thighs brown more quickly, and the final dish will be definitely lighter—but perhaps also less satisfying, since skinless breasts easily overcook and turn stringy. You may also need to add another tablespoon of oil to the pan because the naked meat can stick—so you rob Peter to pay Paul. In no case use boneless skinless breasts; these are better in a quick sauté (see page 39).

What Is Braising?

A braise is a classic technique in which browned protein is simmered at low heat in a small amount of liquid. The name comes from an archaic French word (*braise*, BRAYZ, "live coals"—that is, what the pot rested on in the eighteenth century, back when the French were busy inventing dinner). In a classic braise, some of the meat must remain above the liquid so that it cooks in both liquid and steam. If the protein is submerged, the dish morphs into an expression of a fad from the '50s when Americans were busy inventing convenience: "smothered."

To remove the skin from a chicken thigh, peel it off the meat, starting at one corner and working across the thigh, taking off chunks of fat with the skin.

But the skin can turn depressingly spongy in the braise, no? The best remedy for this problem is this step: adequate browning. If you're still not satisfied with the result, leave the skin on now but remove it at the table.

Slip the chicken into the skillet or pan bone side up and skin side down; then switch on your vent or open a window, step back, and wait. You may need to squeeze the pieces together to fit. Skin on, they need perhaps 5 minutes over the heat; skin off, perhaps 4 minutes. You're waiting for golden brown caramelization on the outside of the chicken and, if the skin is still on, the melted subcutaneous layer of fat to slick the skillet or pan.

Turn with tongs and cook bone side down (and skin side up) for perhaps 3 minutes. Again, wait for the caramelization and now for the taste of the bone to sear into the meat. Then transfer the chicken pieces to a plate. If you happen to have the gizzard and other innards (lucky you), fry them up as well, then chop them finely to return to the braise with the chicken pieces in step 6.

• **STEP 3** Add about 4 cups diced vegetables including perhaps a little chopped dried fruit; cook, stirring often, about 4 minutes. In a French-influenced dish, the natural beginning of the sauce is a diced onion or shallots. (For a discussion of aromatics, see page 40.)

Depending on whether you're working with white- or dark-meat chicken, pair an aromatic with a host of other vegetables, roots, shoots, sweet potatoes, tomatoes, leeks, bell peppers, winter squash, and/or hearty greens like kale, all the while avoiding squishy lettuces, spinach, and greens, which don't hold up to braising. If you're cooking chicken breasts, stick with spring and summer vegetables, such as those used in Biryani (page 25). If you're cooking thighs, try heartier vegetables, such as those used in Beef Stew (page 17).

With the exception of greens, dice everything to about the same size, between ¼ inch and ½ inch. Roughly chop kale and other sturdy greens—and use about twice the amount in the mix because they cook down so dramatically.

If you want to go easy and are working with breasts, toss in one 16-ounce bag of frozen mixed vegetables. The final dish will be less toothsome, but the prep will be nil.

Consider up to ½ cup chopped dried fruit as part of the 4 cups. Fresh fruit breaks down in a low-liquid braise and turns into a jam-like sauce, none too appealing; but dried fruit holds up well to provide a sweet accent against most vegetables. Here are some basic combos: fennel and golden raisins, carrots and prunes, parsnips and dried cherries, or shallots and dried cranberries.

• **STEP 4** Toss in some minced herbs, perhaps some minced garlic, 1 tablespoon plus 1 teaspoon all-purpose flour, and 1 teaspoon salt; cook, stirring frequently, until the flour browns, about 2 minutes. As Brillat-Savarin once wrote: "Poultry is to the cook what canvas is to the painter." Particularly appealing herbs with chicken include parsley, cilantro, marjoram, sage, rosemary, oregano, thyme, and tarragon; particularly appealing spices include ground cumin, ground fenugreek, ground ginger, paprika, and saffron, as well as finely grated lemon zest and lots of freshly ground black pepper. Avoid overpowering dried spices like star anise, cloves, or cardamom pods, except for perhaps ¼ teaspoon grated nutmeg or ground allspice. Figure on about 1 to 2 tablespoons fresh herbs and perhaps ¼ to ½ teaspoon dried spices.

How do you mix and match herbs to make a good combination? Smell them. If you want to put tarragon and nutmeg into the braise, hold them both to your nose. Do they match for your palate? If not, what about tarragon and ground allspice? Or thyme and grated lemon zest?

Since the stew will simmer for at least 25 minutes, feel free to use dried herbs—so long as they're viable. Contrary to what our grandmothers and great aunts thought, dried herbs have a shelf life, perhaps 1 year if stored in a cool, dark place.

Stir everything over the heat until the herbs or spices become aromatic and the flour browns. It will add color and richness; well browned, it will also yield no raw-flour aftertaste. The flour will not thicken the sauce like a gravy; rather, it will just give it heft.

Why salt now? Because you want to leach lots of vegetable flavor—and later, chicken flavor—into the sauce. The salt helps to force out the essential juices.

• **STEP 5** Pour in 2 cups broth or an enhanced broth, scrape up any browned bits on the pan's bottom, and bring to a full simmer. Basically, you have two choices:

1. Chicken broth on its own.
2. Chicken broth mixed with an enhancer like wine, dry vermouth, dry sherry, port, cream, or coconut milk—or perhaps a more complicated, three-part combination like 1 cup chicken broth, ½ cup white wine, and ½ cup heavy cream.

When enhancing broth with another liquid, consider these schematics:

Broth and white wine or dry vermouth—very light
Broth and dry sherry—somewhat more substantial
Broth alone—moderately heavy
Broth and dry Madeira or dry Marsala—heavier still, more aromatic to boot
Broth and red wine—full-bodied
Broth and port—full-bodied yet sweet
Broth and cream—quite heavy
Broth and coconut milk—quite heavy and only for Asian and East Indian dishes

A pot of Easy Bistro Chicken Thighs. Its slow simmer yields just a few bubbles at a time, certainly nothing vigorous.

For this braise, the amounts should be about 1½ cups broth and ½ cup enhancer—but in this, as in nearly everything, there's no reason to stand on ceremony. Yes, more chicken broth will get more chicken taste into the braise. But a 1 cup/1 cup ratio of chicken broth and dry vermouth will yield a light, somewhat sweet dish, perfect with shallots, fennel, and peas. In general, save broth-and-cream mixtures for roots, tubers, and winter squash—although shallots, dried cherries, broth, and cream make an irresistible pan sauce.

All that said, vegetable broth is lighter still, summery and savory—and can be substituted for chicken broth in the lighter half of the pairings in the schematic for this dish.

But always follow this rule: if you buy canned broth, choose a no-salt or reduced-salt version. Why let someone else dictate the sodium in your dish? And we prefer fat-free canned broth at all times. If we're going to go over the top with fat, we'd rather do it ourselves.

• **STEP 6** Return the chicken and any accumulated juices as well as the bacon, pancetta, or its like to the skillet or pan, cover, reduce the heat to low, and simmer slowly, basting occasionally, until an instant-read meat thermometer inserted into the thickest part of the meat registers 165°F, perhaps 20 or 25 minutes—although the thighs should simmer slowly for up to 40 minutes, creating a richer stew. Season with salt and freshly ground black pepper to taste. Put the pieces back in the pan bone side down and skin side up. If left too long in the sauce, the skin can turn gooey. However, it mustn't dry out; baste occasionally.

The sauce should simmer slowly, just a handful of bubbles at a time. Bring the chicken slowly up to the proper temperature, creeping along so lots of the sauce's flavor infuses the meat. Yes, the thighs may reach 165°F as quickly as the breasts, but they should be cooked longer. They are chock full of connective tissue and collagen, which need to melt into the sauce. Plus, you've probably paired them with longer-cooking roots that take more time to get tender.

The dish may or may not need additional salt—depending on whether you've used bacon or pancetta. It will most certainly need a good grinding of black pepper.

Recipes for Braised Bone-In Chicken Breasts or Thighs

	Moroccan Braised Chicken Breasts	Braised Chicken Breasts and Garden Vegetables	Braised Chicken Breasts, Puttanesca Style	Braised Chicken Breasts and Mushrooms with Cream
1. Crisp and transfer to a bowl—or heat	2 Tbs canola oil	2 Tbs olive oil	1 Tbs olive oil 3 ounces pancetta, chopped	1 Tbs unsalted butter 3 ounces bacon, chopped
2. Brown and transfer to a bowl	Four 12-ounce bone-in chicken breasts	Four 12-ounce bone-in chicken breasts	Four 12-ounce bone-in chicken breasts	Four 12-ounce bone-in chicken breasts
3. Add and cook	1 medium red onion, chopped 1 cup canned chickpeas, drained ½ cup chopped dried apricots ½ cup halved pitted green olives	4 ounces shallots, thinly sliced 1 medium fennel bulb, trimmed, halved, and thinly sliced 8 baby artichokes, stems and outer leaves trimmed, top quarter removed	1 medium yellow onion, chopped 1 medium green bell pepper, seeded and chopped 6 Roma or plum tomatoes, chopped (do not seed)	6 ounces shallots, thinly sliced 12 ounces cremini or white button mushrooms, thinly sliced
4. Toss in	1 Tbs plus 1 tsp all-purpose flour 1 tsp salt ½ tsp ground cinnamon ½ tsp ground coriander ½ tsp ground cumin ½ tsp ground ginger 2 garlic cloves, minced	2 Tbs minced dill 1 Tbs plus 1 tsp all-purpose flour 2 tsp minced oregano 1½ tsp finely grated lemon zest 1 tsp salt	2 Tbs chopped, drained capers 1 Tbs plus 1 tsp all-purpose flour 1 Tbs minced rosemary 1 Tbs minced oregano 1 tsp salt 2 anchovy fillets, chopped 1 garlic clove, minced	1 Tbs plus 1 tsp all-purpose flour 1 Tbs minced tarragon 1 tsp salt ¼ tsp grated nutmeg
5. Pour in	1½ cups chicken broth ½ cup white wine	1½ cups chicken broth ½ cup white wine	1½ cups chicken broth ½ cup dry vermouth	1½ cups chicken broth ½ cup cream
6. Add, cover, and simmer	The browned chicken breasts Salt and pepper to taste	The browned chicken breasts Salt and pepper to taste	The browned chicken breasts and the frizzled pancetta Salt and pepper to taste	The browned chicken breasts and the frizzled bacon Salt and pepper to taste

	Easy Bistro Chicken Thighs	Chicken Thighs in a Thai Curry	Jerk Chicken Thighs	Braised Chicken Thighs with Cherries and Port
1. Crisp and transfer to a bowl—or heat	1 Tbs unsalted butter 3 ounces bacon, chopped	2 Tbs canola oil	2 Tbs canola oil	1 Tbs unsalted butter 3 ounces pancetta, chopped
2. Brown and transfer to a bowl	Eight 5-ounce bone-in chicken thighs	Eight 5-ounce bone-in chicken thighs	Eight 5-ounce bone-in chicken thighs	Eight 5-ounce bone-in chicken thighs
3. Add and cook	1 medium yellow onion, halved and thinly sliced 2 medium carrots or 12 baby carrots, sliced 8 pitted prunes, halved	1 small onion, diced 1 red bell pepper, seeded and diced 6 ounces green beans, thinly sliced	1 medium red onion, diced 1 ripe plantain, peeled and sliced into 1-inch rounds	4 ounces shallots, thinly sliced 2 medium parsnips, thinly sliced ½ cup chopped dried cherries
4. Toss in	1 Tbs plus 1 tsp all-purpose flour 1 Tbs chopped rosemary 2 tsp stemmed thyme 1 tsp salt 3 garlic cloves, minced	1 Tbs plus 1 tsp all-purpose flour 1 Tbs fish sauce (see page 388) Up to 1 Tbs Thai green curry paste (see page 386) 2 garlic cloves, minced 1 tsp finely grated lime zest	1 Tbs plus 1 tsp all-purpose flour 1 Tbs jerk seasoning[1] 1 tsp salt 2 garlic cloves, minced	1 Tbs plus 1 tsp all-purpose flour 2 tsp stemmed thyme 1 tsp salt 1 garlic clove, minced
5. Pour in	1½ cups chicken broth ½ cup red wine	1½ cups chicken broth ½ coconut milk	2 cups chicken broth	1½ cups chicken broth ½ cup port
6. Add, cover, and simmer	The browned chicken thighs and the frizzled bacon Salt and pepper to taste	The browned chicken thighs Salt and pepper to taste	The browned chicken thighs Salt and pepper to taste	The browned chicken thighs and the crispy pancetta Salt and pepper to taste

[1]To make your own jerk seasoning paste, place the following in a food processor fitted with a chopping blade: 7 diced medium whole scallions; ½ to 1 habanero chile, seeded and stemmed or not, at will, but quartered; 2 tablespoons red wine vinegar; 1 tablespoon canola oil; 1 tablespoon minced peeled fresh ginger; 1 tablespoon packed light brown sugar; 1½ teaspoons salt; 4 teaspoons dried spices including ground cinnamon, ground allspice, ground coriander, grated nutmeg, ground mace, rubbed sage, dried oregano, or ground cardamom. Our preference is for 1 teaspoon ground coriander, 1 teaspoon ground allspice, 1 teaspoon dried thyme, ½ teaspoon ground cinnamon, and ¼ teaspoon grated nutmeg—but you can experiment with combinations to balance the super-hot habanero. Process to a grainy paste, stopping the machine occasionally to scrape down the canister's insides. Or use a blender for this task, but increase the oil to 2 tablespoons and add 1 tablespoon water. Store, covered, in the refrigrator for up to 2 weeks or freeze indefinitely.

Braised Bone-In Pork Chops

Another bone-in cut, another braise. You'll need a very large Dutch oven, maybe even a 10-quart one, to hold these chops. The rest is all finesse—mostly your own. • MAKES 4 SERVINGS

• **STEP 1** Heat ¼ cup fat in a very large Dutch oven over medium heat. Less a blank canvas than chicken, pork chops take to medium-range fats: olive, peanut, or untoasted nut oils (see page 17 for a schema of fats). Indeed, any neutral oil—canola to corn—will also work because of the more assertive flavor of the meat. But why skimp on flavor? Unsalted butter, which will give a pronounced sourness against the rather sweet pork, should be used in combination with one of the oils to avoid overwhelming the chops. Avoid toasted oils or anything too assertive. But if you don't have a cardiologist appointment anytime soon, try duck fat—or for a real blow-out, 2 tablespoons duck fat and 2 tablespoons unsalted butter.

• **STEP 2** Dredge four 8-ounce bone-in pork loin chops in seasoned flour, slip in the pan, and cook until brown on both sides, about 8 minutes, turning once; transfer to a plate. For this dish, use loin chops if possible, rather than rib chops. Larger and meatier, loin chops will have better collagen in the bone for a juicier cut once braised. That said, rib chops will work, although you should use only quick-cooking vegetables and cut the braising time down to 25 minutes. In any event, avoid shoulder chops, which are stringier and less flavorful and need a very long braise.

Seasoned flour is simply all-purpose flour with various seasonings added to it. While mild paprika is added across the American South (and cayenne in Louisiana), seasoned flour most often refers to all-purpose flour with salt/pepper added to it. Still, ground allspice, cumin, or grated nutmeg adds a sweet, aromatic note.

To make seasoned flour, place about ¾ cup all-purpose flour on a large plate. Do not substitute cake, self-rising, or any other kind of flour. Use a fork to stir in about 1 teaspoon salt, 1 teaspoon freshly ground black pepper, and up to 2 teaspoons of another ground or dried spice if desired. Drag both sides of each chop through the mixture, shake off any excess, and slip the chops into the pan.

Leave undisturbed for 4 minutes. Resist the temptation to poke, prod, or move the chops. They need to sit steady over the heat so the flour turns golden brown, forming a light crust. If you're antsy and need something to do, wash the plate the flour was on.

Turn the chops with tongs, then leave them alone again until a light brown crust forms on the underside, perhaps another 4 minutes.

You can use a variety of spices to season all-purpose flour: here, from front to back, cayenne, ground cloves, paprika, thyme, and ground cumin.

• **STEP 3** Add about 4 cups chopped or diced vegetables to the pot; cook, stirring often, until softened, from 5 to 10 minutes. For the quickest results, stick with vegetables that take a moderate time over the heat, such as fennel, shallots, carrots, or parsnips. Or go with vegetables that will not fall apart in long cooking: leeks, peas, baby artichokes, or frozen lima beans. Zucchini and summer squash should be in hunks, perhaps 1-inch pieces. Even a double portion of kale or thicker, sturdy greens can be used.

Still, savory roots and sweet winter squash are quite appealing with pork, provided they are seeded, if necessary, peeled and diced. For potatoes, chop baby red-skinned, small white, or yellow-fleshed tubers. (Starchy Russets will unnecessarily cloud the stew.)

In total, there'll be about 45 minutes over the heat: onions will sweeten and melt; roots will soften nicely; but asparagus, broccoli florets, and green beans will turn to baby food. If you really want to use broccoli, buy whole heads, save the florets back for another night, and chop the thick stems for this braise.

Properly cut vegetables help assure correct cooking times—largest to smallest, clockwise from bottom left: roughly chopped, chopped, cubed, finely chopped, diced, and minced.

• **STEP 4** Add some minced herbs or dried spices; warm until aromatic, about 20 seconds. About 1 tablespoon (that is, 3 teaspoons) of combined spices and herbs is the top limit. Start with a small amount of dried spice, particularly fennel, celery, or caraway seeds; red pepper flakes; grated nutmeg; saffron; or ground cinnamon, cardamom, and cloves. Then round out the mixture with a complementary, headier, more ethereal fresh herb like cilantro, rosemary, sage, thyme, and oregano. A dried version of any of these is acceptable, if less heady, since the stew is going to simmer about 40 minutes. (For the difference between spices and herbs, see page 230.)

• **STEP 5** Pour in about 2½ cups liquid, deglaze the pan, nestle the chops into the sauce, cover, reduce the heat to low, and braise until very tender, about 40 minutes; season with salt and freshly ground black pepper to taste. Start with a combination of any two of the following: chicken or vegetable broth, white wine, and heavy cream. In 99 cases out of 100, skew the mix to the broth and/or away from the cream. In other words, use more broth when it's paired with wine or cream; use less cream when it's paired with broth or wine.

That said, also consider dry fortified wines with broth or cream, provided these wines are used judiciously—for example, 2 cups broth and ½ cup dry sherry. Or mix them with broth and cream: 1 cup broth, 1 cup cream, and ½ cup dry Madeira.

The notion that alcohol is "boiled away" during cooking is simply false. When alcohol is added to a braise, stew, or sauté, the amount remaining after cooking runs along these lines:

Less than 1 minute—85%
Less than 5 minutes—55%
About 15 minutes—40%
About 30 minutes—35%
About 1 hour—25%
About 2 hours—10%
About 3 hours—5%

For this braise, about 30% of the original alcohol will remain in the sauce. Such a small amount should have no effect on children or the infirm, since wine or even dry fortified wine is low in alcohol; but you should always know an action's consequences, even when you choose to ignore them. If you want to avoid wine, substitute unsweetened apple cider or white grape juice, mixing either of these with 1 teaspoon cider vinegar.

Pour in the liquid, then use a wooden spoon to get any browned or blackened bits off the pot's sides and bottom. Now put the chops back in, partially submerging them in the liquid. They should be half-in, half-out of the water, some perhaps overlapping others. Halfway through cooking, rearrange them so they're evenly braised.

Cover the pan and sit back to anticipate the coming delights of your cooking. Once the dish is done, taste the sauce and season it before napping it over the chops on plates. But do remember that there was some salt and pepper in the seasoned flour.

Chopping, Dicing, and Mincing Guidelines

Roughly chopped: uneven pieces up to 1 inch wide

Chopped: fairly uniform ½-inch pieces

Cubed: small ½-inch cubes

Finely chopped: smaller still but less precise, about ¼ inch

Diced: a small cube, about ¼ inch on all sides

Minced: the smallest of all, about ⅛ inch, made by first dicing the ingredient, then rocking a chef's knife back and forth through the pieces against a cutting board

Autumn Bone-In Pork Chops, ready for dinner

Recipes for Braised Bone-In Pork Chops

	Bone-In Pork Chops with Fennel and Leeks	Asian-Inspired Bone-In Pork Chops	German-Inspired Bone-In Pork Chops	Bone-In Pork Chops with Baby Artichokes
1. Heat	¼ cup olive oil	2 Tbs peanut oil 2 Tbs untoasted sesame oil	2 Tbs canola oil 2 Tbs unsalted butter	2 Tbs olive oil 2 Tbs unsalted butter
2. Dredge, brown, and remove	¾ cup all-purpose flour seasoned with 1 tsp salt and 1 tsp pepper Four 8-ounce bone-in pork loin chops	¾ cup all-purpose flour seasoned with 1 tsp salt, 1 tsp pepper, and 1 tsp five-spice powder (see page 149) Four 8-ounce bone-in pork loin chops	¾ cup all-purpose flour seasoned with 1 tsp salt, 1 tsp pepper, and 2 tsp dry mustard Four 8-ounce bone-in pork loin chops	¾ cup all-purpose flour seasoned with 1 tsp salt and 1 tsp pepper Four 8-ounce bone-in pork loin chops
3. Add and soften	2 medium leeks, white and pale green parts only, halved lengthwise, rinsed carefully, and thinly sliced 1 medium fennel bulb, frond and stalks discarded, the bulb trimmed and thinly sliced	4 ounces snow peas, chopped 4 medium whole scallions, thinly sliced 1 small red bell pepper, seeded and chopped	12 small red-skinned potatoes, halved 1 large green apple, peeled, seeded, and sliced	4 ounces shallots, diced 12 baby artichokes, trimmed
4. Warm	1 Tbs minced sage ½ tsp grated nutmeg	2 Tbs minced peeled fresh ginger 1 star anise pod ½ tsp red pepper flakes	2 Tbs minced dill 1 Tbs caraway seeds	1 Tbs minced oregano 1 Tbs minced rosemary ⅛ tsp saffron
5. Pour in, return chops, cover, and simmer 40 minutes; season	1½ cups chicken broth 1 cup dry white wine Salt and pepper to taste	1¾ cups chicken broth ½ cup shaoxing (see page 374) or dry sherry ¼ cup soy sauce	2 cups chicken broth ½ cup beer Salt and pepper to taste	2 cups chicken broth ½ cup white wine Salt and pepper to taste

	Springtime Bone-In Pork Chops	Summery Bone-In Pork Chops	Autumn Bone-In Pork Chops	Wintry Bone-In Pork Chops
1. Heat	¼ cup olive oil	¼ cup canola oil	2 Tbs olive oil 2 Tbs unsalted butter	¼ cup untoasted walnut oil
2. Dredge, brown, and remove	¾ cup all-purpose flour seasoned with 1 tsp salt and 1 tsp pepper Four 8-ounce bone-in pork loin chops	¾ cup all-purpose flour seasoned with 1 tsp salt and 1 tsp pepper Four 8-ounce bone-in pork loin chops	¾ cup all-purpose flour seasoned with 1 tsp salt and 1 tsp pepper Four 8-ounce bone-in pork loin chops	¾ cup all-purpose flour seasoned with 1 tsp salt, 1 tsp pepper, and ½ tsp grated or ground nutmeg Four 8-ounce bone-in pork loin chops
3. Add and soften	2 cups fresh shelled or frozen peas 2 medium kohlrabi, peeled and diced	1 medium leek, white and pale green parts only, halved lengthwise, washed carefully, and thinly sliced 2 medium zucchini, roughly chopped	1 small acorn squash, peeled, seeded and diced 4 ounces shallots, chopped ½ cup chopped dried cranberries	1 medium onion, chopped 2 medium parsnips, peeled and sliced into thin rings 2 medium carrots, sliced into thin rings
4. Warm	2 Tbs minced chives 1 Tbs minced parsley	2 Tbs minced rosemary ½ tsp red pepper flakes	One 4-inch cinnamon stick 2 whole cloves 1 bay leaf (discard all before serving)[1]	3 garlic cloves, minced 2 bay leaves 1 Tbs minced oregano
5. Pour in, return chops, cover, and simmer 40 minutes; season	1½ cups chicken broth 1 cup dry white wine Salt and pepper to taste	1½ cups dry white wine 1 cup chicken broth Salt and pepper to taste	2 cups chicken broth ½ cup cream Salt and pepper to taste	1½ cups chicken broth 1 cup canned crushed tomatoes Salt and pepper to taste

[1]Bay leaves must always be discarded before any dish with them is served. They will provide an unwelcome, bitter crunch on someone's plate. Also, never store a cooked dish in the refrigerator or the freezer with the bay leaf still in it; the taste will turn markedly bitter over time.

Brunswick Stew

American Southerners wage war over who claims this thick stew: Brunswick, Georgia, or Brunswick County, Virginia. And they fight over its meat, too: chicken or squirrel. No matter: Brunswick stew is a tomato-based, well-stocked rib-sticker, more meat and vegetables than liquid. (No squirrel required.) • MAKES 6 HEARTY SERVINGS

• **STEP 1** Make a dark roux in a large Dutch oven over medium-low heat using ¼ cup all-purpose flour and ¼ cup oil or unsalted butter, stirring occasionally. A roux (French, ROO) is a thickening and flavoring agent, usually made from equal parts fat and all-purpose flour. It's the basis of several, classic French sauces, as well as Southern American classics like gumbo, etouffée, and this stew. A roux is traditionally made with unsalted butter—and it can certainly be so made here. However, a dark roux, named because of its far-beyond-peanut-butter color, is usually made with a fat that can stand up to higher temperatures and longer cooking.

For Southern cooks, that fat more often than not is peanut oil with its mild taste and high smoke point (the temperature at which the oil will volatilize and ignite). Do not use unrefined Asian bottlings, often with peanut particles floating in the oil and cloudy even at room temperature. These may well ignite when heated for prolonged periods.

And prolonged periods are what a dark roux is all about. Indeed, it's the basic flavor; everything in this dish is built off its foundation. (And thus this humble stew contradicts centuries of cookery: here, sweet will be built off bitter, and not the other way around.)

Some Southern cooks identify a roux by how many bottles of beer they can drink before it's ready. This is definitely a two- or even three-bottle event. Whisk the fat and flour together in the pan over medium-low heat, then let it cook for perhaps 8 minutes if using butter, more likely 10 minutes with peanut oil, or even up to 16 minutes if the heat is a little lower, whisking occasionally at first and then more often as the color deepens. Think melted caramel or reddish-brown mud. When whisked, the roux will not instantly flow back into place but may momentarily leave dry, slightly crusty lines in the pot.

• **STEP 2** Raise the heat to medium, add 3 cups mirepoix or a modified mirepoix, and cook just until slightly softened, stirring constantly, about 3 minutes. A *mirepoix* (French, meer-PWAH, named for the culinary expertise of the old Duchy of Lévis-Mirepoix) is a trio of diced vegetables, often referred to as the holy trinity of French cooking: onions, celery, and carrots. For the classic proportions, use twice as much onion by volume as celery and carrot—for example, 1 chopped large yellow onion (about 1½ cups), 1 thinly sliced medium carrot (about ¾ cup), and 2 thinly sliced celery ribs (about ¾ cup). However, the proportions change continuously in modern cooking and the classic ratio is by and large forgotten by everyone except the fussi-

Watch for these three basic stages when cooking a roux—first, a blond or light roux, best for simple braises and easy bistro-inspired stews.

Next, a medium roux—a moderately heavy taste, good against heartier cuts of meat.

And finally a dark roux, well toasted and quite complex, the perfect start for Brunswick Stew.

est chefs. Indeed, modern Western cooking is about breaking eighteenth-century French culinary traditions: keeping them in mind, yes—they still structure the "argument" of a dish and their absence would render most cooking meaningless—but morphing and breaking them at will.

Brunswick Stew often begins with what's sometimes called an "American mirepoix" (aka "the Cajun holy trinity"): onion, celery, and seeded green bell pepper. But once you know the basics of a mirepoix, you, too, can vary its components. For example, substitute 2 to 4 medium shallots or 1 medium leek for the large onion; substitute a parsnip or diced small sweet potato for the carrot. Many modern French chefs substitute diced, peeled celeriac for the celery, a more earthy taste and certainly more sophisticated. Or what of white, juicy, if rather esoteric parsley root? In other words, make a trio of aromatic vegetables that will flavor the stew with an onion or its equivalent as the base. Your only real concern? Since everything will cook for quite a while, make sure all the vegetables are able to stand up to long cooking. Do not use asparagus, broccoli, and other spring vegetables. These can be added later in step 4. Instead, play around with trimmed fennel for the celery, turnips for the carrot—the big flavors of long-cooking vegetables. However, do remember that if you're making a shellfish or fish Brunswick stew, the time over the heat will be markedly less. Hard roots may not have time to soften.

• **STEP 3** Stir in 4 cups (1 quart) broth or an enhanced broth, 3½ cups diced tomatoes, some dried herbs and spices, and 3 to 5 pounds bone-in meat or shell-on large shellfish; bring to a simmer, cover, reduce the heat to low, and cook until the meat or shellfish is cooked through. Use broth in toto or an enhanced version with white wine or dry vermouth. No cream or coconut milk. Of the total amount, use no more than 2 cups wine or dry vermouth; its addition will dramatically lighten the stew, turning it more toward summer, making the flavors less intense and sweeter, too.

If you don't want to use canned diced tomatoes (the amount called for is about a 28-ounce can), try chopped fresh tomatoes, either in combination with canned tomatoes or as an outright substitute. The skins may come off and wrinkle into shards in the stew; but the taste will be decidedly fresher, particularly if you've used 1 cup white wine with 3 cups broth. However, fresh tomatoes will need some time to soften in the stew; the cooking time in step 4 will probably need to be increased by about 10 minutes. Also consider adding ½ extra cup of broth to compensate for their drier texture.

Dried herbs and spices are best because they'll simmer a long time without adding little flecks of blackened green in the tomato-based broth. In general, add either cayenne or red pepper flakes for heat. A bay leaf or a cinnamon stick adds a nice back-taste but should be removed before the stew is served.

The protein, whether meat, fish, or shellfish, is not browned; rather, it's simply stirred into the pot after the liquid, the better to let the flavors of the darkened roux provide most of the caramelized taste. Consider these your basic choices:

One 4- to 4½-pound chicken, skinned and cut up. There's no point in adding the skin; it will simply add a layer of unincorporated fat that skims the pot. The breasts may well be cooked long before the rest of the meat; remove them after perhaps 30 minutes, then let the other pieces stew longer, until falling-apart tender.

One 5- to 6-pound duck, cut up, the skin and fat removed. If you're unsure of its anatomy, have the butcher cut it into 6 pieces for you.

One 4- to 4½-pound rabbit, cut into 6 pieces. Here's a throw-back to that original squirrel: a sweet, rich taste, a little more sophisticated than chicken. The pieces with the rounded loin may well be cooked through before the legs; check it and consider removing them after 20 minutes.

2½ pounds shell-on large shrimp (perhaps 20 per pound), deveined (see page 315). Use large shrimp, about 12 to 20 per pound, so they'll cook at least 10 minutes to flavor the stew and so the meat can be later chopped into bite-sized bits. If you find head-on shrimp, all the better—and use perhaps 3½ to 4 pounds to compensate for the extra weight of the heads (which will be discarded after cooking).

Two 1½-pound lobsters. You'll need to use a very large Dutch oven for this stew, perhaps even a stock pot. Here's a problem: plunging them in boiling water is actually crueler than just quickly killing them outright. Pierce their heads just behind the eye stalks with a chef's knife, the blade facing away from the tail; then slice down so that you cut their heads in half. It's admittedly gruesome, and you can put them to the plunge if you wish, but it may well be an easier death for the creatures. If you're squeamish, use frozen lobster tails, available at most supermarkets. They'll take about 10 minutes to cook once they've been thawed in the refrigerator overnight.

5 pounds whole, live crawfish. With this Cajun version, you can have great, messy fun sucking out the head juices while shelling the tail meat after it's cooked.

There are Brunswick versions that use beef (chuck, arm, or shoulder roasts) and pork (shoulder)—or even ground beef or pork. However, they quickly turn fatty, so they often also include ketchup or barbecue sauce (or both!) to help weigh down and incorporate all that excess fat. If you would like to make a beef or pork version, skip the ketchup and/or barbecue sauce: make the stew the day before, refrigerate it overnight, and skim the pot before reheating over low heat, stirring often to prevent scorching once the stew's been thickened.

Timing here is a matter of the protein you've chosen: duck and rabbit, about 1 hour; chicken breasts about 30 minutes, the other pieces about 25 more minutes; lobster and crawfish, about 20 minutes; and large shrimp, about 10 minutes.

• **STEP 4** Remove the meat or shellfish from the pot; set aside to cool. Stir in 6 cups chopped quick-cooking vegetables; raise the heat to medium-high and simmer, uncovered, for 20 minutes, or until the vegetables are cooked. Use tongs and a slotted spoon to remove the meat or shellfish; all liquid should drip back into the pot so not a drop is wasted.

A well-stocked pot of Brunswick Stew is thickened with minced, toasted, stale bread.

Now's your chance to add those spring and summer vegetables. Okra and corn are traditional—frozen versions work well—but feel free to try sugar snaps, green beans, chunks of zucchini or summer squash, as well diced fennel and radishes, frozen lima beans, or even chopped kale or cabbage. As with all greens, double the amount used; for example, if using 3 cups peas, fill out the vegetable selection with 6 cups packed chopped kale.

While quick-cooking vegetables are most common at this stage, you can skip them altogether and add diced wintry roots like seeded, peeled butternut squash; peeled sweet potatoes; or shredded Brussels sprouts. Harder vegetables should be chopped into ½-inch pieces. If adding these, the stew may well need to cook longer. To do so, simmer uncovered for 20 minutes as directed, then cover the pot and keep simmering until the vegetables are tender when pierced with a fork. Stir occasionally as well. Do not mix them with broccoli, asparagus, or other quick-cookers, which will turn mushy in the prolonged heat required to cook the roots. Also be careful of a double hit: roots earlier in the stew (in step 2) and then again in this step. In general, use roots (celeriac, parsnips, etc.) in one step or the other, but not both. And one more caveat: if the stew needs to simmer a while to get the vegetables tender, you should refrigerate the cooked meat for safety's sake until you're ready to use it in the next step.

• **STEP 5** Meanwhile, debone the meat or shell the shellfish and chop into bite-sized pieces. When the vegetables are tender, stir the meat or shellfish and 2 pieces minced toasted crustless stale bread into the stew. Cook for 5 minutes, stirring constantly, then season with salt and freshly ground black pepper. Lobster claws and knuckles should be cracked open to release the meat inside; the shrimp will need to be peeled and roughly chopped. All meat should be deboned and then chopped so that the stew can be eaten with a spoon, not a knife and fork. Any liquid in the shells—or on the cutting board, for that matter—should be reserved and stirred back into the stew with the meat.

The stale bread will thicken the stew in the way the roux cannot. Once toasted dark brown, the roux loses much of its thickening power and acts primarily as a flavoring agent. So now use a couple pieces of crunchy bread that are well beyond their prime to thicken the stew. Cut off the crusts, then toast the bread until lightly browned. Mince finely by rocking a large knife back and forth through the pieces until they're almost like bread crumbs.

Some old-time Southern cooks butter the bread before chopping and adding it to the stew. Or they toast the bread slices in a skillet with some melted butter. In any case, once the bread bits are in the pot, stir constantly because they can fall out of suspension and burn on the pot's bottom.

If you want an easier solution, stir in ½ cup unseasoned dried bread crumbs. For a deeper taste, toast them on a lipped baking sheet in a preheated 300°F oven, stirring occasionally, until lightly browned, about 6 minutes.

Finally, add salt and pepper to taste, perhaps 1 teaspoon of each and then more by choice. Some cooks also stir in Worcestershire sauce at this point (perhaps 1 or 2 tablespoons, a salty/sweet addition). If you do, adjust the table salt accordingly, perhaps to just ½ teaspoon. Then ladle the stew into bowls and have Tabasco sauce or another hot red pepper sauce on hand for dribbling over individual servings.

Recipes for Brunswick Stews

	Chicken Brunswick Stew	Rabbit Brunswick Stew	Shrimp Brunswick Stew	Lobster Brunswick Stew
1. Make a dark roux with	¼ cup all-purpose flour ¼ cup peanut oil	¼ cup all-purpose flour ¼ cup peanut oil	¼ cup all-purpose flour ¼ cup peanut oil	¼ cup all-purpose flour ¼ cup unsalted butter
2. Add and soften slighlty	1 medium yellow onion, chopped 1 small green bell pepper, seeded and chopped 2 celery ribs, thinly sliced	1 medium yellow onion, chopped 1 medium carrot, thinly sliced 1 small celeriac, peeled and diced	8 ounces shallots, diced 1 medium carrot, thinly sliced 2 celery ribs, thinly sliced	1 medium yellow onion, chopped 1 small red bell pepper, seeded and chopped 2 celery ribs, thinly sliced
3. Add, cover, and cook	4 cups (1 quart) chicken broth 3½ cups canned diced tomatoes 2 tsp dried thyme 2 tsp dried sage ½ tsp cayenne One 4-inch cinnamon stick (discard before serving) One 4½-pound chicken, cut up and the skin removed (the giblets removed as well)	4 cups (1 quart) chicken broth 3½ cups canned diced tomatoes 2 tsp dried oregano 2 tsp minced dried orange peel 1 tsp red pepper flakes 2 bay leaves (discard before serving) One 4-pound rabbit, cut into 6 pieces	2 cups fish stock or clam juice 2 cups dry white wine 3½ cups canned diced tomatoes 2 tsp dried thyme ¼ tsp grated nutmeg 2 bay leaves (discard before serving) 2½ pounds shell-on large shrimp (about 20 per pound)	2 cups vegetable broth 2 cups fish stock or clam juice 3½ cups canned diced tomatoes 2 tsp dried sage 2 tsp minced dried lemon peel ¼ tsp cayenne Two 1½-pound lobsters
4. Remove the meat, add, and cook	3 cups frozen corn kernels 3 cups frozen sliced okra	2 diced peeled medium sweet potatoes 12 ounces green beans, chopped	3 medium yellow-fleshed potatoes, peeled and diced 1 medium fennel bulb, trimmed and thinly sliced 1 cup frozen corn kernels	2 cups fresh shelled or frozen peas 2 cups frozen okra 2 cups frozen pearl onions
5. Add and heat through until thickened; season	The chopped chicken meat 2 pieces minced, toasted, stale bread 1 Tbs Worcestershire sauce Salt and pepper to taste	The chopped rabbit meat 2 pieces minced, toasted, stale bread Salt and pepper to taste	The chopped shrimp meat 2 pieces minced, toasted, stale bread Salt and pepper to taste	The chopped lobster meat 2 pieces minced, toasted, stale bread Salt and pepper to taste

Burgers

Although burgers come in a wide range—beef, turkey, cod, salmon, ostrich, chicken, and halibut, to name a few—we've lumped them together because their cooking techniques are remarkably similar. The only exception? Veggie Burgers (page 391). That said, the variations here are indeed a little different: everything follows the same general pattern, although meat, poultry, and fish burgers deviate in significant ways. • MAKES 6 BURGERS

• **STEP 1** Mix 2 pounds ground meat, poultry, or fish with one of these enhancers: 4 ounces ground mushrooms for meat, ¾ cup cooked grain or couscous for poultry, or ¼ pound peeled and deveined shrimp for fish—or alternatively, grind trimmed meat, poultry, or fish by hand at home with its stated enhancer. Admittedly, this is a little tricky—and so we'll take it burger by burger. But first here's an explanation of the why and wherefore. Ground meat, even ground fish, has two, contradictory tendencies:

1. It is extraordinarily fatty (even fish burgers often have the skin ground with the flesh for added moisture).
2. It loses much of that fat over the heat and ends up exceptionally dry.

Anyone who has ever choked down a dry-as-Egypt-in-August hamburger at a family reunion knows the problem. So ground meat, poultry, and fish are best if they have a little help with their moisture content. Unfortunately, solving the problem usually involves adding fat. One fast-food restaurant in Wisconsin actually cuts butter into every hamburger patty. Um, no. Without turning puritanical, we all need to be eating better than that. So how then do you keep burgers moist without larding them up?

Burgers made from ground meat

Start with 2 pounds ground beef, pork, veal, or buffalo—or a combination of any two. Excellent combos include 1½ pounds ground beef and ½ ground pork or 1 pound ground beef and 1 pound ground veal. Also treat ground ostrich, a beef pretender, as you would any of these ground meats, using it on its own or mixing it with another ground meat. Then mix in ¼ pound ground mushrooms, usually white button or cremini mushrooms, but sometimes shiitake caps, portobello caps, or even exotic forest mushrooms.

The best burgers are a combination of meat, an enhancer, and some spices: here, from top, salmon with shrimp, mustard, and tarragon; ground turkey with couscous and barbecue sauce; and finally ground beef with mushrooms, sun-dried tomatoes, and Worcestershire sauce.

There are two ways to get the job done:

1. Buy already-ground meat, then grind the mushrooms in a food processor fitted with the chopping blade just until they are the consistency of very coarse salt; they must not become a soggy paste. Stir these ground mushrooms into the ground meat.
2. Run trimmed pieces of meat and quartered mushrooms together through your own meat grinder. Trimmed sirloin is exceptional; top or bottom round is also good, if leaner and drier. Veal stew meat can make excellent burgers as can pork loin or boneless country-style ribs—or better yet, a combination of the latter two.

Burgers made from ground poultry

Mix 2 pounds ground turkey or chicken with ¾ cup cooked couscous or a cooked, cooled grain like white rice, brown rice, barley, quinoa, or wheat berries. Rice and most of the other grains must also be hand-chopped or pulsed in a food processor until they're about the size of couscous grains; quinoa is ready to go when cooked. But be forewarned: food processors quickly turn rice into mush.

In truth, the best option is unflavored couscous. Stir it into the requisite amount of boiling water according to the package instructions, cover, set aside for 5 minutes or so, and it's done. By the way, almost all the couscous sold in North American markets is so-called "instant" couscous, meaning it's precooked and dried. Basically, you're just rehydrating a cooked semolina product. If you find real couscous at a North African market, you'll have to go through a complicated process of steaming it (often twice) to get it fluffy—probably not the best pay-off for a burger.

Or consider soaking rolled oats (not quick-cooking or steel-cut) in a bowl with very hot water for 5 minutes before draining and chopping. Or make a whole grain from scratch and add it: about ¼ cup of a dried grain will cook up to the correct amount. Quick-cooking barley is a modern marvel for times like these.

You can indeed grind skinless bird cuts: turkey cutlets, boneless chicken thighs. Or have the butcher grind the cuts you select at the market on the spot. A mix of 1 pound white meat and 1 pound dark works best for burgers. But don't put the grain through the grinder with the meat; instead, stir the ground bird and the grain together in a large bowl.

Burgers made from ground fish

You'll need 2 pounds of fish fillets and ¼ pound raw peeled and deveined medium shrimp (about 30 per pound—or 7 or 8 such shrimp). Since the shrimp will need

Ground Bird

According to the USDA, a package labeled "ground turkey meat" or "ground chicken meat" should contain only the muscle—that is, the meat without the fat or skin. (Note the important word in the label: "meat.") A package labeled "ground turkey" or "ground chicken" has it all: muscle, fat, and skin. (Note the absence of that important word.) If the ground turkey or chicken is solely white meat, it must be labeled as such; all other packaging should be presumed to be a combination of dark and white meat, usually weighted heavily toward the dark. And then comes the obligatory bureaucratic complication: if it says "ground white meat chicken meat" or "ground white meat turkey meat," then there's none of the other stuff you may not want; but if it says "ground white meat chicken" or "ground white meat turkey," it's probably got the skin, fat, and even cartilage in it.

to be ground, do not buy already-ground salmon, tuna, and such at the market.

Still, fish doesn't run through a grinder very well; if you want to try it, make sure you give the internal parts a good coating of non-stick spray. Some markets will grind fish for you; ask to see if yours will accommodate. Failing that (and a simpler solution anyway) put the cut-up fillets and the shrimp in a food processor fitted with the chopping blade; then pulse repeatedly, scraping down the canister's sides once or twice, until the mixture is ground without turning into wallpaper paste.

Firm-fleshed fish works best: salmon, tuna, halibut, cod, or even swordfish. Thin-fleshed white fish fillets like snapper and bass tend to mush up. If you use any of these—including tilapia, drum, and parrotfish—chop the shrimp first to give it a head start in the processor.

All fish should be ground without its skin. Have the fishmonger at your market remove it or do it yourself (page 124). Also, right before it's ground, run your fingers lightly over the meat to check for bones, removing any with a pair of sterilized tweezers.

Mix the ground turkey meat, couscous, and barbecue sauce together in one bowl, taking care not to turn the meat's fibers into mush.

● **STEP 2** Mix in some basic flavorings: herbs, spices, liquids, pastes, or condiments; season with salt and some freshly ground black pepper; and form into 6 patties. Again, there are some basic differences among the burgers, but the technique is the same.

Burgers made from ground meat

Add 2 tablespoons Worcestershire sauce and if desired, *up to* 2 tablespoons chopped herb(s) or a seasoning mix: curry powder (see page 113), garam masala (see page 27), lemon pepper seasoning, bottled jerk seasoning, or another bottled spice mixture. Excellent herbs to match with hamburgers include parsley, oregano, and thyme. Or use a solid flavoring agent such as finely chopped sun-dried tomatoes or pitted olives. Even finely chopped, toasted nuts add lots of flavor. And up to ¼ teaspoon grated nutmeg or ground mace is a sweet, aromatic addition.

Burgers made from ground poultry

Add about 6 tablespoons of a moist, pasty flavoring agent: ketchup, American barbecue sauce, Chinese barbecue sauce, pesto of any variety, canned minced chiles, hoisin or chouhee sauce, applesauce, prepared mustard, chutney, pickle relish, Chinese bean sauce, American chow chow, or pizza sauce. Avoid soy sauce, maple syrup, and the like because they're too wet. Rather, this flavoring agent should add both body and necessary moisture, binding with the whole grain to keep the burger intact. If desired, also add 1 tablespoon minced herb or perhaps 1 teaspoon dried spice— but bird burgers thrive on simplicity, not complicated flavors.

Fish burgers must not be ground to a paste; there should be some chunky graininess in the mixture.

To keep burgers from balling up over the heat, make a fairly deep indentation in one side of each patty with your thumb.

Burgers made from ground fish

Add up to ¼ cup minced fresh herb(s) as well as perhaps 2 tablespoons additional solid flavoring and/or 1 to 2 tablespoons liquid flavoring. For the solid flavoring, consider chopped pitted green or black olives, drained capers, minced pickled sushi ginger, minced peeled fresh ginger, chopped sun-dried tomatoes, or chopped jarred pimientos or roasted red peppers. For the liquid flavoring, there's soy sauce, lemon or lime juice, Worcestershire sauce, Dijon or deli mustard, vinegar of any variety (except flavored vinegars), or even prepared bottled horseradish. Use common sense with the amount: if you're a person who likes milder flavors, two tablespoons of bottled horseradish or spicy mustard is going to blow you out of your seat. In the end, you can add both types of flavoring, the solid and the liquid agents; but you needn't add either and can go with just an herb. A simple fish burger with a single herb is a pleasure indeed. Still, who could argue with tarragon in a salmon burger paired with some chopped sun-dried tomatoes and a little prepared mustard?

For all types of burgers, add some salt and freshly ground black pepper, taking into account that Worcestershire and other flavorings may have already added salt. Then mix the entire thing into a uniform mass. The best way to do this? Wash and use your hands, the best tools you have in the kitchen. If you're squeamish about getting your fingers dirty, use a long-handled wooden spoon. Do not mix until you've got baby food. Rather, leave some texture in the meat—if not much.

Still, you're going to have to get your hands dirty, no matter what you do. Wet them slightly, form the mixture into 6 even balls, and pat them between your palms into circles about 4 inches in diameter and ½ inch thick. One problem: burgers can ball up over the heat. As you form them, put a fairly deep, thumb-shaped indentation in one flat side, a little well that will prevent the patty from curling. Don't be shy, but don't poke through or cause the meat to be too thin in the center.

The patties can now be set on a plate, covered with plastic wrap, and refrigerated for up to 4 hours—or if there's no acid in the mix, up to 24 hours.

• **STEP 3** Heat 2 tablespoons fat in a large skillet or grill pan over medium heat; add the patties and cook until well browned and at the proper temperature, turning once. If you don't have a skillet or grill pan large enough to hold all the burgers, you'll have to cook them in batches, adding more fat the second time around; or else use two skillets or grill pans over two burners, adding 2 tablespoons fat to each.

Sesame oil is a great match to Asian seasonings; unsalted butter, to a rich hamburger. Really, use any fat you'd like, but think about how it mixes with the flavorings in the patties. When in doubt, punt: use a neutral oil like canola or safflower.

Turn the burgers with a wide metal spatula; otherwise, they can chip and break. If you're working in a nonstick skillet, use a spatula specifically designed for its surface.

The various burgers cook to different temperatures. According to the USDA, beef and buffalo should be cooked to 160°F; ostrich, turkey, and chicken, to 165°F; and pork, to 170°F—all 8 to 10 minutes over the heat, turning once. If the patty has a mixture of meats in it, cook it to the highest temperature required. Always use an instant-read meat thermometer inserted into the center of one patty to determine its exact temperature.

Still, most pests are killed above 140°F. And for many people, these recommended temperatures are simply too high, the meat too well-done. Meat burgers are best about 140°F to 150°F; bird burgers, about 160°F, both about 7 minutes, turning once. Yes, you can eat rare beef burgers (at an internal temperature of 120°F), but make sure they're made with certified organic meat you've ground yourself. As in most things, know what you're doing and the consequences of it.

The USDA recommends 145°F for fish burgers, but this temperature may well be too high for those who like sushi or medium-rare salmon. A better alternative is to cook tuna burgers to rare (about 4 minutes, turning once), salmon burgers to medium rare (about 6 minutes, turning once), and cod or halibut burgers until cooked through (about 8 minutes, turning once). Still, eating undercooked shrimp can cause problems for those with compromised constitutions and may simply be unsavory to others.

As a final note, you needn't fry any of these burgers. Instead, preheat the broiler, rub the patties with about 1 teaspoon oil on each side, then place them in the broiler pan and broil 4 to 6 inches from the heat source, turning once, until the desired temperature has been reached.

Once the patties are off the heat, you can build any burger to your heart's desire: on buttered toast slices with sliced, salted radishes; on buns with barbecue sauce and sliced pickled okra; on toasted English muffins topped with ratatouille; or on a large flour tortilla and topped with lots of chopped salad. Then again, why tinker with shredded lettuce, chopped tomato, a slice of red onion, and a smear of deli mustard?

CHEESEBURGERS

Never for fish, rarely for bird, but often for meat: there are two ways to get good cheeseburgers.

1. Once the patty has cooked on one side and been turned, let it cook a couple minutes, then lay a thin slice of cheese over the top, cover the skillet, and cook for 1 or 2 minutes, until the meat is at the proper temperature and the cheese has melted. Don't just think Cheddar or Monterey Jack; consider Gruyère, Emmental, Asiago, or even a mixture of a little blue cheese underneath a thin slice of Parmigiano-Reggiano.

2. Form the meat mixture into 12 thinner patties, not the stated 6. Grate or crumble ½ to 1 ounce hard, semi-firm, or semi-soft cheese onto each of 6 of the patties (see page 175 for an explanation of the various categories for cheese). Top each patty with a second patty, seal the edges well, and cook as directed, thereby melting the cheese inside the burgers.

Recipes for Burgers

1. Combine	Best-Ever Hamburgers	Sun-Dried Tomato Burgers	Southwest Buffalo Burgers	Asian-Inspired Burgers
1. Combine	1½ pounds lean ground beef ½ pound ground pork 4 ounces cremini mushrooms, ground	1 pound lean ground beef 1 pound ground pork 4 ounces portobello mushroom caps, ground	2 pounds ground buffalo 4 ounces cremini mushrooms, ground	1 pound ground pork 1 pound lean ground beef 4 ounces shiitake caps, ground
2. Mix in and form into patties	2 Tbs Worcestershire sauce Salt and pepper to taste	2 Tbs Worcestershire sauce ¼ cup minced sun-dried tomatoes packed in oil 1 Tbs minced oregano Salt and pepper to taste	2 Tbs Worcestershire sauce 1 Tbs chili powder 1 tsp ground cumin ¼ tsp ground cinnamon Salt and pepper to taste	2 Tbs Worcestershire sauce 2 Tbs minced cilantro 2 tsp minced peeled fresh ginger 1 tsp chile oil (see page 375) Salt and pepper to taste
3. Fry in	2 Tbs canola oil	2 Tbs olive oil	2 Tbs canola oil	2 Tbs sesame oil

	Pesto Chicken Burgers	Barbecued Turkey Burgers	Bistro Salmon Burgers	Herbed Halibut Burgers
1. Combine	2 pounds ground chicken, preferably a mix of white and dark meat ¾ cup chopped cooked barley	2 pounds ground turkey, preferably a mix of white and dark meat ¾ cup cooked couscous	2 pounds skinless salmon fillet ¼ pound medium shrimp, peeled and deveined	2 pounds skinless halibut fillet ¼ pound medium shrimp, peeled and deveined
2. Mix in and form into patties	6 Tbs pesto Salt and pepper to taste	6 Tbs barbecue sauce Salt and pepper to taste	2 Tbs minced tarragon 2 Tbs Dijon mustard Salt and pepper to taste	2 Tbs minced parsley 1 Tbs minced oregano 1 Tbs stemmed thyme 1 Tbs lemon juice Salt and pepper to taste
3. Fry in	2 Tbs olive oil	2 Tbs peanut oil	2 Tbs canola oil	2 Tbs olive oil

Cacciatora

Although often called "cacciatore" (that is, "from the hunter"), this tomato-and-mushroom-laced braise is actually *cacciatora* in Italian (cah-chee-ah-TOH-rah—that is, "from the hunter's wife"). It's all too easy to forget who created the modern home-cook food scene, lock, stock, and braise—not the hunter, but the one back home who kept the pots of hearty fare on the stove. • MAKES 6 SERVINGS

• **STEP 1** Heat 2 or 3 tablespoons olive oil and/or unsalted butter in a large Dutch oven over medium heat. At first blush, there's little sense in rearranging the basic flavors of Italian cooking, so olive oil and unsalted butter are the choices and limits. Although a mix is best, using all butter yields a silkier, richer dish; all olive oil, a brighter, lighter taste. If you use only butter, lower the heat in the next few steps if it starts to burn on the pot's bottom.

That said, there's no reason not to mix it up. Untoasted walnut or almond oil makes an interesting, sophisticated dish, tilting Italy toward France, the way Napoleon wanted to. Rendered duck fat is a luxurious indulgence, hard to beat (or to justify). Toasted oils are too heavy; neutral oils like corn and canola add zilch to the pot, a wasted layer in a complex braise.

• **STEP 2** Add about 4 ounces chopped smoked and/or cured pork product or its substitute (see page 18); cook, stirring often, until crisp; transfer to a bowl. Think through the dish before you begin. Where do you want to end up? With a winter braise? Break out the bacon and butter. A springtime supper? Use olive oil and prosciutto. With a rich but still fairly light dish? A mix of olive oil and butter with chopped pancetta. Just remember two things: 1) you're building layers of flavor and 2) you're trying to mitigate an unwarranted complexity. Duck prosciutto is all fine and good in a simple braise with few flavors; it could be downright confusing here without limiting the later selection of vegetables to just a single choice, simplifying the braise a bit so that the taste of that cured duck meat comes through. In other words, the more complex you go early on, the simpler you might want to go in later steps.

• **STEP 3** Dredge 3½ to 5 pounds cut-up chicken, other birds, rabbit, lamb stew meat, or lamb shoulder chops in seasoned flour on a plate, add the pieces to the pot in batches, and fry until lightly browned before transferring to the bowl from step 2. For a discussion of seasoned flour, see page 51 Plan on using 1 teaspoon each salt and freshly ground pepper with about ¾ cup all-purpose flour. One warning: too much flour will turn the stew gummy and cloudy. Turn the meat in the seasoned flour and shake off any excess.

There's no reason to add more spices—again, note the balancing act good cooking requires: you work through a complex braise to simplify the flavors; you work up a simple sauté to make the flavors a little more sophisticated.

The more bone in the meat, the more total weight you'll need to feed six people. For on-the-bone cuts of lamb or guinea hens, plan on 5 pounds; for bone-in chicken, 3½ to 4 pounds. Chicken breasts should be cut in half the short way, each making two pieces.

The pieces should be lightly browned, a creamy dark beige, but still well colored. A little caramelization will enhance the stew; deep browning would weigh it down, adding bitter undertones. Again, it's all trade-offs and balance—like marriage.

If you've got the liver, gizzard, and/or heart from the bird or rabbit, chop them into bite-sized pieces, dredge them in the flour, and cook as well. They'll give the stew a decided richness, a little mineraly. But do not use the rabbit's kidneys, sometimes still hanging inside the carcass; these must undergo a special preparation and would add an unwelcome taste.

• **STEP 4** Cook 1 chopped large yellow onion, several minced garlic cloves, and 2 to 3 cups chopped vegetables in the fat, stirring often until softened. In addition to the onion and garlic, consider a host of aromatic vegetables including baby artichokes (stems and outer leaves trimmed off), chopped celery, seeded bell peppers, cardoons, or even Chinese long beans. Under few circumstances in a braise are vegetables ready for the heat without some preparation: onions must be peeled and diced; scallions must be trimmed and thinly sliced; potatoes may not need to be peeled but definitely must be chopped for quicker cooking. That said, you could take the easy route here and add frozen lima beans, frozen corn, frozen peas, or frozen quartered artichoke hearts.

TO CUT UP A RABBIT: First take off the larger back legs by wiggling them to reveal their joints and then slicing through the ball sockets.

Now remove the smaller front legs the same way, wiggling them before slicing through the joint.

Finally, cut the loin and back into two or three serving-size pieces.

Roots and tubers like parsnips, carrots, sweet potatoes, and potatoes should be used in moderation: perhaps half the total amount. White creamer or red-skinned potatoes are a better choice than Russets, which would add milky starch and detract from the overall lightness. Avoid leafy greens which will turn mushy, as will asparagus or broccoli. Dried beans will not have enough time to cook. But feel free to add perhaps 1 cup canned, drained, and rinsed beans—although they may break down a bit as the stew simmers.

If you want a sweet accent, consider adding ¼ cup chopped pitted prunes; for a little sourness, ¼ cup chopped dried apricots, especially if you're going to use stronger herbs or spices like rosemary or ground cinnamon in step 7.

The mushrooms have given off their liquid and it's been boiled down to a glaze that momentarily holds its shape when the pan is scraped with a wooden spoon.

• **STEP 5** Add about 12 ounces mushrooms, thickly sliced or chopped; cook, stirring often, until they release their liquid and it reduces to a glaze. Clean mushrooms by rinsing them with cold water and blotting dry on paper towels. Or wipe off any dirt with a damp towel or mushroom brush. In general, cut a little off the bottom of the stem, the bit that has dried out—except for shiitakes, whose stems must be removed altogether since they're too fibrous to soften in a braise.

Mushrooms hold a great amount of water and nutrients in their honeycombed cells; they'll release this liquid over the heat as the cells collapse. You're looking for a noticeable pick-up of moisture on the pot's bottom—and then that liquid to simmer away until it becomes a thickened glaze.

• **STEP 6** Pour in about 1 cup wine or dry fortified wine, raise the heat to medium-high, and boil until the total amount of liquid in the pot has been reduced by half, about 3 minutes, scraping up any browned bits on the pot's bottom. As a general rule, use white wine with pancetta or prosciutto; red wine with bacon or other smoked products. Dry Marsala or dry Madeira adds an aromatic sweetness. A rosé is lovely with lamb, prosciutto, peas, and artichoke hearts. The point here is to concentrate the wine's flavor and enrich it with the caramelized bits on the pot's bottom.

If you didn't buy diced canned tomatoes, cut up whole tomatoes in their can with kitchen shears.

• **STEP 7** Stir in about 3½ cups canned diced tomatoes, some herbs and/or other aromatics, the lightly sautéed meat and pork or its substitute as well as any accumulated juices in their bowl. Cacciatora has four basic elements: meat, onion, mushrooms, and wine. What's missing? Tomatoes. (The amount called for here is a 28-ounce can.) They became part of the dish in the twentieth century, thanks largely to restaurants in North America where they were Italian cuisine's signature ingredient.

The browned meat is nestled into the simmering sauce. Note how lightly browned the meat is, just a hint of caramelization.

Still, who could argue with their addition? They balance acid and sweet, a fruity, bright note that makes this a dish for all year round. But there's a wide disparity among canned versions. Some are sweet and juicy; others, tasteless and mealy. Always use the reduced-sodium or no-salt-added variety; there's no reason why someone else should control the sodium in your meal. And price is no Virgil, no guide. Spend a few bucks and do your own taste test. We're constantly amazed by cooks who use everyday ingredients like broth and canned tomatoes without first tasting them. One Saturday afternoon when you're feeling both adventurous and critical (a bad mix for a romantic tryst), buy a few varieties and taste them right out of the can. Your cooking will never be the same.

Diced, canned tomatoes quicken the cooking time considerably. That said, if you use whole canned tomatoes, cut them up before adding them to the stew. The easiest way to do this is with kitchen shears: stick them in the open can and cut away in several directions. Or clean your hands and pour the tomatoes one by one into your palm, crushing each up before dropping it into the pot.

Add one or two herbs, most likely from the Italian family: rosemary, basil, oregano, sage, or flat-leaf parsley. If you've added several garlic cloves in step 4, consider a pinch more herbs for balance. Up to ½ teaspoon red pepper flakes unexpectedly lightens the stew. Also consider other aromatics like chopped pitted black or green olives, drained capers, or minced anchovies. A little goes a long way—and adds lots of salt. Use no more than 1 tablespoon capers and minced anchovies, no more than 2 tablespoons chopped olives.

• **STEP 8** Bring to a simmer, cover, reduce the heat to very low, and simmer slowly until the meat is quite tender, even falling off the bone, stirring occasionally, between 1 and 2 hours. Season with salt and freshly ground black pepper to taste before serving. A slow simmer means you can count the bubbles as they come to the surface. You may have to count quickly; but if you easily lose track, your sauce is at a full simmer, maybe even a low boil. There's no hurry. After all, you're supposed to be waiting for your husband to come in from the hunt. Still, chicken will take about 1 hour; other birds, about 1¼ hours; rabbit, about 1½ hours; and lamb, a little more than 2 hours. But keep checking, poking the meat with a fork to see how tender it is.

Those pesky chicken breasts can easily be overcooked. If you find they're turning stringy after 20 minutes, transfer them to a plate, tent with foil, and set aside until the final 10 minutes when you can add them again to reheat them.

A hearty bowl of Rabbit Cacciatora

Recipes for Cacciatoras

	Rabbit Cacciatora	Chicken Cacciatora	Lamb Cacciatora	Veal Cacciatora
1. Heat	1 Tbs olive oil 1 Tbs unsalted butter	2 Tbs olive oil	2 Tbs unsalted butter	1 Tbs olive oil 1 Tbs unsalted butter
2. Add, cook, and transfer to a bowl	4 ounces chopped bacon	4 ounces pancetta, chopped	4 ounces bacon, chopped	4 ounces pancetta, chopped
3. Dredge, brown, and transfer to a bowl	¾ cup seasoned all-purpose flour 4 pounds cut-up rabbit	¾ cup seasoned all-purpose flour 3½ pounds cut-up chicken	¾ cup seasoned all-purpose flour 3½ pounds lamb stew meat	¾ cup seasoned all-purpose flour 4 pounds veal shoulder chops, cut up into chunks with a bone still in each piece
4. Add and cook	1 large yellow onion, chopped 2 medium green bell peppers, seeded and chopped 2 garlic cloves, minced	1 large yellow onion, chopped 1 pound very small baby artichokes, tops cut off and trimmed of tough outer leaves 2 garlic cloves, minced	1 large yellow onion, chopped 1 small cabbage, cored and shredded 1 medium green bell pepper, seeded and chopped ½ cup chopped dried apricots 2 garlic cloves, minced	1 large yellow onion, chopped 2 medium green sour apples like Granny Smiths, peeled, cored, and chopped 2 garlic cloves, minced
5. Add and cook	12 ounces cremini mushrooms, chopped	12 ounces white button mushrooms, thickly sliced	6 ounces cremini mushrooms, chopped 6 ounces shiitake caps, thickly sliced	9 ounces cremini mushrooms, chopped
6. Pour in and reduce by half	1 cup red wine	1 cup dry white wine	1 cup rosé wine	1 cup dry white wine
7. Add	3½ cups canned diced tomatoes 1 Tbs chopped rosemary 1 Tbs chopped sage The browned rabbit, bacon, and any juices	3½ cups canned diced tomatoes ¼ cup chopped parsley 2 tsp chopped oregano 1 tsp stemmed thyme The browned chicken, pancetta, and any juices	3½ cups canned diced tomatoes 1 Tbs chopped marjoram 2 tsp stemmed thyme The browned lamb, bacon, and any juices	3½ cups canned diced tomatoes 1 Tbs chopped tarragon 1 tsp stemmed thyme ¼ tsp grated nutmeg The browned veal, pancetta, and any juices
8. Cover, simmer slowly, then season	About 1½ hours Salt and pepper to taste	About 1 hour Salt and pepper to taste	About 2½ hours Salt and pepper to taste	About 2½ hours Salt and pepper to taste

	Spring Cacciatora	Summer Cacciatora	Autumn Cacciatora	Winter Cacciatora
1. Heat	1 Tbs olive oil 1 Tbs unsalted butter	2 Tbs olive oil	2 Tbs unsalted butter	2 Tbs unsalted butter
2. Add, cook, and transfer to a bowl	4 ounces prosciutto, chopped	4 ounces prosciutto, chopped	4 ounces pancetta, chopped	4 ounces mild chorizo, chopped
3. Dredge, brown, and transfer to a bowl	¾ cup seasoned all-purpose flour 2 pounds bone-in chicken thighs 2 pounds quail	¾ cup seasoned all-purpose flour 3½ pounds cut-up chicken	¾ cup seasoned all-purpose flour 4½ pounds Cornish game hens, halved	¾ cup seasoned all-purpose flour 2½ pounds bone-in chicken thighs 1 pound lamb stew meat
4. Add and cook	1 large yellow onion, chopped 1 medium green bell pepper, seeded and chopped 1 cup frozen peas 1 cup frozen lima beans 2 garlic cloves, minced	1 large yellow onion, chopped 1 large zucchini, thinly sliced 6 ounces green beans, chopped	1 large yellow onion, chopped 2 medium parsnips, sliced 2 medium carrots, sliced 12 small Brussels sprouts, stemmed and chopped ½ cup chopped pitted prunes	1 large yellow onion, chopped 1 very small butternut squash, peeled and cubed 1 cup canned chickpeas, drained and rinsed 2 garlic cloves, minced
5. Add and cook	12 ounces white button mushrooms, chopped	12 ounces white button mushrooms, chopped	6 ounces cremini mushrooms, chopped 6 ounces wild mushrooms, chopped	12 ounces cremini mushrooms, chopped
6. Pour in and reduce by half	1 cup rosé wine	1 cup dry white wine	1 cup red wine	1 cup red wine
7. Add	3½ cups canned diced tomatoes 2 Tbs chopped parsley 1 tsp stemmed thyme The browned chicken and quail, frizzled prosciutto, and any juices	3½ cups canned diced tomatoes 1 Tbs chopped thyme 1 tsp finely grated lemon zest ¼ tsp red pepper flakes The browned chicken, frizzled prosciutto, and any juices	3½ cups canned diced tomatoes 1 Tbs chopped sage 2 teaspoons green peppercorns ½ teaspoon grated nutmeg The browned game hens, pancetta, and any juices	3½ cups canned diced tomatoes 2 tsp chopped oregano 2 tsp stemmed thyme ⅛ tsp saffron 1 garlic clove, minced The browned chicken and lamb, chorizo, and any juices
8. Cover, simmer slowly, then season	About 1½ hours Salt and pepper to taste	About 1 hour Salt and pepper to taste	About 1½ hours Salt and pepper to taste	About 2 hours Salt and pepper to taste

A pot of Southwestern Chicken and Rice

Chicken and Rice

This oven-baked casserole is endlessly variable, satisfying any time of the year. Although Arroz con Pollo is perhaps its most famous incarnation, there are plenty of ways to turn it into a spectacular dinner. What's more, leftovers are a dream, the flavors even more intense. • MAKES 6 TO 8 SERVINGS

• **STEP 1** Preheat the oven to 350°F. Meanwhile, heat ¼ cup (4 tablespoons) fat in a 6- to 8-quart Dutch oven over medium heat. Since the casserole will be built in layers, consider the fat the first. For the simplest results, use a single kind of fat, rather than a combination, so that the layer is uniform and present, flavoring the dish fully. In general, go with olive oil, unsalted butter, or an untoasted nut oil. For a more complex taste, pair unsalted butter with olive oil or an untoasted nut oil, thereby adding a slightly sour accent to the dish without a butter overdose.

• **STEP 2** Brown one 3- to 4-pound cut-up chicken in batches as necessary; transfer to a plate.

The Right Cookware

Old-fashioned Dutch ovens were relatively shallow, made of cast iron, and meant to hang over an open fire. They bore little resemblance to their modern kin, which are really saucepans on steroids. That said, those high sides are necessary for a good simmer without too much reduction. Avoid flimsy, lightweight competitors.

Cutting up a chicken

There's no reason to pay extra to have your supermarket cut up a chicken. Just follow these steps:

1. Remove the neck and giblets from the cavity. Freeze the neck for stock, the giblets for enrichers in Braised Bone-In Chicken Breasts or Thighs (page 45).
2. Set the chicken breast side up on a cutting board; pull one wing out from the body. Press between the wing and breast until you can feel the joint, a knuckle-like structure in the "arm pit." Place a chef's knife over the joint and slice down. If you meet resistance, adjust the blade to slice directly through the joint, severing the wing from the body. Repeat with the other wing.
3. Position the body on a cutting board so the large opening faces you. Steady the breast with one hand and gently pry the thigh-and-leg quarter away from the body until you hear a pop, thereby disjointing the hip. Place your knife over the joint's center and slice down, taking off the whole thigh-and-leg quarter. Repeat on the other side.
4. Lay the thigh-and-leg quarter skin side down on the cutting board. Wiggle the leg to find the inside corner of its knee joint. Place your knife right over that point and slice down, severing the leg from the thigh. Repeat with the other thigh-and-leg quarter.
5. With the body still breast side up, insert your knife directly into the large opening so the tip extends almost out of the other opening. Position the blade about

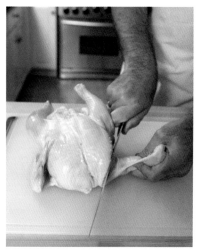
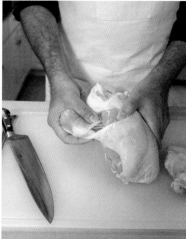
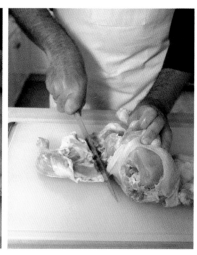

TO CUT UP A WHOLE CHICKEN: Start by removing the giblets and neck, then wiggle each wing until you find its joint and slice through it.

Next, pull the thigh-and-leg quarters away from the body, gently but firmly rotating them until the joint pops out of its socket.

Once the joint has popped loose, slice through it to take off the thigh-and-leg quarter—which can then be cut apart at its knee joint.

2 inches to the side of the backbone and press down, slicing through the ribs and bones. Repeat on the other side of the backbone, thereby taking it off.

6. Lay the breast skin side down on your work surface. Spread the two sides open, pushing down until the breast bone cracks; then cut through the middle of the breast bone. The breast bone of older or larger chickens will not crack easily. In this case, you'll need to eye the breast bone and slice down on one side, thereby leaving one side of the breast with the bone and other without—or else use a sharp cleaver to slice right down through the breast bone. Slice off any extraneous bits of rib and skin. If desired, slice the breast halves themselves in half the short way.

Whether you've cut up a whole chicken or bought one already prepared, trim the pieces to remove all excess skin and fat. Indeed, you can skin the pieces for a more healthy dish. But do not substitute boneless cutlets; they are too quickly cooked and too flavorless against the rice.

• **STEP 3** Add 2 chopped medium yellow onions and, if desired, up to 8 ounces (½ pound) sliced sausage, chopped bacon, or diced pancetta; cook, stirring often, until the onions are soft and the meat, if using, has browned, about 6 minutes. The meat added with the chopped onion is not necessary but lovely. In addition to bacon and its substitutes (all smoky) or pancetta (not smoky but salty), consider mild dried Spanish chorizo, mild fresh Mexican chorizo, turkey sausage, tofu brats, or even wursts like knackwurst or kielbasa. Avoid prosciutto and some of the lighter pork products used as the base of many a sauté or braise—they are too ethereal to stand up to the rice in this casserole. And keep in mind that some hot chorizo or sausage of any variety is often exponentially more fiery than its mild kin.

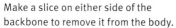

Make a slice on either side of the backbone to remove it from the body.

Finally, slice the breast apart on one side or the other of the breast bone.

• **STEP 4** Add some minced garlic, herbs, spices, and/or flavorings; warm until aromatic, about 20 seconds. Use several herbs or spices here, perhaps about 2 tablespoons in all or even up to ¼ cup for a fresh herb blend—or consider using a purchased dried blend like herbes de Provence, no more than 2 teaspoons.

Other flavorings, while not necessary, include drained capers, chopped pitted olives, chopped dried fruit, chopped sun-dried tomatoes, or even a minced anchovy or two. These should be added with the herbs and spices so their flavors mellow over the heat before the rice is added. Many add quite a bit of salt; make sure you adjust the final seasoning of the dish accordingly.

• **STEP 5** Add about 3 cups vegetables, cut into ½-inch cubes (seeded and peeled, if necessary); cook, stirring often, just until softened. With a few notable exceptions, almost any vegetable will work, even roots and tubers, provided they're peeled and cut into small pieces. Even green beans and asparagus will work if thinly sliced, although they will turn quite soft, more flavor accents than toothsome vegetables. Greens are also a welcome addition—not soft ones, but hearty varietals like kale, chard, or escarole. However, compensate for their wilting by adding more to the pot, doubling—or even tripling—the requisite amount. What about 2 cups diced, peeled, seeded pumpkin and 2 to 3 cups chopped, stemmed chard? If so, make sure your spice mixture includes grated nutmeg.

What vegetables are a definite "no"? Broccoli and cauliflower florets are a couple to leave out. They lose all texture. And fresh tomatoes. Either use sun-dried tomatoes as a flavoring agent in step 4 or use canned crushed tomatoes as part of the liquid in step 7.

• **STEP 6** Stir in 2 cups long-grain rice; cook, stirring constantly, for 1 minute. Basically, you're just softening the outer layer of starch so the rice will cook more quickly in the ambient heat of the casserole. Long-grain rice varietals include basmati, jasmine, Texmati, patna, and Carolina rice, or even the new hybrid popcorn rice, bred as a cross between American long-grain and basmati. For a discussion of what makes a rice a long-grain varietal, see page 231.

• **STEP 7** Pour 4 cups (1 quart) broth, wine, or an enhanced broth into the pot; scrape down the pot's sides and bottom, add the chicken and any accumulated juices, and bring back to a simmer; then cover, place in the oven, and bake until the rice is tender and most of the liquid has been absorbed, about 45 minutes. Season with salt and freshly ground black pepper to taste. The simplest choices? Broth—usually chicken but sometimes vegetable or even beef— white wine, or a combination of the two. Do not use water, juice, or any sugared liquid.

The well-browned chicken and any accumulated juices are added back to the pot.

Dry vermouth is almost always an acceptable substitute for white wine. Indeed, since dry vermouth can be stored for a month or so in a cool, dark place and since white wine starts to go bad within hours of opening, dry vermouth is a more economical— and slightly more herbal—alternative to dry white wine.

Moving beyond the basics for this casserole, don't shy away from red wine. Yes, the rice will be stained; but the flavor will be intense, a stand-up against fiery spice blends or heavy sausage meat. Also consider enhancing the broth with dry sherry or beer (never flavored but a lager or dark beer). An Asian mix can be made with 3 cups broth, ¾ cup shaoxing (see page 374), and ¼ cup soy sauce. However, avoid liqueurs, cream, or coconut milk—all overpowering and unwarranted. If you'd like a tomato-accented casserole, consider using canned crushed (not diced) tomatoes as part of the liquid—say, 2 cups crushed tomatoes and 2 cups broth. And while not necessary, you can also stir in 1 or 2 tablespoons vinegar with almost any combination except straight-on wine. The flavors will intensify considerably while cooking, the sweet accents becoming more pronounced.

Or try this: after about 35 minutes, add some cleaned clams or scrubbed and debearded mussels (see page 203). Nestle them hinge down into the rice, cover, and continue baking the requisite amount of time.

Once the rice is tender and almost all the liquid has been absorbed, season with salt and pepper, then set aside at room temperature, covered, for 10 minutes to meld the flavors.

Recipes for Chicken and Rice Casseroles

	Arroz con Pollo	Southwestern Chicken and Rice	French-Inspired Chicken and Rice	Chicken and Rice with Walnuts and Cherries
1. Preheat the oven; heat	¼ cup olive oil	¼ cup canola oil	2 Tbs canola oil 2 Tbs unsalted butter	2 Tbs untoasted walnut oil 2 Tbs unsalted butter
2. Brown and remove	One 3- to 4-pound cut-up chicken, giblets and neck removed	One 3- to 4-pound cut-up chicken, giblets and neck removed	One 3- to 4-pound cut-up chicken, giblets and neck removed	One 3- to 4-pound cut-up chicken, giblets and neck removed
3. Add and cook	2 medium yellow onions, chopped ½ pound hot or mild Italian sausage, sliced into 1-inch rings	2 medium yellow onions, chopped ½ pound dried mild Spanish chorizo, sliced into 1-inch rings	2 medium yellow onions, chopped	2 medium yellow onions, chopped ½ pound thick-cut bacon, chopped
4. Add and warm	4 garlic cloves, minced ½ cup chopped pitted black olives 2 Tbs drained capers 1 Tbs minced oregano 1 Tbs mild paprika ⅛ tsp saffron	3 garlic cloves, minced ½ to 1 chipotle canned in adobo, stemmed, seeded, and chopped 1 Tbs minced oregano 1 Tbs ground cumin 1 tsp ground cinnamon	2 garlic cloves, minced 1 Tbs minced tarragon 1 Tbs minced sage 1 Tbs stemmed thyme	3 garlic cloves, minced ¼ cup chopped dried cherries ¼ cup chopped walnuts 2 Tbs minced sage ¼ tsp grated nutmeg
5. Add and cook	2 cups peas 1 cup chopped sun-dried tomatoes	1¾ cups canned pinto beans, drained and rinsed 1 medium green bell pepper, seeded and chopped	10 ounces white button or cremini mushrooms, thinly sliced	Two 10-ounce packages frozen artichoke hearts, thawed and squeezed of excess moisture 1 medium yellow squash, diced
6. Stir in	2 cups long-grain rice	2 cups long-grain rice	2 cups long-grain rice	2 cups long-grain rice
7. Stir in, cover, and bake about 45 minutes—then season	2 cups chicken broth 2 cups dry white wine The browned chicken and any accumulated juices Salt and pepper to taste	2½ cups beef broth One 12-ounce bottle of beer The browned chicken and any accumulated juices Salt and pepper to taste	2 cups chicken broth 2 cups dry vermouth The browned chicken and any accumulated juices Salt and pepper to taste	3 cups chicken broth 1 cup dry vermouth The browned chicken and any accumulated juices Salt and pepper to taste

	Italian-Inspired Chicken and Rice	Spanish-Inspired Chicken and Rice	Asian-Inspired Chicken and Rice	Hungarian-Inspired Chicken and Rice
1. Preheat the oven; heat	¼ cup olive oil	¼ cup olive oil	¼ cup peanut oil	¼ cup canola oil or schmaltz
2. Brown and remove	One 3- to 4-pound cut-up chicken, giblets and neck removed	One 3- to 4-pound cut-up chicken, giblets and neck removed	One 3- to 4-pound cut-up chicken, giblets and neck removed	One 3- to 4-pound cut-up chicken, giblets and neck removed
3. Add and cook	2 medium yellow onions, chopped ½ pound pancetta, chopped	2 medium yellow onions, chopped ½ pound mild Spanish dried chorizo, sliced into 1-inch rings	2 medium yellow onions, chopped ½ pound smoked ham, chopped	2 medium yellow onions, chopped ½ pound hot Hungarian-style sausage, sliced into 1-inch rings
4. Add and warm	3 garlic cloves, minced ¼ cup chopped pitted black olives 3 Tbs minced parsley 2 Tbs chopped rosemary 1 Tbs minced oregano	4 garlic cloves, minced ¼ cup chopped cilantro 2 Tbs smoked paprika 1 Tbs stemmed thyme ½ tsp saffron	2 garlic cloves, minced 2 Tbs minced peeled fresh ginger 2 Tbs finely grated orange zest 2 tsp five-spice powder (see page 149)	¼ cup mild paprika 2 tsp stemmed thyme ½ tsp grated nutmeg ½ tsp cayenne
5. Add and cook	2 medium fennel bulbs, trimmed and thinly sliced 6 ounces broccoli rabe, chopped	1 cup canned chickpeas, drained and rinsed ½ cup chopped dried figs 2 whole jarred roasted red peppers or pimientos, chopped	6 ounces snow peas, sliced 6 ounces shiitake mushrooms, stems removed and discarded, caps thinly sliced	1 large green bell pepper, seeded and chopped 1 large red bell pepper, seeded and chopped
6. Stir in	2 cups long-grain rice	2 cups long-grain rice	2 cups long-grain rice	2 cups long-grain rice
7. Stir in, cover, and bake about 45 minutes—then season	3 cups chicken broth 1 cup red wine The browned chicken and any accumulated juices Salt and pepper to taste	3 cups chicken broth 1 cup dry sherry The browned chicken and any accumulated juices Salt and pepper to taste	3 cups chicken broth ¾ cup shaoxing (see page 374) ¼ cup soy sauce The browned chicken and any accumulated juices Salt and pepper to taste	4 cups chicken broth The browned chicken and any accumulated juices Salt and pepper to taste

Chicken Soup

It might well have been your grandmother's cure-all, but the truth is this: chicken soup is comfort food in three easy steps. Nothing's browned: no caramelization, just silky, smooth, richness—all in one pot. • MAKES 6 GENEROUS SERVINGS

• **STEP 1** Put about 8 cups (2 quarts) broth, water and/or wine, about 5 cups chopped vegetables or prepared roots, and one cut-up 3- to 4-pound chicken in a large Dutch oven or soup pot set over high heat; bring to a simmer, cover, reduce the heat to low, and simmer slowly for 1 hour. Once upon a time, frugal grandmothers used only water, but they also let the soup simmer for hours. For modern convenience, the best ratio is 50/50 broth and water—that is, 4 cups (1 quart) chicken broth and 4 cups (1 quart) water. Using 8 cups (2 quarts) chicken broth produces a luxurious soup, best in small cups as the first course of a holiday meal. Equal parts chicken and vegetable broth afford a lighter flavor, although make sure the vegetable broth isn't overpoweringly heavy with the taste of onions, something that will cover up the flavor of the chicken. Using only vegetable broth will yield a much lighter soup, which should probably be given heft with 1 cup dry white wine as part of the total liquid amount.

Speaking of wine, use up to 1 cup as part of the total liquid in any combination. More than 1 cup and the soup will be overwhelmed, too sweet and acidic all at once. Dry white wine or dry vermouth works best, although dry sherry adds a sophisticated note, particularly if used sparingly—say, no more than ½ cup.

All vegetables and roots should be those that can withstand long simmering: for example, shallots, winter squash, celeriac, sweet potatoes, carrots, celery, turnips, or parsnips. Save peas, asparagus, and other spring vegetables for step 3. The point here is to leach flavor into the broth, to color and enrich it.

Start with a chopped mirepoix or a modified mirepoix (onions, carrots, and celery—see page 57), then fill it out by adding peeled roots, tubers, sweet potatoes, or seeded winter squash. All these should be roughly chopped: 1-inch thick rings for carrots and parsnips; 1½-inch cubes for potatoes, turnips, and the like. Small red-skinned potatoes should be halved; extra-small ones can be left whole. Avoid beets: they will stain the soup a garish pink.

Garlic is usually welcome but only in moderation. Minced fresh ginger is particularly appealing in an Asian-based or curried chicken soup. But don't add hot, spicy ingredients at this point: red pepper flakes, Thai curry pastes, and the like. Save these for step 3; they'll maintain more of their vigorous heat if added toward the end of cooking.

Use enough liquid to fully submerge all the chicken and vegetables in the pot.

Use a small strainer to skim off impurities while the chicken and vegetables cook.

Your cleaned hands are the best tools to shred the warm chicken into bite-sized bits. If you've used chicken pieces with the skin on, remove and discard it now.

See page 77 for tips on cutting up a whole chicken on your own. And don't forget the neck. It adds lots of flavor—though you'll discard it with the bones and skin in step 2. If you're lucky enough to find a butcher who sells the feet with the chicken, slip these into the soup, discarding them in step 2 as well. But skip adding the gizzard, heart, and other innards. These will turn the soup a sickly brown.

Reduce the heat so the soup simmers, doesn't boil. Too quick a simmer and the chicken can shred, leaving unattractive bits of skin and bone floating everywhere in the stew.

Bones and meat in a pot inevitably lead to scum and impurities that billow in foamy clouds. No, you don't have to skim them off; but they will eventually dissolve and cloud the soup, leaving some sediment and a slightly bitter backtaste. It's better to skim the soup a few times, particularly early on, pulling the foam and its impurities to the pot's side with a large spoon or a small strainer, then gently lifting them out to discard them.

Finally, if you have the time and the inclination, remove the breasts after 45 minutes, set them in the refrigerator, and let the soup continue simmering slowly for another 45 minutes. The broth will get richer, and the hearty dark meat can withstand much more cooking than the low-fat breasts.

• **STEP 2** Remove the chicken pieces from the pot, set them aside to cool for perhaps 10 minutes while the soup stays warm over very low heat, and then skin and debone the pieces. Before transferring them to a colander set in the sink, pick the pieces up one by one with tongs and shake each one over the pot so that any trapped liquid under the skin and in the joints drips back into the soup.

Some cooks now strain the soup, getting rid of the vegetables which are "spent" (that is, their flavor has leached into the soup). But if the soup is cooked for only an hour or so, there's no need to consider those carrots or parsnips worthless. Yes, straining the soup now makes a clearer broth, but a well-stocked soup is wonderfully satisfying—and more economical, to boot. Why waste the nutrients and vitamins still found in the vegetable fibers?

If you set the soup aside, covered, for about 10 minutes (about the time it'll take for the chicken to cool to a point at which you can handle it), some of the fat will rise to the surface. Skim it with a spoon, pulling it toward the pot's side and tilting the spoon to let the broth flow away while the discardable fat (and any leftover scum) stays put in the spoon.

• **STEP 3** Chop and stir in the chicken meat as well as some fresh herbs or a spice mixture and if desired, about 2 cups chopped, quick-cooking spring vegetables or sliced mushrooms; bring back to a low simmer, cover, and cook until the vegetables are crisp-tender, from 5 to 20 minutes; then season with salt and freshly ground black pepper to taste. The skinned, boneless meat that returns to the pot should be in bite-sized chunks. You usually eat a soup with just a spoon; you may eat a stew with a full complement of cutlery. Indeed, the difference between the a soup and a stew is hairline fine these days. By and large, a stew has less liquid per spoonful. A braise? Much less. But a soup is all about the broth.

Now's your chance to add quick-cooking vegetables: asparagus, zucchini, peas, green beans, corn kernels, or even mushrooms. Even greens or cabbage can be added, provided their tough center stems or cores have been removed. Kale and other sturdy greens should be chopped and the soup may need 15 or 20 minutes at a simmer to get them tender. Spinach and chard, however, will be done in as little as 5 minutes.

Be generous with the spices and herbs: ¼ cup chopped basil, 2 tablespoons minced dill or tarragon. Any fiery spices or flavorings—Thai curry paste (page 386), sambal olek, Tabasco sauce, chile oil—should also be added at this point but in moderation, perhaps no more than 1 teaspoon, often less. Allowing one of them to simmer just a few minutes will preserve its vinegary or spiky taste, a better foil to the chicken.

To season, stir in 1 teaspoon salt and take it from there. You'll probably need at least 2 teaspoons, but adjust to your taste, slurping broth from the spoon to adjudicate its seasoning. Yes, slurping—don't be embarrassed; pull the soup in with gusto, noise, and air. This is the only way to get the aromas volatilized and in your nose, your most sensitive taste organ.

Chicken soup eats up freshly ground black pepper. For a good nose, give the pot several generous grinds, stir well, and taste before adding more. If you don't like black flecks in the broth, consider using white pepper—but remember that it's more piquant, even a little sour.

When reheating leftover or even frozen chicken soup, consider stirring in 1 or 2 teaspoons lemon juice or white wine vinegar, just to brighten the flavors that may have dulled in storage.

A winter warmer: a bowl of Thai Chicken Soup

Recipes for Chicken Soups

	Old-Fashioned Chicken Soup	Thai Chicken Soup	African-Inspired Chicken Soup	Autumn Chicken Soup
1. Add, cover, and simmer	4 cups (1 quart) chicken broth 4 cups (1 quart) water 1 medium yellow onion, chopped 4 medium celery ribs, sliced 2 medium carrots, cut into rings 1 garlic clove, minced One 3- to 4-pound cut-up chicken, giblets and neck removed	4 cups (1 quart) chicken broth 4 cups (1 quart) water 1 medium yellow onion, chopped 3 medium carrots, cut into rings 3 medium celery ribs, sliced 2 garlic cloves, minced 3 Tbs minced peeled fresh ginger One 3- to 4-pound cut-up chicken, giblets and neck removed	4 cups (1 quart) chicken broth 4 cups (1 quart) water 1 medium yellow onion, chopped 2 medium carrots, cut into thick rings 2 medium sweet potatoes, peeled and roughly chopped 2 garlic cloves, minced One 3- to 4-pound cut-up chicken, giblets and neck removed	5 cups chicken broth 3 cups water 1 medium yellow onion, chopped 1 small butternut squash, peeled and cubed 2 parsnips, cut into rings 1 carrot, cut into rings One 3- to 4-pound cut-up chicken, giblets and neck removed
2. Remove the meat	Skin and debone	Skin and debone	Skin and debone	Skin and debone
3. Stir in and simmer—then season	The chopped chicken meat 2 tablespoons minced dill Salt and pepper to taste	The chopped chicken meat 8 ounces shiitake mushrooms, stems removed and discarded, caps thinly sliced ¼ cup shredded basil 1 tsp Thai curry paste (see page 386) Salt and pepper to taste	The chopped chicken meat ½ pound stemmed and chopped turnip, mustard, or collard greens ½ cup chopped, roasted, unsalted peanuts 1 or 2 fresh jalapeño or serrano chiles, seeded and minced Salt and pepper to taste	The chopped chicken meat ½ pound broccoli florets 1 Tbs minced oregano 1 Tbs stemmed thyme Salt and pepper to taste

	Spring Chicken Soup	Italian-Inspired Chicken Soup	Curried Chicken Soup	Winter Comfort Chicken Soup
1. Add, cover, and simmer	4 cups (1 quart) chicken broth 3 cups water 1 cup dry white wine 6 ounces shallots, chopped 4 medium celery ribs, sliced 8 ounces frozen lima beans One 3- to 4-pound cut-up chicken, giblets and neck removed	4 cups (1 quart) chicken broth 3 cups water 1 cup dry white wine 1 medium yellow onion, chopped 8 plum or Roma tomatoes, chopped 2 garlic cloves, minced 1¾ cups canned white beans, drained and rinsed One 3- to 4-pound cut-up chicken, giblets and neck removed	4 cups (1 quart) chicken broth 4 cups (1 quart) water 1 medium yellow onion, chopped 1 medium sweet potato, peeled and cubed 1 medium turnip, peeled and cubed 3 garlic cloves, minced 2 Tbs minced peeled fresh ginger One 4-inch piece lemongrass, crushed but still intact One 4-inch cinnamon stick (remove both the lemongrass and cinnamon before serving) One 3- to 4-pound cut-up chicken, giblets and neck removed	5 cups chicken broth 3 cups water 8 ounces shallots, thinly sliced 2 parsnips, cut into rings 1 medium celeriac, peeled and cubed 1 medium turnip, peeled and cubed One 3- to 4-pound cut-up chicken, giblets and neck removed
2. Remove the meat	Skin and debone	Skin and debone	Skin and debone	Skin and debone
3. Stir in and simmer—then season	The chopped chicken meat 8 thin asparagus spears, thinly sliced ½ cup corn kernels 2 Tbs shredded basil 1 Tbs minced tarragon Several dashes hot red pepper sauce Salt and pepper to taste	The chopped chicken meat 1 medium zucchini, thinly sliced 1 Tbs minced sage 1 Tbs stemmed thyme Salt and pepper to taste	The chopped chicken meat 6 ounces cleaned and sliced white button or cremini mushrooms 1 Tbs curry powder (see page 113) or vindaloo paste (see page 395) ¼ cup minced cilantro Salt and pepper to taste	The chopped chicken meat 8 ounces shiitake mushrooms, stems removed and discarded, caps thinly sliced 3 Tbs chopped parsley 1 Tbs minced tarragon 1 Tbs stemmed thyme Salt and pepper to taste

Technically, it's "chili con carne"—that is, "chiles with meat." Therefore, just say "no" to beans! And while you're at it, to ground beef, too! Because this is the real deal: cubes of meat, loads of chiles and spices, a carnivore's Paradise, a vegetarian's Tartarus. • MAKES 6 TO 8 SERVINGS

• **STEP 1** Stem, seed, devein, and slice about 2 ounces dried chiles; toast in a dry skillet over medium heat, stirring constantly, until pliable and fragrant, 1 to 2 minutes. Watch as the dried chiles toast over the heat; do not let them burn or the flavors will turn astringent. Instead, warm the chiles until pliable and fragrant. But beware: some oils, particularly in fiery varietals, can volatilize (that is, get airborne) and burn your eyes. Stand back.

Chiles

Cultivated and dried since 6200 B.C.E. in the Americas, chiles come in an astounding number of varieties. The best chili takes advantage of this abundance by blending flavors. Here's a basic reference list for dried varietals:

ají (red, brown, or orange): often used in sauces, a little sour with berry notes (the orange are exceptionally hot, up near habanero levels)

ancho: a dried poblano, moderately hot but with raisin, coffee, and licorice accents

cayenne: sour and pungent, quite hot but with mushroomy undertones

chilhaucle (red or black): plummy and figgy, moderately subtle heat

chipotle: a smoked jalapeño, chocolately but banging hot (sometimes canned in adobo sauce—only use the dried here)

guajillo: cinnamon and nutmeg notes, somewhat sweet and a little grassy, a low-grade heat

habanero: the don of heat, a molten spike in the mouth

mora: like the chipotle, a smoked jalapeño, but made of red varietals and thus less sour, far hotter

mulato: like the ancho, a dried poblano but with a low heat, nicely balanced sweet and sour notes, quite smoky

new Mexican (red, green, orange, or black): woodsy cherries and blackberries, moderately low but on-the-tongue heat (the dried greens are the rarest and hottest)

pasilla: a dried chilaca, notes of grassy herbs and raisins, moderate heat

pasilla de Oaxaca: a smoked pasilla, a sophisticated accent but difficult to find

serrano seco: bitingly hot and a little bitter, best in combo with other chiles

Many of these chiles are grown in miniature varietals; avoid these peewees and go for the originals. The miniatures are quite pungent, more biting than their larger kin. Also avoid dried chiles that are miniatures in their own right like pequín, de árbol, and tepín—all too hot and sour for well-balanced chili.

The Heat in Chiles

Although fresh chiles pack more wallop than dried, the naturally occurring capsaicin (cap-SAY-uh-suhn, the chemical burn, $C_{18}H_{27}NO_3$) will come alive via heat and moisture far better than other flavors in the fruit. So compared to fresh chiles, drieds have a savory heat: less sour, less sweet, more earthy, and with notes of dried fruit—a similar difference between white and red wine.

Capsaicin is found mostly in the inner, fleshy veins. When cut, jostled, or dried, the capsaicin packets leak or explode, coating the adjacent seeds (and thus the myth that the heat lies in the seeds). Remove the seeds (they add bitter notes), but keep the veins for a tear-jolting stew.

If you're at all sensitive, wear rubber gloves when working with chiles. Do not touch your eyes, ears, or other sensitive bits. Wash your hands thoroughly when you're done. But take care: trace amounts of oily capsaicin can be left on your skin.

Capsaicin is also a marvelous evolutionary creation. Birds are immune to it; mammals grind the seeds and stop the plant's reproduction—and thus are bitten by the defense. Capsaicin has some other marked effects: it throws off our temperature regulation, pumps up our metabolic rate, and triggers brain signals to suppress the appetite, encouraging us to eat less in an age of abundance.

When shopping for dried chiles, look for perky stems and pliable, whole peppers—no rips or shards. If you find them in bags, most should retain their seeds, there should be little dust (a sign of desiccation), and there should certainly be no fuzzy mold at the stems. Store dried chiles for up to a year in a loosely sealed bag in a cool, dry place; humidity and temperature shifts are their sworn enemies.

• **STEP 2** Place the chiles in a large bowl, cover with boiling water, and set aside for 15 minutes. Make sure they're pressed down into the hot water. If some refuse to take the dive, set a small plate inside the bowl to force them under.

• **STEP 3** Drain the chiles in a colander set in the sink and transfer to a food processor fitted with the chopping blade; then add some quartered garlic cloves and 1 teaspoon salt, as well as a few spices, herbs, and/or other flavorings before processing to a purée. Now you'll make a paste with the rehydrated chiles—and there are myriad flavors to consider: ground ginger, cinnamon, oregano, cumin, dry mustard, Dijon mustard, an all-fruit spread like apricot or raspberry, cilantro, basil, grated orange zest, pitted olives, capers, anchovies, sun-dried tomatoes, and/or ground mace, to name a few. Fresh herbs like oregano, thyme, and parsley will brighten the flavors; dried spices like ground coriander and grated nutmeg will deepen them. Don't be shy: there's hardly an herb or spice in the modern American kitchen to be avoided—except perhaps tarragon (too French) and rosemary (too overpowering), although we can immediately imagine either of these in blends with ground cinnamon, mace, sun-dried tomatoes, minced dried orange peel, and dried cherries.

Follow this guide:

1. Put the chiles in a food processor fitted with the chopping blade—or, failing that, a very large mortar.
2. Add a tablespoon or two of fresh green herbs, followed by perhaps an equivalent amount of another "solid " or "paste" flavoring like olives, mustard, or all-fruit spread.
3. Season with a teaspoon or so of dried spices like ground cumin, nutmeg, or cinnamon.
4. Toss in your peeled or crushed garlic cloves and the salt—and you're locked and loaded to either process or grind with a pestle into a thick, slightly grainy paste.

The rehydrated chiles have enough residual water; there's no need to add oil.

TO MAKE A CHILE PASTE: First, remove the veins and seeds in dried chiles before toasting them in a dry skillet.

Then soak the toasted chiles in warm water until they're quite pliable.

Finally, the paste made from these chiles should still be somewhat grainy but certainly not chunky.

- **STEP 4** Heat 3 tablespoons neutral fat or rendered animal fat in a large pot or Dutch oven set over medium heat. Avoid fats like butter, nut, olive, or sesame oils. All are too fruity or aromatic—and a bad match for the mix of dried chiles you've chosen. Instead, as with most spicy dishes, choose fats from either end of the spectrum (see page 17): either a non competing, neutral taste like canola oil or refined peanut oil; or the full-blown other end of the spectrum with the likes of mustard seed oil as well as rendered bacon fat, drippings saved from your last weekend breakfast.

- **STEP 5** (optional): Add a chopped medium yellow onion and/or a chopped, seeded and cored bell pepper; cook until softened, stirring constantly, about 4 minutes. Strictly optional, this step would be much debated by purists. But you might like the sweet notes an onion brings to the dish and/or the garden-fresh taste a bell pepper affords.

- **STEP 6** Spoon the chile purée into the pan and cook, stirring constantly, until aromatic, about 1 minute. Do not let the purée brown or (God forbid) burn. Get it frying—bubbling at the edges and popping a bit—and then immediately pass on to the next step.

- **STEP 7** Add 3 pounds meat, cut into bite-sized, ½-inch cubes; stir over the heat until the meat loses its raw color, about 2 minutes. Again, no ground beef! And certainly no seafood! This is a hearty dish, best made with good-quality meat. No, not tenderloin or anything so expensive, but a fairly lean cut, certainly not the

GARNISHES

Over each serving, try chopped and seeded bell pepper; chopped avocado tossed with a splash of lime juice; chopped cherry tomatoes; chopped radishes; chopped red onion; chopped, peeled, pitted mango; chopped, seeded jalapeños; corn chips or tortilla chips; grated cheese; minced cilantro; minced parsley; sliced grapes; sliced scallions; regular, low-fat, or fat-free sour cream; toasted slivered almonds or toasted pecan pieces.

TO CUBE MEAT: First, slice it into thick strips.

Then hold some of the strips together and slice into cubes.

fatty, long-braise cuts (chuck and shoulder roasts, for example) that will leave a grease slick on top of the dish.

Select from this list:

beef—bottom round or sirloin
pork—loin
turkey—skinless thigh or leg
chicken—boneless, skinless thighs
lamb—leg or deboned shoulder chops
veal—deboned shoulder chops
alligator—tail
buffalo—round or sirloin
venison—leg
ostrich—steaks

• **STEP 8** Pour in 3 cups broth or an enhanced broth, scrape up any browned bits on the pot's bottom, and bring to a simmer; then cover with the lid askew, reduce the heat to very low, and simmer slowly until the meat is meltingly tender, about 1½ to 3 hours. Season with salt to taste. By and large, beef broth is best, although chicken will make a silky dish. Vegetable? Very light—perhaps best in a chicken or turkey chili. Fish broth or clam juice? No way.

If you'd like to make a combo with the broth, try 1 cup beer or unsweetened apple cider to a proportionally less amount of the broth. However, use neither if you've included an all-fruit spread in the chile paste—the whole thing will become unbearably sweet. And do not use a flavored or fruit beer, but rather a lager or a dark beer.

Wine can also be mixed with the broth with this caveat: the chili will be lighter, less hearty. Or mix in a little purchased barbecue sauce as part of your liquid for a barbecued chili.

Note the absence of tomatoes, again something purists would decry. If you'd like to dare their ire and add them, use 1 cup tomato purée as part of the total liquid in this step.

And now it's just a matter of letting the meat get tender and absorb the flavors. For chicken, turkey, and pork, it'll need 1½ to 2 hours; for beef and buffalo, 2½ to 3 hours. Or try this: pour everything into a slow cooker, cover, set on low, and cook for 6 to 10 hours.

• **STEP 9** (optional); Thicken by stirring in 1 tablespoon cornmeal. Again, you needn't, but if you like a thicker chili, consider whisking in a little cornmeal—yellow or blue—for a slightly thicker but grainier finish.

What else do you need with a pot of Tex-Mex Chili? A couple of beers and plenty of napkins

Recipes for Chilis

	Tex-Mex Chili	Southwestern Chili	Rabbit Chili	Turkey Chili
1. Stem, seed, devein, and toast	4 dried New Mexican red chiles 3 dried guajillos 3 anchos	4 dried New Mexican red chiles 4 pasillas 2 dried chipotles	6 dried New Mexican red chiles 2 anchos 1 dried chipotle	6 dried New Mexican red chiles 4 mulatos 1 serrano seco or pasilla chile
2. Place in a bowl and cover with	Boiling water	Boiling water	Boiling water	Boiling water
3. Drain, then process with	4 garlic cloves 1 tsp salt ¼ cup oregano leaves 1½ tsp cumin seeds	3 garlic cloves 1 tsp salt 2 Tbs sage leaves 2 tsp stemmed thyme 1 tsp ground cinnamon 2 tsp ground cumin	3 garlic cloves 1 tsp salt ½ cup sliced pitted green olives ¼ cup chopped cilantro ½ tsp ground mace	3 garlic cloves 1 tsp salt ¼ cup sage leaves 2 tsp drained capers 1 tsp ground cinnamon ½ tsp ground allspice
4. Heat	3 Tbs canola oil	3 Tbs canola oil	3 Tbs canola oil	3 Tbs canola oil
5. (optional) Cook	Omit	1 medium yellow onion, chopped	1 medium yellow onion, chopped	1 medium yellow onion, chopped
6. Add	The chile paste	The chile paste	The chile paste	The chile paste
7. Add and cook	1½ pounds trimmed, cubed beef bottom round 1½ pounds trimmed, cubed pork loin	2 pounds trimmed and cubed sirloin 1 pound cubed boneless skinless chicken thighs	Two 3-pound rabbits, cut into pieces, the meat removed from the bones and chopped (the bones discarded)	3 pounds cubed, skinless turkey leg or thigh meat
8. Pour in, partially cover, and simmer slowly	1½ cups beef broth One 12-ounce bottle of beer	2½ cups chicken broth ½ cup dry white wine	2½ cups chicken broth ½ cup dry white wine	1½ cups chicken broth One 12-ounce bottle of beer
9. (optional) Stir in to thicken	Omit	1 Tbs cornmeal	1 Tbs cornmeal	Omit

	Mole Chili	Tear-Jolting Chili	Spanish-Inspired Chili	Chicken Chili
1. Stem, seed, devein, and toast	4 ancho chiles 4 mulatos 3 pasillas	7 dried guajillo chiles 3 dried chipotles 1 dried habenero	12 dried New Mexican red chiles	6 dried New Mexican red chiles 5 dried guajillos 1 serrano seco chile
2. Place in a bowl and cover with	Boiling water	Boiling water	Boiling water	Boiling water
3. Drain, then process with	2 garlic cloves 1 tsp salt 2 Tbs unsweetened cocoa powder 2 Tbs sesame seeds 1 Tbs cumin seeds 2 tsp ground cinnamon 2 dried figs, stemmed	3 garlic cloves 1 tsp salt ¼ cup unsweetened dried coconut ¼ cup basil leaves 2 Tbs stemmed thyme 1 Tbs drained capers	4 garlic cloves 1 tsp salt 3 Tbs stemmed thyme 2 Tbs packed oregano leaves 2 Tbs smoked paprika ½ tsp saffron	3 garlic cloves 1 tsp salt ¼ cup packed cilantro leaves 1 Tbs stemmed thyme 1 Tbs packed oregano leaves 1 Tbs Dijon mustard
4. Heat	3 Tbs canola oil	3 Tbs lard or canola oil	3 Tbs canola oil	3 Tbs schmaltz or canola oil
5. (optional) Cook	Omit	1 red bell pepper, seeded and chopped	1 medium green bell pepper, seeded and chopped	1 medium yellow onion, chopped
6. Add	The chile paste	The chile paste	The chile paste	The chile paste
7. Add and cook	3 pounds trimmed, cubed beef bottom round	2 pounds trimmed, cubed buffalo sirloin 1 pound cubed, trimmed pork loin	3 pounds trimmed, cubed pork loin	3 pounds cubed boneless skinless chicken thighs
8. Pour in, partially cover, and simmer slowly	2½ cups beef broth ½ cup unsweetened apple juice	1½ cups beef broth One 12-ounce bottle of beer	2 cups chicken broth 1 cup dry sherry	2 cups chicken broth 1 cup barbecue sauce
9. (optional) Stir in to thicken	1 Tbs cornmeal	Omit	1 Tbs cornmeal	1 Tbs cornmeal

Summer's bliss: a bowl of Chilled Blueberry Soup

Chilled Fruit Soup

A summer treat, a chilled fruit soup is admittedly not a meal on its own. You'll need to pair it with a composed salad or a grilled burger. Or offer it as a tempting starter in chilled shot glasses. You might even spike each serving with 1 ounce vodka. • MAKES 6 LARGE LUNCHEON SERVINGS OR UP TO 12 FIRST-COURSE SERVINGS

• **STEP 1** Bring 4 cups water, 2 pounds pitted or seeded fruit or berries, and a few spices to a boil in a large saucepan over high heat; reduce the heat to low, cover, and simmer slowly until the fruit is meltingly tender, between 10 and 25 minutes. Ever disappointed in peaches or blackberries? The only rule is your nose: if the fruit doesn't smell like anything, it won't taste like anything. If your market's apricots have no fragrance, frozen's a better bet. Besides, frozen fruits—berries, especially—are a wallet-friendly alternative.

In general, go for stone fruits (peaches, nectarines, plums, pluots, cherries, mangoes, apricots, and the like—all actually called "drupes"), apples, pears, or berries (black, blue, and cran). If using apples or pears, consider a pairing with a berry: apples and blueberries, pears and raspberries. A 50/50 ratio is a good bet, although you can tip the scale either way, depending on your taste. Cranberries are, of course, quite tart, nicely balanced by sweet pears.

What fruits won't work? Tomatoes, sour citrus fruits, and melons. Tomatoes won't take to the added sugar, most varieties of citrus (lemons, limes, and such) are too tart, and melons will foam over the heat (see the box for the proper technique). That said, you can make a satisfying fruit soup from orange sections, the peel and any white pith removed. But do not later add heavy or whipping cream; it will curdle. Instead, thicken the soup with crème fraîche, sour cream, or plain, unsweetened yogurt.

For the spices, hard, whole ones first come to mind: cinnamon sticks, fennel seeds, star anise pods, whole cloves, whole cardamom pods, or even a vanilla bean, split lengthwise. That said, you would never toss in a whole nutmeg. Ground or grated versions do offer a concentrated flavor punch: use no more than ¼ to ½ teaspoon of any. And use no more than two dried spices—or three if one's a cinnamon stick.

Or forgo dried spices entirely. A sophisticated, summery treat can be made with fruit and a green herb: peaches and thyme, apricots and rosemary. But keep this in mind: the more present the herb, the sweeter and more assertive the fruit needs to be. Rosemary would KO pluots.

Berries, of course, won't need as long over the heat as, say, nectarines or certainly pears—perhaps just 10 minutes before the berries begin to break down. Peaches and nectarines, about 15 minutes; apples, the full 25.

MELON SOUP

To make a fresh melon soup, omit simmering the chunks in water. Instead, place 4 cups rindless and seeded melon chunks in a large blender with 1 cup white wine, ½ cup sugar, and ½ cup plain yogurt, sour cream, or crème fraîche. If desired, also add up to 1 tablespoon minced herb like basil, oregano, thyme, cilantro, or mint. Blend until smooth, stopping the machine and scraping down the canister's sides as necessary.

The cooked fruit or berries should be quite soft but still retain their basic shape.

Better to leave some soup in the pan for a second blending than to overfill a blender or food processor and have a mess on the counter.

• **STEP** 2 Remove and discard any hard spices, transfer large chunks of fruit or pulp to a bowl, turn the heat to medium-high, and boil the liquid in the pan, uncovered, until its volume has been reduced by half, stirring occasionally. Use a slotted spoon to remove the fruit so most of the liquid stays in the pan. Any berries may have begun to break down, but gather as much of the pulp as you can to transfer to a bowl. The best tool? A handheld strainer, even a large tea strainer.

Natural sugars are now dissolved in the water. Stir the boiling liquid occasionally so nothing sticks to the pan's bottom and so the sugars do not congregate in a heavy layer under the boiling water.

Because of various viscosities, the liquid will take various times to reduce, based on the fruit used. Plan on a little more than 10 minutes, but check the liquid often to make sure it hasn't boiled away too much. You should end up with about 2½ cups liquid.

• **STEP** 3 Purée the fruit, the reduced cooking liquid, ½ cup sugar, ½ cup dairy product, and ¼ to ½ cup wine, fortified wine, brandy, or cognac in a large blender or a food processor fitted with the chopping blades, working in batches as necessary. If you've got a sweet tooth, consider adding more sugar, up to 1 cup. But remember: this is not a dessert; it's an easy lunch or elegant starter. Granulated sugar works best, perhaps even finely ground sugar (sometimes called "bar sugar") that dissolves more quickly. Avoid heavy brown sugar. If you're dead set against sugar, use the equivalent amount of a sugar substitute as called for on the product's packaging. Some are one to one; others have their own ratio—but beware: the soup's body and silkiness will be adversely affected.

For dairy, consider sour cream, crème fraîche, plain unsweetened yogurt, heavy cream, whipping cream, light cream, half-and-half, buttermilk, whole milk, whole goat's milk, or evaporated milk. If you want to save calories, use fat-free sour cream or yogurt but not fat-free milk, which will make the soup watery. If you want to skip the dairy, use rice or soy milk—but if you use the latter, consider cutting down on the sugar because most soy milk is cut with sweeteners. Or try coconut milk, regular or light—an interesting tropical twist with other tropical flavors like fresh mangos and grated lime zest.

Dry white wine is usually the choice, although dry vermouth is equally good, if more herbal. Don't forget red wine, particularly with plums and blackberries. Dry sherry or other dry fortified wines will definitely work; but the taste will be more pronounced, so they should be used only with strong-tasting berries or fruit. Dry Marsala and apples would be pointless. You might as well have a glass of Marsala and call it quits.

If you use brandy or cognac, or a flavored brandy like Grand Marnier, remember that its taste is quite strong—and will not be cooked. No more than ¼ cup should do it, maybe less.

Which brings up the question of alcohol in the soup. No, it's not cooked, so it is indeed full-on alcohol in the final dish. If you need to make a substitution, consider a nonalcoholic white wine, unsweetened white grape juice, or unsweetened apple juice.

If you need to work in batches, apportion the ingredients properly: half the fruit, half the liquid, half the wine, and half the sugar, for example. In a food processor, if the liquid comes up above the blade housing, it can spill out the bottom of the canister and all over the counter. Turn the machine off a couple times while blending or processing to scrape down the inside of the canister or processor so everything's in contact with the blades and you end up with a smooth purée.

GARNISHES

Sprinkle a little aged balsamic vinegar, chopped chives, edible flowers, grated citrus zest, ground walnuts or pecans, lemon juice, or pomegranate molasses over each serving.

• **STEP 4** Transfer to a large, nonreactive container; seal and refrigerate for at least 4 hours or up to 3 days; then season with salt to taste. A high-acid mixture, a fruit soup must be stored in a nonreactive container that will not form harmful compounds when acid comes in touch with a metallic surface. Nonreactive materials include heat-safe glass, stainless steel, enameled iron, enameled steel, or some ceramics (certain glazes are reactive). Reactive cookware is made of tin, copper, and nonanodized aluminum, as well as certain dyes in decorative glass and pottery.

The secret to sweet is always salt, but chilling dulls salt considerably, so forgo adding any until you're ready to serve the soup. Stir in ½ to 1 teaspoon to see how the flavor brightens. Some dairy products like sour cream do have sodium in the mix, so be careful of oversalting the soup.

Once blended or processed, the soup should be quite smooth, not a chunk of fruit or berry in sight.

Recipes for Chilled Fruit Soups

	Spiced Plum Soup	Peach Thyme Soup	Cherry Brandy Soup	Apricot Rosemary Soup
1. Simmer	4 cups water 2 pounds plums, pitted and halved One 4-inch cinnamon stick 4 whole cloves (discard cinnamon stick and cloves after simmering) ¼ tsp grated nutmeg	4 cups water 2 pounds peaches, pitted and quartered 2 tsp thyme leaves	4 cups water 2 pounds sweet cherries, pitted One 4-inch cinnamon stick (discard after simmering)	4 cups water 2 pounds apricots, pitted and halved 1 Tbs chopped rosemary ⅛ tsp red pepper flakes
2. Remove large spices and fruit	Boil down liquid by half	Boil down liquid by half	Boil down liquid by half	Boil down liquid by half
3. Purée	The cooked fruit and the reduced cooking liquid ½ cup sugar ½ cup plain unsweetened yogurt ½ cup red wine	The cooked fruit and the reduced cooking liquid ½ cup sugar ½ cup sour cream ½ cup dry vermouth	The cooked fruit and the reduced cooking liquid ½ cup sugar ½ cup crème fraîche ¼ cup brandy	The cooked fruit and the reduced cooking liquid ½ cup sugar ½ cup sour cream ½ cup fruity white wine
4. Refrigerate and then season	Salt to taste	Salt to taste	Salt to taste	Salt to taste

	Blackberry Chipotle Soup	Pear Ginger Soup	Raspberry Summer Soup	Blueberry Soup
1. Simmer	4 cups water 2 pounds blackberries 1 dried chipotle, stemmed and seeded but left whole (discard after simmering)	4 cups water 2 pounds pears, cored and sliced 1 Tbs peeled minced fresh ginger One 4-inch cinnamon stick (discard after simmering)	4 cups water 2 pounds raspberries 1 Tbs grated orange zest 4 or 5 mint leaves	4 cups water 2 pounds blueberries 1 Tbs minced peeled fresh ginger One 4-inch cinnamon stick (discard after simmering)
2. Remove large spices and fruit	Boil down liquid by half	Boil down liquid by half	Boil down liquid by half	Boil down liquid by half
3. Purée	The cooked fruit and the reduced cooking liquid ½ cup sugar ½ cup plain unsweetened yogurt ½ cup red wine or dry Madeira	The cooked fruit and the reduced cooking liquid ½ cup sugar ½ cup cream ¼ cup Grand Marnier	The cooked fruit and the reduced cooking liquid ½ cup sugar ½ cup half-and-half ½ cup fruity white wine	The cooked fruit and the reduced cooking liquid ½ cup sugar ½ cup crème fraîche ½ cup red wine
4. Refrigerate and then season	Salt to taste	Salt to taste	Salt to taste	Salt to taste

Creamy Vegetable Soup

Based on a velouté (vehl-oo-TAY), one of the foundational French sauces, this easy technique creates any vegetable "cream of" soup: cream of asparagus, cream of mushroom, and the like. For the freshest taste, go simple: one vegetable, one herb. • MAKES 6 SERVINGS

• **STEP 1** Make a blond roux with 3 tablespoons fat and 3 tablespoons all-purpose flour in a large saucepan over low heat. In a cream soup, the roux is traditionally made with unsalted butter. (For a discussion of roux, see page 57.) But don't steer away from other oils like peanut, olive (especially for green vegetable soups like pea or zucchini), or even untoasted nut oils. Or if you're making a root vegetable soup, try even the melted, unseasoned fat trimmings from the last time you had a rib roast. Cream of potato soup made with rendered beef fat? A ridiculous indulgence.

Place the fat in a large saucepan over low heat. The moment the butter has melted or the oil barely ripples, whisk in the flour until smooth. "Blond" refers to the roux's color—that is to say, the absence of any deep color—as opposed to the darker roux used in Brunswick Stew (page 57). The fat and flour should be whisked over the heat into a single mass that's pale beige but smooth, not grainy.

• **STEP 2** Whisk in 4 cups (1 quart) broth until smooth; bring to a simmer. Avoid fish broth or clam juice: they will overpower the vegetables. Instead, use one of these:

> **vegetable broth**—a natural choice, light and flavorful
> **chicken broth**—a silky substantiality, best with broccoli, asparagus, peas, and other green vegetables
> **beef broth**—a good match with roots

Homemade stock is the best bet, but we freely admit to using canned most of the time—but not without discernment. Canned broths vary widely: some are all onion; a few, rich and delicious. An insipid, watery broth will make an insipid, watery soup. Do a taste test of several varieties of broth right from the cans or boxes. More expensive is not necessarily better. But always buy a reduced-sodium version. Watery flavor should never be shellacked with salt.

To avoid lumps, some chefs recommend heating the broth first; however, whisking constantly while adding room-temperature broth in a small, steady stream does the trick. Still, work efficiently, not so slowly that the roux begins to brown.

Cream

The difference between light cream, heavy cream, and whipping cream is negligible outside the discipline of pastry making. In the United States, the first has about 30% fat; the second, up to 36%; and the last, up to 39%. Obviously, any will do here. Don't boil the cream; the taste will be overpowering. Instead, let it cook just until the soup begins to fizz around the pan's edge. Once it does, take the pot off the heat.

Do not use half-and-half or whole milk; both are too thin to give the soup body. And do not use condensed milk, which adds an unwanted and unincorporated "cooked" taste in the soup. So-called "fat-free" creams are loaded with corn syrup; they will turn the soup unbearably sweet.

Finally, creamy dishes always eat up salt. Act like a Gen X college grad: start conservatively but be prepared to go liberally.

Once all of the broth has been added, whisk almost constantly until the soup comes to a simmer. It should look like thin gravy, a watery cream soup. Most of its body will come later from the puréed vegetables.

• **STEP 3** Add 4 cups chopped, prepared vegetable and perhaps a single herb or dried spice; bring to a simmer, reduce the heat, cover, and cook until the vegetables are tender when pierced with a fork, between 15 and 45 minutes. In a good cream soup, nothing is browned. First, it would change the color of the dish. Second, there must be no bitter undertones.

Choose one vegetable—broccoli, asparagus, mushrooms, acorn squash, and the like. If it has a thick skin—rutabaga or butternut squash, for example—peel it before cubing it. Potato and sweet potato skins, while fully edible, will turn the soup depressing colors, so these vegetables should be peeled as well. Also remove any seeds and inner membranes from winter squash, red bell peppers, or other vegetables. Seeding tomatoes is a matter of taste: the seeds (and skins) will later be puréed, but some seeds may be left intact even after the most rigorous blending.

Broccoli stems should be peeled with a vegetable peeler to remove the tough, outer bits, then cut into small chunks; asparagus spears should also be peeled to remove the fibrous outer bits and, like green beans, cut into 2-inch segments. Cauliflower florets should be separated from the head.

Don't neglect greens. They will be puréed, so they won't be gummy. Spinach and stemmed chard are obvious choices—but what of even lettuce or endive? Garnished

There are three ways to purée a vegetable soup: with a food processor. . . .

Or with a blender (note that the center piece in the lid has been removed and the hole covered with folded paper towels to prevent splattering). . . .

Or with an immersion blender right in the pot.

with finely grated lemon zest, cream of escarole is fine lunch fare.

The only vegetables not recommended? Stringy ones like celery or whole artichokes—unless you're willing to strain the soup after it's been puréed in step 4. Asparagus, too, can be quite sinewy; use spears no thicker than a pencil. That said, they all make a delicate, savory soup. For a quick convenience, use frozen artichoke hearts, thawed and squeezed of all excess moisture. And beets, while they produce a sweet cream soup, will also yield one that's an unappetizing pinkish purple. Consider yellow beets for better aesthetics.

One herb is sufficient, fresh or dried. Why not two vegetables and several herbs? This soup is delicate; the cream enhances the flavors so they're fresh and present. Indeed, there's no compelling reason for an herb: a cream of broccoli soup is delicious with thyme but comforting and warm without it.

Timing is a function of the chosen vegetable. Reduce the heat to low and let the soup simmer slowly until the thickest part of the vegetable (broccoli stems, for example) can be pierced with a fork, not a knife. Almost any food can be pierced with a sharp knife. If not, have your knives sharpened.

• **STEP 4** Purée the soup, pour it back into the saucepan, stir in about 1 cup cream, raise the heat to medium, and cook just until simmering at the pan's edge, about 4 minutes. There are three ways to purée the soup:

1. **With a food processor fitted with the chopping blade.** Work in batches, making sure the liquid in the processor bowl doesn't ride over the blade housing and spill under the canister and onto the counter.

   Pro: A food processor runs little risk of scalding and makes a smooth soup every time.

   Con: It yields a slightly thinner soup because of the way the blades juice the vegetables.

2. **With a blender.** Work in batches, pouring in the liquid and vegetables in equal amounts each time. Pour each puréed batch into a large bowl before pouring it all back into the saucepan.

   Pro: A blender usually produces a slightly thicker cream soup.

   Con: Hot soup can spew out of the lid because of air-pressure changes. To avoid nasty splatters, remove the lid's center portion, place a doubled, clean kitchen towel over the opening, and pulse a few times before blending fully.

3. **With an immersion blender.** Submerge the blades in the soup, turn the blender on, and stir it through the soup, keeping the blades away from any nonstick surfaces. Also keep the cord away from the heating element.

   Pro: Clean-up is easier; an immersion blender makes this a one-pot meal.

   Con: An immersion blender may leave small chunks in the soup simply because there's no way to assure that all the material comes in contact with the blades.

Freezing a Cream Soup

If you want to freeze the soup for a future meal, cool the pan in the refrigerator until chilled. Some casein (like a pudding skin) may form over the soup; stir it back into the mixture, then ladle the soup into a sealable plastic container and freeze for up to 2 months. Long freezing dulls the taste of a creamy soup. When you reheat it, consider adding more herbs and salt—and even grating lemon zest over individual servings.

Recipes for Creamy Vegetable Soups

	Cream of Asparagus Soup	Cream of Broccoli Soup	Cream of Potato Soup	Cream of Mushroom Soup
1. Make a blond roux	3 Tbs unsalted butter 3 Tbs all-purpose flour	3 Tbs canola oil 3 Tbs all-purpose flour	3 Tbs unsalted butter or melted beef fat trimmings 3 Tbs all-purpose flour	3 Tbs unsalted butter 3 Tbs all-purpose flour
2. Whisk in	4 cups (1 quart) chicken broth	4 cups (1 quart) vegetable broth	4 cups (1 quart) beef broth	4 cups (1 quart) vegetable or mushroom broth
3. Add, cover, and cook	1 pound thin asparagus spears, peeled and chopped 2 Tbs minced tarragon ¼ tsp ground allspice	1½ pounds broccoli, florets separated and stems chopped 2 Tbs minced rosemary	1½ pounds small white potatoes, preferably Irish creamers, peeled and chopped 2 Tbs minced sage	12 ounces white button or cremini mushrooms, or a mix of wild mushrooms, cleaned and thinly sliced 1 Tbs stemmed thyme
4. Purée, stir in, and reheat	1 cup cream Salt and pepper	1 cup cream Salt and pepper	1 cup cream Salt and pepper	1 cup cream Salt and pepper

	Fresh Pea Soup	Creamy Sweet Potato Soup	Creamy Carrot Ginger Soup	Creamy Tomato Soup
1. Make a blond roux	3 Tbs unsalted butter 3 Tbs all-purpose flour	3 Tbs unsalted butter 3 Tbs all-purpose flour	3 Tbs canola oil 3 Tbs all-purpose flour	3 Tbs unsalted butter 3 Tbs all-purpose flour
2. Whisk in	4 cups (1 quart) chicken broth	4 cups (1 quart) chicken broth	4 cups (1 quart) chicken broth	4 cups (1 quart) chicken broth
3. Add, cover, and cook	4 cups fresh shelled or frozen peas 2 tsp stemmed thyme	1 pound sweet potatoes, peeled and chopped One 4-inch cinnamon stick (discard before puréeing) ¼ tsp grated nutmeg	1¼ pounds carrots, chopped 2 tsp ground ginger	2 pounds very ripe tomatoes, seeded and chopped
4. Purée, stir in, and reheat	1 cup cream Salt and pepper	1 cup cream Salt and pepper	1 cup cream Salt and pepper	1 cup cream Salt and pepper

Duck Breasts with a Fruit Sauce

Ducks take to water in the wild but to fruit in the pan. Pekin—aka "Long Island"—duck breasts are readily available in our supermarkets and surprisingly quick to prepare. The only real surprise is that so few people make this simple but sophisticated dinner. • MAKES 4 SERVINGS

• **STEP 1** Preheat the oven to 375°F. Score the skin and fat on four 7-ounce Pekin or Long Island duck breasts, season with salt and freshly ground black pepper; then set the breasts skin side down in a cold, large, oven-safe skillet and place over medium-low heat. Cook until the skin is golden brown, 10 to 14 minutes. In North America, there are basically two kinds of ducks in our markets: Moulard and Pekin. Moulards, a French favorite, have breasts that are quite large, sometimes over 2 pounds; they have a slightly gamy taste, better suited to braising or roasting. Pekin ducks, by contrast, have breasts that are smaller and so better suited to this quick sauté.

Pekin ducks (the name, a derivative of "Peking") are also called "Long Island ducks" because of the erstwhile preponderance of duck farms on the island, most of which have been overrun by subdivisions. (Most "Long Island" ducks are now raised in Wisconsin and Indiana.)

A duck has one breast in the wild but one or two at the supermarket, depending on how the meat is cut. Like a chicken, the meat on a duck's "chest" has two lobes. When the entire structure is left whole, both lobes together, it's called a "duck breast." However, when the lobes are separated, these are also each called a "duck breast"—as is the case with boneless skinless chicken breasts, which are in fact boneless skinless chicken breast *halves*. Confusing, yes— but it's the latter, those so-called halves, that we mean here.

Thus, you'll need to examine carefully what you've bought. If you've bought frozen duck breasts, chances are they were sold whole, the two lobes together; these must be thawed and separated by cutting through the thin strip of meat between them. If you've bought fresh duck breasts, chances are they have already been separated into lobes, each about 7 or 8 ounces. If not, separate them now so you have two lobes, each of which looks like a compact but more oval boneless chicken breast with thicker skin.

If you're a fan of really crisp skin, air-dry the breasts uncovered on a plate in the refrigerator for 24 hours before cooking them. The skin will dehydrate—and will then get very crunchy over the heat.

Underneath that skin, a duck's thick layer of fat is both a blessing and a curse

Score the skin and fat on the breasts to help them release much of their fat over the heat.

TO MAKE CITRUS SUPREMES: Slice off the top and bottom sections so the fruit will sit flat on a cutting board, then slice off the peel and pith, following the fruit's natural curvature.

Then cut out the individual sections, catching the juice in a bowl. Discard the peel, any white pith, and the connective membranes.

in the kitchen. To avoid the skin's turning gummy, the fat must be rendered (that is, melted away), yet that same fat can crisp the skin and protect the meat over the heat.

Place the breasts "horizontally" on a cutting board (that is, narrower ends to your left and right). First, cut off any skin and fat that lops over the edge of the breasts. Then score the remaining skin and fat with a sharp knife, making three parallel cuts across the breasts at a diagonal from the breast's orientation on the cutting board. Do not cut into the meat; just cut through the skin and into the fat so that the fat itself has run-off channels as the breasts cook. Turn each breast 90 degrees (a quarter turn) and make three more parallel cuts in each, thereby creating a diamond-patterned crosshatch in the skin and fat.

Set the scored breasts skin side down in a large, high-sided sauté pan or skillet, then set the pan or skillet over a burner just now turned to medium-low. The fat will begin to melt gently, slowly softening the skin and turning it golden over the next 10 minutes or so.

● **STEP 2** Turn the breasts over, place the skillet in the oven, and cook until an instant-read meat thermometer inserted into the center of a breast registers 140°F for medium-rare or 165°F for medium (the latter, the USDA recommendation), about 10 to 15 minutes. There will be quite a bit of fat in the pan. Never fear: it will be discarded later. For now, turn the breasts with tongs and slip the pan or skillet into the oven where the skin will dry out and crisp as the meat cooks.

The USDA recommends all poultry be cooked to 165°F. For chicken, we're in accord. However, duck breasts, fatty as they are, can turn stringy at such temperatures; they're often served redder, or just pinker, certainly rarer than chicken, usually around 140°F, just within the range of safety. If you're worried, cook the breasts to the higher temperature.

• **STEP 3** Remove the hot skillet from the oven, transfer the breasts to a plate, tent with aluminum foil, and pour off all but 1 tablespoon fat. Place the skillet over medium-high heat; add about 1 cup finely diced aromatics and perhaps some herbs or spices; and cook, stirring often, until softened. The duck's done; speed's of the essence. Avoid long-cooking roots or wilty, cloying greens. Consider these the basics in order of decreasing volume used:

Once the breasts are browned, most of the rendered fat should be poured off and discarded.

> finely diced yellow onion
> finely diced scallions
> finely diced or very thinly sliced shallots
> minced, stemmed and seeded fresh chiles such as a
>   jalapeño or the hotter serrano
> minced garlic cloves
> minced peeled fresh ginger

One diced medium onion and a few minced garlic cloves are the outer limit in terms of volume. If you want to add other aromatics besides the onion, use a very small yellow onion—or use three to four medium whole scallions, or one to two medium shallots. Add no more than a couple garlic cloves, one prepared chile, and up to 2 tablespoons minced ginger. A little more may make a more vibrant sauce; much more will be overwhelming.

All of these aromatics, with the exception of the chiles, are by nature sweet—and most likely, the fruit you'll soon add will be sweet, too. A green herb or perhaps a dash of ground allspice can help the balance. You needn't add any herb or spice, especially for a simple sauté of, say, shallots and blueberries. Still, even here thyme would be a little aromatic fulcrum in the sauce, balancing everything.

Some spices, like cinnamon, cardamom, cloves, and star anise, work best whole. Break a four-inch cinnamon stick in half to release some of its oils. Whole, they should be used sparingly: just 4 cloves, a few cardamom pods, or one star anise pod. They should also be removed and discarded before serving. Ground, these spices can unnecessarily cloud the sauce.

And speaking of things discarded, don't throw that rendered fat down the drain. To avoid a nasty clog, pour it into a sealable container and throw it out with the garbage. Or don't throw it away at all. Save it, covered, in the freezer for up to 4 months. For a decadent treat, use it the next time you pan-fry diced potatoes or other roots.

• **STEP 4** Add about 1 cup broth, wine, or an enhanced broth and simmer until reduced by half, scraping up any browned bits on the skillet's bottom. Start with the basics: either broth (chicken, vegetable) or wine (red, white)—or a combination of broth and wine. Or combine broth with a dry fortified wine, perhaps in a 50/50 combo: ½ cup chicken broth and ½ dry vermouth. Dry sherry, dry Madeira, and dry Marsala are far stronger but balance the sweet aromatics and fruit; still and all, they should also be tempered, perhaps in a 25/75 ratio with broth. Don't neglect unsweetened apple juice, again best tempered 50/50 with broth.

Cream and coconut milk are simply too rich, adding an unappetizing heaviness. But do consider adding a splash of cognac or Grand Marnier to the mix, keeping it to less than 1 tablespoon—or a little fish sauce and/or soy sauce for Asian flavors.

• **STEP 5** Stir in about 1 cup chopped peeled fresh fruit, about 2 teaspoons vinegar, and about 2 teaspoons honey; then add the breasts skin side up and any accumulated juices. Cook just until warmed through, about 2 minutes; season with salt to taste. Choose from a range of fruits and berries:

apples—peeled, cored, seeded, and chopped
apricots—pitted and chopped
blackberries
blueberries
cherries—sour or sweet, pitted
cherry tomatoes—halved or quartered
figs—quartered
grapefruits—peeled and cut into supremes
lychees—preferably canned, pitted and drained
mangos—pitted, peeled, and chopped
oranges—peeled and cut into supremes
peaches—pitted, peeled, and chopped
pears—peeled, cored, seeded, and chopped
raspberries

Avoid lemons and limes—too strong. And skip papayas and kiwis—too subtle.

Use any vinegar you prefer: red wine vinegar if you've used red wine; white wine vinegar, if white wine; sherry vinegar, if sherry. Or don't stick to the basics. Balsamic is good in any mix—but save the aged, syrupy stuff for salads. White balsamic is quite sweet, a match to sour fruit. Apple cider vinegar is a hearty, sturdy stand-up against blackberries.

The better the honey, the better the dish. Look for nosy, fragrant honeys, not laced with artificial flavorings but actually flavored by the plants from which they're taken. Star thistle, eucalyptus, or other herbal honeys are nice matches with duck.

Taste before you salt. Remember: the breasts have already been salted in step 1. The sauce may need just a pinch more before it's ready.

Pan-Seared Duck Breasts with Pears and Ginger

Recipes for Duck Breasts

	Pan-Seared Duck Breasts with Blackberries and Sage	Pan-Seared Duck Breasts with Apricots and Rosemary	Pan-Seared Duck Breasts with Plums and Chiles	Pan-Seared Duck Breasts with Cherries and Port
1. Preheat the oven; score, season, and cook	Four 7-ounce Pekin or Long Island duck breasts Salt and pepper	Four 7-ounce Pekin or Long Island duck breasts Salt and pepper	Four 7-ounce Pekin or Long Island duck breasts Salt and pepper	Four 7-ounce Pekin or Long Island duck breasts Salt and pepper
2. Turn and roast to	140°F—medium-rare and our preference 165°F—medium and the USDA guideline	140°F—medium-rare and our preference 165°F—medium and the USDA guideline	140°F—medium-rare and our preference 165°F—medium and the USDA guideline	140°F—medium-rare and our preference 165°F—medium and the USDA guideline
3. Transfer to a plate, pour off almost all fat, and cook	4 ounces shallots, diced 2 tsp minced peeled fresh ginger 2 tsp minced sage	4 ounces shallots, diced 2 Tbs minced rosemary	1 medium yellow onion, chopped 1 or 2 red Thai hot or serrano chiles, seeded and minced	1 medium red onion, chopped 1 garlic clove, minced 2 tsp stemmed thyme ¼ tsp ground cloves
4. Pour in and reduce	1 cup red wine	1 cup white wine	½ cup chicken broth ½ cup red wine	½ cup chicken broth ½ cup port
5. Add, warm, and season	½ pint (1 cup) fresh blackberries 2 tsp red wine vinegar 2 tsp honey Duck breasts and accumulated juices Salt to taste	½ pound apricots, pitted and thinly sliced 2 tsp cider vinegar 2 tsp honey Duck breasts and accumulated juices Salt to taste	½ pound red plums, pitted and thinly sliced 2 tsp balsamic vinegar 2 tsp honey Duck breasts and accumulated juices Salt to taste	½ pound pitted sweet cherries 2 tsp balsamic vinegar 2 tsp honey Duck breasts and accumulated juices Salt to taste

	Pan-Seared Duck Breasts with Oranges	Pan-Seared Duck Breasts with Pears and Ginger	Pan-Seared Duck Breasts with Figs and Madeira	Pan-Seared Duck Breasts with Mango and Basil
1. Preheat the oven; score, season, and cook	Four 7-ounce Pekin or Long Island duck breasts Salt and pepper	Four 7-ounce Pekin or Long Island duck breasts Salt and pepper	Four 7-ounce Pekin or Long Island duck breasts Salt and pepper	Four 7-ounce Pekin or Long Island duck breasts Salt and pepper
2. Turn and roast to	140°F—medium-rare and our preference 165°F—medium and the USDA guideline	140°F—medium-rare and our preference 165°F—medium and the USDA guideline	140°F—medium-rare and our preference 165°F—medium and the USDA guideline	140°F—medium-rare and our preference 165°F—medium and the USDA guideline
3. Transfer to a plate, pour off almost all fat, and cook	4 medium whole scallions, thinly sliced 2 garlic cloves, minced 1 Tbs minced peeled fresh ginger 1 star anise pod (discard before serving) ¼ tsp red pepper flakes	2 ounces shallots, diced 1 Tbs minced peeled fresh ginger One 4-inch cinnamon stick, broken into thirds (discard before serving)	2 ounces shallots, diced 1 Tbs stemmed thyme ¼ tsp ground mace	4 medium whole scallions, thinly sliced 2 Tbs chopped basil
4. Pour in and reduce	½ cup chicken broth ½ cup shaoxing (see page 374) or dry sherry	1 cup white wine	½ cup chicken broth ½ cup dry Madeira	1 cup white wine
5. Add, warm, and season	1 cup orange supremes (about 2 medium oranges) 2 tsp rice vinegar 2 tsp honey Duck breasts and accumulated juices Salt to taste	1 large pear, peeled, seeded, and sliced thin 2 tsp honey 2 tsp lemon juice Duck breasts and accumulated juices Salt to taste	3 to 4 fresh figs, quartered 2 tsp honey 2 tsp sherry vinegar Duck breasts and accumulated juices Salt to taste	1 medium ripe mango (about 12 ounces), peeled, pitted, and chopped 2 tsp honey 2 tsp white wine vinegar Duck breasts and accumulated juices Salt to taste

East Indian Curry

Curry is not one thing but a multitude. The word itself is the Anglicization of the Tamil word *kari,* which means a secondary dish (eaten with the rice, the primary dish). Over the years, that secondary dish has overwhelmed its starch. Today, curries are global fare with variations across India, Asia, the Pacific rim, the Caribbean, and even Africa. There are quite literally thousands of curries—we make no claims to authenticity but have adapted a basic technique for the American kitchen. Still, these many dishes are based on the original: a long, slow braise best eaten over a bowl of fragrant basmati rice. • MAKES 6 SERVINGS

• **STEP 1** Heat 2 tablespoons fat in a large Dutch oven or soup pot over medium heat. Despite common perceptions, curry is not necessarily fiery. It is, however, aromatic. The best choice for a fat is a pale, noncompeting flavor such as one of the neutral oils like safflower, sunflower, or canola oil; refined peanut oil; or ghee (that is, clarified butter—for an explanation and tips on making your own, see page 25). These will let the spices' fragrance come through without the competing tastes found in other oils.

That said, almond oil makes a lovely complement to a well-balanced curry—not toasted almond oil, but the pale, slightly fruity, untoasted oil, a sweet finish without competing fragrances. For a pungent, sour, and somewhat bitter taste, some East Indian curries begin with mustard seed oil, an acquired taste but definitely Turkish Delight once acquired.

• **STEP 2** Add 2 to 3 cups chopped aromatics; cook, stirring often, until softened. The basic choices are onions, shallots, and leeks. A red onion would give a little peppery bite; a yellow onion, soft sweet undertones. A large version of either should do the trick. Four to six shallots, of course, would add their garlic-like flavor; two large leeks, a few herbal notes.

Do watch out for those leeks: they're quite sandy. Use only the white and pale green sections (the dark green bits can be frozen and saved back for stock making). Slice the usable parts lengthwise, then open up the inner chambers under running water to remove sand and grit. Yes, the cellular fibers will expand in the water, doping the leek with unnecessary moisture; but it's a small price to pay to avoid the crunch of sand. Once washed, slice each part into very thin half-moons and fan the slices out so the layers are separated when they hit the heat.

Basic Meat Choices for Curry

beef—bone-in short ribs, arm roast, shoulder roast, flanken, or oxtails, all in large pieces

pork—cut-up bone-in country-style ribs, blade chops, shoulder arm roast cut into steaks, shoulder arm steaks, or bone-in shoulder chops

lamb—bone-in arm or shoulder chops, cut into large hunks, each with a section of bone

veal—bone-in shoulder chops, cut into large pieces; or arm roast, left whole

goat—bone-in shoulder chops, cut up

rabbit—cut up

chicken—skinless bone-in thighs and/or skin-on wings

roots—peeled and seeded if necessary, then roughly chopped into 2-inch pieces

You can use a combination of these aromatics (a large shallot and a leek, for example), or you can accent these with minced peeled fresh ginger or minced garlic cloves. However, these latter two may already be in the spice blend to come in the form of ground ginger or garlic powder. Watch out for a double hit.

• **STEP 3** Add about 2 tablespoons curry spice blend and perhaps ½ teaspoon salt; cook until aromatic, stirring constantly, about 30 seconds.

Bottled curry powder

The path of least resistance is to use a bottled, dry curry blend (not a wet blend as for Vindaloo, page 395, and Thai Curry, page 385). Despite what it may seem at the local grocery store, curry powder comes in an astounding array. Common yellow curry powder is often just an excuse for too much turmeric. However, some yellow blends are mild, sweet, and fragrant, a good match to aromatic basmati rice.

But why settle for the common? Madras curry powder is laced with cayenne and very hot; West Indian, often quite mild; Jamaican varieties, influenced by jerk and cayenne-heavy (see page 50); Masaman, fiery and fragrant. These are available at high-end markets and spice suppliers on the Web.

Check your bottling for salt. Some have it in the mix; others don't. If yours doesn't, add ½ teaspoon salt to the pot as well as the spice blend.

If you use a bottled blend, particularly the common yellow variety, try using only 1 tablespoon and doctoring it with 2 teaspoons ground coriander; about ½ teaspoon ground cinnamon, mace, or ginger; and ½ teaspoon cayenne. Or consider doctoring it your own way with other ground spices including rubbed sage, ground cinnamon, ground fenugreek, ground fennel seeds, or grated nutmeg.

Homemade curry powder

Many curry powders are developed over generations in East Indian families, a secret rarely told. But don't be daunted; just follow some easy rules. You'll need about 2 tablespoons total volume—that is, 6 teaspoons. Follow these steps:

1. Start with 2 or 3 teaspoons of a base dried spice, usually turmeric, ground coriander, cumin, or ginger. Don't like this list? What about rubbed sage or thyme, more Western European in taste but also quite aromatic. You can also mix the

TO CHOP A LEEK: Take off the root end, then slice the white and pale green section lengthwise to reveal its inner chambers, most often filled with sand and grit that must be washed away.

Then lay the cleaned leek cut side down and slice off thin half-moons.

base: 1½ teaspoons ground coriander and 1½ teaspoons ground ginger, for example.

2. Add ½ teaspoon salt. Salt will help the meat leach its juices into the sauce, making the best curry imaginable. You will probably have to add more at the end; this is not enough salt for 6 servings under normal conditions.

3. If desired, add up to ½ teaspoon cayenne for heat.

4. Finally, make up the remaining 2 or 4 teaspoons with a wide array of ground, dried spices and herbs: thyme, sage, nutmeg, mace, cinnamon, cloves, and fenugreek, to name a few. In some cases, you may have to grind your own in a spice grinder: fennel, mustard, or celery seeds, for example, as well as dried lemon or orange peels, a nice citrus burst in the mix. Don't use more than 1 teaspoon of any added spice, preferably ½ teaspoon of each. And make notes in the margin here. What was your blend? Did you like it? Would you increase the heat? Would you add more ginger, more nutmeg?

One Southeast Asian additive to curry blends is ground toasted rice. Put about 3 tablespoons of dry rice kernels in a dry skillet and toast them over medium-low heat, stirring often, until golden and fragrant. Cool to room temperature, then grind in a spice grinder until powdery. Since toasted rice adds a strong, nutty taste, blend in no more than 1 teaspoon, probably just ½ teaspoon until you get used to the taste; save the rest back in a small bottle for the next time you make curry.

• **STEP 4** Add about 4 pounds bone-in meat or root vegetables; stir over the heat until well coated with the spices. Not both meat and roots, but either. A curry, if

A curry powder starts with a basic ground spice—here, ground coriander (in the spoon).

Some curry powders use toasted rice, the grains heated until aromatic and brown in a dry skillet before being cooled and ground in a spice grinder or mini food processor.

The curry powder must coat the aromatics before any protein or vegetables are added.

you recall, started out as a side dish to the rice. Keep it that way by using one basic ingredient: pork curry, chicken curry, etc. If you want a vegetable with the curry, steam spinach, kale, or collards and stir them into the cooked basmati rice just before serving.

With the exception of the roots, you're looking for a braising meat with the bone—in other words, not quick-cooking tenderloin and not a boneless brisket.

• STEP 5 Pour in 2 cups broth or an enhanced broth and bring to a simmer, scraping up any browned bits on the pot's bottom; cover, reduce the heat to low, and simmer slowly until tender, skimming occasionally if desired, about 1½ to 3½ hours, depending on the cut. Season with salt to taste. In general, the liquid used is broth—but wine or unsweetened apple juice can be used for up to half the liquid for a sweeter dish. Coconut milk can also be added, up to 1 cup, for a Southeast Asian taste. Avoid cream and dry fortified wines: all too Western and not a good match to the spice blend.

SERVING SUGGESTIONS

Although it's common to serve curry over basmati rice (or any of its kin, like Texmati—see page 25), try it over cooked and drained red lentils, steamed greens like chard or spinach, or on a purée of roasted sweet potatoes, beaten smooth with some chicken or vegetable broth. Serve in bowls with sour cream, yogurt, or crème fraîche on the side; chopped, peeled, and seeded mangos or cucumbers; and/or chopped parsley, cilantro, and/or mint.

As the meat cooks, it will give off lots of fat as well as dissolved collagen and connective tissue. If desired, skim the fat once in a while, catching it with a large spoon against the side of the pot. We find it best to skim after the first hour and then leave the stew alone. Some fat is necessary: the spice blend will be more aromatic in its presence. Also, much of the spice blend has incorporated with the fat—and to skim too much is to lose flavor.

The various cuts take different amounts of time: chicken thighs and roots, about 1½ hours; goat, short ribs, and shoulder chops, about 2½ hours. In the end, look at the meat you've added. If there are more sinewy bits between the muscle planes, the cut will take longer over the heat. A lamb, pork, or beef shoulder roast, loaded with those connective membranes, will need the full 3½ hours over the heat.

Because the timing can be a tad unpredictable, it's best to make the curry earlier in the day—or even the day before—storing it in the fridge until dinner. That said, refrigeration unyieldingly dulls a curry. Consider adding about 1 teaspoon additional dried spices when you reheat it—or squeeze in a little lemon juice to brighten the flavors.

And don't forget more salt. If you're storing the braise in the fridge or the freezer, don't add any more now—just salt the dish as you reheat it. But if you're serving it now, you'll need to add extra. Start with ½ teaspoon and take it from there.

At the very end, once the braise has been skimmed and just before you're ready to ladle the meat or roots and sauce into bowls, it's your chance to turn it into a South African curry. Stir in about ½ cup regular or low-fat buttermilk, then balance that tartness with 1 to 2 tablespoons all-fruit spread. A sweet/sour note with apricot, raspberry, or blackberry spread works best; strawberry and blueberry spreads are too sweet—no balance, all sugar. Stir in these two ingredients, cover the pot, and set it aside off the heat for 5 minutes to blend the flavors.

Recipes for East Indian Curries

	Lamb Curry	Duck Curry	Curried Beef Stew	South African-Inspired Curry
1. Heat	2 Tbs ghee (see page 25)	2 Tbs ghee (see page 25)	2 Tbs canola oil	2 Tbs canola oil
2. Cook	2 medium yellow onions, chopped	2 medium yellow onions, chopped 1 Tbs minced peeled fresh ginger	9 ounces shallots, chopped	7 ounces shallots, chopped 1 Tbs minced peeled fresh ginger
3. Add	1½ tsp ground coriander 1½ tsp turmeric 1½ tsp ground ginger ½ tsp ground fenugreek ½ tsp ground mace ½ tsp salt ¼ tsp ground cloves ¼ tsp cayenne	2 tsp ground coriander 1 tsp ground ginger 1 tsp dry mustard 1 tsp pure chili powder ½ tsp ground cinnamon ½ tsp ground allspice ½ tsp salt	1½ tsp ground coriander 1½ tsp ground cumin 1 tsp ground cardamom 1 tsp ground mace ½ tsp cayenne ½ tsp salt	2 tsp turmeric 1 tsp ground cumin 1 tsp ground coriander 1 tsp ground cinnamon ½ tsp cayenne ½ tsp salt
4. Stir in	4 pounds bone-in lamb shoulder chops, cut into large chunks	One 6-pound duck, cleaned and cut into 10 to 12 pieces (perhaps by your butcher)	4 pounds beef arm roast, cut into large chunks	4 pounds skinless bone-in chicken thighs
5. Pour in, cover, and simmer slowly—then season	2 cups chicken broth Salt to taste	1½ cups chicken broth ½ cup rosé wine Salt to taste	1½ cups beef broth ½ cup red wine Salt to taste	2 cups chicken broth Salt to taste (at end, add ½ cup buttermilk and 1 Tbs apricot all-fruit spread)

	Tamil-Inspired Curry	Kashmiri Rogan Josh	Punjabi-Inspired Curry	Bengali-Inspired Curry
1. Heat	2 Tbs almond oil	2 Tbs canola oil	2 Tbs ghee (see page 25)	2 Tbs mustard oil
2. Cook	2 medium yellow onions, chopped	2 medium yellow onions, chopped	2 medium leeks, white and pale green parts only, halved lengthwise, carefully washed, and thinly sliced 2 Tbs minced peeled fresh ginger	2 medium yellow onions, chopped 3 garlic cloves, minced
3. Add	1½ tsp ground cumin 1 tsp ground coriander 1 tsp ground ginger ½ tsp ground fennel seeds ½ tsp garlic powder ½ tsp salt ½ tsp ground black pepper ¼ tsp grated nutmeg ¼ tsp cayenne	2 tsp ground cumin 1 tsp ground coriander ½ tsp ground ginger ½ tsp pure chili powder ½ tsp turmeric ½ tsp ground cinnamon ½ tsp ground allspice ½ tsp salt	2 tsp ground coriander 1 tsp ground celery seeds 1 tsp ground dried orange peel ½ tsp ground fenugreek ½ tsp ground cinnamon ½ tsp salt ¼ tsp garlic powder ¼ tsp ground mace	1½ tsp ground black poppy seeds 1 tsp ground fenugreek 1 tsp ground cinnamon ½ tsp ground cardamom ½ tsp ground cumin ½ tsp ground cloves ½ tsp salt ½ tsp ground black pepper
4. Stir in	4 pounds bone-in veal shoulder chops, cut into large pieces	4 pounds bone-in lamb arm chops, cut into large chunks	3 pounds skinless bone-in chicken thighs 1 pound chicken drumettes	4 pounds bone-in goat shoulder chops, cut into large pieces
5. Pour in, cover, and simmer slowly—then season	2 cups beef broth Salt to taste	2 cups beef broth Salt to taste	2 cups chicken broth Salt to taste	1½ cups beef broth ½ cup coconut milk Salt to taste

Enchiladas

Enchiladas—literally, "in chiles"—are now global fare like East Indian Curry (page 112) or Mediterranean Fish Stew (page 193), with just as many regional and even personal variations. This technique is modeled on the Tex-Mex incarnation: a traditional Mexican sauce with American-style fillings, all rolled and covered with cheese before baking. • MAKES 8 ENCHILADAS

• **STEP 1** Stem, seed, and devein 12 dried chiles; toast them in a large dry saucepan over medium heat until fragrant, stirring occasionally, about 3 minutes. Transfer to a large bowl. For the classic taste, at least half the chiles should be dried New Mexican reds. In general, all the dried chiles should be red or black, although a few yellow or orange in the mix will create a more complex—and oft-times more biting—heat. For a full inventory, see the reference list under Chili (page 89).

• **STEP 2** Heat 3 tablespoons oil into the saucepan; add 1 chopped large onion and several minced garlic cloves; and cook, stirring often, until translucent, about 5 minutes. In general, use a neutral oil like canola or corn. However, aromatic oils like walnut or olive can add an interesting taste to nouveau enchiladas; almond oil is particularly nice against the chiles.

But far more than the oil, the onion varietal you use will change the nature of the sauce. A yellow onion will give the classic sweet, slightly bitter undertones; a white onion, a bit of an acidic spike; and a red, more sour, a light spark, often a good foil to the earthy taste of dried chiles. Most hip varietal hybrids—Vidalia, Walla Walla, and Maui—are considerably sweeter, some with more sugar than complexity. They should be balanced with bitter notes (spinach, chard, diced turnip), earthy tastes (mushrooms, carrots, potatoes), or sour accents (lemon zest, cheese).

That all said, you can substitute 2 to 4 medium shallots or 2 large leeks, white and green parts only, for the onion; but you'll skew the dish away from the Southwest and more toward Europe. Still, a walnut, tarragon, and chicken enchilada filling will definitely be enhanced by some shallots in the sauce.

• **STEP 3** Stir in the toasted chiles, 3½ cups broth or enhanced broth, 1 or 2 tablespoons minced herb, 1 teaspoon salt, and several grinds of black pepper; bring to a simmer, cover, reduce the heat to low, and simmer slowly for 20 minutes—then purée the contents of the saucepan, working in batches as necessary. Now you turn the base (the onions, garlic, and chiles) into a sauce. The broth should be chicken, beef, or vegetable—no fish broth, even for shrimp enchiladas. It will partially mask the chiles' flavors without dousing the fire; you'll end up with unsophisticated, fishy heat.

Although oregano is the traditional herb here, there's no reason not to try others, particularly thyme, parsley, and rosemary (that last, especially for California cuisine).

To purée the sauce, use an immersion blender in the pot—or pour the sauce into a standard blender or into a food processor fitted with the chopping blade. For a discussion of the pros and cons of all three methods, see the puréeing instructions for Creamy Vegetable Soup (page 101).

Once the sauce has been puréed, it can be placed in a nonreactive bowl (see page 99) and refrigerated for up to 3 days. Or it can be frozen in a similar container for up to 6 months—which is why you might consider making a double batch of enchilada sauce and squirreling half in the freezer. However, cold storage compromises the chiles' fire and flavors. Compensate by serving sliced pickled jalapeños on the side.

There are two ways to soften tortillas: by heating them briefly in a dry skillet (left) or by dipping them in the enchilada sauce.

• **STEP 4** Preheat the oven to 350°F and make 4 cups filling for the enchiladas. Here's where your creativity can really come into play. Baking enchiladas is all about melding the sauce to the tortillas and melting the cheese into gooey gorgeousness—but not about cooking the filling. Thus, it should be ready to eat.

As a starting point, cook up 1½ pounds lean ground beef, pork, veal, turkey, or even lamb with 2 tablespoons fat in a large skillet over medium heat. Add up to 2 tablespoons dried spices—chile powder, ground cumin, ground mace—and perhaps a diced and seeded red bell pepper. Voilà—a classic.

Or steam about 1½ pounds peeled, deveined, medium shrimp in a vegetable steamer set over 1 inch of simmering water until pink and firm, about 5 minutes. Cool for 10 minutes, then mix with ½ cup peas and a diced medium carrot.

Or try the path of least resistance and forgo cooking altogether. How about 2½ cups shredded meat from a precooked rotisserie chicken, 1½ cups canned black beans, and a little ground cinnamon? Or cubed firm tofu, minced ginger, and sliced scallions? Or pasteurized lump crabmeat, checked for any shell fragments and cartilage, and mixed with some minced herbs and perhaps ¼ teaspoon grated nutmeg?

You can also add up to 2 cups shredded cheese to any filling, deducting that amount from the cheese used in step 5. Just be sure the other ingredients are cooled to room temperature so the cheese doesn't melt.

Or make a cheese filling with 3½ cups shredded semi-firm or semi-soft cheese and a sautéed minced large onion. (For a list of various cheeses in these categories, see page 175.) Or even try a little soft cheese like chèvre (goat) or ricotta (do not use fat-free—too watery). Or mix about 1 cup soft cheese with 3 cups chopped rotisserie chicken meat and 1 teaspoon finely grated lemon zest for a new twist. After all, the sauce is traditional; everything else, up to your imagination. For any cheese-heavy filling, put only a moderate dusting of cheese over the top of these enchiladas in the next step.

Place the filling down the center of the sauce-coated tortilla, then roll the tortilla closed before placing it in the baking dish.

Spoon the remaining enchilada sauce over the filled tortillas.

Grate the cheese over the enchiladas just before baking.

• **STEP 5** Roll ½ cup of the filling into each of eight 8-inch tortillas, lay them seam side down in a 9 x 13-inch baking dish, pour the puréed sauce over the top, and grate up to 12 ounces cheese over the entire dish. Bake uncovered until the cheese has melted and the sauce is bubbling, about 30 minutes. While corn tortillas are the most traditional, we prefer well-stuffed flour tortillas, a little chewy texture against the filling. If you use corn, you may have trouble finding 8-inch ones without shopping at a Mexican or Latin American market. You can use the smaller 6-inch corn tortillas; but you'll then make perhaps 15 enchiladas, not the 12 called for here.

The tortillas must be softened before they can be rolled. You can do this in two ways:

1. Pour the puréed sauce back into its saucepan. Dab the tortillas into the sauce one by one, coating them lightly before transferring them to a cutting board to fill. Watch out: if the sauce is still hot, it can burn your fingers. Also, you'll have capsaicin all over your hands; wash up carefully.
2. Place the tortillas one by one in a microwave and heat on high for 10 to 20 seconds, just until pliable.

To fill them, lay the tortillas one at a time on a cutting board, place ½ cup filling in a line down the center of the tortillas, and roll closed parallel to the line of the filling. Place the enchiladas one by one in the baking dish seam side down so they stay closed.

If you've used cheese in the filling, consider cutting down on the amount of cheese you spread over the sauce—say, only 6 to 8 ounces. The cheese here should be any of the semi-soft or semi-firm varieties: Monterey Jack is traditional, but also try Cheddar, Emmental, Gouda, or Gruyère. For most of these, 4 ounces = 1 cup shredded. (Thus, 1 pound or 16 ounces = 4 cups shredded.) Avoid hard cheeses like Parmigiano-Reggiano or Pecorino in favor of a gooey, irresistible topping.

Recipes for Enchiladas

	Chicken and Black Bean Enchiladas	Smoky Beef Enchiladas	Mushroom Enchiladas	Spinach Enchiladas
1. Stem, seed, devein, and toast	8 dried New Mexican red chiles 4 guajillos	7 dried New Mexican red chiles 4 mulatos 1 dried chipotle chile	8 dried New Mexican red chiles 4 pasillas	10 dried New Mexican red chiles 2 mulatos
2. Heat, then cook	3 Tbs canola oil 1 large yellow onion, chopped 3 garlic cloves, minced	3 Tbs canola oil 1 large yellow onion, chopped 2 garlic cloves, minced	3 Tbs almond oil 1 large red onion, chopped 3 garlic cloves, minced	3 Tbs almond oil 1 large yellow onion, chopped 4 garlic cloves, minced
3. Stir in, cover, and simmer—then purée	The toasted chiles 3½ cups chicken broth 1 Tbs minced oregano 1 tsp salt Freshly ground black pepper to taste	The toasted chiles 3½ cups beef broth 2 Tbs minced oregano 1 tsp salt Freshly ground black pepper to taste	The toasted chiles 3½ cups chicken broth 1 Tbs minced tarragon 1 tsp salt Freshly ground black pepper to taste	The toasted chiles 3½ cups vegetable broth 2 Tbs minced oregano 1 tsp salt Freshly ground black pepper to taste
4. Preheat the oven and make a filling	2¼ cups chopped cooked chicken 1½ cups drained, canned black beans ¼ cup pickle relish	3 cups cooked ground beef 4 ounces shredded Cheddar 2 Tbs chili powder 2 tsp ground cumin 1 tsp smoked paprika	1½ pounds sliced mushrooms, preferably a mix, sautéed until they release their liquid and it evaporates in a large skillet over medium heat with 2 Tbs canola oil 4 ounces shredded Gruyère	Two 10-ounce packages frozen chopped spinach, squeezed of excess moisture 8 ounces crumbled Queso Blanco or Oaxaca cheese 1 medium red bell pepper, seeded and diced ½ cup toasted pine nuts ¼ tsp grated nutmeg
5. Roll the enchiladas, top, and bake	The puréed sauce 12 ounces Monterey Jack cheese, shredded	The puréed sauce 8 ounces Cheddar, shredded	The puréed sauce 8 ounces Gruyère, shredded	The puréed sauce 6 ounces Emmental, shredded

	Turkey and Walnut Enchiladas	Crab Enchiladas	Vegetable Enchiladas	Tomato and Goat Cheese Enchiladas
1. Stem, seed, devein, and toast	8 dried New Mexican red chiles 4 pasillas	12 dried New Mexican red chiles	8 dried New Mexican red chiles 4 guajillos	12 dried New Mexican red chiles
2. Heat, then cook	3 Tbs canola oil 1 large red onion, chopped 1 garlic clove, minced	3 Tbs olive oil 1 large yellow onion, chopped 1 garlic clove, minced	3 Tbs canola oil 1 large yellow onion, chopped 3 garlic cloves, minced	3 Tbs canola oil 1 large yellow onion, chopped 3 garlic cloves, minced
3. Stir in, cover, and simmer—then purée	The toasted chiles 3½ cups chicken broth 1 Tbs minced parsley 1 tsp salt Freshly ground black pepper to taste	The toasted chiles 3½ cups vegetable broth 1 Tbs minced oregano 1 tsp salt Freshly ground black pepper to taste	The toasted chiles 3½ cups vegetable broth 2 Tbs minced oregano 1 tsp salt Freshly ground black pepper to taste	The toasted chiles 3½ cups chicken broth 2 Tbs minced oregano 1 tsp salt Freshly ground black pepper to taste
4. Preheat the oven and make a filling	1½ pounds ground turkey, sautéed with 2 Tbs canola oil in a large skillet ¾ cup finely chopped walnut pieces ¼ cup chopped raisins ½ tsp ground cinnamon	1½ pounds purchased lump crabmeat, picked over for shell and cartilage 1 cup crumbled chèvre (goat cheese) ¼ tsp grated mace	1 medium red bell pepper, seeded and diced 1 medium carrot, diced 1 cup shredded snow peas 1 cup peas All these sautéed with 2 Tbs olive oil in a large skillet until fairly soft	1 pound plum or Roma tomatoes, chopped 1¾ cups chèvre (goat cheese) 2 Tbs stemmed thyme 1 Tbs minced parsley 1 Tbs minced marjoram ¼ tsp grated nutmeg
5. Roll the enchiladas, top, and bake	The puréed sauce 12 ounces Cheddar, grated	The puréed sauce 8 ounces Emmental, grated	The puréed sauce 12 ounces smoked Gouda or Swiss, grated	The puréed sauce 6 ounces Gruyère, grated

Escabeche

This cold fish dish came to Spain via the Middle East (from the Persian *sikbag,* or "acid food"), but it's now found in incarnations all over the world (*escovitch* in the Caribbean, *scapece* in Italy, and *scabetche* in Morocco). The fish fillets are first fried, then marinated and chilled in a vinegar-based sauce. A terrific starter on a summer night, it's also a light lunch anytime of the year. • MAKES 4 SERVINGS

• **STEP 1** Heat 2 tablespoons fat in a large skillet set over medium heat. Because the vinegar is potent in this dish, choose a neutral oil like sunflower, corn, or canola—or olive oil if the marinade will bend toward the Mediterranean, peanut oil or untoasted sesame oil if it will be Asian-inspired. Yes, you could use untoasted nut or seed oils, unsalted butter, or even mustard seed oil. However, these are all strong tastes, skewing the dish this way and that. They must be balanced by strong aromatics and sweet, flavorful vegetables—and perhaps several minced garlic cloves. Forgo any rendered animal fat—this is a fish dish, after all—as well as toasted nut oils, slightly bitter.

• **STEP 2** Dredge 2 pounds skinned, thin, white-fleshed fish fillets in seasoned flour spread on a plate, slip the fillets into the skillet, and cook until golden brown, about 3 minutes; then turn and cook until golden, about 2 more minutes. Transfer to a cutting board and set aside. For a discussion of seasoned flour, see page 51. Use perhaps ¾ cup all-purpose flour, 1 teaspoon salt, and 1 teaspoon freshly ground black pepper—but no other dried herbs. These should be in the sauté to come, not here in the flour. If you have a gluten allergy, substitute cornstarch—but season it lightly. Its finer powder will encourage more salt and pepper to stick to the fillets.

Basically, go to the market and choose what's fresh, any one of a number of thin, white-fleshed fish fillets, including

> any drum
> flounder
> fluke
> freshwater bass
> orange roughy
> perch
> rockfish
> any snapper
> sole
> tilapia
> turbot

Most are sold without the skin. If not, have the fishmonger remove it.

TO REMOVE THE SKIN ON A FISH FILLET: Place the fillet skin side down on your work surface and begin to slice the skin down and away from the flesh, keeping a firm tension on the skin.

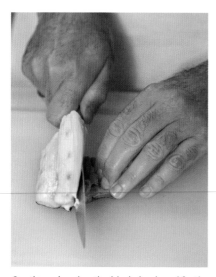

Continue drawing the blade back and forth, always holding the skin against the work surface and angling the knife to get farther and farther into the seam between the flesh and the skin.

Or do it yourself. To remove the skin from a fish fillet, you'll need a long, thin, very sharp knife and a steady hand. Put a fillet skin side down on a cutting board. Pick up the narrow tip of the fillet and run a long, thin, sharp knife between the flesh and the skin, angling the blade toward the skin without slicing through to the cutting board. Draw the blade back and forth, slicing between the flesh and skin. Once you have some of the skin detached, hold it against the cutting board with one hand and continue to work the knife between the flesh and skin, thereby taking the flesh off the skin (rather than the skin off the flesh). You may have to reposition the blade once or twice, but keep the tension on the skin constant against the cutting board.

Once the fillets are in the skillet, use a wide spatula to turn them when one side is lightly browned, a spatula large enough so they don't fall off, chip, or break. When lightly browned on both sides and the thinnest part can be flaked with a fork, transfer them to a clean plate.

• **STEP 3** Add another 2 tablespoons fat to the skillet and stir in about 1 cup chopped aromatics; cook, stirring often, until softened. In general, use the same fat you used in step 1. See page 17 for a list of the basic aromatics. Add a spark from minced peeled fresh ginger, minced garlic cloves, crushed and minced lemongrass (white ends only), or finely grated lemon or lime zest. And don't forget a seeded and minced fresh chile like a serrano, poblano, or jalapeño.

• **STEP 4** Stir in about 2 cups chopped vegetables and/or dried fruit or berries as well as at most a couple teaspoons herbs or spices; cook until softened and aromatic, stirring often. The list is limitless so long as you understand that the vegetable must be thoroughly cooked before you move on to step 5. If you use potatoes, sweet potatoes, or other hard vegetables, peel them and dice them very small so they'll cook quickly in the skillet. Thus, diced and seeded bell peppers, diced fennel, chopped zucchini, corn kernels, or peas are among the easiest vegetables to toss into the mix.

As far the herbs or spices go, consider one or two, rarely three (usually done if one of them is saffron). If you use whole seeds—cumin, fennel, celery, mustard, and the like—crush them in a mortar with a pestle, in a sealed plastic bag with the bottom of a large heavy saucepan, or with a rolling pin so they'll release more flavor into the sauce.

If you use cinnamon, cloves, star anise, or cardamom, use them in their "whole" form: sticks, pods, and the like. That way, you can remove them before you serve the dish and they won't cloud the sauce (as they would if ground).

Dredge the skinless fillets just so they're coated only with a fine dusting of flour.

Seeds like those for cumin or fennel should be crushed—as here, under a rolling pin—before they're used in the sauce.

The fillets are lightly browned, just a couple minutes over medium heat.

• **STEP 5** Pour in 1 cup vinegar and simmer for 1 minute, scraping up any browned bits on the pan's bottom. Remove from the heat. Don't limit your choices to just white wine or red wine vinegar. Consider sherry, apple cider, or even low-acid Asian rice vinegar. White balsamic will lend a sweet note, but avoid flavored vinegars, best for foofy salad dressings. Also avoid syrupy aged balsamic, best as a condiment and far too sweet to create the necessary bite.

• **STEP 6** Slice the fish fillets into 1-inch pieces; place them in a large nonreactive bowl or a glass baking dish. Pour the vinegar-based sauce over them, toss well, and check for salt. Cover and refrigerate at least 4 hours or up to 4 days. The longer the dish marinates, the more intense the taste. Keep the time within reason, of course. It will not keep forever— nor will it freeze well. See page 99 for types of nonreactive cookware.

Discard any whole spices or bay leaves before serving. Spoon the pieces of dish and the sauce over a bed of lettuce, shredded radishes and carrots, or minced seeded cucumbers and thinly sliced onions.

The marinade is ladled and poured over the browned fillets before chilling.

Recipes for Escabeches

	Spanish-Inspired Escabeche	Sweet-and-Sour Escabeche	Mexican-Inspired Escabeche	Filipino-Inspired Escabeche
1. Heat	2 Tbs olive oil	2 Tbs canola oil	2 Tbs olive oil	2 Tbs peanut oil
2. Dredge, cook, and transfer	¾ cup all-purpose flour seasoned with 1 tsp salt and 1 tsp ground black pepper 2 pounds thin white-fleshed fish fillets	¾ cup all-purpose flour seasoned with 1 tsp salt and 1 tsp ground black pepper 2 pounds thin white-fleshed fish fillets	¾ cup all-purpose flour seasoned with 1 tsp salt and 1 tsp ground black pepper 2 pounds thin white-fleshed fish fillets	¾ cup all-purpose flour seasoned with 1 tsp salt and 1 tsp ground black pepper 2 pounds thin white-fleshed fish fillets
3. Add and cook	2 Tbs olive oil 1 medium yellow onion, chopped 3 garlic cloves, minced	2 Tbs canola oil 1 medium yellow onion, chopped 1 Tbs minced peeled fresh ginger 1 tsp finely grated lemon zest	2 Tbs olive oil 1 medium yellow onion, chopped 1 chipotle chile canned in adobo sauce, chopped 2 tsp finely grated lime zest	2 Tbs peanut oil 1 medium yellow onion, chopped 3 garlic cloves, minced 1 Tbs minced peeled fresh ginger
4. Stir in and cook	3 jarred roasted red bell peppers or pimientos, thinly sliced 1 cup canned chickpeas, drained and rinsed 2 tsp stemmed thyme ½ tsp saffron	1 small fennel bulb, trimmed and chopped 5 dried figs, chopped 1½ tsp crushed fennel seeds 1 tsp crushed mustard seeds	1 large firm banana, peeled and diced 1 large tomato, seeded and chopped 1 tsp ground black pepper 2 bay leaves (discard before serving) 4 whole cloves	2 medium Yukon Gold potatoes, peeled and cubed ½ cup unsalted roasted peanuts 2 tsp minced mint 1 tsp fish sauce (see page 388) 1 tsp finely grated lime zest
5. Pour in	1 cup sherry vinegar	1 cup white balsamic vinegar	1 cup white wine vinegar	1 cup rice vinegar
6. Slice the fish, place the pieces in a bowl or dish, pour in the marinade, season, and refrigerate	Salt to taste	Salt to taste	Salt to taste	Salt to taste

	Portuguese-Inspired Escabeche	Miami-Inspired Escabeche	Southwestern Escabeche	Moroccan-Inspired Escabeche
1. Heat	2 Tbs olive oil	2 Tbs olive oil	2 Tbs canola oil	2 Tbs mustard seed oil
2. Dredge, cook, and transfer	¾ cup all-purpose flour seasoned with 1 tsp salt and 1 tsp ground black pepper 2 pounds thin white-fleshed fish fillets	¾ cup all-purpose flour seasoned with 1 tsp salt and 1 tsp ground black pepper 2 pounds thin white-fleshed fish fillets	¾ cup all-purpose flour seasoned with 1 tsp salt and 1 tsp ground black pepper 2 pounds thin white-fleshed fish fillets	¾ cup all-purpose flour seasoned with 1 tsp salt and 1 tsp ground black pepper 2 pounds thin white-fleshed fish fillets
3. Add and cook	2 Tbs olive oil 1 medium yellow onion, chopped 6 garlic cloves, minced 2 tsp finely grated lemon zest	2 Tbs olive oil 1 medium yellow onion, chopped 1 Tbs finely grated grapefruit zest 1 fresh jalapeño, seeded and minced	2 Tbs canola oil 6 ounces shallots, chopped 1 small jalapeño, seeded and chopped 2 medium garlic cloves, minced	2 Tbs mustard oil 2 medium leeks, white and pale green parts only, halved lengthwise, washed carefully, and thinly sliced 3 garlic cloves, minced 1 Tbs minced peeled fresh ginger
4. Stir in and cook	1 small red bell pepper, seeded and chopped 1 cup chopped skinned toasted hazelnuts (see page 217) 10 whole black peppercorns 2 bay leaves (discard before serving)	1 medium mango, peeled, seeded, and chopped 1 jarred roasted red pepper or pimiento, chopped ¼ cup minced mint	1 cup fresh or frozen corn kernels ½ cup chopped golden raisins 4 cherry tomatoes, quartered 2 tsp minced oregano 1 tsp crushed cumin seeds	1 cup pomegranate seeds 1 cup toasted slivered almonds 2 tsp crushed cumin seeds 1 tsp crushed fennel seeds ¼ tsp red pepper flakes One 4-inch cinnamon stick (discard before serving)
5. Pour in	1 cup sherry vinegar	¾ cup white vinegar ¼ cup grapefruit juice	1 cup cider vinegar	1 cup white balsamic vinegar
6. Slice the fish, place the pieces in a bowl or dish, pour in the marinade, season, and rerigerate	Salt to taste	Salt to taste	Salt to taste	Salt to taste

Filets Mignons and Other Red-Meat Medallions with a Pan Sauce

Nothing's better for easy entertaining elegance—or simply a quick dinner after work. If you don't want to make a sauce, complete the recipe through step 3, then let the medallions rest at room temperature for 5 minutes to assure their tenderness.

• MAKES 4 SERVINGS

• **STEP 1** Preheat the oven to 400°F; heat a very large cast-iron or heavy stainless-steel skillet over medium-high heat until smoking—then swirl in about 2 tablespoons oil. A modern oven takes about 10 minutes to heat up, so you can start it at the same time you fire up the skillet—which should be smoking hot: say, 5 minutes over medium-high heat. A drop of water must instantly ball up and dance across the skillet's surface. At such high temperatures, avoid nonstick cookware.

There's no reason to get obsessive about the exact amount of fat. A thin layer will help the meat caramelize without sticking. That said, don't use butter, animal fats, or toasted nut oils—all of which have low smoke points. These can ignite before the meat has a good crust. Even canola and olive oil may combust at such high temperatures. Instead, use oils with very high smoke points: grapeseed oil (420°F), refined almond oil (420°F), refined peanut, canola, corn, or soybean oil (all, 450°F).

• **STEP 2** Slip four seasoned 6- to 8-ounce filets mignons or red-meat medallions into the skillet and sear for 3 minutes per inch of thickness. The medallions should be about 2 inches thick. Consider any of these cuts:

> beef or buffalo filets mignons
> elk or venison tenderloin medallions
> ostrich or emu medallions

Before cooking, do the last two or all three of these things to the filets or medallions:

1. **Wrap them.** Utterly unnecessary but classic, a thin strip of bacon is wrapped around the filets or medallions to give them a beautiful appearance—and add a smoky flavor to the rather mild meat. For pitch-perfect aesthetics, trim the strips of bacon lengthwise so they're exactly as wide as the filets are thick.

Three Main Temperature Points for Beef or Other Red Meats

1. 120°F. Some of the proteins coagulate, causing the fibers to collapse and release trapped liquid.

2. 140°F. Most of the proteins have coagulated and any liquid lies in thin sheaths throughout the meat's fairly firm fibers.

3. 150°F. The collapsing proteins squeeze out all moisture; above this temperature, meat is tough and leathery. (That said, stewed meats go to higher temperatures than this, but these are fattier cuts with more collagen, which breaks down above 160°F and makes the meat appear more juicy than it in fact is.)

2. **Tie them.** Lay them flat side down on your cutting board. Tie a piece of butcher's twine around their "equators"—that is, around their circumferences, halfway between the two cut sides, securing any bacon in place if you've used it. This step will keep the filets or medallions from flattening over the heat.

3. **Pat them dry and season them.** Use paper towels to blot off excess surface moisture, then add salt and a couple grinds of black pepper. A thin layer of salt not only becomes part of the crunchy crust, it also helps pull water out of the surface cells, thereby creating that prized outer layer of charred meat, reminiscent of grilled steaks. With its mineral taste, kosher salt is best; about ½ teaspoon salt per side is sufficient.

Never put cold meat in a hot skillet. Let the filets or medallions sit at room temperature for 10 to 15 minutes before they hit the heat. True, bacteria can proliferate between 40°F and 140°F, but cool meat will not sear properly. If the filets or medallions are too cool and the skillet is not hot enough, the liquid will fall out of suspension too soon—and the meat will stew in its own juices instead of developing a crust.

The instantly volatilized juices in the skillet will smoke terribly. Make sure you have the vent on high—or the window open. If the filets mignons or medallions have been wrapped in bacon, first set them edge side down in the pan, the bacon against the heat, turning often so the bacon crisps all around—then set them cut side down to sear.

> **Filets Mignons**
>
> Filets mignons (French, fee-LAY mee-NYON—note the two unpronounced s's in the plural—"small fillets") are cut from the beef tenderloin. (Oddly, in France, "filet mignon" refers to a cut of pork, not beef.) The tenderloin is a long, tubular muscle (the psoas muscle) that runs along a cow's spine near the rump. The muscle has two ends, a thicker one (often called the "chateaubriand") and the smaller end, from which filets are usually cut.

Rather than buying individual beef filets, buy a center-cut tenderloin, slice off any surface fat and the translucent silver skin, then cut the trimmed tenderloin into 2-inch-thick medallions.

The classic filets mignons have bacon strips wrapped around their edges.

The bacon is held in place with butcher's twine. Even without this bacon wrapping, it's best to tie the filets so they hold their shape over the heat.

• **STEP 3** Turn the filets with tongs and place them in their skillet in the oven until they're cooked to the proper temperature, perhaps 3 to 4 minutes per inch of thickness for rare. Transfer the meat to a plate and tent with aluminum foil. Filets mignons or other medallions cooked directly over the heat the whole time toughen considerably, so the oven's radiant heat gently (even at 400°F) finishes the job.

The only way to tell exactly if the filets or medallions are done is to take their internal temperature. Insert an instant-read meat thermometer on the diagonal into the thickest part of the center.

There's a wide difference between the USDA's notions of doneness and ours. The government has regulated temperatures only with pests in mind; we care about both pests and taste. That said, many bacterial problems are not solved at temperatures below 140°F. If you cook meat below this temperature, buy certified organic cuts and know what you're up to and against.

Ostrich and emu medallions, although red, are not "red meat." They should not be cooked to the blue, rare, or medium-rare stages. Around 160°F is perfect for them, juicy but still tender.

Much has been written about taking meat off the heat when the internal temperature is 5°F lower than desired and letting the temperature rise while the meat rests. These cuts are not large enough to retain such a high level of heat and the temperatures for blue and rare are so low that the residual heat will not continue to cook the meat, since the meat's temperature is below protein coagulation anyway. That said, meat should rest a few moments off the heat—not so the internal temperature will rise but so the fibers can relax and any juice can reinfiltrate them.

• **STEP 4** After setting the very hot skillet over medium heat, add some minced aromatics, a minced herb or two, and perhaps some thinly sliced mushrooms; then cook, stirring often, until softened. The skillet is very hot—scalding, in fact. Forewarned, begin to build a simple sauce. There's no need for any extra oil; there's already rendered fat in the skillet.

Use simple aromatics like shallots, onions, scallions, and/or garlic. A little is enough—this is not the beginning of a sauté, after all. Try one or two minced shallots or perhaps ½ cup minced red onion and 2 minced garlic cloves.

That said, there's no reason not to push the boundaries of the customary. What about adding some finely grated lemon or orange zest if red wine will be added in step 5? Or try berries: blackberries or blueberries pair beautifully with game, particularly if reduced in port or dry Marsala.

Herbs enhance a sauce—in moderation: one or two minced teaspoons. Steer clear of bitter or musky dried spices like turmeric or saffron. That said, ¼ teaspoon grated nutmeg blends beautifully with cream and brandy. Marjoram, oregano, rosemary, parsley, and thyme are all scrumptious with beef or any of these medallions.

Mushrooms will require more time over the heat because they must release their liquid and it must boil down to a glaze, perhaps 3 minutes.

• **STEP 5** Pour in about ¾ cup broth, red wine, a dry fortified wine, or a combination of broth and wine; raise the heat to high; and boil until reduced to 3 tablespoons liquid. Choose a full-flavored liquid to match the meat: beef broth, chicken broth, red wine, dry Madeira, dry Marsala, port, or a mix of broth and wine or dry fortified wine. Vegetable broth and white wine are simply too wimpy for this preparation, but dry vermouth, because of its herbal notes, does indeed add a lovely finish to a light sauce.

As the liquid boils, make sure to loosen any browned bits on the skillet's bottom with a wooden spoon. The total amount of ingredients in the skillet may well be more than 3 tablespoons—but any liquid should have reduced to about that amount.

Because this dish comes together quickly over the heat, have everything prepped and ready to go before you start cooking.

• **STEP 6** Add a little cream, unsalted butter, liqueur, or a sweet or sour accent; stir until smooth, check for salt-and-pepper seasoning, then spoon over the filets or medallions. A quarter cup heavy or whipping cream, two or three tablespoons unsalted butter, 2 tablespoons Grand Marnier, 2 tablespoons chutney, 1 tablespoon syrupy balsamic vinegar—use something that will enhance the natural flavors of the sauce you've built, something syrupy or thick so that it adds body. For an over-the-top treat, swirl in 2 tablespoons foie gras, particularly from a long torchon that can be cut into rounds; it will melt into incredible richness.

The rule is this: if there's alcohol in step 5, there shouldn't be any here. Wine would not pair well with cognac—but beef broth and cognac are a perfect match, like Steve and Eydie. If one of the enhancers you've chosen is cream, consider pairing it with a liqueur in this step: cream and brandy, cream and Armagnac.

And check for salt. The sauce may need a little but keep in mind that there's a salt crust on those filets or medallions. No more than ¼ teaspoon should do the job.

The finished medallions are well browned, even if rare inside; the sauce has thickened quite a bit.

Recipes for Filet Mignons and Other Red-Meat Medallions

	Brandy Cream Filets Mignons	Classic Filets Mignons	Venison Medallions	Ostrich Marsala
1. Preheat oven and skillet before swirling in	2 Tbs refined peanut oil	2 Tbs grapeseed oil	2 Tbs grapeseed oil	2 Tbs grapeseed oil
2. Season and sear	Salt and ground black pepper Four 6- to 8-ounce filets mignons	Salt and ground black pepper Four 6- to 8-ounce filets mignons, each wrapped and tied with 1 bacon strip	Salt and ground black pepper Four 6- to 8-ounce venison medallions	Salt and ground black pepper Four 6- to 8-ounce ostrich medallions
3. Turn and roast to	120°F	120°F	120°F	160°F
4. Add and soften	1 small onion, diced 2 garlic cloves, minced	4 ounces shallots, minced 2 garlic cloves, minced	1 small onion, minced ½ cup blueberries	4 ounces shallots, minced 1 Tbs stemmed thyme 1 Tbs minced rosemary
5. Pour in and reduce	¾ cup beef broth	¾ cup red wine	½ cup red wine ¼ cup beef broth	½ cup dry Marsala ¼ cup chicken broth
6. Finish with	3 Tbs heavy or whipping cream 1 Tbs brandy Salt to taste	2 Tbs unsalted butter Salt to taste	1 Tbs unsalted butter 1 Tbs brandy Salt to taste	1 Tbs unsalted butter 1 Tbs aged balsamic vinegar Salt to taste

	Filets Mignons Rossini	Filets Mignons with a Cranberry Glaze	Curried Buffalo Filets Mignons	Filets à l'Orange
1. Preheat oven and skillet before swirling in	1 Tbs grapeseed oil 1 Tbs unsalted butter	2 Tbs almond oil	2 Tbs peanut oil	2 Tbs almond oil
2. Season and sear	Salt and ground black pepper Four 6- to 8-ounce filets mignons	Salt and ground black pepper Four 6- to 8-ounce filets mignons, each wrapped and tied with 1 bacon strip	Salt and ground black pepper Four 6- to 8-ounce buffalo filets mignons	Salt and ground black pepper Four 6- to 8-ounce filets mignons
3. Turn and roast to	120°F	120°F	120°F	120°F
4. Add and soften	4 ounces shallots, minced 1 garlic clove, minced 2 Tbs minced black truffle	4 ounces shallots, minced ¼ cup chopped cranberries 1 Tbs minced rosemary	4 ounces shallots, minced 1 Tbs minced peeled fresh ginger 2 tsp curry powder (see page 113) 1 garlic clove, minced	1 small yellow onion, minced 1 Tbs finely grated orange zest 2 tsp minced rosemary
5. Pour in and reduce	¾ cup red wine	¾ cup red wine	½ cup red wine ¼ cup beef broth	¾ cup beef broth
6. Finish with	2 Tbs foie gras torchon[1] Salt to taste	1 Tbs white balsamic vinegar 1 Tbs unsalted butter 1 tsp red currant jelly Salt to taste	2 Tbs mango chutney Salt to taste	2 Tbs Grand Marnier or Cointreau Salt to taste

[1]Or make the sauce, then lay a thin round of foie gras on each filet, napping the sauce over each on the plates.

Fish Fillets with a Pan Sauce

Here's a simple but still elegant dinner, suited for weeknights with the family or weekends with company. The fish is sautéed, then put on a platter awaiting the easy sauce you make in the pan. To keep the fish hot, consider warming the serving platter—provided it's oven-safe—in a slow (200°F) oven for 10 minutes or so, just to take off the chill. • MAKES 4 SERVINGS

Fish fillets should smell mild and fresh, like an ocean bay at high tide on a May morning.

The best way to store fish at home is in the refrigerator on paper over a colander of ice set in a bowl to catch the drips.

• **STEP 1** Heat 1 tablespoon fat in a large skillet over medium heat. Almost any simple fat will do: olive oil, canola oil, refined peanut oil, unsalted butter, or an untoasted nut oil (almond oil is particularly appealing with fish). But do not use a toasted nut oil, seed oil, or animal fat like lard, all too complex.

Check out your skillet's size to make sure it's large enough. Before you begin, perhaps you should lay the fillets in it to give them a trial run. You need a skillet big enough to hold them comfortably—perhaps a 14-inch skillet or even a similarly sized sauté pan, although with its high, straight sides, the sauce may have to simmer over the heat a couple minutes longer to achieve the desired consistency. If the fillets don't all fit, you'll need to work in batches—or even cut one so that it fits at the pan's edges.

• **STEP 2** Dredge four 5- to 6-ounce, skinless, thin, white-fleshed fish fillets in seasoned flour on a plate and slip the fillets into the skillet. Cook until lightly browned, then turn and continue cooking until golden and cooked through. Transfer to a serving platter or perhaps individual plates. You'll need about ½ cup all-purpose flour and ½ teaspoon each salt and freshly ground black pepper. For an explanation of seasoned flour, see page 51. You won't use all of this flour mixture; some of it will turn gummy during dredging. But better to waste a little on the plate than to have a skimpy coating.

Choose thin, white-fleshed fish fillets, the same as you would use for Escabeche (page 123). Place one fillet flat side down in the flour, pat gently, turn over, pat again, and then pick the fillet up by one end, shaking it gently over the plate to knock off excess flour. Holding it by one end, lay it in the skillet—work slowly to prevent splatters. Place the first fillet farthest from the skillet's center and work your way across its surface.

The fillets will brown and cook quickly, perhaps in 2 to 3 minutes; they should then be turned with a large metal spatula or a spatula designed for a nonstick surface if you're working on one.

Once turned, let the fillets cook until the thickest part will flake with a fork, perhaps 2 to 4 more minutes. The fillets should be cooked all the way through; they will not return to the heat. Use a wide spatula to transfer them one by one to a serving platter.

• **STEP 3** Add 2 tablespoons fat to the skillet, then ¼ cup diced aromatics; cook, stirring often, just until softened, 1 to 2 minutes. As a general rule, add the same fat you used in step 1, although unsalted butter makes a nice pairing with an oil in the first step, particularly if you've used olive or almond oil. There's more fat here than in step 1 because you're now building a sauce, the fat actually becoming part of its body. For that reason, unsalted butter is often an excellent choice at this juncture.

Now add the diced aromatics: onion, shallot, leek, or scallions—perhaps any mixed with minced garlic cloves, finely grated citrus zest, and/or minced peeled fresh ginger. This is not a sauté; it's a sauce, so the amount should be small, just a flavoring.

• **STEP 4** Add 1 cup chopped or diced vegetables and/or fruit; cook, stirring often, until softened. Any number of quick-cooking vegetables will do the trick: peas, seeded and chopped bell peppers, thinly sliced celery, peeled and very thinly sliced carrots, broccoli florets, sliced asparagus, and the like.

Yes, you can indeed add potatoes, sweet potatoes, or even a winter squash; but before they can be used, all these need to be peeled (the squash seeded as well), then diced into ½-inch cubes and parboiled in a large saucepan of boiling water until almost tender, 5 to 10 minutes. It's best to get this done before you start the recipe.

Fresh or dried fruit works here, too, a natural pairing with the vegetables: pitted cherries with fennel, orange supremes (see page 106) with leeks, dried currants with zucchini. There's no need to add fruit—it simply brightens the sauce (but is perhaps an unwelcome addition on a cold winter evening).

In this case, stay away from leafy greens, which will wilt and glom together. Again, this is a simple sauce, not a vegetable sauté.

But do consider chopped pitted olives, thinly sliced sun-dried tomatoes, drained capers, or even sliced Moroc-

Buying Fresh Fish Fillets

For most dishes that call for thin, white-fleshed fish fillets, there's no need to choose a certain kind in advance; rather, go to the market and see what's fresh, what smells clean and bright, and what lacks any opalescent sheen. If the fillets still have the skin on them, ask that it be removed (it will curl when cooked)—or try removing it yourself at home (see page 124).

Most fish is flash-frozen at catch, a step that improves its quality, keeping the flesh safe in transport. Fresh fish is usually so labeled (although "fresh" can mean "freshly thawed"). Sometimes, whole fish are frozen on the trawler, defrosted at the processing plant, trimmed into fillets, and then refrozen. Twice-frozen fillets often have ice crystals in the flesh and thus turn mushy when cooked. A reputable fishmonger knows what's what. Ask questions before you buy; there are few government standards for labeling or advertising. If your fishmonger seems uninformed or surly, find another market.

If possible, don't buy fish in a sealed package. If your market only carries fish this way, never purchase a package with liquid in it, a potential sign of bacterial breakdown. Keep the fillets cold on the trip home by putting an ice pack in a cooler in your car. And get them in the refrigerator at once. Fresh fish stores best below 40°F, a temperature perhaps below that of your refrigerator. For the best results, store fish in the refrigerator in its paper wrapper on top of a colander filled halfway with ice that's then set over a bowl to catch drips. In most cases, cook fish fillets the day you buy them. Run your fingers over the fillets to check for bones—but be careful; they can pierce your skin. Remove any with sterilized tweezers.

For the best taste, the fillets are very lightly browned, only a minute or two over the heat, with just the hint of color around their natural ridges.

A properly reduced sauce will momentarily leave the skillet's surface dry as a spoon is dragged across it.

can preserved lemon as part of the vegetable medley—but no more than 2 tablespoons of any of these. Again, the sauce for the fish needs to be delicate, not overwhelming. Save heavy combinations for more complicated braises.

• **STEP 5** Stir in a little minced herb and/or dried spices and perhaps some minced garlic until fragrant. Less is more. For a good guideline, consider up to 1 tablespoon minced herb and perhaps ½ teaspoon dried spice as its mate. But even less will do: 2 teaspoons herb, ¼ teaspoon spice.

Excellent herb choices with fish fillets include dill, tarragon, oregano, and marjoram. In moderation ground cinnamon or cardamom can add a sophisticated touch; fennel or celery seeds add a piquant bite; and ¼ teaspoon red pepper flakes is a nice bit of heat in this simple dish. A pinch of grated nutmeg is almost always welcome with green vegetables like peas, broccoli, and zucchini.

• **STEP 6** Pour in ½ cup wine, broth, or an enhanced version of either, scraping up any browned bits on the skillet's bottom. Raise the heat to high, bring to a boil, and cook until the volume of the liquid in the skillet has reduced by half. Season with salt and freshly ground black pepper before pouring over the fillets. Wine or broth are the usual additions. Try vegetable or even chicken broth; fish broth, while seemingly a natural, can overpower the sauce. Let the fish carry its own taste. Although white wine is perhaps the first choice, don't neglect red wine, an earthy addition, particularly if there are earthy vegetables or mushrooms in the mix.

Of course, you can use a 50/50 wine/broth combo—or you can enhance either wine or broth with heavy cream, coconut milk, or a dry fortified wine like dry Madeira. Use no more than ¼ cup of any of these in the total volume.

Now turn the heat to high and let the sauce boil, thereby concentrating its flavors as the liquid evaporates. The total amount of liquid should be boiled down by half. When a wooden spoon is dragged through the sauce, exposing the surface of the skillet, the line should stay stable for a second before the liquid flows back into place. In general, it will take 2 minutes, certainly no more than 3 minutes at a full boil.

Remove the skillet from the heat and check the sauce for seasoning—it can probably use salt and several grinds of black pepper. Then pour the sauce over the fish on the platter, covering all the fillets and rewarming them considerably.

Recipes for Fish Fillets

	Fish Fillets with Cherries and Roasted Red Peppers	Fish Fillets with Figs and Zucchini	Fish Fillets with Eggplant, Olives, and Capers	Fish Fillets with Fennel and Shallots
1. Heat	1 Tbs olive oil	1 Tbs almond oil	1 Tbs olive oil	1 Tbs olive oil
2. Dredge, cook, and transfer	½ cup all-purpose flour seasoned with ½ tsp salt and ½ tsp ground black pepper Four 5- to 6-ounce thin, skinless, white-fleshed fish fillets	½ cup all-purpose flour seasoned with ½ tsp salt and ½ tsp ground black pepper Four 5- to 6-ounce thin, skinless, white-fleshed fish fillets	½ cup all-purpose flour seasoned with ½ tsp salt and ½ tsp ground black pepper Four 5- to 6-ounce skinless, white-fleshed fish fillets	½ cup all-purpose flour seasoned with ½ tsp salt and ½ tsp ground black pepper Four 5- to 6-ounce thin, skinless, white-fleshed fish fillets
3. Add and soften	2 Tbs unsalted butter ½ small yellow onion, diced 2 garlic cloves, minced	2 Tbs unsalted butter ½ small yellow onion, diced 1 garlic clove, minced	1 Tbs olive oil 1 Tbs unsalted butter ½ small yellow onion, diced 2 garlic cloves, minced	2 Tbs olive oil 2 ounces shallots, diced
4. Add and cook	½ cup jarred roasted red bell peppers or pimientos, thinly sliced ½ cup pitted sweet cherries	1 medium zucchini, chopped 4 fresh figs, quartered	1 small eggplant, preferably a long Japanese eggplant, peeled and diced ¼ cup chopped pitted green olives 1 Tbs drained and chopped capers	1 medium fennel bulb, trimmed, halved, and thinly sliced
5. Stir in	2 tsp stemmed thyme	2 tsp minced rosemary ¼ tsp grated nutmeg	1 Tbs stemmed thyme ¼ tsp red pepper flakes	2 tsp minced tarragon
6. Pour in, reduce, and season	¼ cup vegetable broth ¼ cup dry red wine Salt and pepper to taste	½ cup dry white wine Salt and pepper to taste	¼ cup vegetable broth ¼ cup dry white wine Salt and pepper to taste	¼ cup vegetable broth ¼ cup dry white wine Salt and pepper to taste

	Fish Fillets with Fresh Corn "Relish"	Fish Fillets with Summer Squash, Almonds, and Lemon	Stir-Fry-Style Fish Fillets	Fish Fillets with Mustard and Cream
1. Heat	1 Tbs canola oil	1 Tbs unsalted butter	1 Tbs peanut oil	1 Tbs unsalted butter
2. Dredge, cook, and transfer	½ cup all-purpose flour seasoned with ½ tsp salt and ½ tsp ground black pepper	½ cup all-purpose flour seasoned with ½ tsp salt and ½ tsp ground black pepper	½ cup all-purpose flour seasoned with ½ tsp salt and ½ tsp ground black pepper	½ cup all-purpose flour seasoned with ½ tsp salt and ½ tsp ground black pepper
	Four 5- to 6-ounce thin, skinless, white-fleshed fish fillets	Four 5- to 6-ounce thin, skinless, white-fleshed fish fillets	Four 5- to 6-ounce thin, skinless, white-fleshed fish fillets	Four 5- to 6-ounce thin, skinless, white-fleshed fish fillets
3. Add and soften	2 Tbs canola oil	2 Tbs almond oil	2 Tbs sesame oil	2 Tbs unsalted butter
	½ small yellow onion, diced	2 ounces shallots, diced	3 medium whole scallions, diced	3 ounces shallots, diced
	2 garlic cloves, minced	2 tsp finely grated lemon zest	2 Tbs minced peeled fresh ginger	
			1 garlic clove, minced	
4. Add and cook	1 small red bell pepper, seeded and diced	2 medium yellow crookneck summer squash, chopped	1 small red bell pepper, seeded and diced	6 ounces thinly sliced cremini or white button mushrooms
	½ cup fresh or frozen corn kernels	¼ cup sliced toasted almonds	½ cup thinly sliced snow peas	
5. Stir in	1 Tbs minced basil	2 tsp stemmed thyme	½ tsp five-spice powder (see page 149)	1 Tbs minced tarragon
	½ tsp celery seeds	¼ tsp red pepper flakes	¼ tsp red pepper flakes	
	¼ tsp red pepper flakes			
	¼ tsp dry mustard			
6. Pour in, reduce, and season	6 Tbs chicken broth	7 Tbs vegetable broth	¼ cup vegetable broth	¼ cup chicken broth
	2 Tbs white wine vinegar	1 Tbs lemon juice	2 Tbs soy sauce	3 Tbs cream
	Salt and pepper to taste	Salt and pepper to taste	2 Tbs rice vinegar	1 Tbs Dijon mustard
			Salt and pepper to taste	Salt and pepper to taste

Fricassee

This hearty, cream-laced, stovetop braise is made with white wine or dry vermouth, some kind of white meat on the bone, and plenty of vegetables. Serve it in bowls on its own or over white rice, brown rice, cooked egg noodles, or well-toasted pieces of stale whole-grain bread. • MAKES 6 SERVINGS

• **STEP 1** Heat 2 tablespoons unsalted butter and 1 tablespoon neutral oil in a large Dutch oven. A little oil allows the butter to come to a higher temperature without its milk solids burning. Any neutral palette will do: canola, corn, safflower, sunflower, or even grapeseed. Avoid olive, nut, and toasted nut oils—too many flavors spoil the stew.

• **STEP 2** Lightly brown 4 pounds skin-on, bone-in, cut-up bird, rabbit, or veal; transfer to a plate. Fricassee (FRIH-cuh-see in English and free-cah-SAY in French) comes from two French verbs: *frire,* "to fry"; and *casser,* "to break". In other words, a sauté of cut-up meat. Nothing in the name says anything about white meat—that's an additional stricture accrued over centuries.

The modern classic is made with chicken, using all the parts, even the back and neck. Cut the back into two or three pieces so the bones bring the most flavor to the sauce. But do not add the giblets; they'll turn the sauce a sickly, pinkish brown.

Also consider pheasant, game hens, guinea hens (aka pintades), or squabs. (See page 290 for a fuller discussion of these birds.) They should be halved or quartered so there's one meaty piece per serving. Unfortunately, quail are too small: a saucy braise needn't be finger-food. And a turkey is simply too large; the chunky pieces won't cook evenly and will sit too far out of the simmering sauce. If you want the taste of turkey, try a small capon (a gelded rooster), cut into 8 or 9 pieces.

With less fat and more tooth, rabbit is a wonderful alternative. Its anatomy can admittedly be tricky; unless you're sure of its bone structure (see page 70), ask the butcher to cut it into 8 to 10 pieces. He or she will also have a chance to check the meat for freshness. Rabbits don't move off the shelf very fast and are sometimes sold beyond their prime.

Or move well beyond the classic and use bone-in veal, preferably a cut off the shoulder or neck, rather than the much more delicate veal loin or veal chops. For the richest fricassee imaginable, use breast of veal; have your butcher cut it up into 3-inch chunks, keeping the bones attached.

All modern fricassees must have these ingredients: mushrooms, cream, and pearl onions.

MUSHROOM FRICASSEE

This traditional French dish omits the meat and any other vegetables. Beyond that, follow the recipe as indicated but use 2½ pounds thinly sliced mushrooms, 2 tablespoons all-purpose flour, and 2 cups liquid (not three), preferably red wine. Simmer uncovered in step 7 so the sauce reduces quite a bit, just to a thickened glaze.

The chicken is very lightly browned—just a little flavor for the sauce without the chicken later turning this creamy dish beige or brown.

The pearl onions are lightly browned in the fat. Again, nothing should stick to the pan to discolor the cream sauce to come.

There are even shellfish versions (see the recipe chart) as well as mushroom varieties (see page 139). These are riffs off the original, somewhat akin but far afield nonetheless.

Red meats like beef or venison are not traditional and usually not recommended. The delicate cream sauce will turn reddish brown and be lost on stronger-tasting cuts. All that said, and aesthetics aside, a satisfying fricassee can be made with cubed lamb stew meat. It will have to simmer a good long time, perhaps up to 3 hours.

Although the best browning happens with room-temperature meat, never leave cuts or pieces on the counter for more than 20 minutes. Take them out of the fridge to knock off the chill as you gather your other ingredients. Partially frozen meat, a real no-no here, will barely brown; chilled meat will leak too many internal juices as it comes up to the proper browning temperature, stewing the pieces rather than allowing them to brown.

Pat the pieces dry with paper towels to remove surface moisture, then slip a few into the pan and sear until well browned, about 4 minutes per side, turning with tongs to keep their skin and/or crust intact. Don't crowd the pot. If you add too many pieces, they'll stew, their fat and juices filling the pot before these can incorporate and/or evaporate. The point here is to get a barely brown crust on the meat—that will happen only with a fairly dry pan. If you find the pieces stewing, take some out and let the liquid boil off.

That said, in some classic interpretations of this dish, the meat is never browned so the sauce maintains a pure-white look. Still, the sauce and braise, as a whole, benefit from the meat's surface sugars being caramelized first; this light browning enhances the flavors and offers some balance against the cream to come.

Once the pieces are out of the pan and on a large plate, skim off all but about 3 tablespoons fat. You needn't, of course, but it makes for a somewhat healthier dish—although we doubt you're making a fricassee for health reasons.

• **STEP 3** Add 30 to 36 peeled pearl onions and brown well, stirring often, about 4 minutes. If desired, also add 2 to 3 ounces chopped thick-cut bacon, cooking until crisp. Pearl onions are a small-onion varietal, often about 1 inch in diameter; you can substitute boiling onions (tiny versions of yellow or white onions) or small cippolini. All need to have their papery skins removed. Drop them in boiling water for 2 minutes, then pop them out of their skins by squeezing the narrow stem end and ejecting the insides via the wider, root end. Or forgo this mess and buy frozen pearl onions, skinned and ready to go. Drop them into the pot frozen; if first thawed, they can turn mushy. In a pinch, use two medium yellow onions, roughly chopped.

Bacon is not traditional or necessary; smoky and assertive, it easily overpowers veal or guinea hens. Yet it adds a lush taste, especially with chicken and potatoes.

• **STEP 4** Add 12 ounces (¾ pound) thinly sliced mushrooms and 1 to 1½ cups of another chopped vegetable; cook until the mushrooms give off their liquid and it reduces to a glaze. Cremini or white button mushrooms are naturals, but a more luxurious stew can be made with a combination like 2 ounces chanterelles, 2 ounces hen of the wood, and 8 ounces white button; or 2 ounces porcini, 4 ounces shiitake caps, and 6 ounces cremini.

Mushrooms, mostly water, throw off a lot of liquid; it should be reduced to a shiny glaze. Most of the bits of caramelized flavor will be lifted off the pan's bottom, thanks to the mushrooms' liquid.

As for the second vegetable, cubed and peeled roots seem the obvious choice: turnips, celeriac, parsley root, rutabagas, carrots, acorn squash, butternut squash, or sweet potatoes. If you add cut-up potatoes, the preparation becomes a classical French one: *grand-mère* (grandmother—as if anyone's ever stewed a bird in wine and cream). Steer clear of beets; they'll turn the sauce an unpleasant pink. But do try certain quick-cooking vegetables that can hold up in a braise, like roughly chopped fennel, shredded Brussels sprouts, frozen lima beans, corn kernels, or shelled peas.

Most softer vegetables won't work in this braise. Stay away from greens, spinach, or chard. Broccoli florets or cauliflower? Mushy. And okra? Depressingly slimy. Still, seeded, chopped tomatoes can be a nice addition, turning the stew into a creamy, pseudo-Cacciatora (page 69).

• **STEP 5** Add some herbs and/or spices and 3 tablespoons all-purpose flour; cook, stirring often, until the flour browns. Plan on between 2 teaspoons and 2 tablespoons herbs and spices in total. And add a garlic clove or two for flavor. But stay away from blends like curry powder or jerk seasoning. You want a clean taste mostly from leafy herbs. This is a winter dish, but it calls to spring, just around the corner.

Sprinkle the flour evenly over the vegetables. It should brown and start to sizzle, drying up any residual liquid on the pan's bottom.

• **STEP 6** Stir in 3 cups broth or an enhanced broth until smooth; then bring to a simmer, scraping up any bits on the pan's bottom. Start out by trying one of these:

The mushrooms must cook until they release their liquid and it mostly boils away so that the sauce is not watery.

Slow and Easy

Although cartilage breakdown is the secret to a successful braise, there's a problem. Cartilage, full of collagen, dissolves above 160°F; however, almost all white meat turns tough and stringy at temperatures not too far above that. The secret is to keep the braise at a low, small-bubble simmer, certainly no boil, so the cartilage slowly comes up to the right temperature while the meat stays moist.

chicken broth
vegetable broth
white wine
dry vermouth
a combination of broth and wine in a 2/1 ratio (2 cups broth to 1 cup wine)
a mixture of 2¾ cups broth and ¼ cup brandy or cognac

The lightly browned chicken is nestled back into the sauce. No cream has yet been added.

Once you get the hang of the tastes, play with several at once: broth, white wine, and brandy, for example.

There is a tradition in rural France of making a fricassee simply with water; however, this parsimonious version is quite limp and hardly worth the time. Besides, if it's made with water, much more cream is added to compensate, hardly a frugal measure.

• **STEP 7** Stir the meat plus any accumulated juices back into the sauce; cover, reduce the heat to low, and simmer slowly until tender at the bone. The meat should be partially submerged so that it remains moist during the long braising. Rearrange the pieces with tongs once or twice during its time over the heat, stirring the pot gently so as to keep the skin on the meat and the meat on the bones.

Chicken and smaller birds will be done in about 45 minutes; capon or rabbit, perhaps 1 hour 20 minutes. The pieces shouldn't fall apart, but the cartilage in the bones should have softened to enrich the sauce. Veal or lamb stew meat? Between 2½ and 3 hours.

• **STEP 8** Stir in about ½ cup heavy or whipping cream, bring back to a simmer, and season with salt and pepper to taste. Or use these substitutes: half-and-half, whole milk, goat's milk, evaporated milk, or even evaporated fat-free milk. All will make a less-rich dish. However, this is not a Creamy Vegetable Soup (page 101), so even less-fat versions of the dairy addition will enhance the dish.

If using any of these lower-fat alternatives, make the dish richer either by stirring a beurre manié (see page 209—made from 1 tablespoon softened unsalted butter and 1 tablespoon all-purpose flour) into the sauce just as it comes to a final simmer or by ladling some of the sauce into a bowl with a beaten egg yolk, whisking until smooth, and then whisking this mixture back into the sauce for about 15 seconds over the heat.

Finally, add some salt and ground black pepper to taste, then cover the pot and let the stew stand off the heat for 10 minutes. A braise, while a wet environment, nonetheless dries the meat out as the slow simmering leaches internal moisture into the stew. Ten minutes and the meat will have reabsorbed some of the liquid that now lies at the edge of its fibers.

Once you've done that, ladle the sauce and pieces of meat into serving bowls. Use a large spoon so the meat doesn't fall apart on its way out of the pot.

French Provincial meets the modern American kitchen: Chicken Fricassee

Recipes for Fricassees

	Chicken Fricassee	Capon Fricassee	Cornish Game Hen Fricassee	Rabbit Fricassee
1. Heat	2 Tbs unsalted butter 1 Tbs canola oil	2 Tbs unsalted butter 1 Tbs canola oil	2 Tbs unsalted butter 1 Tbs grapeseed oil	2 Tbs unsalted butter 1 Tbs canola oil
2. Brown and transfer	One 4-pound cut-up chicken, back and neck included	One 5- to 6-pound cut-up capon, back and neck included	Four 1-pound Cornish game hens, halved	One 4- to 5-pound cut-up rabbit
3. Add and brown	30 to 36 pearl onions	30 to 36 pearl onions 3 ounces bacon, chopped	30 to 36 pearl onions	30 to 36 pearl onions
4. Add and reduce the mushroom liquid to a glaze	12 ounces white button mushrooms, cleaned and thinly sliced 1 large turnip, peeled and cubed	12 ounces white button mushrooms, cleaned and thinly sliced 1 medium sweet potato, peeled and cubed	6 ounces cremini mushrooms, cleaned and thinly sliced 6 ounces lobster or oyster mushrooms, cleaned and chopped 6 to 8 small Roma or plum tomatoes, seeded and chopped	12 ounces cremini mushrooms, cleaned and thinly sliced 1 small rutabaga, peeled and cubed
5. Add and cook	3 Tbs all-purpose flour 1 Tbs stemmed thyme 1 Tbs minced sage 2 garlic cloves, minced	3 Tbs all-purpose flour 2 Tbs minced parsley 1 Tbs minced oregano 2 garlic cloves, minced	3 Tbs all-purpose flour 2 Tbs minced oregano 3 garlic cloves, minced	3 Tbs all-purpose flour 3 Tbs minced parsley 1 Tbs minced marjoram 2 garlic cloves, minced
6. Stir in	2 cups chicken broth 1 cup dry white wine	2¾ cups chicken broth ¼ cup Armagnac	2 cups chicken broth 1 cup dry vermouth	2¾ cups chicken broth ¼ cup brandy
7. Return the meat to the pan, cover, and simmer slowly	About 45 minutes	About 1 hour 20 minutes	About 50 minutes	About 1 hour 20 minutes
8. Stir in, simmer, and season with salt and pepper to taste	½ cup cream	½ cup cream	½ cup cream	½ cup cream

	Pheasant "Grand-mère"	Veal Fricassee	Lamb Fricassee	Shellfish Fricassee
1. Heat	2 Tbs unsalted butter 1 Tbs canola oil	2 Tbs unsalted butter 1 Tbs canola oil	2 Tbs unsalted butter 1 Tbs canola oil	2 Tbs unsalted butter 1 Tbs canola oil
2. Brown and transfer	Two 3-pound pheasants, quartered 3 ounces chopped bacon	4 pounds cubed veal shoulder steaks, bones attached	4 pounds cubed lamb stew meat	Omit
3. Add and brown	30 to 36 pearl onions	30 to 36 pearl onions	30 to 36 pearl onions	30 to 36 pearl onions
4. Add and reduce the mushroom liquid to a glaze	12 ounces white button mushrooms, cleaned and thinly sliced 2 medium yellow-flesh potatoes, such as Yukon Golds, cubed	12 ounces cremini mushrooms, cleaned and thinly sliced 2 medium carrots, thinly sliced	12 ounces white button mushrooms, cleaned and thinly sliced ½ pound white potatoes, cubed 1 small leek, white and pale green parts only, halved, washed, and thinly sliced	12 ounces white button mushrooms, cleaned and thinly sliced 1 small fennel bulb, trimmed and thinly sliced 3 or 4 Roma or plum tomatoes, seeded and chopped
5. Add and cook	3 Tbs all-purpose flour 2 Tbs stemmed thyme 2 bay leaves (discard before serving)	3 Tbs all-purpose flour 3 Tbs minced parsley 2 tsp finely grated lemon zest ½ tsp grated nutmeg 1 bay leaf (discard before serving)	3 Tbs all-purpose flour 3 Tbs minced parsley 1 Tbs stemmed thyme 2 garlic cloves, minced	3 Tbs all-purpose flour 2 Tbs minced tarragon 2 garlic cloves, minced 1 bay leaf (discard before serving)
6. Stir in	3 cups dry white wine	3 cups dry white wine	2 cups beef broth 1 cup dry white wine	2 cups dry white wine 1 cup fish broth
7. Return the meat to the pan, cover, and simmer slowly	About 1 hour	About 2 hours 30 minutes	About 3 hours	3 frozen lobster tails (about 6 ounces each), thawed and halved lengthwise ½ pound medium shrimp, peeled and deveined ½ pound sea scallops 2 pounds scrubbed clams—simmer only 10 minutes or until the clams open
8. Stir in, simmer, and season with salt and pepper to taste	½ cup cream	½ cup cream	½ cup cream	½ cup cream

Autumn Fried Rice

Fried Rice is not a make-ahead dish; it's a think-ahead dish. There must be left-over rice. Make it while you get ready in the morning, saving it in the refrigerator during the day. Or make it an hour or so before dinner. Or just stop off at a Chinese restaurant on your way home and buy a couple cartons. Unfortunately, the rice cannot be left more than 24 hours in the refrigerator or it will dry out and turn hard, a less-than-satisfying base for this Chinese-American favorite. • MAKES 4 SERVINGS

• **STEP 1** Heat a large wok over medium-high heat, then swirl in 2 tablespoons peanut or sesame oil. The wok should be preheated until it's fairly hot, then the oil should be swirled around the upper rim so that it drizzles down into the wok's bowl.

Chinese dishes often begin with either peanut oil or the more aromatic sesame oil. It's simply a matter of the dish itself—as a general rule, chiles and other deep aromatics dictate a more neutral base like peanut oil, less competition for their fire. Sesame oil is a sure way to gussy up less aromatic (or stinging) ingredients.

Save toasted sesame oil mostly as a drizzle for appetizers and salads. The wok's intense heat will get most of the toasted flavor airborne. Your kitchen will smell terrific; the fried rice, not so much. Use regular sesame oil, less aromatic but more economical.

In many Asian dishes, it's traditional to use unrefined peanut oil that has bits of solids and sediments floating in it and is sometimes still cloudy at room temperature. However, the unrefined oil does have a relatively low smoke-point, easily igniting over the heat. For American home cooking, use refined peanut oil, a safer if less aromatic alternative. It should be stored in the refrigerator to prevent its going rancid. It will indeed cloud; squeeze a little out into a bowl and let it come to room temperature while you gather the other ingredients together.

• **STEP 2** Add 4 chopped medium whole scallions and 1 tablespoon minced peeled fresh ginger; stir-fry for 15 seconds. For a discussion of the exact technique of stir-frying, see page 371. Just remember to keep everything moving. This is a quick dish; you cannot leave the wok unattended. Have all the ingredients ready before you begin cooking. Although the basis of the dish—scallions and ginger—rarely changes, you could, of course, substitute a diced, small yellow onion or a couple shallots sliced into thin rings. The dish will become sweeter, less aromatic, less traditional, but also perhaps more to your taste.

Dried Tofu

In general, tofu is too soft to stir-fry, even the fairly new varieties of "firm silken." Instead, search out pressed, dried tofu from Asian markets or high-end supermarkets. Cut the block into matchsticks before adding to the wok.

You can also press it yourself. Set a block of extra-firm tofu on a paper-towel-lined cutting board. Lay more paper towels over the tofu and set a second cutting board on top. Set a saucepan or a few 14-ounce cans on the upper board to weigh it down and place the whole thing in the refrigerator for at least 4 hours or overnight.

FRIED RICE IN MINUTES: Fried rice happens fast once the wok is hot—here, the meat is browned over the heat.

The vegetables are diced for quick cooking.

Everything is quickly tossed with two spoons, just until the vegetables are crisp-tender.

• **STEP 3** Add ½ pound finely chopped or ground protein; stir-fry until lightly browned, 1 to 2 minutes. At this stage, the protein does not need to be cooked through. In fact, it shouldn't be. It will have at least 5 more minutes over the heat.

Look for a tender cut of meat or shellfish, one that can stand up to the intense tossing and cooking (fish fillets will shard impossibly), but not one that needs long cooking to get tender (no pork shoulder or beef chuck). The pieces should be bite-size—no knife required at the table. Consider these your options:

> **peeled and deveined medium shrimp,** roughly chopped
> **peeled frozen salad or cold-water shrimp** (often misnamed "baby" shrimp), thawed
> **sea scallops,** chopped
> **frozen lobster tail meat,** thawed, taken out of its shell, and chopped
> **pork loin or tenderloin,** sliced into thin rings and these cut into matchsticks
> **purchased Char Siu or Chinese barbecued pork,** chopped
> **ground pork**
> **pork belly,** chopped
> **ground lamb**
> **sirloin,** thinly sliced against the grain (see page 270) and cut into ¼-inch matchsticks
> **diced boneless skinless chicken thighs**
> **ground turkey**
> **purchased Chinese barbecued duck,** skinned, the meat shredded
> **pressed tofu**

• **STEP 4** Add about 2 cups chopped vegetables and about 1 teaspoon spice mixture; stir-fry until aromatic, 1 to 2 minutes. One vegetable will most likely do it, maybe two. A seeded and diced large bell pepper can fill up 2 cups. But make sure

A well is made in the wok's center, just at the hottest spot; the well-beaten egg is poured in and scrambled quickly.

The cooked rice is added, then tossed just until well combined and heated through.

everything's cut to bite-sized portions. Broccoli florets should be halved or quartered; cauliflower, too. Green beans, Chinese long beans, and asparagus should be cut into ½-inch segments. The vegetable needs to cook quickly and be mixed well with the rice to come. You're looking for quick-cookers: snow peas, sugar snaps, carrots shredded through the large holes of a box grater, thinly sliced celery, or thinly sliced mushrooms.

With minimal fuss, you can use a 10- or 12-ounce bag of frozen mixed vegetables. Do not thaw the vegetables; rather, leave them on the counter while you're prepping and laying out the other ingredients. They may need an extra minute over the heat to cook, but their texture will be less compromised, more toothsome.

For the best results, use a purchased blend of dried spices. The classic is five-spice powder, said to replicate the five basic tastes of Chinese cuisine: sweet, salty, sour, savory, and bitter. More authentic varieties are made from ground cinnamon, powdered cassia buds, powdered star anise, ground ginger, and ground cloves. A common variant uses Szechwan peppercorns, star anise, fennel, cinnamon, and cloves.

Or use another spice blend: curry powder of almost any stripe (see page 113) or garam masala (see page 28). These will, of course, skew the flavors away from traditional Chinese cooking and more toward India, but the results are quite savory. Or try a spice paste like a Thai curry paste (see page 385).

Finally, consider doctoring any bottled spice blend with a little finely grated orange zest, some spicy ground Vietnamese cinnamon, a little additional cayenne, or a pinch of ground mace—just to make sure the flavors aren't too dull.

MAKING YOUR OWN FIVE-SPICE POWDER

Toast 2 tablespoons Szechwan peppercorns (or black peppercorns for a less piquant taste), 2 tablespoons fennel seeds, 10 whole cloves, 5 star anise pods, and a 2-inch cinnamon stick broken into several pieces in a dry skillet over medium heat, stirring constantly until aromatic and lightly browned, about 4 minutes. Cool to room temperature, then transfer to a spice grinder; grind until powdery. Pour through a fine-mesh sieve or strainer to get rid of any hard bits; seal in a jar for up to 6 months.

- **STEP 5** Push the ingredients to the sides of the wok, pour in 2 well-beaten large eggs, and scramble in the well at the wok's center. Beat the eggs in a small bowl with a small whisk or fork until quite foamy, no unincorporated clear bits in the mix. Pour them in and keep scraping them off the hot surface. Don't worry about making fluffy curds. You want to cook the egg quickly and get little threads throughout the dish.

- **STEP 6** Add 4 to 5 cups cooked rice; stir-fry to heat through, about 2 minutes. Use a long-grain rice, white or brown, one with lots of amylose (see page 231), even Basmati, Texmati, or jasmine rice. Do not use converted rice, a convenience product that will not stand up to stir-frying.

The cooked rice should be cooled, preferably at room temperature, never hot. Crumble it into the pan, separating the grains. Keep tossing and stirring until the grains are evenly coated in the spices. You're not cooking the rice, just heating it through.

- **STEP 7** Pour in 2 tablespoons soy sauce, 2 tablespoons rice vinegar, and about 2 tablespoons of another liquid; stir-fry until incorporated, about 30 seconds. Toss with toasted sesame oil or chile oil just before serving, if desired. For a discussion of soy sauce, see page 168. A low-acid vinegar, rice vinegar is sold in two varieties: regular and "seasoned." Use regular here—that is, not seasoned, not cut with sugar (which is the "seasoning" in "seasoned rice vinegar"). Regular rice vinegar is usually just labeled "rice vinegar"; seasoned has the word "seasoned" somewhere on the label, even if in very small type. If you can't find regular rice vinegar, use 1 tablespoon white balsamic or white wine vinegar.

The final flavoring is a matter of preference, fairly substantial in its taste, perhaps a thick Chinese condiment (see page 168 for a list), but certainly something with an aromatic finish: broth, whether chicken, vegetable, or beef; shaoxing (page 374) or its substitute, dry sherry; hoisin or chouhee sauce (the latter, a somewhat stronger version of hoisin); oyster sauce; orange juice, particularly undiluted orange juice concentrate; dry white wine or its substitute, dry vermouth; or Chinese barbecue or bean sauce.

Keep in mind that Chinese condiments are quite salty. If you prefer less salt, use less. And keep in mind that this addition is barely cooked, just warmed through. In other words, dry sherry will not blend but simply mix with the flavors.

Finally, you can add a drizzle of toasted sesame oil or fiery hot chile oil (page 375), a final spark. This addition is unnecessary—and maybe unwanted. You can simply pass bottles of both, allowing everyone to doctor the dish as they choose.

Fried Rice is done when all the liquid has been absorbed, probably not more than 1 minute.

Ginger

When shopping for ginger, look for firm rhizomes with a taut skin and without any spongy, soft bits, particularly in the joints. Wrinkled skin or open cracks are signs it's well beyond its prime.

Store ginger at room temperature for a week (after all, it's not refrigerated at the store); in a plastic bag in the refrigerator for about 3 weeks; or in a plastic bag in the freezer for up to 6 months (slice off what you need and stick the rest back in the freezer). A 1½-inch section will yield about 1 minced tablespoon.

To chop ginger, remove the husk gently with a vegetable peeler, taking care to keep the flesh under the skin intact. The flesh within ⅛ inch of the skin is the most aromatic part. Cut the peeled ginger into thin matchsticks, then slice these into very small cubes.

Or forget the knife technique altogether. Thickly slice the peeled rhizome, place the bits in a plastic bag, seal closed, then mash with the pointy side of a meat mallet.

Recipes for Fried Rice

	Fried Rice with Shrimp and Peppers	Vegetarian Fried Rice	Beef and Mushroom Fried Rice	Curried Fried Rice
1. Heat	2 Tbs peanut oil	2 Tbs sesame oil	2 Tbs sesame oil	2 Tbs peanut oil
2. Stir-fry	4 medium whole scallions, chopped 1 Tbs minced peeled fresh ginger	4 medium whole scallions, chopped 1 Tbs minced peeled fresh ginger	4 medium whole scallions, chopped 1 Tbs minced peeled fresh ginger	4 medium whole scallions, chopped 1 Tbs minced peeled fresh ginger
3. Stir-fry	½ pound peeled and deveined medium shrimp, chopped	½ pound dried tofu, cut into matchsticks	½ pound beef sirloin, sliced into thin strips and then these into ¼-inch matchsticks	½ pound ground pork
4. Stir-fry	1 large yellow bell pepper, seeded and diced 1 tsp five-spice powder (see page 149)	12 ounces broccoli florets (do not use frozen), chopped 1 tsp five-spice powder (see page 149)	8 ounces shiitake mushrooms, stems removed and discarded, caps thinly sliced 1 tsp five-spice powder (see page 149)	12 ounces cauliflower florets, chopped 1 tsp curry powder (see page 113) ¼ tsp red pepper flakes
5. Scramble	2 large eggs, well beaten	2 large eggs, well beaten	2 large eggs, well beaten	2 large eggs, well beaten
6. Stir-fry	4 to 5 cups cooked and cooled long-grain rice	4 to 5 cups cooked and cooled long-grain rice	4 to 5 cups cooked and cooled long-grain rice	4 to 5 cups cooked and cooled long-grain rice
7. Pour in and toss	2 Tbs soy sauce 2 Tbs rice vinegar 2 Tbs oyster sauce	2 Tbs soy sauce 2 Tbs rice vinegar 2 Tbs hoisin sauce 1 tsp toasted sesame oil	2 Tbs soy sauce 2 Tbs rice vinegar 2 Tbs hoisin sauce	2 Tbs soy sauce 2 Tbs rice vinegar 2 Tbs dry white wine 1 tsp chile oil (see page 375)

	Springtime Fried Rice	Autumn Fried Rice	Japanese-Inspired Fried Rice	Thai-Inspired Fried Rice
1. Heat	2 Tbs peanut oil	2 Tbs sesame oil	2 Tbs sesame oil	2 Tbs peanut oil
2. Stir-fry	4 medium whole scallions, chopped 1 Tbs minced peeled fresh ginger	4 medium whole scallions, chopped 1 Tbs minced peeled fresh ginger	4 medium whole scallions, chopped 1 Tbs minced peeled fresh ginger	4 medium whole scallions, chopped 1 Tbs minced peeled fresh ginger 1 serrano chile, seeded and minced
3. Stir-fry	¼ pound peeled and deveined medium shrimp, chopped ¼ pound bay scallops or sea scallops, chopped	½ pound ground turkey	½ pound boneless skinless chicken breast, thinly sliced	½ pound boneless skinless chicken thighs, chopped
4. Stir-fry	4 ounces pencil-thin asparagus spears, thinly sliced 4 ounces snow peas, thinly sliced 1 tsp five-spice powder (see page 149)	1 cup quartered jarred roasted or steamed chestnuts 4 ounces Chinese long beans or green beans, thinly sliced 1 tsp curry powder (see page 113) ½ tsp ground cinnamon	1 cup frozen peeled edamame (soybeans) 1 cup diced yellow pickled daikon radish 1 tsp wasabi paste	8 ounces bean sprouts, chopped 1 tsp Thai curry paste (see page 386)
5. Scramble	2 large eggs, well beaten	2 large eggs, well beaten	2 large eggs, well beaten	2 large eggs, well beaten
6. Stir-fry	4 to 5 cups cooked and cooled long-grain rice	4 to 5 cups cooked and cooled long-grain rice	4 to 5 cups cooked and cooled long-grain rice	4 to 5 cups cooked and cooled long-grain rice
7. Pour in and toss	2 Tbs soy sauce 2 Tbs rice vinegar 2 Tbs dry white wine	2 Tbs soy sauce 2 Tbs rice vinegar 2 Tbs shaoxing (see page 374) or dry sherry 1 tsp toasted sesame oil	2 Tbs soy sauce 2 Tbs rice vinegar 2 Tbs mirin	2 Tbs soy sauce 2 Tbs rice vinegar 2 Tbs frozen orange juice concentrate, thawed 1 tsp toasted sesame oil

Frittata

A quick brunch, lunch, or dinner, a frittata is like a simplified omelet—no flipping required. Because the oven's radiant heat can compromise the eggs' tenderness, the best frittatas are made stovetop. • MAKES 4 SERVINGS

• **STEP 1** Heat about 4 tablespoons (¼ cup) fat in a 12-inch skillet over medium heat. Although a frittata is most easily made in a Teflon®-coated skillet, such pans have come under attack for being unsafe, even carcinogenic. According to the FDA, a pan with a Teflon® surface should not be heated above 350°F and should be discarded if nicked or scratched. To keep your nonstick pans safe, don't use them in the oven, don't stack other pans in them, and use only cookware designed for their special surface (never metal utensils).

That all said, you can't use a nonstick skillet for the frittata if you're going to later brown cheese on top of it under the broiler. In that case, make sure you use the full amount of fat here—or even a little more. Or invest in the time and energy it takes to season a cast-iron skillet until it becomes a full-fledged omelet pan, following the manufacturer's instructions for your model.

For the frittata, choose a fat that complements the other ingredients:

Neutral oils. Simpler sautés often work best with simpler oils. If the frittata will have only a few ingredients—softened onions and herbs, for example—choose a pale palette like grapeseed, canola, refined peanut, corn, or another vegetable oil.

Unsalted butter. Its slightly sour taste is well balanced by sweet aromatics like scallions, shallots, leeks, and celery; by smoked meats like bacon, lox, or ham; or by an assortment of herbs (parsley, oregano, rosemary, and thyme, for example).

Olive or nut oils. These nosy flavors are suited to the bolder flavors of shrimp, chicken, sausage, and many vegetable combinations.

Animal fats. Try fats like duck fat or rendered, smoky bacon fat, saved back from the last time you fried a panful. Pair these gorgeously big flavors with creamy vegetables like diced potatoes, rutabagas, or thinly sliced parsnips. Double the herbs and toss in some chopped garlic for balance.

• **STEP 2** Build a simple sauté with protein and/or vegetables. A frittata is an egg dish; it shouldn't be overloaded with other ingredients. If it's laden with filler, it will break into chunks when sliced. Use no more than 1½ cups diced ingredients for an eight-egg frittata.

Most sautés begin with a chopped onion. And although the onion's natural sweetness is terrific with creamy eggs, you needn't

Don't pour the beaten eggs into the center of the skillet; pour them all around the hot surface so the eggs don't clump.

Covering the skillet and cooking a frittata stovetop is the easiest—and best—way to get a tender egg dish every time.

A properly set frittata will come off the skillet in one piece without any uncooked egg mixture puddled across its surface.

start there. How about a shallot? Or simply bacon and garlic? Or peas and chopped spinach?

Evenly dice and slice the ingredients to about the size of an almond. That way, they'll cook at about the same rate, so you can add them all to the pan at the same time. Yes, there are subtleties among proteins and vegetables as to how fast they cook; but remember that everything will have at least 10 more minutes over the flame in the next steps—with these two exceptions:

1. Hard vegetables like carrots, potatoes, turnips, and parsnips will need longer to soften, so toss them into the skillet several minutes before you add any protein.
2. Ready-to-eat meats should only be warmed through—as in, say, a salami and onion frittata. Mince the onion so it cooks quickly—or put it in the pan first. Pasteurized lump crabmeat and smoked salmon should be barely warmed over the heat, so as to prevent the release of their fishy oils.

All this said, look for visual cues to tell if the sauté is done. Onions should be translucent; diced potatoes, browned and softened. Ground meat should have lost its raw, red color; chicken pieces should be almost cooked through.

But how do you know what to choose for this simple sauté? Think this way: the four basic tastes—sweet, sour, bitter, and salty—are the corners of a square, balanced over a central point (aka, the fat). Don't load up one corner—for example, everything on the sweet part of the square, tipping the thing off balance. Since caramelized onions and shrimp are both quite sweet, they should be balanced by a bitter herb like rosemary or a dash of balsamic vinegar. Nor should everything lie on the bitter corner: no spinach with parsley, escarole with browned butter. But an absolute "yes" to spinach with thyme and shrimp or escarole with simple, melted butter. You want a balance over the central point.

And that central point—the fat—can be off-center as well. Neutral oils are evenly centered, but unsalted butter inches toward the sour corner; therefore, it's best balanced by sweet or bitter ingredients. Nut oils move toward the bitter corner; animal fats, toward the sweet. Compensate with the vegetables and protein. In good cooking, balance is everything.

• STEP 3 Warm the fresh herbs and/or spices in the pan for less than a minute. If the protein has thrown off quite a bit of fat—boneless chicken thighs or mild dried Spanish chorizo, for example—first drain off all but 2 tablespoons.

In general, avoid dried herbs. A quick dish like this is enhanced by the more present flavors in fresh herbs. Latch their flavors and those of dried spices to the other ingredients, relying on classic combinations: oregano with shrimp, thyme with bacon; nutmeg with sausage. Or use classic blends: rosemary, oregano, and parsley; or marjoram, thyme, and chives. Chili powder works wonders with scallions, mushrooms, and shrimp; curry powder, with onions, garlic, minced peeled fresh ginger, and chopped stemmed chard. Mace is particularly appealing in a spinach frittata.

But limit your selection of herbs and spices. Start out using one or two to get the hang of their flavor before moving on to more complicated combinations. After all, is this the last frittata you're going to make? If so, we suggest lobster tail meat and tarragon topped with crème fraîche and beluga caviar.

If you use grated cheese, sprinkle it evenly across the frittata's surface. Remember that nonstick skillets should not be placed under a broiler.

• **STEP 4** Whisk 8 large eggs with 2 tablespoons cream, wine, or broth; pour into the skillet. For the most tender frittata, start out with room-temperature eggs. (The protein chains need to be uncoiled, relaxed from the cold.) Either set the eggs out on the counter for 15 minutes before you begin cooking, or set them (unbroken) in a bowl of warm—not hot—water for 5 minutes.

Whisked, the eggs should be quite foamy and light. Don't break out the mixer, but do give your forearm a good workout.

You can substitute a pasteurized egg substitute for the eggs, although the frittata won't be as creamy. Our best advice is to use 1¾ cups pasteurized egg substitute and 1 large egg, replacing 7 of the eggs in the dish.

Why add 2 tablespoons of another liquid? Direct heat toughens eggs, so their proteins need to be encased for protection. Cream is the usual candidate—and a good choice to be sure. In fact, since most chefs make frittatas in the oven, the radiant heat mandates that the eggs get cream's heavy dose of fat for protection. But by cooking stovetop, we are free to use a host of other liquids. Half-and-half yields a luxurious, velvety finish. But milk, even fat-free milk, will work well, particularly if the flavors in the sauté are bucked up with bolder tastes like minced clams, chives, or chopped leftover brisket. What's more, there's no reason to limit the liquid to dairy. Try white wine, dry vermouth, dry Madeira, or vegetable broth.

As you pour this mixture into the skillet, move the bowl evenly over the hot surface. Pouring straight into the center can cause a toughened lump as the eggs pile onto themselves over the heat. Also, pouring directly into the center of the pan will push the sautéed ingredients to the side, causing uneven distribution.

• **STEP 5** Cover, reduce the heat to low, and cook until the top is set, 8 to 10 minutes; season with salt and freshly ground black pepper to taste. Keep the heat low and leave the skillet alone. A closed lid stabilizes the humidity inside to create the best texture.

On an electric stove, the burner temperature may not change quickly enough to keep the eggs from browning. The solution? Set a second burner on low during step 4, then move the skillet from the higher temperature one to the low-temperature one at this point.

Check the frittata after 8 minutes. There should be no runny liquid on top. Slip a heat-safe rubber spatula under one side and gently lift up. The custard should appear set but flexible, not stiff.

Add salt and pepper only after the frittata's set. Salt toughens eggs considerably if added while they're raw; pepper will lose some of its nose-spike in the moist humidity of a closed skillet. If adding cheese in the next step, you may want to forgo any salt because of the sodium in the cheese.

A mushroom frittata, browned under a broiler and ready to eat.

• **STEP 6** (optional): Top with about ½ cup grated cheese (about 4 ounces) and brown under a pre-heated broiler about 4 inches from the heat source. Preheat the broiler while the frittata cooks. The cheese, like the eggs, should be at room temperature. It will thus melt quickly so the frittata's top doesn't brown too deeply or turn rubbery.

Use a hard or semi-firm cheese, like Cheddar, Gruyère, Emmental, or Swiss, finely grated, preferably through a microplane. (For a generalized list of cheese categories and varieties, see page 175.) Choose a cheese that builds on the flavors you've chosen: Parmigiano-Reggiano for more delicate tastes, Asiago for bolder flavors. Avoid blue cheeses, runny double-creams, or cream cheeses; they're better on their own anyway.

Recipes for Frittatas

	Bacon-and-Egg Frittata	Herb Frittata	Mushroom Frittata	Garden Vegetable Frittata
1. Heat	4 Tbs unsalted butter	¼ cup canola oil	4 Tbs unsalted butter	¼ cup olive oil
2. Sauté	4 ounces shallots, diced 4 ounces bacon, diced	4 ounces shallots, diced	6 ounces cremini mushrooms, cleaned and thinly sliced 2 garlic cloves, minced	4 ounces shallots, thinly sliced 4 ounces thin asparagus spears, chopped ½ cup frozen peas
3. Warm	1 tsp stemmed thyme	2 Tbs parsley 1 Tbs marjoram 2 tsp stemmed thyme	2 tsp chopped tarragon ¼ tsp grated nutmeg	2 tsp chopped parsley
4. Whisk and pour in the skillet	8 large eggs 2 Tbs heavy cream	8 large eggs 2 Tbs white wine	8 large eggs 2 Tbs brandy	8 large eggs 2 Tbs heavy cream
5. Reduce the heat	Cover and cook until set	Cover and cook until set	Cover and cook until set	Cover and cook until set
6. (optional) Top and brown	½ cup grated Asiago	Omit	½ cup finely grated Parmesan	½ cup finely grated Parmesan

	Crab and Spinach Frittata	Smoked Salmon Frittata	Sausage Frittata	East Indian-Inspired Frittata
1. Heat	¼ cup olive oil	3 Tbs canola oil	3 Tbs olive oil	4 Tbs almond oil or ghee
2. Sauté	½ pound lump crabmeat, picked over for shell and cartilage 6 ounces chopped frozen spinach, thawed and squeezed almost dry	1 small yellow onion, minced 1 large Roma or plum tomato, seeded and chopped ¼ pound smoked salmon, chopped	6 ounces sausage meat, casings removed 1 small onion, diced 1 small red bell pepper, seeded and thinly sliced	1 small yellow onion, minced 6 ounces cauliflower florets 1 Tbs peeled minced fresh ginger
3. Warm	¼ teaspoon grated nutmeg Several dashes hot red pepper sauce	¼ tsp ground allspice	2 tsp thyme 1 tsp fennel seeds 1 tsp finely grated lemon zest	1 Tbs curry powder (see page 113)
4. Whisk and pour in the skillet	8 large eggs 2 Tbs milk	8 large eggs 2 Tbs half-and-half	8 large eggs 2 Tbs milk	8 large eggs 2 Tbs coconut milk
5. Reduce the heat	Cover and cook until set	Cover and cook until set	Cover and cook until set	Cover and cook until set
6. Top and brown	Omit	Omit	½ cup finely grated Gruyère	Omit

Garden Vegetable Gratin

A layered potato casserole, a *gratin* (French, grah-TAN) is named for both the technique and the dish it's baked in: a fairly shallow, oval, oven-safe baking dish. Nonetheless, you can make it in a standard 9 x 13-inch baking dish, more in keeping with standard American kitchenware. Perhaps this use of a standard baking dish is why the casserole's gotten hitched to "scalloped potatoes" in the United States. In fact, the real thing is less thick, has no cheese, and is more a centerpiece for the potatoes themselves. • MAKES 8 SIDE-DISH SERVINGS

• **STEP 1** Preheat the oven to 350°F. Peel and thinly slice 3 pounds Russet potatoes, place them in a large bowl, cover with cool water, and set aside. Russets are the best varietal for the best gratin. Sometimes called Russet Burbanks, they're an American hybrid with white flesh, brown skin, and plenty of natural sugars; they are also full of starch, making them quite fluffy when cooked. That starch will also make a gratin exactly what it is: a casserole thickened with the potatoes' starch, sort of a potato version of Risotto (which is a sauce thickened with rice starch, page 284).

The potatoes need to be cut into slices about ⅛-inch thick—cut lengthwise, to boot, so the strips are as a long as possible. There are three ways to do this:

1. **A sharp knife.** You need a hefty knife, no cleaver of course, but a chef's knife for sure. The weight of the tool will help keep the slices even; your steady hand will keep them thin. If you haven't sharpened the knife in a while, now's the time to get out the sharpener—or at least get out the steel and hone the blade. Slice off about ½ inch from one side of the peeled potato, so it will sit flat on the cutting board. Now spray the knife blade with nonstick spray so the starchy potato doesn't stick to it. (You may need to do this several times during slicing if you notice pieces sticking.) Slice down in slow, steady, thin cuts, a little thicker than a piece of elementary-school construction paper. Remove each slice before making the next.

2. **A mandoline** (pronounced MAN-doh-lin but not to be confused with the stringed instrument, a mandolin). This kitchen tool is an angled plane with an adjustable, razor-sharp blade; items are run repeatedly down the slope and over the blade, thin slices falling through the crack and onto the counter below. Set the blade to ⅛-inch thickness and use a food grip to run the peeled potatoes their long way over the blade, thereby making long, thin strips. Unlike the technique for using a knife, there's no benefit here in going slowly—indeed, it's a hindrance. Instead, run the items across the blade at a good, steady clip,

For the best gratin, peeled Russets should be sliced as thinly as possible.

pressing down gently but firmly so they come in contact with the blade. Do not attempt to slice the potatoes without using the food grip; many a person has shorn the skin off their fingers thanks to a mandoline (and probably to a mandolin, too). Cheap knock-offs are sometimes sold without the safety grip; invest in a higher-end, professional mandoline or work with a metal glove that can resist the blade.

3. **A food processor** fitted with the 2-millimeter slicing blade. Place a potato in the slot, turn the machine on, and use the plunger to press the spud down over the spinning blades. You won't be able to get long slices; the potato will have to go in short end first. And the food processor will "juice" the potato somewhat, its moisture leached out of the whacked-open cells. Still, it's hard to argue with convenience.

Put the potato slices in water to leach a little of their starch and help them remain white, rather than oxidizing to a pale brown in the open air. But not too long because too much starch will be lost. Just keep them in the water while you make the following vegetable sauté.

• **STEP 2** Heat 3 tablespoons fat in a large skillet over medium heat. In general, if the gratin will be made with milk or cream, use unsalted butter; if it will be made with broth and/or wine, use either olive oil, an untoasted nut oil, or a neutral oil like canola or vegetable oil. However, a broth-based gratin made with butter is silky and smooth; a milk-based gratin with olive oil is light and less palate-drenching. Just remember that the fat you use will also probably be the one dotted or drizzled over the dish just before baking. In all cases, stay away from toasted nut and seed oils.

A gratin is a layered casserole; the potato slices perform the same dividing act noodles do in lasagna.

The potato slices, kept in water to halt discoloration, are placed in an overlapping layer in the baking dish.

The liquid—here, milk and cream—is poured over the casserole, moistening the top layer as it soaks into those below.

And that all said, many a traditional French gratin is made with duck fat, then dotted with unsalted butter. Wow.

• **STEP 3** Add 4 cups packed diced aromatics, a mirepoix, or a modified mirepoix (see page 57); cook, stirring often, until softened, from 3 to 8 minutes. The mix here is entirely dependent on what you want the final effect to be. Treat all these vegetables as the "spices" of the gratin. How about shredded Brussels sprouts, diced onion, diced zucchini, and shredded carrots? Or a shallot and one or two peeled, cored, and diced apples? Or some chopped, stemmed chard with about 2 ounces chopped bacon? All these bring new flavors to the gratin—some sweeter (carrots and the like); others, more bitter (like Brussels sprouts and chard). None will be used to excess; all must be cooked until almost ready to eat so they continue to dissolve in the casserole as it bakes.

Wet vegetables—sliced mushrooms, diced summer squash—must give off their moisture over the heat; dry, hard vegetables—carrots or seeded winter squash—must be diced into very small pieces so they'll cook quickly. Oddly, 2 cups diced onion and 2 cups sliced mushrooms will actually take longer over the heat than 1 cup diced onion and 3 cups diced carrot because of the difference in moisture content, the time it takes for the mushrooms to give off their liquid. Since leafy greens are mostly air, you'll need a double amount because of the way they cook down over the heat. Chopped, they fill the pan too full; add them in batches.

Yes, you can make a gratin with tomatoes, but they must be cooked down thoroughly so as not to water-log the casserole. In truth, if you want a tomato taste with the potatoes, it's easiest to add tomato paste or sun-dried tomatoes in the next step.

• **STEP 4** Add some minced garlic, perhaps a chopped flavoring agent like pitted olives or sun-dried tomatoes, and up to 2 tablespoons minced herbs and/or ½ teaspoon dried spice—as well as 1 teaspoon salt and ½ teaspoon freshly ground black pepper; cook for 30 seconds to warm through. Then layer the vegetables and the drained potatoes in a 10-cup au gratin dish or a 9 x 13-inch baking dish. Garlic is almost irresistible with potatoes; just make sure it's minced so it doesn't dot the casserole with nose-spanking bites. Also consider other flavorings: a minced, seeded fresh chile; some sliced sun-dried tomatoes; a dab of tomato paste; a minced, jarred, roasted red pepper; some minced peeled fresh ginger; chopped, pitted black olives; or even a minced anchovy. No more than 1 or 2 tablespoons of any, just as a flavoring. This is a potato dish, after all. Everything else is ornamentation.

As a gratin bakes, press down occasionally with a large spoon to scoop up juices that then can baste the top layer.

Those juices will brown the potatoes as the casserole bakes.

Fresh herbs work best—parsley, rosemary, oregano, or a simple combination—but there's no reason not to pair them with a little dried spices, particularly the sweeter ones like ground mace, grated nutmeg, ground ginger, or ground cumin.

Once you've got the vegetable medley softened and aromatic, layer the casserole. Start by blotting the potato slices dry on paper towels to remove any moisture that will increase the cooking time and leach too much liquid into the casserole. Place an overlapping layer of slices in the bottom of the baking dish. Then spread ¼ to ⅓ cup vegetable mixture over the potatoes. There's no reason to get crazed over amounts, but remember that this is not a true layer as in, say, a lasagna. Rather, this is a flavoring to the potatoes.

Keep layering, pressing down and compacting as you build the dish, overlapping the slices and using small amounts of vegetable filling each time. There's no way to say exactly how many layers you'll make: the potato slices may have been different sizes and there may be slightly different amounts of the vegetable mixture, depending on which vegetables you used. When you see you have enough potato slices for one more layer, add the rest of the vegetables, spread them evenly over the slices, and top with an overlapping layer of these last potato slices.

One thing you may have noticed: the baking dish is not greased or buttered. You want crunchy, browned bits all over the edges. If this sort of thing bothers you, consider giving the inside of the baking dish a quick shot of nonstick spray or a light coating of unsalted butter before you build the casserole. But realize you've lost the pleasure of pulling little bits of browned potatoes off the baking dish.

• **STEP 5** Pour 4 cups (1 quart) milk, broth, or an enhanced version of either over the contents of the baking dish; drizzle or dot with 2 tablespoons fat. Bake uncovered, basting occasionally, until golden and most the liquid has been absorbed, about 2 hours. Either milk (regular, low-fat, or even fat-free) or chicken, beef, or vegetable broth (avoid fish broth) can be enhanced with up to 1 cup dry white wine, dry sherry, dry vermouth, or heavy cream. However, bear this in mind: too much wine and the dish will be too sweet; too much cream, too heavy.

The fat that goes over the top of the dish is most likely the same one you used to cook the vegetables. However, feel free to mix it up: unsalted butter to cook the vegetables and untoasted walnut oil over the top layer of potatoes; olive oil for the vegetables, unsalted butter over the top.

After the casserole has baked about 45 minutes, start basting it by pressing a large spoon down onto the potatoes, compacting them a bit, and scooping up any juices that bubble up. Drizzle these back over the contents of the baking dish, perhaps every 10 or 15 minutes. In the end, the casserole should be golden brown; there should be little unthickened liquid in the dish.

Recipes for Gratins

	Creamy Potato and Leek Gratin	Savory Potato and Cabbage Gratin	Potato and Brussels Sprouts Gratin	Curried Potato, Cauliflower, and Pea Gratin
1. Preheat the oven; thinly slice, cover with water, and set aside	3 pounds Russet potatoes, peeled	3 pounds Russet potatoes, peeled	3 pounds Russet potatoes, peeled	3 pounds Russet potatoes, peeled
2. Heat	3 Tbs unsalted butter	3 Tbs olive oil	3 Tbs olive oil	3 Tbs unsalted butter
3. Add and cook	4 large leeks, white and pale green parts only, halved lengthwise, washed carefully, and thinly sliced	1 medium yellow onion, diced 1 pound green cabbage, cored, halved, and thinly sliced into shreds (see page 166)	1 medium yellow onion, diced 1 celery rib, thinly sliced 1 pound Brussels sprouts, cored and thinly sliced into shreds	4 ounces shallots, diced 1 small head cauliflower, trimmed, cored, and chopped into small florets 2 cups fresh shelled or frozen peas
4. Add, then layer with the potatoes in the baking dish	2 garlic cloves, minced 1 Tbs minced tarragon 1 tsp salt ½ tsp ground black pepper	2 garlic cloves, minced 1 Tbs minced parsley 1 Tbs minced oregano 1 tsp salt ½ tsp ground black pepper	1 garlic clove, minced 1 tsp salt 1 tsp ground black pepper	2 Tbs minced peeled fresh ginger 1 Tbs curry powder (see page 113) ½ tsp salt (if none is in the curry powder)
5. Pour on, drizzle or dot, and bake, basting often	3 cups milk 1 cup heavy cream 2 Tbs unsalted butter	4 cups (1 quart) chicken broth 2 Tbs olive oil	3 cups chicken broth 1 cup dry white wine 2 Tbs unsalted butter	3 cups vegetable broth 1 cup coconut milk 2 Tbs unsalted butter or ghee (page 25)

	Garden Vegetable Gratin	Potato and Apple Gratin	Potato and Greens Gratin	Curried Potato and Carrot Gratin
1. Preheat the oven; thinly slice, cover with water, and set aside	3 pounds Russet potatoes, peeled	3 pounds Russet potatoes, peeled	3 pounds Russet potatoes, peeled	3 pounds Russet potatoes, peeled
2. Heat	3 Tbs unsalted butter	3 Tbs untoasted walnut oil	3 Tbs olive oil	3 Tbs canola oil
3. Add and cook	4 ounces shallots, diced 1 medium carrot, diced 1 small zucchini, diced 1 cup fresh shelled or frozen peas	1 large yellow onion, diced 2 large tart green apples, such as Pippins or Granny Smiths, peeled, cored, seeded, and diced	4 ounces shallots, diced 1 celery rib, thinly sliced 12 ounces chard leaves, stemmed and roughly chopped 8 ounces baby spinach leaves	4 ounces shallots, diced 1 pound carrots, peeled and shredded though the large holes of a box grater
4. Add, then layer with the potatoes in the baking dish	2 garlic cloves, minced 2 Tbs stemmed thyme ¼ tsp grated mace 1 tsp salt ½ tsp ground black pepper	2 garlic cloves, minced ½ tsp ground cinnamon 1 tsp salt ½ tsp ground black pepper	1 garlic clove, minced ¼ tsp grated nutmeg 1 tsp salt 1 tsp ground black pepper	1 Tbs minced peeled fresh ginger 2 tsp curry powder (see page 113) 1 tsp salt (less if some exists in the curry powder) ½ tsp ground cinnamon Up to ½ tsp cayenne
5. Pour on, drizzle or dot, and bake, basting often	3 cups chicken broth 1 cup heavy cream 2 Tbs unsalted butter	4 cups (1 quart) milk 2 Tbs unsalted butter	3 cups vegetable broth 1 cup dry white wine 2 Tbs unsalted butter	4 cups (1 quart) chicken broth 2 Tbs unsalted butter

Lo Mein

This Chinese favorite is somewhat like a good noodle soup—but without the soup. All the vegetables and meat are there, but bound up with the tender-chewy noodles in a one-wok meal. By the way, "lo" (*lao* in Mandarin) refers to something scooped out of water; "mein" (*me-an*) are wheat noodles. • MAKES 4 SERVINGS

• **STEP 1** Cook and drain ¾ pound dried noodles or 1 pound fresh noodles; set aside. Traditionally, lo mein is made with either Chinese wheat or egg noodles. Wheat noodles—made without eggs and occasionally flavored with shrimp or fish in Asian packagings—have a bit more tooth and are a paler yellow than traditional egg noodles. A good Asian market will carry an abundance; there are even choices in the Asian aisle of most supermarkets.

Still, you could use fresh or dried udon, a Japanese wheat noodle known for its chewy texture. Or try Japanese soba noodles, made from buckwheat flour, earthier, more toothsome, and far from traditional. Or even use Italian noodles, round, not flat, egg or wheat—all of which will not be as chewy as their Asian counterparts.

Dried or fresh, the noodles should come out of the cooking water slightly undercooked, with a little "tooth," a little chew right at their centers; there's more cooking in the steps ahead. Give dried noodles perhaps 5 to 6 minutes in a large pot of boiling water over high heat to get tender, stirring occasionally to forestall sticking. Fresh noodles will need no more than 1 minute; do not let them turn soft or they will fall apart in the wok.

• **STEP 2** Heat a large wok over high heat, then swirl in 1 tablespoon oil. As with a stir-fry, you'll need a deep wok, one whose sides allow constant contact between the heat and the ingredients. Set the wok over the heat for a couple minutes to get very hot, then swirl in the oil and proceed immediately to the next step. For a discussion of woks, see page 373.

As with Fried Rice (page 147), use peanut or sesame oil. No need for toasted sesame oil, which will lose much of its aroma over the heat. That said, don't buy a pale imitation of sesame oil: it should smell like sesame seeds. If you must account for peanut allergies and don't want the sesame taste, use a neutral vegetable oil, from corn to canola.

• **STEP 3** Add 1 cup diced aromatic vegetables and stir-fry for 1 minute. For a discussion of the technique of stir-frying, see page 371.

Sold wound into balls, Chinese egg noodles (in the wok) are the basis of an authentic lo mein. Use chopsticks or a long, bamboo skewer to unwind them after they've been dropped in boiling water.

TO CORE AND SHRED A CABBAGE: First, slice the cabbage in half through the root, then cut out its pyramidal root stalk.

Next, place the cabbage cut side down on your work surface and make thin slices through the head, releasing the leaves into long strands. Some may need to be broken up by hand.

The classic Chinese aromatics are scallions, minced peeled fresh ginger, and minced garlic cloves; but also consider minced shallots, pickled or fresh chiles, finely grated orange or lemon zest, Szechwan peppercorns, or even canned preserved Chinese vegetables, available at most Asian grocery stores. Preserved Szechwan cabbage, mustard greens, or radishes are particularly appealing, a vinegary, hot bite in the mix. However, they should be used sparingly—perhaps at the very most ¼ cup of the total aromatics and well balanced by scallions and ginger. In fact, use good judgment for all these strong aromatics: scallions are the base of the mix—perhaps as much as ¾ cup—followed by dribs and drabs of the others.

• **STEP 4** Add ½ pound thinly sliced, diced or shredded protein; stir-fry for 1 minute. In this step, the meat should be heated through and almost cooked, although it will have several more minutes over the heat in the steps ahead. Thus, the protein 1) must not need long cooking (no bottom round, no pork shoulder) and 2) must not fall apart over the heat (no soft tofu, no thin-fleshed fish fillets). Still, within these horizons, the sky's the limit:

trimmed pork loin or tenderloin, cut into thin rounds and then into ¼-inch-thick matchsticks
purchased roast pork or Char Siu from a Chinese restaurant, chopped
lamb sirloin, cut into long strips and then these into small matchsticks
beef sirloin, cut against the grain (see page 270) into long strips
boneless skinless chicken breasts, cut into thin slices
boneless skinless chicken thighs, chopped
boneless skinless turkey breast cutlet, cut into thin slices or chopped
peeled and deveined medium shrimp, perhaps chopped if they are large
scallops, cut into quarters if they are large
frozen lobster tail meat, thawed and cut into bite-sized chunks
pressed tofu (see page 147), cut into thin slices and then into ¼-inch wide matchsticks

• **STEP 5** Add 3 cups diced or shredded quick-cooking vegetables; stir-fry until the meat is almost cooked through and the vegetables have started to soften. In truth, take a use-up-the-hydrator attitude to the dish. Got half a bell pepper in plastic wrap? Slice it up and toss it in. A bit of cabbage left over? Shred it and toss it in. A mélange of vegetables is both the best way to get this favorite to the table and the most healthful way to include a wide range of vitamins, nutrients, and fiber.

Consider these choices:

thinly sliced mushrooms (particularly shiitake caps)
seeded bell peppers, cut into thin strips
bean sprouts
sliced snow peas or sugar snap peas
broccoli florets
cauliflower florets
thinly sliced water chestnuts
thinly sliced silk squash (sometimes called Chinese okra)
chopped long beans
bamboo shoots, cut into matchsticks
diced summer squash
thinly shredded and cored bok choy, cabbage, or another leafy
   green like water spinach or Chinese flowering cabbage

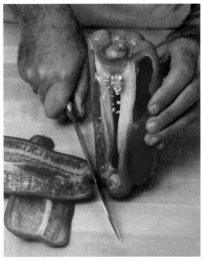

Don't rely on fancy techniques to core a bell pepper. Just slice the flesh right off the core, leaving the white membranes still attached to the stem at the top.

Avoid roots, tubers, and such—except for carrots, a modern favorite in this dish. Shred these through the large holes of a box grater so the threads cook quickly. Peeled zucchini and cucumber can also be shredded through the large holes of a box grater; grate them down to their seedy centers, discarding these rather than letting their juice packets water down the sauce. Also consider folding the zucchini or cucumber threads in paper towels and squeezing them over the sink to remove even more moisture.

• **STEP 6** Stir in the cooked noodles; ½ cup broth; 3 tablespoons vinegar, shaoxing, or dry sherry; 3 tablespoons of another thick Chinese condiment or flavoring; and 2½ tablespoons soy sauce. Stir-fry until almost all the liquid has been absorbed. It's common culinary practice to whisk the broth, vinegar, the thick condiment, and the soy sauce together in a bowl before pouring them into a wok. This extra step is up to you. If you have the ingredients prepped and in little bowls next to your stove, you can just quickly dump them in one at a time, much the way a chef at a Chinese restaurant would do it.

Use chicken, beef, or vegetable broth, depending on the protein you've used in the dish. Do not use fish broth or clam juice, which are too overpowering; accent shrimp and scallops with chicken or vegetable broth instead.

Rice vinegar will work well and is more traditional if you're not going to use shaoxing (see page 374) or its substitute, dry sherry. But it's hard to miss the extraordinary abundance of vinegars in Asian markets and from their online sites. Consider the pale, delicate fragrance of red rice vinegar; the plummy aroma of Chinese black vinegar, a cross between balsamic vinegar and Worcestershire sauce; or even the tart sourness of Chinese white vinegar. Do not use a "seasoned" version of any of these Chinese vinegars; they are all laced with sugar and not a good match for this stir-fry. Of course, you can also use plain white or red wine vinegar.

A fermented sauce of soybeans, water, and flour, soy sauce isn't one thing but a multitude with as many variations and shades of flavor as wine in Western culture. In use for over 3,000 years of documented Chinese history, it was once declared one of the seven essentials for life (along with firewood, oil, salt, rice, vinegar, and tea).

There are two basic varieties: light and dark. "Light" does not refer to calories or sodium content. (In North America, low-sodium soy sauce is usually labeled "lite.") Rather, "light" is a reference to the sauce's color, which can range from pale to dark oaky brown. This is the soy sauce most familiar to North Americans. In Asian bottlings, it is often labeled "superior soy sauce."

Dark soy sauce, by contrast, is more pungent and almost black in color, aged for several months, even a year or so in some bottlings. It's a savory, musky condiment, not for the faint of heart, but an acquired taste over time.

Still, there are labeling confusions because of international, regional, and even North American packaging. If you're standing in the market and want to know what you've got, hold the bottle up to the light and shake it. If the mixture is watery and thin, it's light soy sauce; if it's thick enough to coat the inside of the bottle, it's dark soy sauce.

Mushroom soy sauce, available in all Asian markets, is dark soy that has been soaked with dried mushrooms for an even deeper, earthier taste.

Chinese thick condiments

Here's a little bit of Chinese extravagance, a way to thicken the sauce somewhat. Consider this a basic list:

Chinese bean sauce—the mother of all Chinese condiments, available hot, sweet, mild, and sugary, made from brined yellow or black soy beans and spices.

oyster sauce—made from fried oysters, boiled with soy sauce, spices, and salt until they're a thick, pasty seasoning that mellows beautifully over the heat.

hoisin sauce—a sweet, thick condiment in the bean sauce family made with soy paste, vinegar, and lots of sugar, familiar in North America as the sauce for the pancakes in various Moo Shoo dishes.

chouhee sauce—a more pungent variation of hoisin, musky and darker.

Chinese barbecue sauce—a sweet bean sauce, sometimes made with sweet potatoes, always viscous and aromatic.

plum sauce—a sweet, tart jam made from very soft plums, ginger, and loads of spices, as well as sometimes chiles for heat.

duck sauce—an orange version of plum sauce, very mild in comparison, mostly sweet, not very aromatic, and often used as an egg-roll dip in many restaurants. There is no duck in duck sauce.

A wok full of Vegetable Lo Mein

Recipes for Lo Meins

	Shrimp and Mushroom Lo Mein	Shrimp and Cabbage Lo Mein	Pork Lo Mein	Roast Pork Lo Mein
1. Cook and drain	¾ pound dried or 1 pound fresh round egg or wheat noodles, preferably Chinese noodles	¾ pound dried or 1 pound fresh round egg or wheat noodles, preferably Chinese noodles	¾ pound dried or 1 pound fresh round egg or wheat noodles, preferably Chinese noodles	¾ pound dried or 1 pound fresh round egg or wheat noodles, preferably Chinese noodles
2. Heat a wok and swirl in	1 Tbs sesame oil	1 Tbs peanut oil	1 Tbs sesame oil	1 Tbs peanut oil
3. Add and stir-fry	6 medium whole scallions, chopped 2 Tbs minced peeled fresh ginger	5 ounces shallots, thinly sliced 2 garlic cloves, minced 1 fresh serrano or jalapeño chile, stemmed, seeded, and minced	1 medium yellow onion, thinly sliced 3 garlic cloves, minced 1 Tbs minced peeled fresh ginger	4 medium whole scallions, chopped ¼ cup canned preserved Chinese vegetables 2 Tbs minced peeled fresh ginger
4. Add and stir-fry	½ pound peeled, deveined, and roughly chopped medium shrimp	½ pound frozen cold-water, baby, or salad shrimp (no need to thaw)	½ pound trimmed pork loin, cut into ¼-inch matchsticks	½ pound purchased Char Siu or Chinese roast pork, thinly sliced
5. Add and stir-fry	8 ounces white button mushrooms, cleaned and thinly sliced 1 cup canned sliced bamboo shoots	1 pound Savoy, Napa, or Chinese cabbage, cored and shredded 1 medium carrot, shredded through the large holes of a box grated	6 ounces broccoli florets 6 ounces shiitake mushrooms, stems removed and discarded, caps thinly sliced 3 ounces snow peas, thinly sliced	8 ounces broccoli florets (do not use frozen) 1 large yellow bell pepper, seeded and cut into thin matchsticks
6. Stir in and cook briefly	The cooked and drained noodles ½ cup vegetable broth 3 Tbs shaoxing (see page 374) or dry sherry 3 Tbs oyster sauce 2½ Tbs soy sauce	The cooked and drained noodles ½ cup chicken broth 3 Tbs shaoxing (see page 374) or dry sherry 3 Tbs jarred Chinese bean sauce 2½ Tbs soy sauce	The cooked and drained noodles ½ cup chicken broth 3 Tbs rice vinegar 3 Tbs hoisin sauce 2½ Tbs soy sauce	The cooked and drained noodles ½ cup chicken broth 3 Tbs shaoxing (see page 374) or dry sherry 3 Tbs Chinese barbecue sauce 2½ Tbs soy sauce

	Szechwan Lo Mein	Vegetable Lo Mein	Cantonese Beef Lo Mein	Seafood Lo Mein
1. Cook and drain	¾ pound dried or 1 pound fresh round egg or wheat noodles, preferably Chinese noodles	¾ pound dried or 1 pound fresh round egg or wheat noodles, preferably Chinese noodles	¾ pound dried or 1 pound fresh round egg or wheat noodles, preferably Chinese noodles	¾ pound dried or 1 pound fresh round egg or wheat noodles, preferably Chinese noodles
2. Heat a wok and swirl in	1 Tbs sesame oil	1 Tbs peanut oil	1 Tbs peanut oil	1 Tbs peanut oil
3. Add and stir-fry	5 medium whole scallions, chopped 2 garlic cloves, minced 6 to 10 dried Chinese red chiles (discard before serving) ¼ cup canned preserved Chinese vegetables 1 Tbs Szechwan peppercorns	6 medium whole scallions, chopped 2 garlic cloves, minced 1 Tbs finely grated lemon zest	6 medium whole scallions, chopped 3 garlic cloves, minced	4 medium whole scallions, chopped 3 Tbs canned preserved Chinese vegetables 2 Tbs minced peeled fresh ginger
4. Add and stir-fry	½ pound boneless skinless chicken thighs, chopped	Omit	½ pound trimmed beef sirloin, cut into thin strips against the grain (see page 270)	¼ pound peeled, deveined, and roughly chopped medium shrimp ¼ pound sea scallops, quartered
5. Add and stir-fry	8 ounces baby bok choy, cored and shredded 1 medium red bell pepper, seeded and diced	1 pound small Savoy, Napa, or Chinese cabbage head, cored and roughly chopped 6 ounces snow peas, thinly sliced 1 medium carrot, peeled and shredded through the large holes of a box grater	12 ounces baby bok choy, cored and roughly chopped 1 cup canned sliced water chestnuts	8 ounces bean sprouts 6 ounces cremini or white button mushrooms, cleaned and thinly sliced
6. Stir in and cook briefly	The cooked and drained noodles ½ cup chicken broth 3 Tbs rice vinegar 1½ Tbs oyster sauce 1½ Tbs jarred Chinese hot bean sauce 2½ Tbs soy sauce	The cooked and drained noodles ½ cup vegetable broth 3 Tbs rice vinegar 3 Tbs jarred Chinese plum sauce 2½ Tbs soy sauce	The cooked and drained noodles ½ cup chicken broth 3 Tbs shaoxing (see page 374) or dry sherry 3 Tbs jarred Chinese plum sauce 2½ Tbs soy sauce	The cooked and drained noodles ½ cup vegetable broth 3 Tbs shaoxing (see page 374) or dry sherry 3 Tbs oyster sauce 2½ Tbs soy sauce

Classic Macaroni and Cheese

Macaroni and Cheese

This is the real thing: a thickened cream sauce (technically, a béchamel—French, besh-ah-MEHL) with lots of pasta and grated cheese. But don't stop there. Try adding vegetables: shredded Brussels sprouts, frozen peas, or broccoli florets—as well as perhaps some sliced deli ham or cooked cocktail shrimp. • MAKES ABOUT 6 SERVINGS (UNLESS YOU HAVE A TEENAGER)

• **STEP 1** Preheat the oven to 350°F. Cook and drain 12 ounces dried pasta in a large pot of boiling water. Fresh pasta doesn't have the tensile strength to hold up in this dish: it will break into maddening, little threads. Use only dried pasta; almost any shape will do. Yes, elbow macaroni is customary; but Macaroni and Cheese can be made with ziti, farfalle, or even wide fettuccine noodles. Our only caveat: stay away from angel-hair pasta, orzo (rice-shaped pasta), and orecchiette (little ear-shaped pasta). And as usual when making pasta, do not salt the water.

Whole wheat pasta has better texture and certainly better nutrition. Read the label for cooking instructions; whole wheat pasta often needs to cook significantly longer than regular pasta. Gluten-free noodles are a necessary alternative for increasingly many. However, these specialty noodles are a difficult matter in this casserole: they often turn to mush when baked. To solve the problem, dramatically undercook them before adding them to the sauce.

In truth, all pasta should be undercooked. Consider it a balancing act: the pasta should not be so soft as to be instantly edible, but also not so hard that it will absorb too much of the sauce as it bakes. There should be a little tooth, a little bite—perhaps a little harder than the classic Italian marker of *al dente* (ahl DEN-tay—"to the tooth": in other words, "with some chew") but certainly not so hard as to offer any crunch on the outside of the pasta.

Once drained, do not rinse the noodles. They will come unstuck when stirred into the sauce, grabbing up more of the liquid with their starchy coating.

• **STEP 2** Make a blond roux by melting 4 tablespoons (½ stick) unsalted butter in a large saucepan and then whisking in ¼ cup all-purpose flour over medium-low heat. See page 57 for an explanation of a roux in general and page 58 for a photo of a blond roux. Can you use another fat for the roux? Yes, peanut or canola oil come to mind; even untoasted almond or walnut oil adds a subtle delicacy. However, unsalted butter and grated cheese are a time-tested combo: from the same flavor family and so silky, quite indulgent.

More about Roux

A roux works because the minuscule grains of flour are separated from one another by a fine film of fat. With the grains isolated, they can each absorb more liquid than when packed together, even loosely so.

As a general rule, a blond roux thickens while a dark roux enriches. The darker the roux, the more the flour has broken into dextrins (full-fledged sugars) that have slowly caramelized over the heat. And outside of the complex chemistry of pastry making, sugar doesn't thicken as well as flour.

The sauce for macaroni and cheese begins with a classic sauce, a béchamel—first, milk is whisked into a blond roux.

Then the sauce is cooked and stired until thick, creamy, and smooth.

The cooked macaroni (or other pasta) should still have a little tooth, a little chew—it will cook fully in the oven.

• **STEP 3** Turn off the heat and whisk in 4 cups (1 quart) milk in a slow steady stream; turn the heat back to medium and whisk the mixture constantly until thickened, about 2 minutes. Use whole or low-fat milk, even 1%, but not fat-free, which doesn't have enough body without adding a copious amount of cheese later on.

Do not leave the pan unattended: whisk constantly, steadily, and efficiently until the sauce looks a little looser than gravy, about like melted premium ice cream. At the right thickness, the whisk's movement should create noticeable, rounded, little valleys or troughs (not just wavelets), which quickly, almost instantly, close up.

The sauce will thicken more quickly if the milk is not cold. Set it out on the counter and let it come to room temperature while you prep the other ingredients and make the roux. Or place it in a microwave-safe container and heat in the microwave on high for 15 or 20 seconds, just to knock off the chill. Do not boil or simmer—the milk will develop a "cooked" taste, not at all appealing in this casserole.

As for substitutions, goat's milk and soy milk will work, but avoid thin, watery rice milk. Most soy milk is sweetened; the resulting casserole will be much sweeter, what with the pasta and those crafted sugars in the roux. For the best taste, search out unsweetened soy milk at health-food stores.

And for a more sophisticated, fondue-like flavor, use 3 cups whole milk and 1 cup dry white wine or dry vermouth.

● **STEP 4** Stir in some herbs, spices, solid flavoring agents like chopped pitted olives, and/or other seasonings; 12 ounces (¾ pound or about 3 cups) shredded or crumbled cheese; the cooked and drained pasta; some salt and freshly ground black pepper; and if desired, about 2 cups cooked, prepared vegetables and/or meat. Now's your chance to customize the casserole. Start out with mustard, either 2 teaspoons dry or 1 tablespoon Dijon. Also, consider a little salty Worcestershire sauce, more of a sweet, earthy, complex taste than ordinary table salt.

Fresh herbs are better than they're dried kin, a more present, brighter taste against the cheese; use 1 or 2 minced tablespoons. Dried spices like ground cumin or grated nutmeg offer subtle undertones but should be used sparingly—perhaps ½ teaspoon. Don't be afraid of herbs and spices, just prudent. There's no reason to bury the dish with ¼ cup minced parsley, but 1 teaspoon will add little more than green flecks.

Don't forget a generous grind of black pepper. And not just pepper alone. Heat's welcome, too: red pepper flakes, a little cayenne, or even a few dashes of hot red pepper sauce.

Also, consider chopped sun-dried tomatoes, drained capers, chopped pitted black olives, or even a minced anchovy. Or try a little sweet/savory condiment like mango chutney. But remember that all these add lots of salt and there's already sodium in the cheese. Proceed judiciously.

Any meat or vegetable additions must be fully cooked and bite-sized: medium peeled and deveined shrimp, Spanish dried mild chorizo, deli ham, the meat from a rotisserie chicken, sautéed mushrooms or onions, or cooked cubed sweet potatoes. A thoroughly delicious macaroni and cheese can be made with sautéed or boiled, diced, peeled, and seeded butternut squash, frozen peas, shredded Gruyère and grated Parmigiano-Reggiano, tossed with whole wheat pasta.

However, those butternut squash cubes must first be sautéed or boiled until tender. To circumvent this extra step, use ready-to-eat vegetables: broccoli florets, shredded Brussels sprouts, or chopped baby bok choy, as well as canned or frozen products like artichoke hearts, baby corn, peas, or lima beans.

Macaroni and cheese is often made with a combination of cheeses: usually two, maybe three or four. However, the primary cheese should be semi-soft or semi-firm. Cheddar provides an all-American natural but should be paired with European cheeses like Asiago, Gruyère, Emmental, or Appenzell to avoid a too-creamy texture.

Types of Cheese

Although categorizing thousands of cheese varieties verges on the nonsensical, and a good many kinds slip between categories or change among them depending on their age and/or the process used to make them, much of the world's production can nonetheless be divided into five categories:

1. Fresh: soft mozzarella, ricotta, and cottage cheese—all are quite wet and should be used sparingly in macaroni and cheese, no more than 2 or 3 ounces, if at all.

2. Soft: goat cheese, Queso Blanco, Brie, Camembert, Gorgonzola, many blues, and most feta—all should also be used sparingly here, no more than a quarter of the total amount used.

3. Semi-soft: Havarti, Oaxaca, Muenster, Emmental (the original Swiss), Edam, Gouda, Jarlsberg, and Gruyère—all are excellent in this casserole.

4. Semi-firm: Cheddar, Cheshire, Cotija, Gloucester, Asiago, Monterey Jack, and Colby—all are pressed into molds and make up the other excellent group for this dish.

5. Hard: Parmigiano-Reggiano, aged Asiago, Pecorino, Grana Padano, and aged Gouda—all are packed in forms and aged for months, usually grated over the top of the dish but an excellent choice when mixed in moderation with softer cheeses.

The casserole's mixture is ready to go the moment the cheese starts to melt. Take the pan off the heat at once to keep any fat from falling out of suspension.

Smoked cheeses add a distinct nutty taste. But use no more than 4 ounces to prevent overwhelming the dish, making it taste like your barbecue grate. All blues, Gorgonzola to Danish, are equally overpowering; more than 3 ounces will produce an oily slick because of their high fat content.

The best macaroni and cheese often includes a little grated Parmigiano-Reggiano, a hard, aged, Italian cheese made from raw grass-fed cow's milk produced between April 1st and November 11th of any year. Grate it using a cheese plane or the small holes of a box grater. Buy small chunks, cut off larger wheels. The rind should be stamped with the cheese's name and origin.

• **STEP 5** Lightly butter a 2½- to 3-quart high-sided round casserole or baking dish, pour in the pasta mixture, and top with a little extra grated cheese, if desired. Bake until lightly browned and bubbling, about 35 minutes. The best way to butter a baking dish is to use the butter left on the wrapper once the stick has been removed. Simply run the inside of the wrapper around the inside of the dish, taking care to coat the angled seam between the side and the bottom. Make sure the sides are quite high enough to hold all the cheese and noodles. An improper baking dish will result in a badly burned or undercooked casserole.

If you like a final grating of cheese on the contents of the baking dish, consider using a hard, aged cheese. Other varieties (semi-firm, etc.) tend to brown and burn in the oven.

To make a crunchy bread crumb topping, omit the cheese grated on top of the casserole and instead mix ⅔ cup plain dried bread crumbs; 2 tablespoons unsalted butter, melted; 2 teaspoons dried herb (parsley, thyme, oregano, etc.), and ½ teaspoon salt in a small bowl. (Do not use fresh herbs; they will singe in the oven, releasing few oils.) Sprinkle this mixture over the casserole after it has baked for 10 minutes, then continue until the topping is deeply browned and the cheesy filling is bubbling through the crust, about 30 more minutes.

Once out of the oven, the casserole is best if it sits at room temperature about 10 minutes. The sauce will set up a bit and the taste of the cheese will be markedly improved.

Recipes for Macaroni and Cheese Casseroles

	Classic Macaroni and Cheese	Baked Ziti and Cheese with Ham and Peas	Four-Cheese Macaroni and Cheese	Swiss-Style Macaroni and Cheese
1. Preheat the oven; cook and drain	12 ounces dried elbow macaroni	12 ounces dried ziti	12 ounces dried elbow macaroni	12 ounces dried egg noodles
2. Whisk together over the heat	4 tablespoons (½ stick) unsalted butter ¼ cup all-purpose flour	4 tablespoons (½ stick) unsalted butter ¼ cup all-purpose flour	4 tablespoons (½ stick) unsalted butter ¼ cup all-purpose flour	4 tablespoons (½ stick) unsalted butter ¼ cup all-purpose flour
3. Whisk in	4 cups (1 quart) whole milk	4 cups (1 quart) whole milk	4 cups (1 quart) milk	4 cups (1 quart) milk
4. Stir in	2 tsp dry mustard 1 tsp celery seeds ½ tsp salt ½ tsp ground black pepper 8 ounces Cheddar, shredded 4 ounces Parmigiano-Reggiano, shredded The cooked and drained pasta	1 Tbs Dijon mustard 1 Tbs Worcestershire sauce 2 tsp minced sage 2 tsp stemmed thyme ½ tsp ground black pepper 6 ounces Cheddar, grated 6 ounces Emmental, grated The cooked and drained pasta 1 cup fresh shelled or frozen peas 4 ounces smoked deli ham, diced	1 Tbs minced rosemary 2 garlic cloves, minced ½ tsp salt ½ tsp red pepper flakes 3 ounces Pecorino, grated 3 ounces Parmigiano-Reggiano, grated 3 ounces fresh mozzarella, crumbed 3 ounces Fontina, grated The cooked and drained pasta ½ cup chopped sun-dried tomatoes	2 tsp caraway seeds 2 tsp stemmed thyme 1 tsp onion powder ½ tsp dry mustard ½ tsp salt 6 ounces Gruyère, grated 4 ounces Emmental, grated 2 ounces aged hard goat cheese (chèvre), grated The cooked and drained pasta 6 ounces cooked and drained sausage, sliced into thin rings
5. Bake	Unsalted butter for the baking dish	Unsalted butter for the baking dish Finely grated Parmigiano-Reggiano on top	Unsalted butter for the baking dish Finely grated Parmigiano-Reggiano on top	Unsalted butter for the baking dish Finely grated hard aged goat cheese on top

	Chicken and Noodle Cheese Casserole	Pasta, Cheese, and Artichoke Casserole	Macaroni and Blue Cheese	Cheese-Shop Macaroni and Cheese
1. Preheat the oven; cook and drain	12 ounces dried farfalle (bow-tie pasta)	12 ounces dried elbow ziti	12 ounces dried rigatoni	12 ounces dried elbow macaroni
2. Whisk together over the heat	4 tablespoons (½ stick) unsalted butter ¼ cup all-purpose flour	4 tablespoons (½ stick) unsalted butter ¼ cup all-purpose flour	4 tablespoons (½ stick) unsalted butter ¼ cup all-purpose flour	4 tablespoons (½ stick) unsalted butter ¼ cup all-purpose flour
3. Whisk in	4 cups (1 quart) milk	3 cups milk 1 cup dry vermouth	4 cups (1 quart) milk	3 cups milk 1 cup dry white wine
4. Stir in	1 Tbs Dijon mustard 1 Tbs minced oregano ½ tsp salt ¼ tsp hot red pepper sauce ¼ tsp garlic powder 6 ounces Gruyère, grated 6 ounces Gouda, preferably an aged Gouda, grated The cooked and drained pasta 2 cups skinless, boneless, purchased rotisserie chicken meat in cubes	3 Tbs chopped pitted black olives 2 Tbs minced chives or the green part of a scallion 1 Tbs minced oregano 6 ounces Pecorino, grated 6 ounces Havarti, grated The cooked and drained pasta 6 canned artichoke hearts packed in water, quartered	2 Tbs minced parsley 1 Tbs Worcestershire sauce ¼ tsp garlic powder Several dashes hot red pepper sauce 5 ounces Gruyère, grated 4 ounces Parmigiano-Reggiano, grated 3 ounces Gorgonzola, crumbled The cooked and drained pasta 8 ounces broccoli florets, chopped	2 tsp dry mustard 2 tsp Worcestershire sauce 2 tsp stemmed thyme ½ tsp ground black pepper 4 ounces Brie, frozen 1 hour, rind removed, and shredded 4 ounces Asiago, grated 2 ounces Camembert, frozen 1 hour, rind removed, and grated 2 ounces Parmigiano-Reggiano, grated
5. Bake	Unsalted butter for the baking dish Finely grated Gouda for the top	Unsalted butter for the baking dish Finely grated Pecorino on top	Unsalted butter for the baking dish	Unsalted butter for the baking dish Finely grated Parmigiano-Reggiano on top

Marinara

Unlike Pasta in a Cream Sauce (page 241), this is not a souped-up sauté, the noodles and sauce tossed together for a full meal. Rather, this is a basic Italian red sauce—to be tossed with cooked and drained pasta and topped with grated Parmigiano-Reggiano in serving bowls. Or fry up some Meatballs (page 187) and add them to the pot of simmering Marinara. One note: this recipe makes enough for crowds—because who doesn't want more red sauce on hand? Marinara freezes beautifully, a meal in minutes from the microwave, the heated sauce tossed with cooked pasta. • MAKES ABOUT 10 CUPS RED SAUCE

• **STEP 1** Heat 2 tablespoons fat in a large Dutch oven set over medium heat. Olive oil and unsalted butter—these are the basic choices. In truth, the best choice is a combination: 1 tablespoon olive oil and 1 tablespoon unsalted butter, a sweet/sour flavor at the sauce's base. But Pomodoro, a sauce of almost all tomatoes with only onions and garlic, is traditionally made solely with butter. Forgo various toasted oils—they are too strong; neutral oils like safflower are just not flavorful enough. That said, you can make marinara with 1 tablespoon untoasted walnut oil and 1 tablespoon unsalted butter.

A sauce made with all olive oil is lighter, brighter by far. For thoughts on olive oil in general, see page 193. Use a fragrant, cold-pressed oil with a fruity aroma, not overpowering but present. Pour a drip into your hand, let it warm up while you count to 10, and then take a taste. With most decent bottlings, you'll taste olives.

• **STEP 2** (optional): Add 6 ounces chopped, smoked and/or cured pork product or its substitute—or 6 ounces crumbled sausage meat; brown well, about 4 minutes. Not all tomato sauces include meat; many, if not most, don't. However, its addition definitely turns this sauce into a full meal. See page 18 for a list of smoked and/or cured pork products and their substitutes.

If using sausage, choose a mild Italian version; you can add heat later on with red pepper flakes. Either buy sausage meat without the casings—or buy whole sausages, slit and remove the casings, and crumble the meat into the pot. Or substitute turkey sausage meat or even seasoned textured soy protein, made to look like ground beef.

• **STEP 3** Add 1 chopped medium yellow onion or 6 to 8 ounces chopped shallots; cook, stirring often, until softened, about 3 minutes. In this technique, add the onion or shallot before anything else. In quick sautés, the onion can be added with the other veg-

Sweet Onions

Following on the heels of Vidalia onions' commercial success, there are all sorts of fancy onion varietals on the market. But remember the original concept of the Vidalia: a sweet, eating onion. There's no sense in wasting money on exotic or gourmet varietals when the thing's going to stew in the pot for over an hour. A standard yellow onion works best for long cooking.

MUSSELS MARINARA

Ladle about 2 cups marinara sauce into a large pot, bring to a simmer, add up to 4 pounds mussels, scrubbed and debearded (see page 203), cover, reduce the heat to low, and simmer until the mussels open, about 6 minutes. Discard any that do not open. The same technique can be used for scrubbed clams; simmer until opened, about 10 minutes.

etables (compare Boneless Skinless Chicken Breasts with a Pan Sauce, page 39). But in Marinara, the onion or shallot needs time to soften and sweeten. By the end, it should have almost melted; giving it a head-start aids that process.

To chop an onion, first peel off the outer, papery layer, then slice it in half through its root. Lay one half cut side down on a cutting board with the root end pointing away from you. With the knife's tip facing the root, make parallel, ½-inch slices through the onion without cutting through the root. Turn the onion 90 degrees (a quarter turn) and again make parallel, ½-inch slices across the onion, thereby letting the small bits fall off and onto the cutting board. Discard the root end and repeat with the other half.

To dice an onion, follow this same technique, only making the cuts ¼ inch apart in all cases; to roughly chop an onion, about 1 inch apart. To mince, finely chop.

Storing Chopped Onion

If you're cutting up an onion, consider doing two or three. Once chopped, freeze the others in a small, sealable plastic bag for up to 3 months; use them straight from the freezer the next time you need chopped onion in these proportions: ½ cup for a small onion, 1 cup for a medium, and 1½ to 2 cups for a large.

However, the same cannot be done for shallots; chopped, they do not freeze well, losing some of that aromatic, sweet, garlicky taste and coming out of the freezer tasting about like an onion but more bitter. Leeks are even more problematic: they freeze well, but must first be washed. The extra moisture dopes their cells, which swell considerably; freezing them then turns them into mush when they thaw, even directly over the heat. To skip their washing and freeze them full of grit is simply not an option.

TO CHOP, DICE, OR MINCE AN ONION: First, peel off the onion's papery, outer hull.

Then slice the onion in half through its root.

With the onion placed cut side down on your work surface, make parallel cuts through the onion, the knife's tip pointed toward the root.

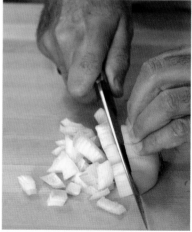

Finally, slice down perpendicular to these cuts to release the little cubes. Some may need to be broken apart by hand.

- **STEP 4** Stir in a couple minced garlic cloves and if desired, up to 4 cups chopped vegetables; cook, stirring often, until softened, about 4 minutes. Garlic is almost always necessary for a successful red sauce. You needn't add anything else, but vegetables make a lovely counterpoint in a red sauce. Conside these the basics:

> **bell peppers,** seeded and chopped
> **fava beans,** shelled, parboiled, and peeled
> **fennel bulbs,** trimmed and chopped
> **hot peppers like cubanels or Italian frying peppers,** seeded and chopped
> **lima beans,** frozen
> **mushrooms,** cleaned and sliced
> **peas,** fresh shelled or frozen

Steer clear of vegetables that turn mushy in long stewing: broccoli, cauliflower, green beans, and asparagus. Zucchini and squash are fine if chopped—although they'll add lots of moisture and the sauce will need to simmer longer to reduce properly. Remember this: it's *up to* 4 cups chopped vegetables. Add 1 or 2 cups for a light taste. Whatever you do, stay away from roots, tubers, or winter squash. These add too much starch, an unwelcome interloper in a bright tomato sauce.

Although you will add canned tomatoes in step 7, there's no reason not to add several chopped, seeded plum or Roma tomatoes now, particularly if you've omitted the smoked or cured product in step 2 and/or any other vegetable in this step. Fresh tomatoes will give the sauce a brighter, sweeter taste.

Seed fresh tomatoes so their taste permeates the sauce without a lot of added liquid. To seed tomatoes, cut them into quarters, then gently but firmly squeeze them cut side down over the sink, forcing out the seeds and pulp. If you want the fibers intact, less squished, hold the tomato over the sink and run your finger into the chambers to release the seeds and pulp.

- **STEP 5** Warm a fair amount of minced herbs or a little bit of dried spices in the pot until aromatic. For a red sauce, the classics are minced basil, oregano, rosemary, thyme, sage, and/or parsley, a total amount between 3 and 6 tablespoons—as well as very small amounts of celery seeds, fennel seeds, and/or grated nutmeg. Canned tomatoes have a sour edge; they're best balanced by fairly sweet herbs, rather than more bitter or savory ones like dill, chervil, or sage.

But even though tomatoes add acid to the pot, consider also adding finely grated lemon zest, zip without bitterness. Avoid tarragon (too French), star anise (too Asian),

RAGÙ

This classic Italian meat sauce can be made the same way as a standard red sauce—with these exceptions. In step 2, add 6 ounces lean ground beef, 4 ounces ground pork, and 1 cup milk; then raise the heat to high, and simmer until almost all the liquid has been absorbed. In step 4, use only thinly sliced carrots and celery; in step 5, add some basic Italian herbs (rosemary, oregano, thyme, and maybe fennel seeds). Pour in ½ cup dry white wine in step 6. Add the crushed tomatoes but omit the broth and simmer very slowly, just the barest bubble, partially covered, until quite thick, about 1 hour.

Utterly optional but often indispensable, a little vinegar or lemon juice will brighten up a pot of marinara or most of its variants, provided they don't contain cream or milk.

and cloves or cinnamon (too weird). Curry blends, chili powder, and other spice mixtures also have no place in this sauce.

In the end, consider 3 tablespoons of a single minced herb or up to 6 tablespoons of various herbs as your base, then add a dried spice if you want to, particularly red pepper flakes if you haven't added a fresh chile in step 4.

• **STEP 6** **Pour in ½ cup wine or cream; bring to a simmer, scraping up any browned bits on the pot's bottom.** White wine or dry vermouth produces a delicate, fruit-laced tomato sauce. Other dry, fortified wines—dry Marsala, dry Madeira, and the like—offer sophisticated accents, far from traditional and certainly not for the tame of culinary spirit. Red wine, not often used, adds a sweet earthiness, particularly if there's any meat in the sauce. But steer clear of port and other sweet wines, all a bad match for tomatoes.

Cream should be added now if you're making, say, a vodka sauce (see step 7). However, although the wine should come to a simmer, don't let cream reduce before passing on to the next step.

• **STEP 7** **Add about 6½ cups canned crushed tomatoes with their juice and 1 cup broth; bring to a simmer, cover, reduce the heat to low and simmer slowly for 30 minutes. Uncover, stir well, and simmer until slightly thickened and the vegetables are meltingly tender, about 15 more minutes; then stir in salt and freshly ground black pepper to taste.** Marinara—literally, "as the sailor's wives"—was at its origin most likely made with fresh tomatoes, which are pulpy enough to thicken the sauce without a roux (see page 57), beurre manié (see page 209), cornstarch, flour, or any of the other likely candidates. The only trick? Time. These tomatoes must break down considerably.

Which is why canned crushed tomatoes are a time-saver. They're already partly broken down; there's no need to simmer the sauce for hours. However, just like canned whole tomatoes or diced tomatoes, they vary widely in quality. They should not be seasoned (many cannings add basil to make up for poor-quality tomatoes), nor should they be pumped with salt.

Broth is added with the tomatoes because it will concentrate and focus the flavors as it, too, reduces. Plus, it will help those fleshy bits of the tomatoes break down further as more liquid simmers around them. Chicken or vegetable broth is often used, although beef broth will make a hearty, wintry sauce. Even fish stock is a fine addition if a sauce is to be paired with shrimp, mussels, clams, and the like. Here's where you'd add liquor if you were making a vodka sauce: use ½ cup broth and ½ cup vodka.

The sauce should bubble at the slightest rate, just a few gurgles at a time, certainly within the realm of counting them as they appear.

Finally, a little secret to brightening tomato sauce: if you haven't used cream or lemon zest, stir in *up to* 2 tablespoons wine vinegar, balsamic vinegar, or lemon juice with the added salt. The taste will be remarkably fresher, more summery.

Classic Pasta Sauce on spaghetti

Recipes for Marinara Sauces

	Classic Pasta Sauce	Fra Diavolo	Vodka Sauce	Red Sauce with Mushrooms
1. Heat	1 Tbs olive oil 1 Tbs unsalted butter	2 Tbs olive oil	1 Tbs olive oil 1 Tbs unsalted butter	1 Tbs olive oil 1 Tbs unsalted butter
2. (optional) Brown	6 ounces sweet Italian sausage meat, crumbled	Omit	Omit	6 ounces bacon, chopped
3. Add and cook	1 medium yellow onion, chopped	1 medium yellow onion, chopped	1 medium yellow onion, chopped	1 medium yellow onion, chopped
4. Stir in and cook	2 garlic cloves, minced	4 garlic cloves, minced	1 garlic clove, minced	1 garlic clove, minced 4 cups sliced mushrooms
5. Add and warm	1 Tbs minced basil 1 Tbs minced oregano 2 tsp minced rosemary 2 tsp fennel seeds	1 Tbs minced oregano 1 Tbs stemmed thyme 2 tsp red pepper flakes	2 Tbs minced parsley 1 Tbs stemmed thyme ¼ tsp grated nutmeg	1 Tbs minced oregano 2 tsp celery seeds ½ tsp grated nutmeg ¼ tsp red pepper flakes
6. Pour in	½ cup dry vermouth	½ cup dry white wine	½ cup heavy or whipping cream	½ cup dry vermouth
7. Add, cover, and simmer slowly; then uncover, thicken, and season	6½ cups canned crushed tomatoes 1 cup chicken broth Salt and pepper to taste	6½ cups canned crushed tomatoes 1 cup chicken broth Salt and pepper to taste	6½ cups canned crushed tomatoes ½ cup vegetable broth ½ cup vodka Salt and pepper to taste	6½ cups canned crushed tomatoes 1 cup chicken broth Salt and pepper to taste

	Puttanesca	Garden Pasta Sauce	Tuscan Red Sauce	Sauce Piquante (a Cajun sauce for shrimp or seafood)
1. Heat	2 Tbs olive oil	2 Tbs olive oil	1 Tbs olive oil 1 Tbs unsalted butter	2 Tbs olive oil
2. (optional) Brown	Omit	Omit	Omit	6 ounces bacon, chopped
3. Add and cook	1 medium yellow onion, chopped	4 ounces shallots, chopped	1 medium yellow onion, chopped	1 medium yellow onion, chopped
4. Stir in and cook	2 garlic cloves, minced ¼ cup chopped pitted black olives 2 Tbs drained capers 4 chopped anchovy fillets	2 garlic cloves, minced 2 plum or Roma tomatoes, seeded and chopped 1 medium fennel bulb, trimmed and chopped 1 cup fresh shelled or frozen peas	3 garlic cloves, minced 4 plum or Roma tomatoes, seeded and chopped 2 celery ribs, thinly sliced 1 medium carrot, thinly sliced	2 garlic cloves, minced 1 large green bell pepper, seeded and chopped 3 celery ribs, thinly sliced
5. Add and warm	3 Tbs minced basil 2 tsp fennel seeds ½ tsp red pepper flakes	2 Tbs minced basil 2 Tbs minced parsley 1 Tbs minced marjoram	3 Tbs minced basil 2 Tbs minced parsley 1 tsp red pepper flakes	2 Tbs minced chives or the green part of a scallion 1 Tbs minced oregano 1 tsp fennel seeds Up to 2 tsp red pepper flakes
6. Pour in	½ cup dry white wine	½ cup dry vermouth	½ cup red wine	½ cup dry white wine
7. Add, cover, and simmer slowly; then uncover, thicken, and season	6½ cups canned crushed tomatoes 1 cup chicken broth Salt and pepper to taste	6½ cups canned crushed tomatoes 1 cup vegetable broth Salt and pepper to taste	6½ cups canned crushed tomatoes 1 cup chicken broth Salt and pepper to taste	6½ cups canned crushed tomatoes 1 cup bottled clam juice Salt and pepper to taste

Classic Italian Meatballs have been browned and are now ready to simmer in a pot of tomato sauce

Meatballs

They come in all varieties: Turkish *köfte* to Mexican *albóndigas,* Italian-American meatballs to Danish *frikadeller*. But they all make a lovely dinner: dropped in soup, served over buttered noodles, offered on their own, or ladled into Marinara (page 179). • MAKES 14 TO 20 MEATBALLS

• **STEP 1** Soak 2 cups torn-up crustless bread in 1 cup milk, broth, wine, or an enhanced version of any in a small bowl for 30 minutes; drain and gently squeeze out the excess moisture. As with Burgers (page 63), meatballs need added moisture to improve their texture. To that end, choose any bread you like: wheat, oatmeal, baguette, or even rye for a "deli" taste. Just keep in mind that the better the bread, the better the meatball. Do not use whipped bread, it's too gummy and fatty. Instead, choose a bread with texture or crumb: 7-grain, country white, or some version of a French or Italian bread. It should not be rock-stale; you want moisture, after all. Do not substitute bread crumbs, fresh or dried.

Although milk (regular, low-fat, or even fat-free) is traditional the world over, the soaking liquid can fall in a wide range, divided into two camps:

1. Liquids used straight, without additions. Cow's milk, yes; but also consider goat's milk, condensed milk, or even half-and-half. Or forgo the dairy altogether and soak the bread in broth, beer, or wine, red or white.
2. Liquids used as enhancements to milk, broth, or wine. Dry fortified wines—vermouth, sherry, etc.—can be used in small amounts, say 14 tablespoons milk and 2 tablespoons dry sherry. (There are 16 tablespoons in 1 cup. But the easiest way to make these odd-increment additions is to pour 2 tablespoons of some chosen liquid in a 1-cup measuring cup, then fill with milk, wine, or what you have.) Cream or coconut milk can also be up to ¼ cup of the total liquid used. Or what about a 75/25 mix of broth and a liquor like brandy or rum? Or a 50/25/25 mix of broth, soy sauce, and shaoxing (page 374) for an Asian meatball? Or a 50/50 combo of apple cider or tomato juice with milk or broth? Don't use sweetened juices, flavored liquids, maple syrup, or soft drinks—although there is a tradition in some parts of the South of using 7-Up® for meatballs.

The lightest meatballs begin with cubed bread, first soaked in liquid, then gently squeezed dry.

After 30 minutes, wash your hands and pick up the bread. Squeeze gently, just to remove the excess moisture. You'll most likely get out about ⅓ cup liquid. Don't make a hard baseball. The bread should be quite damp, just not sopping wet—damp enough to adhere into a loose ball when so formed.

• **STEP 2** Heat 1 tablespoon fat in a medium skillet over medium heat. Almost any will do: walnut, sesame, peanut, or canola oil, as well as unsalted butter. Skip toasted nut or seed oils as well as most animal fats, which are all quite strong in flavor. And remember that you should probably use the same fat here that you will later use to brown the meatballs in step 6.

• **STEP 3** Add 1 cup diced aromatics or a modified mirepoix (see page 57); cook until softened, stirring often; and then set aside off the heat to cool for 15 minutes. The aromatics should be diced very small, until they're about the same size as the grains of ground meat. Start with onion, shallots, leek, or finely minced scallions. Then build out with garlic, ginger, bell pepper, fresh chile, fennel, or celery.

Avoid carrots—too sweet and hard—as well as most roots. Still, a very finely diced sweet potato adds a nice touch, but the pieces must be quite small, about ⅛ inch—or better yet, grated through the large holes of a box grater. At the end of this step, everything in the skillet should be ready to eat. If the leek is chewy, it's not ready.

Cool the ingredients before adding them in the next step. Hot, they'll brown the meat and scramble the egg.

• **STEP 4** Mix the contents of the skillet, the soaked bread, and 1½ pounds ground meat or poultry in a large bowl. Choose from

> **ground beef**
> **ground pork**
> **ground veal**
> **ground buffalo**
> **ground venison**
> **ground ostrich**
> **ground lamb**
> **ground turkey**
> **or ground chicken**

The best Italian meatballs are made with a combination: beef and veal, pork and veal, or even all three: beef, pork, and veal. Ground lamb can be quite strong, even gamy, and is often best if cut with a little ground veal or beef.

Since the bread's been soaked, feel free to buy lean ground beef, 93% or even 95% lean. That said, 80% lean ground beef will yield more luxurious (if less healthful) meatballs. Most of that fat will not be rendered off, as it is with burgers; instead, the bread will soak it up, enriching the meatballs considerably. If you choose to go with fattier ground meat, the meatballs are probably best served on their own. Dropped in a soup or sauce, they can leave an oily slick.

And what of using ground fish? Yes, meatballs can be made with ground tuna or salmon, but the texture will be depressingly pasty, even gummy. If you go this route, these "meatballs" should be steamed or boiled, not fried.

• **STEP 5** Mix in 1 large egg, well beaten; about 2 tablespoons minced herbs or about 1 teaspoon dried spices; salt and freshly ground black pepper to taste; and perhaps one or two other flavoring agents. Dampen your hands and form the mixture into balls using about 3 tablespoons at a time. After the egg, don't get overly ornate with the herbs and spices: one of either will do, perhaps two that are good complements: rosemary or oregano and grated lemon zest, tarragon or parsley and grated nutmeg, mint and ground coriander.

As for the salt and pepper, consider the outer limit 1 teaspoon of each—although that much pepper will certainly spice up the meatballs. Plan on salting them again when served.

For the other flavorings, all optional, consider these your choices and their limits:

> **cheese,** finely crumbled or grated: ¾ cup
> **minced dried fruit:** ⅓ cup
> **mashed cooked potatoes, sweet potatoes, mashed roots, or cooked winter squash:** ¼ to ⅓ cup
> **ground nuts and peanuts:** ¼ cup
> **minced firm flavoring agents like sun-dried tomatoes, pitted olives, or drained capers:** 2 tablespoons
> **pasty condiments like barbecue sauce, ketchup, prepared mustard, hoisin sauce, and Chinese bean sauce:** 1½ tablespoons

Form meatballs by hand, rolling the mixture between your hands, compacting it without squeezing out any moisture.

One or at most two will add a nice spark, but there's no reason to add any—and certainly no reason to add them to their limit. Rather, think through the pairings you might use, all the ingredients in this step forming a single canvas: grated feta with sun-dried tomatoes and dill or perhaps minced dried cranberries with sage and nutmeg.

• **STEP 6** Heat 2 tablespoons fat in a large skillet; add as many meatballs as will comfortably fit, working in batches as necessary; and brown on all sides, turning occasionally, about 10 minutes. Meatballs should be browned before they're added to a sauce—or certainly before they're cooked off on their own. In general, use the same fat here that you used in the step 2—although unsalted butter there and olive oil here are a classic pairing. If you're making an Asian-inspired meatball, try peanut oil there and sesame oil here.

Heat the oil until you get a good sizzle from a droplet of water, then add the meatballs and leave them untouched for perhaps 2 minutes. Use a spatula to turn them, not tongs. Brown the other side, then work your way around the circumference, browning those edges, too.

• **STEP 7** Either add ¼ cup wine or broth, cover the skillet, reduce the heat to medium-low, and cook until an instant-read meat thermometer inserted into the center of one ball registers 165°F, about 5 minutes; or drop the meatballs into a simmering sauce or soup to cook thoroughly. Once browned, the meatballs can be finished off in the pan with some broth or wine; or they can then be transferred to another sauce, like a pot of Marinara (page 179) to make spaghetti and meatballs. The longer they stew, the softer their texture will become. Within limits, of course. They can start to fall apart if you simmer them over an hour.

If you'd like to make them ahead and refrigerate them for the next day or freeze them for several months, cook the meatballs thoroughly, not partially. Add the broth and wine and steam them as directed, then place in a sealable container in the refrigerator or freezer for storage. Reheat them in a little oil in a preheated skillet—or drop them straight from the freezer into a pot of simmering tomato sauce.

Recipes for Meatballs

	Classic Italian Meatballs	Walnut Meatballs	Köfte (Turkish Meatballs)	Turkey Meatballs
1. Soak	2 cups torn-up crustless Italian white bread 1 cup milk	2 cups torn-up crustless whole wheat or whole-grain bread 1 cup red wine	2 cups torn-up crustless whole wheat or whole-grain bread 1 cup milk	2 cups torn-up crustless country white bread 1 cup dry vermouth
2. Heat	1 Tbs unsalted butter	1 Tbs unsalted butter	1 Tbs canola oil	1 Tbs olive oil
3. Add, cook, and cool	2 ounces shallots, minced ½ cup minced fennel	3 ounces shallots, minced	1 medium yellow onion, diced 2 garlic cloves, minced	1 small yellow onion, diced 2 celery ribs, halved lengthwise and thinly sliced
4. Mix with	The soaked bread ½ pound ground beef ½ pound ground pork ½ pound ground veal	The soaked bread 1 pound ground buffalo ½ pound ground pork	The soaked bread 1 pound ground lamb ½ pound ground beef	The soaked bread 1½ pounds ground turkey
5. Mix in and form into balls	1 large egg, well beaten 1 Tbs minced oregano 1 Tbs minced rosemary 1 tsp salt 1 tsp ground black pepper 2 Tbs minced sun-dried tomatoes	1 large egg, well beaten ¼ cup ground walnuts 1 tsp salt ½ tsp ground cinnamon ½ tsp ground black pepper ¼ tsp ground allspice	1 large egg, well beaten 1 Tbs minced mint 2 tsp turmeric 1 tsp ground coriander 1 tsp salt	1 large egg, well beaten 2 Tbs minced sage 1 tsp salt ½ tsp ground black pepper ¼ tsp grated nutmeg ⅓ cup minced dried cranberries
6. Heat and brown the meatballs	2 Tbs olive oil	2 Tbs canola oil	2 Tbs canola oil	2 Tbs olive oil
7. Finish off with	¼ cup dry Marsala or a simmering pot of tomato sauce	¼ cup white wine or a simmering pot of vegetable soup or beef broth	¼ cup beef broth	¼ cup red wine

	Greek-Inspired Meatballs	Danish Frikadeller	Chinese-Style Meatballs	Romanian Chiftele
1. Soak	2 cups torn-up crustless country white bread 1 cup milk	2 cups torn-up crustless country white bread 1 cup milk	2 cups torn-up crustless country white bread ¾ cup shaoxing (see page 374) or dry sherry ¼ cup soy sauce	2 cups torn-up crustless country white bread 1 cup milk
2. Heat	1 Tbs olive oil	1 Tbs unsalted butter	1 Tbs peanut oil	1 Tbs unsalted butter
3. Add, cook, and cool	1 small yellow onion, diced 1 celery rib, halved lengthwise and thinly sliced 2 garlic cloves, minced	1 small yellow onion, diced 1 celery rib, halved lengthwise and thinly sliced	2 whole medium scallions, minced 3 garlic cloves, minced 1 Tbs minced peeled fresh ginger	1 small yellow onion, minced 4 garlic cloves, minced
4. Mix with	The soaked bread 1 pound ground lamb ½ pound ground pork	The soaked bread 1 pound ground pork ½ pound ground veal	The soaked bread 1½ pounds ground pork	The soaked bread 1 pound ground beef ½ pound ground chicken
5. Mix in and form into balls	1 large egg, well beaten 1 Tbs minced dill ½ Tbs minced oregano ½ Tbs minced mint 1 tsp salt ¾ cup crumbled feta	1 large egg, well beaten 1 tsp salt ½ tsp ground allspice	1 large egg, well beaten 1½ Tbs hoisin or bean sauce ½ tsp salt	1 large egg, well beaten ⅓ cup mashed potatoes 2 Tbs minced parsley 1 tsp salt 1 tsp ground black pepper
6. Heat and brown the meatballs	2 Tbs olive oil	2 Tbs unsalted butter	2 Tbs sesame oil	2 Tbs olive oil
7. Finish off with	¼ cup white wine or a simmering pot of tomato sauce	¼ cup unsweetened apple cider	¼ cup shaoxing (see page 374) or dry sherry—or a large pot of vegetable–Chinese noodle soup	¼ cup beef broth

Mediterranean Fish Stew

Although there are differences aplenty, most Mediterranean fish stews are made with a similar technique: an herb and tomato broth for the fish, topped with one of several aromatic thickeners that varies them considerably and extravagantly.

• MAKES 4 TO 6 SERVINGS

• **STEP 1** Heat 3 tablespoons olive oil in a large Dutch oven over medium heat. Although the nostalgia of olive oil from Italy is pronounced and enticing, all that shimmers isn't green. Over 40% of the world's production comes from Spain, most of it shipped to Italy where it is then repackaged with the words "imported from Italy" stamped on the bottle. Yes, it traveled here from Italy; but it originally came from Spain—or perhaps Greece where 60% of the arable land is given over to olive trees, yielding another 20% or so of the world's production.

Globally, there are at least three grades of olive oil: extra virgin, virgin, *lampante* (meaning, literally, "fit for lamps," too acidic for human consumption), and then others from pomace olives, many of which have the oil extracted via chemical additives, sometimes even industrial solvents, but all sold for human consumption.

Since extra virgin is so delicate and aromatic, virgin olive oil is best suited to this fresh fish stew. But that said, the difference between extra virgin and virgin oil is slight and has little to do with production methods. Yes, it's common parlance to say that extra virgin olive oil is made only from pressed olives, even "cold-pressed olives," no chemicals or heat used in the process. But these strictures have nothing to do with the definitions from the International Olive Oil Council (the IOOC). Their labeling guidelines are only concerned with the difference in the acid content between the two varieties (not more than 0.8 gram oleic acid per 100 grams for extra virgin and not more than 2.0 grams per 100 grams for virgin olive oil). Nothing is stated here about extraction—including the use of industrial solvents. Thus, extra virgin olive oil may indeed have had heat or chemicals applied to it during its production.

And all that said, these are all international standards. In Canada, Australia, and other countries, they apply—but not in the United States, the only olive oil producing and consuming country that does not belong to the IOOC. Other countries (Italy, Spain) have their own independent councils or oversight boards that work in conjunction with the IOOC. But the United States relies solely on the USDA, which recognizes only four varieties of olive oil: fancy, choice, standard, and substandard. In other words, the label "extra virgin" has no legal force in the United States and is often mere window-dressing on oils

Almost all Mediterranean fish stews begin with a balanced mélange of vegetables: here, clockwise from bottom, shallots (sweet), Yukon Gold potatoes (savory), and chiles (spicy).

Before any broth is added, the diced tomatoes must break down, almost like a sauce. Note that the potatoes are in small cubes so they'll cook quickly.

dumped from other countries. Recently, a California trade association petitioned the USDA to change its 1948 standards to conform with international practices. We can only hope that the United States begins to comply and that savvy consumers demand that the quality strictures become more meaningful.

For now, beware of what you're buying. Look for words that detail the manufacturing process like "from hand-picked olives" (meaning that the fruit was not mechanically picked and probably not left on the tree too long so the olives come off more easily but are also partially fermented) and "first cold pressed" (meaning that the olives were not subjected to heat and chemicals). Beware of labels that claim the oil is "from refined olives." The taste has been chemically modified to produce the bottled oil: the fragrance may well be fake.

One final note: so-called "light" olive oil is simply a second, third, or further extraction of the oil from the already-pressed olives, sometimes via chemicals and heat. It's light in taste, not in calories. All olive oil, regardless of grade, has about 120 calories per tablespoon.

• **STEP 2** Add about 3 cups chopped, diced, minced, or prepared vegetables; cook, stirring often, until somewhat softened. Choose one item each from these three categories, stated in terms of decreasing volume from one category to another, not within the categories themselves:

1. Sweet aromatics
   diced onions
   diced shallots
   thinly sliced white and pale green parts of a leek (halved lengthwise and washed carefully to remove any sand)
   peeled pearl onions or frozen pearl onions

2. Savory aromatics and vegetables
   thinly sliced celery
   trimmed and sliced fennel
   seeded and diced bell pepper
   peeled and diced potatoes
   chopped tomatillos
   thinly sliced carrots
   peeled and diced celeriac
   peeled and cubed eggplant
   finely chopped zucchini
   chopped summer squash

3. Spicy accents
    minced garlic
    minced peeled fresh ginger
    seeded and minced fresh chiles

For example, use 2 cups diced onion, 1 cup finely chopped zucchini, and a minced garlic clove or two. Or use 6 ounces diced shallots, 1 trimmed and thinly sliced small fennel bulb, and 1 seeded minced fresh serrano. There will be enough fat in the pan to keep the garlic, ginger, or chile from singeing if you stir almost constantly.

• **STEP 3** Add 2 cups diced fresh tomatoes as well as some minced fresh herbs, spices, and/or chopped pitted olives or drained capers. Cook until the tomatoes begin to break down, stirring often, about 6 minutes. In equivalencies, 2 cups diced fresh tomatoes comes out to about 8 Roma or plum tomatoes or 3 large globe tomatoes. For a fresh taste, try chopped cherry tomatoes; you'll need about 30. Don't seed the tomatoes. Those juicy pockets will add necessary liquid.

Why not use canned tomatoes in this stew? You're looking for a fresh taste; canned tomatoes are often more sour than their fresh kin. Plus, canned tomatoes are too pulpy; they'll thicken the broth, rather than lighten it.

In general, limit your selection of herbs and spices to no more than 2 tablespoons in total, with the major amount weighted heavily toward the fresh herbs. Also consider having more minced herbs on hand to sprinkle over the finished stew in the bowls.

As a fit fit for fish, both olives and capers add a Mediterranean touch—but not both together: too salty and sour. Try ¼ cup chopped pitted olives or no more than 1½ tablespoons drained capers.

• **STEP 4** Pour in 6 cups broth or an enhanced broth and bring to a simmer; cover, reduce the heat to low, and simmer slowly until the vegetables are meltingly tender, between 20 and 50 minutes, depending on whether you've used hard roots or softer aromatics. Any broth for Mediterranean Fish Soup can be enhanced with wine, dry vermouth, or dry sherry. Steer clear of juices, which become too sweet, and beer, too heavy. As a general rule, use up to 1½ cups wine in the mix so that the broth carries the flavors forward without too much acid. There are already lots of tomatoes, after all.

If you want to twist the stew toward Brazil (like Vatapa, a national favorite), the Caribbean, or Southeast Asia, consider up to

FISH BROTH

If Voltaire had thought about stews, his best-of-all-possible worlds would surely have included a high-quality, ready-to-use fish broth. It's still a dream. As a good substitute, look for fish "demi-glace" in the freezer case of high-end supermarkets. Follow the package directions to dilute it to the right proportions. Bottled clam juice, the usual substitute, is quite salty and fishy. A better substitute is a 50/50 mix of clam juice and vegetable broth, lighter and more aromatic.

Of course, the best option is to make your own fish stock. Freeze all the shrimp shells you ever peel, any crab bodies you ever use, as well as any fish bones and heads, sealing them all in a large plastic bag and adding to it over 2 to 3 months. Once you have about 6 to 7 cups, dump the bag's contents into a large soup pot, add 2 quartered medium onions, several chopped carrots and celery ribs, as well as a couple bay leaves, some whole black peppercorns, and perhaps 2 to 4 allspice berries. Fill with water to cover everything by a depth of 2 inches, bring to a boil over high heat, cover, reduce the heat to very low, and simmer slowly for 1½ hours. Cool to room temperature, then strain into small, 1- to 2-cup containers that can be sealed and stored in the freezer for up to 6 months. Use either on its own or as an enhancement to vegetable broth.

1½ cups coconut milk as part of the total liquid. Or forgo the fish broth altogether and make a lighter soup with a good-flavored vegetable broth.

Done, the mixture should look about like a spectacular vegetable soup. The vegetables should have softened; some of them will have melted into the sauce. But don't let it reduce until it's tomato sauce. It should definitely be a soup. The fish or shrimp will stock it up and turn it into a stew.

• **STEP 5** Add about 3 pounds fish fillets, cut into 1-inch pieces, and/or prepared shellfish; simmer uncovered just until the fish is cooked through, between 5 and 10 minutes. Choose either thick-fleshed white fish fillets like halibut, hake, cod, grouper, sturgeon, or pollock; or thin-fleshed white fish fillets like red snapper, any bass, orange roughy, or any drum. But don't mix the two. The thick-fleshed fillets can take up to 8 minutes to get tender; the thin-fleshed ones, perhaps less than 5 minutes. Do not stir the stew too much at this point for fear of breaking up the fish.

Or forgo the fish altogether and use shrimp, scallops, squid, or baby octopus. Peeled and deveined shrimp shouldn't be too large—about 35 per pound, or even 50 a pound if you can find them. Sea scallops work better than bay scallops, which turn chewy quickly. Cut each sea scallop into two disks. Squid should be cut into rings, the tentacles separated but chopped into pieces or left intact if small. Baby octopus is a pain to clean; have your fishmonger do it for you.

Or mix and match fish and shellfish. If you do, use the thicker-fleshed fish like cod and halibut; they'll take about as long as the shrimp or scallops, perhaps 8 minutes. However, if you mix thin-fleshed fillets with shrimp or scallops, consider chopping the shellfish into bite-sized bits to promote even cooking times.

Or here's a much fancier presentation altogether: heat the bowls you'll use to serve the soup in a 200°F oven until fairly warm. (Make sure your dinnerware is oven-safe. Do not use bone china.) Lay one or two skinless, raw, whole thin fish fillets in each bowl, letting its warmth begin to cook them. (Do not use shellfish or thick-fleshed fillets with this method.) Then ladle the simmering stew over the fillets in the bowl and wait 5 minutes to serve. The heat of the bowls and the soup will cook the fish. Pass the thickeners in step 6 on the side so each person can add his or her own as a topping.

• **STEP 6** Season with salt and top with a finisher or a thickener when serving. Mediterranean fish stews have some sort of thickening and/or enriching agent stirred in as they're served, usually right in the individual bowls. Here are eight to choose from:

1. **Rouille** (French, roo-EE, traditional in Bouillabaisse). Process 2 whole jarred roasted red peppers, 3 quartered garlic cloves, and 1 teaspoon salt in a food processor until smooth. Add ½ cup unseasoned dried bread crumbs and process again until fairly smooth. Scrape into a bowl and stir in ½ cup olive oil in a slow, steady stream.
2. **Romesco** (Catalan, roh-MEHS-coh, traditional in many Spanish stews). Process ⅓ cup unseasoned dried bread crumbs, 1 tablespoon water, 2 seeded

and quartered fresh jalapeño chiles, 3 quartered garlic cloves, ½ cup toasted slivered almonds, ½ cup skinned toasted hazelnuts (see page 217), and 1 teaspoon salt in a food processor. Scrape into a bowl and stir in ⅓ cup olive oil in a slow, steady stream.

3. **Burrida** (Sicilian, burr-EE-dah). Process 1 cup toasted walnuts, 2 tablespoons packed parsley leaves, and 2 quartered garlic cloves in a food processor until a grainy paste. Scrape into a bowl and stir in 1 tablespoon red wine vinegar followed by ⅓ cup olive oil in a slow, steady stream.

4. **Picada** (Catalan, pee-CAH-dah, less traditional but simpler). Process 1 cup toasted slivered almonds, ¼ cup packed parsley leaves, 2 tablespoons unseasoned dried bread crumbs, 1 teaspoon salt, and 3 quartered garlic cloves in a food processor until grainy but smooth. Scrape into a bowl and stir in ⅓ cup olive oil in a very thin, steady stream until paste-like.

5. **Gremolata.** See page 33.

6. **Aioli** (Provençal, ay-OH-lee, a flavored mayonnaise). Crush 2 peeled garlic cloves into a paste with the side of a chef's knife against a cutting board; scrape into a small bowl and whisk in 2 large egg yolks, 1 teaspoon lemon juice, and 1 teaspoon salt. Whisk in ⅔ cup olive oil just a few drops at a time. Be patient. If the mixture gets too thick, like jarred mayonnaise, add a teaspoon or two of water to thin it out, then continue whisking in more olive oil.

7. **Beurre manié** (see page 209). Mix together 1 tablespoon all-purpose flour and 1 tablespoon room-temperature unsalted butter. Do not mix this into individual serving bowls; rather, drop it by tiny bits into the simmering soup, stirring each addition until fully incorporated and slightly thickened.

8. **Croutons.** Heat about 3 tablespoons walnut, grapeseed, olive, or canola oil in a large skillet over medium heat. Add 1 or 2 minced garlic cloves and/or 1 tablespoon minced rosemary, oregano, parsley, or thyme. Cook until aromatic, about 30 seconds; then add 2 cups cubed, crustless day-old white, sourdough, whole wheat, or multi-grain bread. Reduce the heat to low and cook, stirring constantly, until crunchy and lightly browned. Season with salt and freshly ground black pepper. Ladle the soup over the croutons in a bowl.

To make the picada or other herbal thickener, place everything in a small food processor. . . .

Then process until still grainy but without any chunks.

Catalonian-Inspired Suquet with a picada thickener

Recipes for Mediterranean Fish Stews

	No-Fuss Bouillabaisse	Italian Zuppa di Pesce	Catalonian-Inspired Suquet	Brazilian-Inspired Vatapa
1. Heat	3 Tbs olive oil	3 Tbs olive oil	3 Tbs olive oil	3 Tbs olive oil
2. Add and cook	4 ounces shallots, diced 1 medium fennel bulb, trimmed and thinly sliced 1 garlic clove, minced	1 medium yellow onion, diced 2 celery ribs, thinly sliced 2 garlic cloves, minced	1 medium yellow onion, diced 2 medium yellow-fleshed potatoes, diced 1 serrano chile, seeded and minced	1 medium yellow onion, diced 1 medium carrot, thinly sliced 1 Tbs minced peeled fresh ginger
3. Add and cook until the tomatoes break down	2 cups diced fresh tomatoes 2 Tbs minced parsley 1 Tbs stemmed thyme 1 Tbs finely minced orange zest ½ tsp saffron 2 bay leaves (discard before serving)	2 cups diced fresh tomatoes 2 Tbs minced parsley 1 Tbs minced rosemary 1 Tbs finely minced lemon zest 2 tsp fennel seed	2 cups diced fresh tomatoes 2 Tbs minced oregano 2 Tbs chopped pitted olives ⅛ tsp saffron	2 cups diced fresh tomatoes 3 Tbs minced cilantro 1 Tbs finely minced lime zest 1 tsp red pepper flakes
4. Pour in, cover, and simmer	6 cups fish broth	4½ cups fish broth 1½ cups dry white wine	4 cups fish broth 2 cups dry white wine	4 cups fish broth 2 cups coconut milk
5. Add and simmer, uncovered	2 pounds thick-fleshed fish fillets, cut into 2-inch pieces 1 pounds medium shrimp, peeled and deveined	1 pound thick-fleshed white fish fillets, cut into 2-inch pieces 1 pound cleaned squid, cut into rings 1 pound medium shrimp, peeled and deveined	3 pounds thick-fleshed white fish fillets, cut into 2-inch pieces	3 pounds medium shrimp, peeled and deveined
6. Season and thicken or enrich	Salt to taste Rouille (see step 6 above)	Salt to taste Aioli (see step 6 above) or purchased pesto	Salt to taste Picada (see step 6 above)	Salt to taste 3 tablespoons finely ground peanuts

	Sicilian-Inspired Burrida	San Francisco–Style Cioppino	Catalan-Inspired Shrimp Stew	Provençal-Inspired Fish Stew
1. Heat	3 Tbs olive oil	3 Tbs olive oil	3 Tbs olive oil	3 Tbs olive oil
2. Add and cook	1 medium yellow onion, diced 1 yellow bell pepper, seeded and minced 2 garlic cloves, minced	1 medium yellow onion, diced 1 green bell pepper, seeded and minced 4 garlic cloves, minced	8 ounces shallots, diced 2 celery ribs, thinly sliced 3 garlic cloves, minced	1 medium yellow onion, diced 1 medium carrot, thinly sliced 6 garlic cloves, minced
3. Add and cook until the tomatoes break down	2 cups diced fresh tomatoes 2 Tbs minced oregano 2 Tbs minced rosemary ½ tsp red pepper flakes	2 cups diced fresh tomatoes 2 Tbs minced basil 1 Tbs minced oregano ½ tsp red pepper flakes 2 bay leaves (discard before serving)	2 cups diced fresh tomatoes ¼ cup chopped pitted black olives 2 Tbs minced oregano	2 cups diced fresh tomatoes 2 Tbs minced parsley 1 Tbs stemmed thyme 2 tsp celery seeds ¼ tsp saffron
4. Pour in, cover, and simmer	4½ cups fish broth 1½ cup dry Marsala	4½ cups fish broth 1½ cups red wine	4 cups fish broth 2 cups dry sherry	4½ cups fish broth 1½ cups dry white wine
5. Add and simmer, uncovered	3 pounds thick-fleshed white fish fillets, cut into 2-inch pieces	1 pound thick-fleshed white fish fillets, cut into 2-inch pieces 1 pound medium shrimp, peeled and deveined 1 pound sea scallops, cut into two disks each	3 pounds medium shrimp, peeled and deveined	3 pounds thin-fleshed white fish fillets, cut into 2-inch pieces
6. Season and thicken or enrich	Salt to taste Burrida (see step 6 above)	Salt to taste 2 Tbs tomato paste Croutons (see step 6 above)	Salt to taste Romesco (see step 6 above)	Salt to taste Rouille (see step 6 above)

Mussels

A Belgian favorite, this is the perfect dinner for a long evening that includes a good movie. As long as you don't have white carpet, just bring the pot to the coffee table with lots of crunchy bread to sop up every drop of sauce. As the first course of a larger meal, this technique will easily yield enough for 6 hearty eaters—or 8 average appetites. • MAKES 4 SERVINGS

• **STEP 1** Heat 2 tablespoons fat in a large soup pot or Dutch oven over medium heat. Be careful of fats that overpower tender mussels. Sesame or toasted nut oils are too strong, a bad match to the mussels' briny sweetness. Even the sour hint of unsalted butter can be too much, unless balanced by sweet, spring vegetables. In most cases, use canola or one of its kin; however, go for olive oil in Mediterranean preparations and peanut oil in Asian-inspired ones.

• **STEP 2** Add and cook a selection of 1 to 2 cups diced aromatics and vegetables, perhaps 3 to 4 cups. There's no reason to be obsessive about amounts: a chopped yellow onion, a few minced garlic cloves, some sliced mushrooms. The point here is to get a simple stew brewing before the mussels take a dive. The usual starters in the mix—if not in all stews—are onions, shallots, or scallions; but there's no necessity. What about a stew of 2 minced garlic cloves, some chopped apple, and diced zucchini? Or peas and diced carrots with a diced shallot for flavor? In general, use quick-cookers like summer squash, green beans, Chinese long beans, or asparagus. Avoid greens, which are impossible to eat after they wilt and stick on the shells. If you want to add tubers or roots like potatoes, parsnips, or carrots, they must be diced into small, ¼-inch cubes. Otherwise, they'll take too long to get tender.

Avoid frozen vegetables: these, by and large, turn to mush in a stew. That said, frozen lima beans or frozen shelled edamame (soybeans) would make an interesting addition with some chopped ginger, a little soy sauce, and some broth mixed with shaoxing (see page 374).

If you like, and it's utterly optional, you can add a little chopped cured or smoked pork product or its substitute here: bacon, pancetta, and the like (see page 18). This is just to give the dish flavor; don't add more than a couple ounces, particularly if you're using tomatoes as the base of the stew.

• **STEP 3** Toss in some fresh minced herbs, dried spices, or a spice paste; warm until aromatic, about 20 seconds, stirring constantly. One to two tablespoons is enough for minced herbs—or perhaps a common blend like chili or curry powder (see page

STEWED CLAMS OR COCKLES

Clams or cockles can be made with the same technique. Use 8 pounds of clams or 6 pounds of cockles. Neither needs to be debearded; the shells of both must be scrubbed for sand. Again, discard any that do not close when tapped; add the rest in step 5, just as you would the mussels. Exceptionally small (and tender), cockles need perhaps 3 minutes in the pot; clams, between 8 and 10 minutes depending on their size. Discard any that do not open.

113). The best herbs for mussels include tarragon, sage, thyme, or parsley, none of which will knock the delicate meat for a loop; the best dried spices include ground coriander, grated nutmeg, fennel, or celery seeds. No more than 1 teaspoon wasabi powder is an agreeable addition on its own or in combination with minced peeled fresh ginger or even pickled "sushi" ginger.

Always moderate your use of Thai or Indian curry pastes—even 1 teaspoon can turn the dish into a fiery farrago. And use far less of strong spices like ground cinnamon or cloves, maybe just ½ teaspoon. Indeed, these are often better in their "whole" or original forms: a cinnamon stick, three or four whole cloves, a couple of cardamom pods. (No whole nutmegs, however.) Any of these can then be discarded before you serve the stew without their having clouded—or overpowered—the broth. A star anise pod is a lovely addition to a mussel stew of scallions, chopped snow peas, and a little minced peeled ginger.

To debeard a mussel, pull the wiry strands up and along the shell's seam with a firm, taut pressure until they release.

• **STEP 4** Pour in 2 to 2½ cups liquid, raise the heat to high, and bring to a full simmer. Here's the way the choices shake out:

1. Broth makes a savory dish, instantly autumnal and hearty. In general, chicken or vegetable broth makes a light dish; bottled clam juice or fish stock can add heft, enhancing the mussels' natural flavor—but always "cut" fish broth and especially clam juice with wine or another liquid so it's not too strong. Avoid beef broth: too heavy.
2. Wine makes a sweeter dish, a little more aromatic, too. Although white wine seems a natural, don't avoid red wine, a stronger taste, better paired with stronger herbs and spices like rosemary or cinnamon. Of course, you can mix wine and broth, perhaps in a 50/50 ratio, or tipped toward the sweet (more wine than broth) or the savory (more broth than wine), depending on your preference.
3. Beer is an even sweeter but hearty stewing liquid. Use a 12-ounce bottle (1½ cups) and then supplement with the remaining liquid with broth or even heavy cream.
4. Heavy cream or coconut milk should be used only in moderation, mixed into broth or wine—perhaps just ½ cup of the creamy addition, certainly no more than 1 cup of the total volume.
5. Finally, a set of salty or sweet accents can be added to broth, up to ¼ cup of the total volume: soy sauce, fish sauce, pomegranate molasses, or apple cider, as well as pineapple, white grape, or cherry juice. Avoid citrus juices, which are too sour. In no instance should you ever use a sweetened juice for this technique.

If you've added some diced hard vegetables like potatoes, parsnips, or carrots, put the lid on the pot, back the heat down to low, and cook for perhaps 5 minutes, until the vegetables are almost tender. Raise the heat back to high before continuing.

• STEP 5 Stir in 4 pounds cleaned and debearded mussels, cover, reduce the heat to medium-low, and simmer until the mussels have opened, about 6 minutes. Wait for the liquid in the pot to come to a full boil, not just a light simmer. Then stir the mussels, cover, and reduce the heat to low so that the liquid simmers slowly. The heat will weaken the muscle that holds the shells closed. As the mussels open, they will release a lot of their salty liquid into the stew—thus you most likely do not need to salt the dish.

Check on the pot after 5 minutes. Stir gently to get the mussels lying on the top down into the liquid—but be careful: you can knock the meat out of opened shells.

The dish is done the moment the mussels have all opened. If any do not after 10 minutes, discard these. Some culinary gurus insist you can eat unopened, cooked mussels—but there's absolutely no reason to take a chance. Besides, some haven't opened because too much mud is clogging the shell shut.

Pour the stew into a giant bowl, break out the bread, and have a feast.

Mussels fra Diavolo

Recipes for Mussels

	Cajun–Style Stewed Mussels	Mussels Fra Diavolo	Manhattan Chowder–Style Stewed Mussels	Asian-Inspired Stewed Mussels
1. Heat	2 Tbs peanut oil	2 Tbs olive oil	2 Tbs unsalted butter	2 Tbs peanut oil
2. Add and cook	1 medium yellow onion, diced 1 medium red pepper, seeded and diced 2 celery ribs, thinly sliced	1¾ cup canned diced tomatoes 1 medium yellow onion, diced 2 garlic cloves, minced	1 large yellow onion, diced 1 medium yellow-fleshed potato, finely diced 1 celery rib, thinly sliced 1 garlic clove, minced	4 thinly sliced scallions 1 large red bell pepper, seeded and diced 3 garlic cloves, minced 2 Tbs minced peeled fresh ginger
3. Toss in and warm	2 tsp mild paprika 1 tsp minced oregano 1 tsp stemmed thyme 1 tsp fennel seeds ¼ tsp cayenne	2 Tbs minced basil 1 Tbs minced oregano ½ tsp red pepper flakes	1 Tbs stemmed thyme	1½ Tbs finely grated orange zest ½ tsp five-spice powder (see page 149)
4. Pour in and bring to a full simmer	2 cups chicken broth ½ cup beer	1 cup chicken broth 1 cup white wine	1½ cups clam juice or fish broth ½ cup canned tomato juice	1½ cups vegetable broth ½ cup dry sherry ¼ cup soy sauce
5. Stir in, cover, and simmer slowly	4 pounds debearded and cleaned mussels	4 pounds debearded and cleaned mussels	4 pounds debearded and cleaned mussels	4 pounds debearded and cleaned mussels

	Southwest Stewed Mussels	Thai Yellow Curry Mussels	Portuguese-Inspired Mussels	Mussels with Mushrooms and Cream
1. Heat	2 Tbs canola oil	2 Tbs peanut oil	2 Tbs olive oil	1 Tbs unsalted butter 1 Tbs olive oil
2. Add and cook	1 medium yellow onion, diced 1¾ cup canned diced tomatoes, drained 1 cup canned pinto beans, drained and rinsed ¼ cup canned, diced green chiles	1 large yellow onion, halved and sliced into thin rings 1 red bell pepper, seeded and diced 2 Tbs minced peeled fresh ginger 2 garlic cloves, minced 1 large lemongrass stalk, white and pale green parts only, cut into thirds and crushed (discard when serving)	1 large yellow onion, diced 1 large yellow bell pepper, seeded and diced ½ cup chopped toasted skinned hazelnuts (see page 217) 2 garlic cloves, minced	4 ounces shallots, diced 2 strips bacon, diced 2 cups thinly sliced mushrooms
3. Toss in and warm	2 Tbs chili powder 1 tsp ground cumin ¼ tsp ground cinnamon	1 Tbs packed dark brown sugar 2 tsp yellow Thai curry paste (see page 386)	2 Tbs stemmed thyme 1 Tbs mild paprika ⅛ tsp saffron	1 Tbs minced tarragon ¼ tsp grated nutmeg
4. Pour in and bring to a full simmer	1½ cups vegetable broth 1 cup beer	2 cups clam juice or fish broth ¼ cup fish sauce (see page 388) ¼ cup lime juice	1½ cups clam juice or fish broth 1 cup red wine	1½ cups white wine ½ cup heavy or whipping cream
5. Stir in, cover, and simmer slowly	4 pounds debearded and cleaned mussels	4 pounds debearded and cleaned mussels	4 pounds debearded and cleaned mussels	4 pounds debearded and cleaned mussels

New England Chowder

Not all purists agree on the ingredients of creamy chowder. Truth be told, no matter what you put in it, chowder is a rich, satisfying meal, especially on a cold day. The best way to make it? Avoid the glop of too much flour, which yields wallpaper paste masquerading as soup. Instead, take it back to its simpler roots, the cream an enhancer to the seafood. • MAKES 4 SERVINGS

• **STEP 1** Cook 2 ounces chopped, smoked and/or cured pork product or its substitute (see page 18) with 1 tablespoon unsalted butter or neutral oil in a large saucepan over low heat; once somewhat crunchy, transfer to a bowl, leaving the fat behind. Unsalted butter is the standard: a slightly sour finish against the cream to come. But if you're making a curried or Asian-style chowder, you'll want to use a neutral oil like canola so as not to compete with the other spices.

A smoky chowder made from bacon and its like or a plain one from pancetta or prosciutto? That's the real question, and it's really a matter of taste. Work over low heat so that the fat renders without the meat's browning; nothing should need deglazing off the pan's bottom. The flavors will not come from caramelization but rather from the cream and seafood combination.

Some insist that there can be no pork in chowder; others, that it's mandatory. If you too are unconvinced, skip this step, melt 2 tablespoons unsalted butter, and continue with next step.

CORN CHOWDER

Omit the fish entirely in step 5 and use about 3 cups corn kernels and about 3 cups diced vegetables in step 2. To remove the corn kernels from the cob, trim off the large end so the cob will stand up straight on your cutting board. Grasp its tip and run a chef's knife down along the cob, slicing off the kernels as close to the cob as you can and working your way around the cob, one strip at a time.

• **STEP 2** Add 3 to 4 cups diced vegetables; cook, stirring occasionally, until softened but not browned, about 10 minutes. Let there be no browning—just a gorgeous, pale yellow, especially if you've used butter. An onion, potato, and corn, weighted in about equal portions, make up the classic combination. Use a yellow-fleshed potato like a Yukon Gold, a mix of both starchiness and waxiness. A Russet will cloud and thicken the soup with unwanted starch; a red-skinned potato is just too waxy, better for roasting.

Or try other white vegetables: shallots rather than onions; cauliflower florets or canned, drained chickpeas instead of the corn or potatoes. Forgo colored roots and rhizomes like beets, carrots, and sweet potatoes in favor of pale but aromatic vegetables like turnips, rutabagas, and parsnips, all substitutes for the potato. This is white food, after all.

Still, there's no reason to stand on ceremony. Trimmed and chopped fennel, thinly sliced celery, frozen peas, or a seeded and diced green bell pepper—any of these would make a lovely addition or substitution, even if you lose the white canvas.

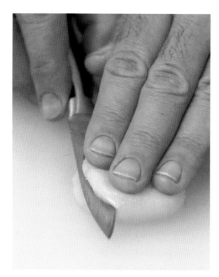

Two ways to cut a scallop for chowder: either into two disks through its middle. . . .

Or into quarters. The end result is a matter of your aesthetics.

Make sure everything's diced small so it cooks quickly—and so you can get several vegetables on a spoon at one time.

• **STEP 3** Toss in some herbs and perhaps a bay leaf; cook until aromatic, about 20 seconds. One or two leafy herbs is sufficient as well as a bay leaf. Avoid dried spices, most of which are too piquant. Fresh herbs will definitely dot the white canvas—although they will get painted somewhat white as the soup cooks. Still, use them generously—perhaps 2 minced tablespoons, maybe even more.

• **STEP 4** Raise the heat to medium-high and pour in 4 cups broth, wine, and/or milk; bring to a simmer, reduce the heat to low, and cook until the vegetables are meltingly tender, stirring occasionally, about 20 minutes. Once again, think clean and simple: chicken, fish, or vegetable broth, white wine or dry vermouth, and/or whole milk. Avoid red wine, beef broth, other dry fortified wines, or liquids that will color the soup.

Still, a combination is best, weighted toward the broth, with wine or milk as the accents: 3 cups fish broth and 1 cup dry white wine; or 2½ cups chicken broth and 1½ cups whole milk. For an even creamier chowder, consider 2 cups white wine and 2 cups whole milk. One caveat: if you're going to finish off the soup with coconut milk, making an Asian-inspired dish, keep the cow's milk out of this step, using here only broth and wine.

• **STEP 5** Stir in 5 to 7 cups chopped fish and/or shellfish, the frizzled pork product, and ½ to 1 cup cream or a creamy enricher; raise the heat to medium and simmer uncovered for 5 minutes, stirring often—then season with salt and pepper to taste. Now add the fish or shellfish. Hake, crab, haddock, lobster, cod, scallops, or shucked oysters each make a rich, luscious soup—as would a combination: crab and hake, lobster and cod. Shrimp are fine as well, despite their pink hue; but no salmon, no tuna.

Five to seven cups shellfish or fish is, of course, an impossible measure at the grocery store. Figure on about 3 pounds shell-on medium shrimp, perhaps 2½ pounds fish. There's no reason to be exact—a well-stocked pot is a delight. As with friends, more within reason is better.

Clams are often used canned—and in this soup, it's not a bad quick-fix. But also search out frozen, chopped clams, sometimes available at high-end markets.

Still, nothing beats freshly steamed clams or mussels—although you'll need to prepare them before you start the soup. Put about 1 cup dry white wine in a very large pot or a Dutch oven and bring to a boil over high heat. Add 5 or 6 pounds cleaned clams or cleaned and debearded mussels (see page 203), cover, reduce the heat to low, and simmer until opened, about 8 minutes for large clams, or 5 minutes for smaller clams or mussels. Drain the pot in a colander over the sink—but don't waste the juice in the pot. Catch it in a small saucepan, then boil it down over high heat to a glaze, about ¼ cup. Take the clam or mussel meat out of the shells, discard them, chop the meat, and stir it along with this boiled-down wine mixture into the chowder at this point.

Or failing all that, just ask the fishmonger at a high-end market to shuck 5 to 6 pounds clams for you. They won't be cooked, should be kept well chilled, and must be used within a few hours.

Other than clams or mussels, chop any fish or shellfish into bite-sized bits—with this caveat: thin-fleshed fish fillets like turbot or snapper will break down quickly. No matter what you do, you'll end up with some fish shards. Do not stir the soup vigorously but just enough to keep any roots or bacon from sticking.

Heavy or whipping cream is the natural enricher, but also consider half-and-half, light cream, or coconut milk. Avoid milk of any variety at this stage—it should have been added earlier. Now, it will yield a watery soup.

Shellfish are quite salty, especially in combination with bacon or pancetta; so beware of adding too much salt. Perhaps no more than ½ teaspoon? If you insist on pitch-perfect aesthetics, use ground white pepper.

• **STEP 6** (optional): Reduce the heat so the soup simmers slowly. Make a beurre manié with 2 or 3 tablespoons room-temperature unsalted butter and 2 or 3 tablespoons all-purpose flour; add to the soup in 5 or 6 additions, stirring in each to incorporate before adding the next. After all the paste has been added, simmer slowly, stirring constantly, until slightly thickened, about 3 minutes. Adding a thickener is a matter of taste. If you like more body, proceed. But if you like a lighter soup, one less rich and cleaner in its taste, skip the thickening and go with the soup as it stands.

A *beurre manié* (French, burr mahn-YAY, "kneaded butter") is a classic thickener made from equal parts butter and flour. The unsalted butter must be quite soft, left out on the counter for several

To remove the lobster meat from its tail, cut through the thinner, bottom section of the shell with kitchen shears before pulling the meat free from the feathery tail sections.

hours—but not melted. If melted, the floury bits will not be coated correctly and may not fully dissolve in the soup, resulting in grainy chowder. Add the flour to the softened butter and use a rubber spatula to make a paste. Stir it into the pot in several additions—but not quickly. If you're making a fish chowder, you'll tear apart the fish.

Creamy comfort indeed: Mixed Shellfish Chowder

Recipes for New England Chowders

	Clam Chowder	Lobster Chowder	Crab Chowder	Oyster Chowder
1. Crisp and remove	1 Tbs unsalted butter 2 ounces bacon, chopped	1 Tbs unsalted butter 2 ounces pancetta, chopped	1 Tbs unsalted butter 2 ounces pancetta, chopped	1 Tbs unsalted butter 2 ounces bacon, chopped
2. Add and cook	1 medium yellow onion, chopped 1 medium yellow-fleshed potato, diced 1 cup corn kernels	1 medium yellow onion, chopped 1 medium celeriac, peeled and diced	1 medium yellow onion, diced 1 medium yellow-fleshed potato, diced 1 parsnip, peeled and thinly sliced	4 ounces shallots, thinly sliced 1 medium turnip, peeled and diced
3. Toss in	2 Tbs minced sage 2 tsp fennel seeds 1 bay leaf (discard before serving)	¼ cup minced parsley 1 Tbs stemmed thyme	2 Tbs minced tarragon 1 Tbs minced sage 1 bay leaf (discard before serving)	2 Tbs minced tarragon 1 bay leaf (discard before serving)
4. Pour in and simmer	3 cups fish broth or clam juice 1 cup dry vermouth	3 cups chicken broth 1 cup whole milk	2 cups fish broth or clam juice 2 cups whole milk	2 cups fish broth or clam juice 2 cups whole milk
5. Along with the frizzled pork product if it's been used, stir in	5 cups clam meat (with any juices) 1 cup heavy or whipping cream Salt and pepper to taste	4 to 5 frozen lobster tails, thawed, shelled, and chopped ½ cup heavy or whipping cream Salt and pepper to taste	1¼ to 1½ pounds pasteurized lump crabmeat, picked over for shell and cartilage ½ cup heavy or whipping cream Salt and pepper to taste	About 50 shucked oysters, the liquid reserved, or about 1½ quarts purchased shucked oysters ½ cup heavy or whipping cream Salt and pepper to taste
6. (optional) Thicken with	2 Tbs unsalted butter mixed with 2 Tbs all-purpose flour	2 Tbs unsalted butter mixed with 2 Tbs all-purpose flour	2 Tbs unsalted butter mixed with 2 Tbs all-purpose flour	Omit

	Seafood Chowder	Mixed Shellfish Chowder	Thai Basil Chowder	Corn Chowder
1. Crisp and remove	1 Tbs unsalted butter 2 ounces bacon, chopped	1 Tbs unsalted butter 2 ounces bacon, chopped	1 Tbs canola oil 2 ounces pancetta, chopped	1 Tbs unsalted butter 2 ounces bacon, chopped
2. Add and cook	4 ounces shallots, diced 2 celery ribs, thinly sliced 1 cup corn kernels	1 medium yellow onion, chopped 1 celery rib, thinly sliced 1 small red bell pepper, seeded and diced 2 garlic cloves, minced	4 medium whole scallions, thinly sliced 1 Tbs minced peeled fresh ginger	1 medium yellow onion, chopped 1 medium yellow-fleshed potato, diced 3 cups corn kernels
3. Toss in	¼ cup minced parsley 1 Tbs stemmed thyme 1 bay leaf (discard before serving)	2 Tbs minced marjoram 2 bay leaves (discard before serving)	¼ cup minced basil, preferably Thai basil 1 tsp yellow Thai curry paste (see page 386)	1 Tbs minced marjoram 2 tsp finely grated lemon zest 1 tsp celery seeds 1 bay leaf (discard before serving)
4. Pour in and simmer	3 cups fish broth or clam juice 1 cup whole milk	2½ cups fish broth or clam juice 1½ cups dry white wine	2 cups chicken broth 2 cups dry white wine or dry vermouth	3 cups chicken broth 1 cup dry white wine
5. Along with the frizzled pork product if it's been used, stir in	8 ounces cod, chopped 8 ounces hake, chopped 8 ounces bay scallops ½ cup heavy or whipping cream Salt and pepper to taste	1 pound medium shrimp, peeled, deveined, and chopped 9 ounces sea scallops, quartered 2 frozen lobster tails, shelled and the meat chopped 1 cup heavy or whipping cream Salt and pepper to taste	1 pound cod, cubed 1 pound medium shrimp, peeled, deveined, and chopped ½ cup coconut milk Salt and pepper to taste	½ cup heavy or whipping cream Salt and pepper to taste
6. (optional) Thicken with	Omit	2 Tbs unsalted butter mixed with 2 Tbs all-purpose flour	Omit	2 Tbs unsalted butter mixed with 2 Tbs all-purpose flour

Omelet

Time was, a well-made omelet was the sign of a great chef. But there's no mystery to the technique, just practice. Sure, on the first try you might make scrambled eggs—but how bad are scrambled eggs anyway? In fact, if you follow these simple steps, you'll cook like a pro and have a terrific breakfast—or lunch or dinner, too, because an omelet with a glass of red wine and a tossed salad is a sophisticated, easy meal. Unfortunately, you can make at most 2 servings at a time. But one omelet can wait two or three minutes while the second cooks, provided you've got everything prepped and ready. • MAKES 2 SERVINGS

• **STEP 1** Whisk 5 large eggs in a large bowl until foamy and light. To whip up the fluffiest, lightest eggs, they need to be at room temperature, somewhere between 65°F and 75°F. Leave them out on the counter for 15 to 20 minutes—or immerse them in a bowl of warm (not hot!) water for 3 to 5 minutes. However, bacteria can proliferate at these temperatures. Don't dally, use certified organic eggs, and understand the consequences of your actions.

You can also use a pasteurized egg substitute, the resulting omelet almost indistinguishable from one made with whole eggs, particularly if it's a well-stocked omelet. But the best alternative is to use 1 cup pasteurized egg substitute with 1 large egg.

In all honesty, you can't overbeat the eggs. Go at them for about 3 minutes with the whisk, attacking the eggs in the bowl in easy, even strokes. There's an old trick of making a figure eight with the whisk, but it's mostly stuff and nonsense. Instead, tilt the bowl toward you—even cradle it next to your body with one arm. Whisk the eggs along the side of the bowl, using the seam of the walls at the bottom as a deep well into which the whisk and beaten eggs fall time and again, whipping the eggs in a circular motion up and out of that well and occasionally rotating the bowl a quarter turn. A balloon whisk is the traditional tool; but in truth, any whisk will get the job done.

• **STEP 2** Heat 2 tablespoons fat in a 10-inch nonstick skillet over medium heat; pour in the eggs and begin pulling them back from the skillet's sides. Chefs guard seasoned, traditional, high-carbon steel omelet pans with their lives—and it may well be worth investing in an old-fashioned omelet pan, seasoning it repeatedly, never washing it, oiling it after each use, and getting a natural nonstick coating on it, much as one does with a cast-iron pan (see page 350). However, there's no gainsaying the modern convenience of a nonstick skillet for an omelet. Besides, you can clean it up with soap and water. (A seasoned omelet pan must never be cleaned, only heated and oiled.)

Egg Safety

Never crack an egg on the rim of a bowl; doing so can drive tiny bits of shell into the yolk or white—and the shell is the most likely place any residual salmonella lurks. Besides, cracking an egg on a bowl's rim is the easiest way to break the yolk—not a problem for an omelet, but not a good habit to get into for other egg dishes. Instead, rap the egg on a flat surface like the counter, then open the shell by pulling it apart and away from what's inside, in this case letting the whole egg drop into a large bowl.

The fluffiest omelets begin with well-beaten eggs. Secure the bowl against your body and beat the eggs vigorously, giving your forearm a good workout.

Nine times out of ten, use unsalted butter. Eggs and butter are a time-tested match-up. Slip the butter into the skillet, let it melt, then swirl the skillet to coat the bottom and about 1 inch of the inside walls.

A rich, satisfying omelet can also be made with olive oil or an untoasted nut oil. Steer clear of neutral oils (they add no taste) as well as any toasted oils (they add too much). Sesame oil is better as a condiment, drizzled over an omelet of several minced scallions and 2 teaspoons minced peeled fresh ginger. Various animal fats (duck, chicken, bacon fat, or lard) offer over-the-top spikes, but are they really necessary for this simple dish? Well, OK, a little schmaltz never killed everyone.

Give the eggs one more whisk, then pour them into the skillet—not right in the center, lest you end up with a lump right where they hit the heat, but instead moving the bowl evenly around the hot surface. Also tilt the skillet in several directions so that the eggs coat it evenly; then set it onto the heat and count slowly to 5, just to give the eggs time to start to set.

Using a rubber spatula or other cookware designed for nonstick surfaces, start gently pulling the set egg off the skillet, working from the outside edge and toward the middle. Don't pull so hard the partially set eggs break apart, but do slip the spatula under the eggs and crimp them toward the center, tilting the skillet so more unset egg flows down and comes in contact with the hot surface. Slip the spatula under the set edge and pull the eggs back all around the skillet, about like wrinkling a sheet toward the center of a bed, always letting more raw egg flow into the empty space you've created. Do not mound the curds in the center as you would with scrambled eggs; instead, keep slipping the spatula under the omelet's rim and wrinkling it back. As you do all this, shake and jiggle the skillet occasionally, too, to make sure the omelet stays loosened from the hot surface.

• **STEP 3** Once the top of the eggs are almost set and only if desired, add a little ready-to-eat filling in a straight line across the eggs, perpendicular to the skillet's handle. In any case, fold the omelet over and slide the whole thing onto a serving plate. Season with salt and freshly ground pepper to taste. The filling will have almost no time over the heat. If you're using a precooked filling—say, ratatouille—consider giving it a few seconds in the microwave on high, just to take off the chill. Consider this a basic canvas of fillings:

> **ready-to-eat meat and/or vegetable mixtures,** ½ to ¾ cup, less if mixed with cheese
>
> **finely grated semi-soft, semi-firm, or hard cheese** (see page 175), about ½ cup (that is, 2 or 3 ounces, grated)

As the eggs begin to set, pull them back from the edge of the skillet, letting more egg flow into the space provided.

Once the omelet is almost set, place the filling in a line right down the center of the eggs.

Fold the omelet over onto itself, lifting the skillet higher and higher until the omelet slides out.

minced herbs, about 3 tablespoons on their own or about 1 tablespoon mixed with cheese or other fillings

pesto, jam, chutney, salsa, Marinara (page 179), or other soupy or pasty condiments, about 2 tablespoons

Once the filling lies in a line perpendicular to the handle or once the plain omelet is almost set, loosen the edge of the omelet all the way around with the spatula, shake the skillet gently to make sure the omelet has thoroughly come unstuck from the skillet (but do not shake so hard that the filling lying on top goes everywhere). If it has not, gently run the rubber spatula underneath to loosen the set eggs. Then tilt the skillet up 10 or 20 degrees by its handle. Slip your spatula under the highest part of the omelet, the part nearest the handle, and begin folding the omelet down over itself and toward the side of the skillet that's still against the burner, tilting up more and more all the while as you roll down so that the omelet basically falls over onto itself and its filling.

Once the omelet is folded down and resting against that one portion of the skillet still on the burner, place the skillet over a serving plate, lift the handle up almost vertical, and let the omelet roll out onto the serving plate, tilting the skillet even further so that the last bit of set egg flaps over the omelet to close it. Only now season the omelet with salt and pepper to taste.

Recipes for Omelets

1. Whisk	Basic Omelet	Herb Omelet	Crab and Scallion Omelet	Sun-Dried Tomato and Goat Cheese Omelet
1. Whisk	5 large eggs	5 large eggs	5 large eggs	5 large eggs
2. Heat, pour in the eggs, and begin forming the omelet	2 Tbs unsalted butter	2 Tbs unsalted butter	2 Tbs olive oil	2 Tbs unsalted butter
3. Fill and roll closed—then season once out of the skillet	Salt and pepper to taste	1 Tbs minced tarragon 1 Tbs minced parsley 1 Tbs stemmed thyme Salt and pepper to taste	¾ cup pasteurized lump crabmeat, picked over for shells and cartilage 2 medium scallions, minced and sautéed with 1 tsp olive oil in a small skillet over medium heat until softened 2 Tbs finely grated Parmigiano-Reggiano Salt and pepper to taste	½ cup crumbled soft chèvre (goat cheese) ⅓ cup chopped drained sun-dried tomatoes packed in oil 1 Tbs minced dill Salt and pepper to taste

	Western Omelet	Spinach and Bacon Omelet	Mushroom Omelet	Shrimp Omelet
1. Whisk	5 large eggs	5 large eggs	5 large eggs	5 large eggs
2. Heat, pour in the eggs, and begin forming the omelet	2 Tbs unsalted butter	2 Tbs unsalted butter	2 Tbs unsalted butter	2 Tbs olive oil
3. Fill and roll closed—then season once out of the skillet	¼ cup diced onion and ¼ cup diced seeded green bell pepper, sautéed with 1 Tbs unsalted butter in a small skillet until softened and fragrant ¼ cup diced thick-sliced deli ham ¼ cup shredded Cheddar Salt and pepper to taste	3 bacon strips, chopped and cooked in a medium skillet over medium heat until crispy 4 ounces baby spinach, wilted in the rendered bacon fat in the skillet ¼ cup finely grated Parmigiano-Reggiano ¼ tsp grated nutmeg Salt and pepper to taste	8 ounces sliced mushrooms, cooked with 1 Tbs unsalted butter in a small skillet over medium heat until they release their liquid and it evaporates ¼ cup grated Emmental or Swiss cheese ¼ tsp ground allspice Salt and pepper to taste	8 cooked, peeled, and deveined medium shrimp, chopped ¼ cup purchased cocktail sauce Several dashes hot red pepper sauce Salt and pepper to taste

This technique removes some—but only some—of the fat used in pan-frying. But one thing's for sure: oven-frying takes away most of the mess! Nuts are added to assure the coating gets crisp in the oven's radiant heat. • MAKES 4 TO 6 SERVINGS

• **STEP 1** Preheat the oven to 375°F; grease a large, lipped baking sheet. Nonstick spray is certainly the easiest, most convenient way to go. Make sure the baking sheet is well coated, not just a light spray. If you don't want to use nonstick spray, any neutral-flavored oil like canola or corn will do—dabbed on a paper towel and smeared generously on the sheet. Just do not waste a nut, seed, or olive oil for this task.

Because of the prolonged cooking, you need to bake all the food at once, not in batches. Make sure the baking sheet is large enough to hold everything. Lipped, it can also prevent things from rolling onto the floor.

• **STEP 2** Fill three wide, shallow bowls with the coating materials: the first with ½ cup all-purpose flour; the second with 1 cup buttermilk or its substitute; and the third with a mixture of 1½ cups chopped nuts, 1 cup seasoned yellow cornmeal or dried bread crumbs, some dried herbs or spices if desired, and 1 or 2 teaspoons salt. Why these three bowls? The liquid in the second, necessary for moisture, can only evenly adhere to the food if there's first a fine film of all-purpose flour—and the dry ingredients in the third bowl (that is, the crust itself) can only latch on via an even coating of that liquid.

> **Skinning Hazelnuts**
>
> Heat them in a dry skillet over medium heat until lightly browned, about 4 minutes; then place them in a large, clean kitchen towel, cool a few minutes, gather the towel together, and abrade the skins off, rubbing the nuts against the towel and each other. There's no need to remove every bit of skin, just most of it.

The first bowl

This contains simply all-purpose flour, preferably unbleached so it has fewer chemical additives released under the hot temperatures. Do not substitute self-rising, cake, or any other flour. If you have gluten allergies, try a 50/50 combination of brown rice flour and soy flour.

The second bowl

The most traditional oven-frying liquid is whole, low-fat, or even fat-free buttermilk. Regular milk, less rich, also works well although fat-free milk yields a very light coating. Or forgo the dairy altogether and try white wine or broth, particularly chicken broth. Neither will produce a coating as thick as buttermilk, but both will lighten the dish considerably.

For a coating suitable for oven-frying, the nuts should be ground to the consistency of very coarse cornmeal.

Having been coated using the three-bowl technique, the pieces are placed on a large, greased, lipped baking sheet.

The third bowl

Use a fine-ground cornmeal or fine, dried bread crumbs. If you think what you have is a little coarse, give it a whir in a mini food processor or a standard food processor fitted with the chopping blade. Do not make dust and do not use seasoned bread crumbs.

Whisk either the cornmeal or the dried bread crumbs in the third bowl with the ground nuts—which themselves should be finely ground in a processor until the consistency of soft sand. Do not overprocess the nuts or they can break down and turn into a nut butter.

The fat from the nuts will protect the meat, thereby mimicking the action of pan-fried food. Walnuts, almonds, or pecans are naturals, but don't neglect hazelnuts—although they'll need to be skinned (see page 217).

Also consider unsalted but roasted peanuts (not actually nuts, but legumes) or unsalted but roasted cashews (not actually nuts, but fruit seeds). Either will give a more pronounced taste to the final dish: less subtle but also more aromatic.

Before you grind the nuts, also add 2 teaspoons salt. And if desired, add some dried herbs or spices, including spice blends like garam masala (see page 27) or chili powder. Ground cumin, onion powder, garlic powder, dried thyme—these are the naturals, most used in small quantities. Garlic powder can quickly overwhelm the coating—use very sparingly.

• **STEP 3** Dip the food to be oven-fried first in the flour, then in the liquid, and then in the nut mixture, shaking off the excess. Lay on the prepared sheet and bake until crispy and cooked through. Consider these the foods you can oven-fry:

> **About 4 pounds chicken pieces or one 4-pound cut-up chicken**, giblets and neck removed
> **Four 8-ounce bone-in pork chops**
> **Four 6-ounce skinless, thin, white-fleshed fish fillets such as tilapia, any snapper, or any drum**
> **2 pounds medium shrimp**
> **2 pounds sea scallops**
> **2 large yellow or sweet white onions**, cut into ½-inch-thick slices and the various rings in each layer divided

Although most vegetables will not work for this technique (they leach too much moisture and the coating turns soggy), onion rings hold up surprisingly well, turning crunchy but still moist in the oven.

First dip and turn the food lightly in the flour, shaking off any excess; then dip it in the liquid, coating it all over without drowning it, letting any excess drip back into the bowl. Finally, place the wet ingredient in the dry nut mixture; roll it around to coat all sides before laying it on the prepared baking sheet. All the while, practice a one-handed technique for moistening and rolling the food around the nut mixture. There's an old rule in culinary school: keep one hand dry in case the president walks in and wants to shake your hand. Actually, a clean hand is always a welcome tool in the kitchen.

Space everything on the baking sheet at least 1 inch apart so there will be even airflow. How long it takes in the oven is a matter of the food itself:

> **shrimp, scallops, and onion rings:** about 20 minutes
> **fish fillets:** about 25 minutes
> **chicken and pork:** about 40 minutes

If you're in doubt about the chicken or pork, take their internal temperature with an instant-read meat thermometer inserted into the thickest part of the meat without the probe's touching bone. The pork should be about 160°F; the chicken, about 170°F. Transfer everything to a wire rack and give it a generous sprinkling of salt. Just like pan-fried foods (see page 235), oven-frieds need salt, more than you think.

Cleaning a Spice Grinder

Wipe it out with a dry paper towel, then pour in some dry white rice kernels and give them a whir until blended to a powder. Wipe it out and go for it again if you notice a distinct aroma in the grinder.

Oven-Fried Fish Fillets

Recipes for Oven-Frying

	Oven-Fried Chicken	Oven-Fried Pork Chops	Oven-Fried Rabbit	Oven-Fried Corn Dogs
1. Preheat the oven; grease a baking sheet	Nonstick spray	Nonstick spray	Nonstick spray	Nonstick spray
2. Prepare three bowls for the coating process	½ cup all-purpose flour 1 cup buttermilk 1 cup dried bread crumbs and 1½ cups chopped walnut pieces ground with 2 tsp onion powder, 2 tsp dried thyme, 2 tsp mild paprika, 1 tsp celery seeds, 1 tsp ground allspice, 1 tsp garlic powder, 1 tsp ground black pepper, and 2 tsp salt	½ cup all-purpose flour 1 cup milk 1 cup yellow cornmeal and 1½ cups chopped pecan pieces ground with 1 Tbs mild paprika, 2 tsp ground cumin, 2 tsp fennel seeds, 1 tsp ground cinnamon, 1 tsp ground black pepper, ½ tsp grated nutmeg, and 2 tsp salt	½ cup all-purpose flour 1 cup buttermilk 1 cup dried bread crumbs and 1½ cups chopped, skinned hazelnuts (see page 217) ground with 1 Tbs ground coriander, 2 tsp dry mustard, 2 tsp ground ginger, 2 tsp fennel seeds, 1 tsp ground cinnamon, ¼ tsp ground cloves, and 2 tsp salt	½ cup all-purpose flour 1 cup buttermilk 1 cup yellow cornmeal and 1½ cups chopped pecan pieces ground with ¼ cup chili powder
3. Dip, coat, and bake	One 4-pound chicken, cut up Salt to taste	Four 8-ounce bone-in pork chops Salt to taste	One 4-pound rabbit, cut into 6 to 8 pieces Salt to taste	8 hot dogs Salt to taste

	Oven-Fried Shrimp	Oven-Fried Scallops	Oven-Fried Fish Fillets	No-Guilt Onion Rings
1. Preheat the oven; grease a baking sheet	Nonstick spray	Nonstick spray	Nonstick spray	Nonstick spray
2. Prepare three bowls for the coating process	½ cup all-purpose flour 1 cup dry white wine 1 cup dried bread crumbs and 1½ cups chopped almonds ground with 1 Tbs chili powder, 2 tsp dried oregano, 2 tsp ground cumin, 1 tsp cayenne, and 2 tsp salt	½ cup all-purpose flour 1 cup dry white wine 1 cup dried bread crumbs and 1½ cups chopped, skinned hazelnuts (see page 217) ground with 2 tsp celery seeds, 2 tsp dried thyme, 2 tsp dried parsley, 2 tsp Old Bay seasoning, and 1 tsp salt	½ cup all-purpose flour 1 cup buttermilk 1 cup yellow cornmeal and 1½ cups chopped walnut pieces ground with 1 Tbs dried dill, 1 Tbs lemon pepper seasoning (see page 355), 1 tsp dried thyme, 1 tsp garlic powder, and 2 tsp salt	½ cup all-purpose flour 1 cup buttermilk 1 cup dried bread crumbs and 1½ cups chopped unsalted peanuts ground with 2 tsp celery seeds, 2 tsp fennel seeds, 2 tsp mild paprika, 1 tsp onion powder, 1 tsp ground black pepper, ½ tsp garlic powder, and 2 tsp salt
3. Dip, coat, and bake	2 pounds medium shrimp, butterflied (see page 238) Salt to taste	2 pounds sea scallops Salt to taste	Four 6-ounce skinless, thin, white-fleshed fish fillets Salt to taste	Two large yellow onions, sliced into rings Salt to taste

Packets

No technique is easier, despite the use of fussy parchment paper. Using this classic method—*en papillote* (French, ahwn pah-pee-OAT, "in paper")—you seal fish, chicken, pork, tofu, and/or vegetables in parchment paper packets and then bake them in a hot oven. The great thing is that you can prepare dinner to everyone's taste with little folderol. If you prefer fish but your partner likes chicken, it's no problem: simply make different packets with different proteins, each with similar (if not exactly the same) vegetables and herbs. • MAKES 1 SERVING—OR CAN BE MULTIPLIED TO HOWEVER MANY YOU DESIRE

• **STEP 1** Position the rack in the center of the oven and preheat the oven to 450°F. Lay two 16-inch sheets of parchment paper on top of each other on your work surface; top with about 1 tablespoon minced herbs, a minced garlic clove, and/or minced peeled fresh ginger, then top with 5 to 6 ounces protein. Doubling the parchment sheets, while not necessary, helps secure the seal and makes it easier to get the hot packet off the baking tray. Position the sheets on top of each other with a long side facing you. Work off this axis, placing everything in a line parallel to the paper's long side.

If you're making more servings, simply make more packets, as many as you like, the doubled sheets of parchment serried across your work surface. If you don't add any acid in the next step, you can make several packets and keep them sealed and on a baking sheet in the refrigerator for up to 6 hours—a meal ready when you are. Pop these straight from the freezer into the oven on a baking sheet and increase the baking time by 3 to 5 minutes.

Sprinkle the herbs, spices, and flavorings down the center of the packet, in a line about as long as the protein you'll use. Any fresh herb will do: oregano, mint, rosemary, thyme, marjoram, dill, or parsley. Some pairings are classic: rosemary with chicken and cherry tomatoes; dill with a fish fillet and artichoke hearts. Others are at your whimsy: parsley with tofu and ginger; mint with shrimp and sliced fennel. Or consider a pairing of herbs in the mix like rosemary and oregano, mint and thyme. Rarely use more than 1 minced garlic clove per packet; a teaspoon or two of minced peeled fresh ginger offers a nice spark to Asian-inspired dishes.

For protein, consider 5 to 6 ounces per packet of any one of the following:

Fish fillets. Thick- or thin-fleshed, the question is just a matter of timing; all should be skinless so they don't curl or warp in the heat. (Either ask your fishmonger to skin the fillets or do it yourself—see page124). Thin-fleshed white fish fillets like tilapia, snapper, bass, or a drum will take about 15 minutes;

Parchment Paper

Heavy-duty parchment paper is resistant to almost all liquids, including melted fat; it's the perfect vehicle for creating these steam packets. Although available in rounds and oblong sheets at high-end markets, the best bet here are the rolls commonly found in the supermarket near the plastic wrap and aluminum foil. The paper may not tear off the roll like plastic wrap; instead, you may have to roll out 16 inches and cut the section with scissors.

thicker-fleshed fillets like hake and cod, about 20 minutes. Avoid tuna and swordfish steaks, both of which are simply too thick and meat-like. However, skinless salmon fillets, particularly those cut the width of the salmon fillet into strips, work well in this simple preparation. Do not use salmon steaks.

Medium shrimp (about 30 per pound). They should be peeled and deveined; larger shrimp will take 3 to 5 extra minutes to cook.

Sea scallops. See page 238 for a discussion of how to shop for scallops.

Boneless skinless chicken breasts. These should be sliced for even cooking. Set them on your cutting board with the "ends" pointing to your left and right. Slice them at a 45-degree angle to get the longest cuts, each about ½-inch thick. Whole boneless skinless breasts can seize into a ball in the packet.

Thinly sliced pork tenderloin. Either slice it into ½-inch-thick coins or cut it into long strips like the boneless skinless chicken breasts. Do not substitute beef or lamb tenderloins. The former will be overcooked and the latter, undercooked.

Sliced silken firm tofu. This relatively new product will hold its shape but remain soft and luxuriant in the packet. Slice it into ½-inch-thick sections.

Set the protein right over the herbs so they'll infuse it as everything cooks.

Of course, you needn't add any protein. If not, double or even triple the vegetables in the next step.

• **STEP 2** Add about 1 cup chopped quick-cooking vegetables or even some fruit; 1 tablespoon broth, wine, fortified wine, or an acid; perhaps 1 tablespoon spicy or salty condiment, as well as salt and freshly ground black pepper to taste. Fold and crimp the packet closed. Although 1 cup is a good measure for all the vegetables, it's certainly no rule, just a guideline. Packets help the vegetables stay crisp-tender; the fruit, if used, will hold its shape. When properly cooked, the vegetables are just slightly steamed/poached in the naturally created sauce. Choose ones you wouldn't mind eating crisp-tender:

pitted, sliced apricots or plums
very thin asparagus spears, cut into 1-inch sections
canned or frozen artichoke hearts, quartered
seeded and diced bell pepper
canned beans, drained and rinsed
broccoli or cauliflower florets
shredded carrot
thinly sliced celery
Chinese water spinach, Chinese broccoli, or other leafy greens, roughly chopped
corn kernels, frozen or fresh
diced eggplant, preferably peeled
trimmed and thinly sliced fennel
fresh figs, quartered
frozen lima beans

green beans or Chinese long beans, cut into 1-inch sections

orange supremes (see page 106)

peas, fresh shelled or frozen

diced or thinly sliced red onion

baby spinach or other tender, small greens

sugar snap peas, tough inner thread zipped off

diced summer squash

cherry or plum tomatoes, quartered

diced zucchini

All the ingredients are laid in a line on top of the protein in the packet. Note that everything forms a line parallel with the paper's long side.

Sprinkle one or several of these over the protein on a line parallel to the packet's long side.

The one quick-cooker that doesn't seem to work in packets: mushrooms. Most of them give off too much liquid and still stay on the near side of raw, a little spongy. That said, enoki mushrooms, a Japanese favorite, will definitely work. These long, thin mushrooms are cultivated in a CO_2-rich environment, stunting their growth and rendering them colorless.

Also consider chopped pitted green or black olives, chopped sun-dried tomatoes, drained capers, or minced seeded chiles as part of this aromatic mélange—but no more than 1 or 2 tablespoons, at most, of the total volume.

Finally, add 1 tablespoon of some liquid:

white wine

broth of almost any kind (beef broth wouldn't go well with
    anything but pork; fish stock, only with fish or shellfish)

lemon juice

any unflavored vinegar (white wine, white balsamic, or rice
    vinegar, or the like)

or even a dry fortified wine, vermouth to Madeira.

A little liquid assures that the protein will steam to perfection in the sealed packet.

Red wine, unfortunately, turns the sauce a depressing pink, as would a "red" version of a fortified wine such as port. Better to stick to lighter-colored liquids for aesthetics. If you're making an Asian-inspired packet, try shaoxing (page 374) or mirin (page 258).

You can also add 1 tablespoon cream for richness; it will not incorporate fully into the sauce, but rather sit in blobs throughout. You can stir it together after baking to make a richer sauce, but the whole effect seems like wasted effort. Besides, if you add any acid—lemon juice or vinegar, for example—or any fruit with a digestive enzyme—figs, for example—the cream will curdle and clot during baking.

Rather than worrying about such richness, sprinkle on up to 1 tablespoon of a spicy or salty condiment over the ingredients in the packet: hot red pepper sauce,

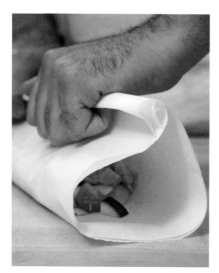

To seal the packet closed, first roll and crimp the long sides together over the protein and vegetables....

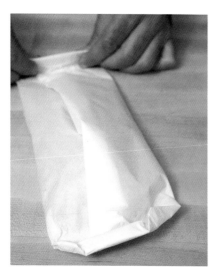

Then roll and crimp the ends closed so no steam can escape.

Asian chili sauce or chile oil, red pepper flakes, or Worcestershire sauce. All these will be quite strong in this delicate dish and should be used sparingly. One tablespoon prepared Asian chili sauce over a pork loin would be lovely—but it would cast a fish fillet into oblivion.

Many classic preparations ask you to sprinkle oil or butter over the food. In truth, there's no need. This simple technique should also remain a healthful preparation. The protein and vegetables will release their liquids, creating a natural sauce.

To fold the parchment packet closed, bring the long sides together and securely crimp them shut by rolling the paper over onto itself and pressing it closed, leaving about 1 inch of air space between the seal and the food below. Then roll up the two short sides, pulling them up as you do so, thereby creating a gentle curve in the packet just at the ends. The paper on top should not lie on the food below. Working with two sheets is a little tricky, but you'll be safer later on. Make sure there are no holes or gaps in your seals. Moisture lost is flavor lost.

• **STEP 3** Place the packet on a large, lipped baking sheet; bake until the protein has been cooked through, 15 to 20 minutes. Let stand for 5 minutes at room temperature before serving. Lift the packet, supporting its bottom with a flat spatula; lay the packet on the baking sheet, which will cradle it in the oven, keeping it from sagging on the rack.

The baking time depends on the protein you've chosen: fish, shellfish, and tofu, about 15 minutes; chicken and pork, about 20. There's no way to tell, of course, without opening the packet and checking, which will in turn ruin the steam chamber inside. Trust the times given and let the packet rest for a few minutes to cool and meld the flavors.

The only real concern is if you see leaked liquid on the baking sheet. Remove the packet from the oven and immediately start again making another packet for those ingredients inside the leaking one. You'll have to reduce the baking time proportionately since the food is now partially cooked, but the loss of the liquid will eventually lead to a dry and unsatisfying meal.

Transfer the packets to plates. Never let a child open her or his own. Steam burns are particularly nasty. In fact, warn all adults to open their packets carefully. In the classic preparation, you put the packet on a plate, open it up, and eat right out of the parchment paper. Frankly, we prefer to open everything in the kitchen and serve the food in bowls, pouring the sauce in each packet over each serving.

Mediterranean Fish in Packets

Recipes for Packets

	Mediterranean Fish in Packets	Ratatouille-Style Fish Fillets in Packets	Thai Fish Packets	Asian Scallops in Packets
1. Preheat the oven. Prepare the packet and top with	Two 16-inch parchment paper sheets 1 Tbs minced rosemary One 5- to 6-ounce skinless, thin-fleshed white fish fillet	Two 16-inch parchment paper sheets 1 Tbs minced basil ½ Tbs minced marjoram One 5- to 6-ounce skinless, thin-fleshed white fish fillet	Two 16-inch parchment paper sheets One 4-inch piece of lemongrass, white and pale green parts only, bruised with the bottom of a pot 2 Tbs minced cilantro One 5- to 6-ounce skinless, thick-fleshed white fish fillet such as hake or cod	Two 16-inch parchment paper sheets 1 Tbs minced cilantro 6 ounces sea scallops, each cut crosswise into two disks
2. Add and seal	½ cup diced zucchini 3 cherry tomatoes, quartered 2 canned artichoke hearts, quartered 1 Tbs dry white wine ½ tsp salt ½ tsp ground black pepper	½ cup diced, peeled eggplant ¼ cup diced seeded red bell pepper 3 cherry tomatoes, quartered 1 garlic clove, minced 1 Tbs lemon juice 1 Tbs Worcestershire sauce ¼ tsp salt ¼ tsp ground black pepper	2 ounces shallots, diced ¼ cup small red bell pepper, seeded and diced 2 Tbs chopped roasted peanuts 1 Tbs coconut milk 1 Tbs lime juice ½ Tbs soy sauce	2 medium whole scallions, minced ⅓ cup sliced snow peas ⅓ cup diced seeded red bell pepper 1 garlic clove, minced 1 star anise pod 1 Tbs rice vinegar ½ Tbs soy sauce 1 tsp Asian red chili sauce ½ tsp ground black pepper
3. Bake	15 minutes	15 minutes	20 minutes	15 minutes

	Chicken with Fresh Corn Relish in Packets	Japanese-Style Chicken Breasts in Packets	Pork and Beans in Packets	Tofu with Garden Vegetables in Packets
1. Preheat the oven. Prepare the packet and top with	Two 16-inch parchment paper sheets 1 Tbs minced parsley One 5- to 6-ounce boneless skinless chicken breast, sliced	Two 16-inch parchment paper sheets 1 Tbs minced pickled "sushi" ginger One 5- to 6-ounce boneless skinless chicken breast, sliced	Two 16-inch parchment paper sheets 1 Tbs minced parsley One 5- to 6-ounce piece pork tenderloin, trimmed and cut into ½-inch rounds	Two 16-inch parchment paper sheets ½ Tbs minced tarragon ½ Tbs stemmed thyme One 5- to 6-ounce tofu square, cut into bite-sized cubes
2. Add and seal	½ cup corn kernels ¼ cup minced red onion ¼ cup minced seeded red bell pepper 1 Tbs chicken broth ¼ tsp red pepper flakes ½ tsp salt ½ tsp ground black pepper	½ cup shredded carrot ½ cup enoki mushrooms, cleaned and separated 1 tsp wasabi powder 1 Tbs mirin (see page 258) 1 Tbs soy sauce	½ cup drained canned pinto beans 1 celery rib, thinly sliced 1 small shallot, thinly sliced 1 Tbs mirin (see page 258) 1 Tbs barbecue sauce ½ tsp salt ½ tsp ground black pepper	2 ounces shallots, thinly sliced 1 medium carrot, shredded through the large holes of a box grater ¼ cup diced summer squash 1 Tbs white wine Several dashes hot red pepper sauce ½ tsp salt ½ tsp ground black pepper
3. Bake	20 minutes	20 minutes	20 minutes	15 minutes

Note: Each recipe makes 1 packet. Double, triple, or make in multiples as you desire, provided you have enough space on the baking sheet (or use more than one) and provided you make each packet individually according to the design for one. Do not double the amount of ingredients in individual packets. Because the amounts for each serving are small, many ingredients are not listed in this chart as their market equivalents—one small red bell pepper, seeded and diced—but rather as volume amounts: ¼ cup seeded and diced red bell pepper.

A plate of Sausage, Shrimp, and Fennel Paella

Paella

Although we think of this Spanish rice casserole as a fish and shellfish dish, the only invariable components are medium-grained rice, olive oil, and saffron, along with the technique of cooking the rice uncovered. An elegantly simple meal—one of those peasant dishes that got swamped with pretensions to authenticity—paella is quite versatile, a show-stopper every time. • MAKES 6 SERVINGS

• **STEP 1** Heat 4 cups broth, ½ teaspoon salt, and ¼ teaspoon saffron in a covered, medium saucepan just until warm, not boiling; meanwhile, preheat the oven to 350°F. Traditionally, paella is made in a wide, concave pan, shallower than a wok, set on a ring or well over an open fire. The paella pans sold in North America, by contrast, have flat bottoms so they sit on stovetop burners—a necessity if not the best invention. Without the pan's well, the rice dries out over the heat, often tough, even desiccated. The answer? Since it's hard to find an authentic paella pan—and harder still to build a fire well at home—use this technique: a stovetop sauté finished in the oven's ambient heat, which keeps the rice grains tender without their turning chewy or tough.

Use any broth: chicken, beef, vegetable, or even fish—as well as bottled clam juice (in moderation and in combination with broth). Or perhaps any combination of these: 2 cups vegetable broth and 2 cups fish broth, or 3 cups chicken broth and 1 cup bottled clam juice. Beef broth is preferred for heartier combinations of, say, chicken thighs, sausage, and shrimp; vegetable broth and clam juice, with a lighter paella of lobster and mussels.

• **STEP 2** Brown up to 3 pounds meat and/or sausage in 2 tablespoons olive oil in a 13-inch paella pan or a 15-inch cast-iron skillet; transfer to a plate and pour off all but 2 tablespoons fat. Since tougher cuts (pork shoulder, London broil, or beef chuck) won't have time to tenderize and more delicate cuts (filet mignon, veal loin, or chicken breasts) will lose all finesse and toughen considerably in the moderately long cooking, choose from a range of moderately fatty but still tender meats like

> **bone-in skinless chicken thighs**
> **cut-up rabbit pieces**
> **cut-up pheasant**
> **duck breasts**, cut into quarters and the skin scored
> **duck confit**, the meat shredded off the bones
> **quartered Cornish game hens**
> **quail**, halved or at least butterflied open
> **dried mild Spanish chorizo**, sliced

Saffron

Saffron threads are the stamens of the crocus savitus, which once grew exclusively in southern Eurasia; the plants flower in mid-autumn and are harvested by hand, back-breaking work to remove Lilliputian bits from flowers low to the ground. The dry threads will soften and partially dissolve in the broth, infusing it with a musky flavor and that distinctive yellow-orange color.

mild Italian sausage or other coarse-grained sausage, cut into sections
pork or beef meatballs
smoked pork chops

The amount of meat—*up to* 2 pounds—will be determined by how much seafood you intend to add later on. Little meat and more seafood, more meat and little seafood? That's your call. A lighter dish can be made with, say, ¾ pound bone-in chicken thighs and then lots of shrimp, scallops, and mussels. Still, the best paella is made with a mix of meat and fish or shellfish.

Once browned, transfer the meat to a plate and set aside. In general, you'll need to pour off all but 2 tablespoons fat; but if the pan is dry, add more olive oil to compensate.

If available, dice the bird or rabbit liver, heart, and/or gizzard; add them with the onion in the next step to make a richer casserole. (However, discard the rabbit's kidneys if attached.)

Herb vs. Spice

An herb is the green, leafy part of a plant used to flavor foods—for example, parsley, rosemary, or marjoram. A spice is a dried root, bark, seed, fruit, or other vegetative material used the same way—for example, cumin, nutmeg, or peppercorns. That said, once the leafy plant is dried and ground, it is often considered a spice. To wit, minced sage leaves are an herb but rubbed sage is often considered a spice.

Sweating Vegetables

Technically, vegetables sweat over the heat; they are not sautéed. Sweating reduces the amount of liquid, softens the cellular structure, and concentrates the flavors; sautéing sears the outside, caramelizing the juices.

• **STEP 3** Add one chopped large yellow onion and cook, stirring often, until softened, about 3 minutes. The onion should be chopped so that the pieces are about the size of the grains of rice.

• **STEP 4** Pour in 1 cup wine, raise the heat to medium-high, and boil until the amount of liquid in the pan has been reduced by half, perhaps 3 or 4 minutes. In general, lighter-flavored wines pair better with lighter-tasting ingredients. So soft, floral Spanish whites from the Rueda region are perfect with shrimp, cubed halibut, or shucked oysters. With a little more body, a French or American rosé complements a paella of turkey sausage, fennel, asparagus, and clams. And a Spanish red like one from Rioja or Ribera del Duero adds a deep, complex flavor to match sausage, lamb, or sirloin. Still, a moderately heavy lamb and shrimp paella made with white wine would be a springtime treat, bright yet comforting. In other words, wine is a complement—or perhaps a balance. But not too far. Red wine will overpower lobster.

• **STEP 5** Add up to 2 tablespoons minced herbs perhaps complemented by ½ teaspoon or so dried spices, as well as 2 teaspoons mild smoked paprika and perhaps some minced garlic cloves; then pour in 1¾ cups canned diced tomatoes and if desired, ½ cup fresh shelled or frozen peas or another quick-cooking vegetable before bringing to a simmer. Leafy, green herbs have a brighter taste, better with the sweet rice. Choose one or perhaps two. To make a combo, start with either thyme or oregano, then add a second herb like parsley or marjoram.

Also, ¼ teaspoon grated nutmeg is a delightful and autumnal

addition—and you might add it as well as comparable amounts of ground coriander, mace, or cinnamon. These small accents, barely noticeable, will bring the more ethereal, aromatic herbs back down to land with their nutty, earthy tastes.

Within the past 60 years, smoked paprika (that is, smoked dried chiles ground into a powder) has become synonymous with Spanish cooking, thanks first to a cadre of Iberian wannabes on the global food scene and then in some weird reversal to its wholesale adoption among Spanish (and particularly Madrid) chefs. It's not that smoked paprika hasn't been in Spain for centuries; it's just that it hasn't been in every dish in Spain until recently. Still, we begrudgingly acknowledge its benefit in paella, a pleasant muskiness—although with this warning: a little goes a long way. Smoked paprika is hardly subtle, more like a smoked hammer. Look for it in gourmet markets or from suppliers on the Web; do not substitute mild or hot Hungarian paprika.

As a base for paella, the tomatoes break down somewhat, the sauce thus becoming quite soupy.

• **STEP 6** Stir in 2 cups medium-grain rice until most of the liquid has been absorbed and the grains have turned translucent except for a little white kernel at one end. There are three types of rice used for paella:

1. **Valencia,** a highly prized Spanish rice, traditional but sometimes difficult to find in North America
2. **Granza,** another Spanish varietal that now shows up more frequently in high-end markets
3. **Arborio,** not traditional but much more readily available and more familiar from Risotto (page 284).

Although often mistakenly called short-grain, these are in fact all medium-grained rices. The grain's length is indeed somewhat determinative for the distinctions among short, medium, and long; however, the real difference lies in the starch content.

However, the rice will absorb much of the liquid as it begins to soften.

Almost all rice has two starches: a fairly uniform variety that packs densely into layers, only to loosen and tenderize after long cooking (amylose) and a gangly variety that won't lay flat and clumps into awkward bundles (amylopectin). By and large, the shorter the grain of rice, the less amylose—and so the less heat and moisture needed to unlock the starch from its layers and tenderize it. Since medium-grain rices have about 15% less amylose than long-grain varieties (like basmati), medium-grains need less cooking to soften (despite the problem of stirring and stirring Arborio in Risotto—see page 286). By the way, short-grain rices like sushi rice have little amylose and so soften quickly and clump together because of all that gangly, sticky amylopectin.

The rice grains will quickly turn opaque, almost a milky translucence with a

Mussels and clams should be added to the paella hinge down so they'll open as the rice bubbles away in the sauce. Here's your chance to art-direct the dish to your heart's desire!

PAELLA CAKES

For leftovers, take the meat off the bones or out of the mollusk shells and chop up any large pieces of meat or whole shrimp. Stir it all together in the rice, then refrigerate. When cold, mix in 1 beaten large egg until well combined, then form the mixture into rice cakes between your cleaned and damp palms. These cakes can be fried in a skillet of olive oil until brown, about 10 minutes, turning once.

white kernel at one end. If the pan's hot, this should happen within 30 seconds.

• **STEP 7** Pour in the warm broth mixture, reduce the heat to medium-low, and simmer very slowly for 10 minutes. If the broth is warm enough, the sauce should be at a simmer almost instantly. Quickly reduce the heat. There must be no full boil.

• **STEP 8** Tuck the browned meat, up to 2 pounds thick-fleshed fish or shellfish, and up to 2 pounds clams or mussels into the simmering rice; place in the oven and bake until the meat is at the proper internal temperature, the mollusks are open, and the rice is tender, about 15 minutes. Think of paella as an open-skillet braise. Everything should be partially submerged in the simmering liquid so that it all has a chance to come to full temperature in the oven.

If you've used less than 2 pounds meat, use the full amount of shellfish here, like

large shrimp, peeled and deveined (about 15 per pound)
large sea scallops
cubed halibut
cubed swordfish
frozen lobster tails, thawed
Jonah or stone crab claws
soft-shell crabs
shucked oysters
or 1-pound lobsters, cut in half lengthwise while alive

For the mussels and clams to open properly, they should be put seam side down in the liquid. (To clean mussels, see page 203.) For a decorative design, line them around the perimeter of the skillet.

Once in the oven, do not disturb the paella. It needs to simmer slowly; the rice will begin to stick slightly. After 15 minutes, pull the grains back from one side of the pan, see how much liquid is left, and taste a spoonful to see if the rice is tender.

Paella is best if allowed to stand at room temperature for 5 to 10 minutes before serving—enough time to open the wine and get everyone to the table.

One final note: in Spain, the most highly prized bits are the slightly burned, clumped grains of rice on the pan's bottom, called the *socarrat*. Unfortunately, you won't get much of it in this oven-based method. If you want a little *socarrat* in your paella, take the pan out of the oven, set it over medium heat, and cook just until the rice on the pan's bottom starts to pop and sizzle, about 3 or 4 minutes.

Recipes for Paellas

	Sausage, Shrimp, and Fennel Paella	Duck and Shellfish Paella	Lobster Paella	Spring Paella
1. Heat in a covered saucepan; preheat the oven	4 cups (1 quart) chicken broth ½ tsp salt ¼ tsp saffron	4 cups (1 quart) beef broth ½ tsp salt ¼ tsp saffron	2 cups fish broth or clam juice 2 cups chicken broth ½ tsp salt ¼ tsp saffron	2 cups chicken broth 2 cups vegetable broth ½ tsp salt ¼ tsp saffron
2. Brown and transfer	2 Tbs olive oil 1½ pounds mild sausage	2 Tbs olive oil 2 duck breasts, quartered and skin scored	2 Tbs olive oil ½ pound mild turkey sausage, cut into 2-inch pieces	2 Tbs olive oil 1½ pounds cleaned quail or bone-in skinless chicken thighs
3. Add and soften	1 large yellow onion, chopped	1 large yellow onion, chopped	1 large yellow onion, chopped	1 large yellow onion, chopped
4. Pour in and reduce	1 cup rosé wine	1 cup red wine	1 cup fruity white wine	1 cup dry white wine
5. Add the herbs, then the vegetables; bring to a simmer	1 Tbs minced oregano 2 tsp stemmed thyme 2 tsp mild smoked paprika 1 garlic clove, minced 1¾ cups canned diced tomatoes 1 small fennel bulb, trimmed and thinly sliced	1 Tbs minced rosemary 2 tsp stemmed thyme 2 tsp mild smoked paprika 1¾ cups canned diced tomatoes ½ cup fresh shelled or frozen peas	1 Tbs minced parsley 1 Tbs minced chives 2 tsp mild smoked paprika 1¾ cups canned diced tomatoes 1 small red bell pepper, seeded and diced	1½ Tbs minced parsley 2 tsp mild smoked paprika 1¾ cups canned diced tomatoes ½ cup fresh shelled or frozen peas
6. Stir in	2 cups medium-grain rice	2 cups medium-grain rice	2 cups medium-grain rice	2 cups medium-grain rice
7. Pour in and simmer slowly 10 minutes	The warm broth mixture	The warm broth mixture	The warm broth mixture	The warm broth mixture
8. Tuck in and bake	The browned sausage 1½ pounds large shrimp, peeled and deveined 2 pounds cleaned clams	The browned duck breasts 2 pounds Jonah or stone crab claws 2 pounds mussels, cleaned and debearded (see page 203) ½ pound shucked oysters	The browned sausage 2 pounds mussels, cleaned and debearded (see page 203) 1 pound large shrimp, cleaned and deveined Two 1-pound lobsters, cut in half down the middle while alive or two 1-pound frozen lobster tails, thawed	The browned quail or chicken thighs 2 pounds large shrimp, peeled and deveined 2 pounds clams, cleaned

	Game Paella	Lamb Paella	Scallop and Pancetta Paella	Pork and Clam Paella
1. Heat in a covered saucepan; preheat the oven	4 cups (1 quart) veal demi-glace or beef broth ½ tsp salt ¼ tsp saffron	4 cups (1 quart) chicken broth ½ tsp salt ¼ tsp saffron	4 cups (1 quart) chicken broth ½ tsp salt ¼ tsp saffron	4 cups (1 quart) chicken broth ½ tsp salt ¼ tsp saffron
2. Brown and transfer	2 Tbs duck fat scraped from duck confit legs One 3-pound rabbit, cleaned, inner organs removed, kidneys discarded, and the meat cut into 8 pieces ½ pound venison sausage, cut into 1-inch rings	2 Tbs unsalted butter Two 1½-pound lamb loins, whole and tied around their circumference in two places each with butcher's twine	2 Tbs olive oil 1 pound pancetta, cut into ½-inch pieces	2 Tbs olive oil 1½ pounds pork tenderloin, trimmed and tied twice around its circumference with butcher's twine
3. Add and soften	1 large yellow onion, chopped	1 large yellow onion, chopped	1 large yellow onion, chopped	1 large yellow onion, chopped
4. Pour in and reduce	1 cup red wine	1 cup white wine	1 cup white wine	1 cup red wine
5. Add the herbs, then the vegetables; bring to a simmer	1 Tbs minced rosemary 1 Tbs stemmed thyme 2 tsp mild smoked paprika 1 garlic clove, minced 1¾ cups canned diced tomatoes	1 Tbs minced sage 1 Tbs stemmed thyme 2 tsp finely grated lemon zest 2 tsp mild smoked paprika 2 garlic cloves, minced 1¾ cups canned diced tomatoes 12 small baby artichokes, halved through the stems and outer leaves trimmed	2 Tbs minced parsley 1 Tbs stemmed thyme 2 tsp fennel seeds 2 tsp mild smoked paprika 1¾ cups canned diced tomatoes ½ cup fresh shelled or frozen peas	2 Tbs minced parsley 1½ Tbs minced oregano 1 Tbs stemmed thyme 2 tsp mild smoked paprika 4 garlic cloves, minced 1¾ cups canned diced tomatoes ½ cup fresh shelled or frozen peas
6. Stir in	2 cups medium-grain rice	2 cups medium-grain rice	2 cups medium-grain rice	2 cups medium-grain rice
7. Pour in and simmer slowly 10 minutes	The warm broth mixture	The warm broth mixture	The warm broth mixture	The warm broth mixture
8. Tuck in and bake	The browned rabbit and sausage 2 duck confit legs, meat removed and broken up into small chunks	The browned lamb loins, twine removed and the loins cut into 2-inch-thick pieces	The browned pancetta 2 pounds sea scallops 2 jarred roasted red peppers, thinly sliced	The browned pork, twine removed, the tenderloin cut into 2-inch pieces 24 cherrystone clams, scrubbed 1 cup chopped toasted skinned hazelnuts, see page 217)

Nutrition fads and carb-phobes notwithstanding, nothing beats fried chicken, fried shrimp, or onion rings. Crunchy, juicy, salty—all for so little effort (if not quite a bit of clean-up). Still, there are a few tricks to this trade that you should ply once in a while, hardly every evening, but surely on occasion, particularly in the summer when the corn and melons are sweet, the perfect side and dessert.

• MAKES 4 TO 6 SERVINGS

• **STEP 1** Set a large sauté pan over medium-high heat, clip a deep-frying thermometer to the inside of the pan, pour in enough oil to get a depth of ½ inch, and heat until the temperature reaches 365°F. This pan-frying technique is actually a bit of a cross, somewhere between deep-frying and traditional pan-frying. There's more oil here than is often used for pan-frying, but certainly not as much as for deep-frying. The food will not float in the oil; rather, it will rest near the pan's bottom, lifted up only slightly by the bubbles of moisture burbling off its underside. In other words, it's the best of both worlds: the golden crust from deep-frying, the caramelization from pan-frying.

The equipment

A high-sided sauté pan works best, one that's 14 inches in diameter with 3-inch-high sides. You'll need up to 6 cups (1½ quarts) oil to get the required depth. Yes, you can use a skillet; but when the food is added, the oil may well rise up to the skillet's rim. Compensate by using a very large skillet—at least 14 inches in diameter—or perhaps two skillets. In fact, to preclude making two batches of fried chicken, one waiting 20 minutes while the other cooks, consider using two pans anyway, whether sauté pans or skillets, each filled with oil to a depth of ½ inch.

Use equipment designed for deep-frying: a heat-safe metal spatula and a deep-frying thermometer. An instant-read meat thermometer, designed for readings around 140°F, can melt at pan-frying temperatures, which reach beyond 350°F. Make sure the deep-frying thermometer's bulb—or one of those new-fangled probes—sits in the oil, doesn't simply rest on the pan's bottom.

The oil

It must have a smoke point—the point at which the oil volatilizes and can ignite—well higher than 365°F. Thus, no lard, schmaltz, butter, or other animal fats like rendered bacon fat, all of which begin to smoke at about 320°F, sometimes lower. Never use any unrefined oil—the moisture and by-products left in the oil can lower the smoke point considerably. Unrefined peanut oil, common in Asian cooking, has a smoke point of 320°F. Unrefined sunflower oil has a relatively low smoke point: just 290°F.

Yes, you can pan-fry in a more exotic oil. Refined hazelnut and almond oils have a smoke point of about 420°F; ghee (clarified butter, see page 25), about 485°F. But why use such costly fats? Their taste will be lost; the aroma, in the air.

Instead, go for the basics: refined corn oil, safflower oil, or soybean oil, all of which have a smoke point at about 420°F. Refined peanut oil, our favorite oil for frying, is common to the North American market and has a smoke point around 450°F, more than high enough for this technique and beyond the danger zone.

• STEP 2 Set up three bowls for coating what's to be fried: 1) a bowl with 1 cup all-purpose flour, 2) a bowl with 3 large egg whites whisked with ½ cup water until foamy, and 3) a bowl with 2 cups seasoned yellow cornmeal, dried bread crumbs, or a combination of both, mixed with up to 2 tablespoons dried herbs or seasonings and 1 or 2 teaspoons salt. Use wide, shallow bowls so the food to be fried is easily set into these various ingredients. Set the bowls in a line with the third nearest the pan on the stove so you can move straight from that last bowl to the hot oil. If coated food sits around before it hits the oil, the flour's glutens can activate, turning the crust gummy.

The first bowl
As for Oven-Frying (page 217), use only all-purpose flour.

The second bowl
The egg whites are whisked with water so that there's more moisture. Frying is actually a dehydrating process. The coated food hits the oil and immediately all moisture goes far above its natural boiling point. That popping and splattering is actually moisture being lost from the coating or the food; it's not something that's happening with the oil—although little droplets of oil get tossed up in the fireworks. As the moisture boils from and through the crust, lots of tiny holes are created, forming an airy lace.

The third bowl
Here's the coating itself: cornmeal, dried bread crumbs, or a 50/50 combination. Or consider panko bread crumbs, a high-fat Japanese specialty that yields a spectacularly crunchy crust.

Season the items to be fried with up to 2 tablespoons dried herbs or spices and up to 2 teaspoons salt, preferably common table salt, better in the blend than coarse kosher or sea salt. In the American South where pan-frying was perfected as an art, many cooks add mild paprika and ground black pepper; but you can mix it up with dry mustard, a little ground cinnamon, perhaps some dried thyme or ground cumin. Or use a standard spice blend: chili powder, curry powder (see page 113), or even lemon pepper seasoning (see page 355).

Do not use fresh herbs, which can singe and turn bitter in the high heat of frying.

A THREE-BOWL TECHNIQUE TO GET PAN-FRIED FOODS PROPERLY COATED: Start by dipping them in all-purpose flour. . . .

Then dip them in egg whites well beaten with water. . . .

And finally, coat them with cornmeal, dried bread crumbs, or a 50/50 combination.

• **STEP 3** When the oil's temperature reaches 365°F, coat the protein or vegetable with the substance or mixture in each of the three bowls—first the flour, then the egg whites, then the dry mixture—before slipping the coated food into the skillet without crowding. Fry until golden brown and cooked through, turning once or twice and adjusting the heat to keep the temperature fairly constant. Transfer to a wire rack and season with salt while very hot. Continue making more fried food as need be. And now for what's to be fried. Consider these:

> About 4 pounds chicken pieces or one 4-pound cut-up chicken, giblets and neck removed
> Four 8-ounce bone-in pork chops
> Four 6-ounce thin, white-fleshed fish fillets such as tilapia, any snapper, or any drum
> 2 pounds medium shrimp
> 2 pounds sea scallops
> 1½ pounds semi-firm mozzarella, cut into ½-inch sticks
> 2 pounds broccoli or cauliflower florets
> 2 large yellow or sweet white onions, cut into ½-inch-thick slices and the various rings in each layer divided
> 4 medium zucchini, cut into ½-inch-thick rings

Here are a few notes on these ingredients:

Kitchen Safety

Frying is always dangerous, pops and splatters aplenty. Practice basic kitchen safety. Turn the pan's handle away from you; never have it sticking over the rim of the stove where you can inadvertently knock the whole thing to the floor. Keep a constant eye on the oil's temperature, making sure it doesn't rise too high. And keep kids and pets from under-foot. Get any burn immediately in ice, and do not hesitate to seek medical help.

1. The amount of chicken seems considerably higher than that of the other foods, but it all has to do with exposed surface area as well as the bone-to-meat ratio. In the end, chicken meat is thick, often balled up around the bone, with less

To butterfly a peeled shrimp, leave a tiny bit of the shell at the tail section intact, just where the split fins come off the tail. Make a cut about two-thirds of the way through the shrimp along the outside curve, just where the vein was removed. Spread the meat open, pressing gently against a cutting board.

Don't drop the pieces into the hot oil. Gently lower them for safety's sake.

exposed surface area than, say, a fish fillet. Skin on or skin off? Given this coating, it's your choice. For tips on cutting up a whole chicken, see page 78.

2. Fish fillets can be long, large, and hard to handle. To ease your task, consider cutting them in half the short way, just so they're easier to get into the oil.

3. Shrimp are better if butterflied.

4. Sea scallops are most often sold out of their shells, cleaned and ready to cook. If yours have a small, tubular muscle still attached to the round disk, remove that muscle and either fry it separately or discard it; it's slightly tougher than the more familiar disk but fully edible. When purchasing scallops, look for firm, pale beige to pink meat. If starkly white, they have been soaked in water to increase their weight. Use unfrozen scallops within a day of purchase, but it's more economical to get them frozen in large bags and thaw them yourself, just as your fishmonger did. There are almost no "fresh" scallops sold in the United States.

5. Cheese sticks often work best if the cheese is first frozen. Cut it into ½-inch sticks, then place on a large baking tray in the freezer for at least 6 hours if not overnight. The cheese will thaw rather than melt in the hot oil. Do not use fresh, soft mozzarella.

Dip and turn one piece in the flour, coating all sides; then tap off any excess against the bowl. Dip and turn the piece immediately into the egg-white mixture, again coating all sides before gently shaking off the excess. Finally, set the piece of food in the dry ingredients and press gently, rolling it on all sides to coat thoroughly.

Hold the piece of coated food by one side and lower it gently into the oil (without your touching the hot oil, of course). Do not drop anything into the pan. And do not crowd the pan: perhaps only six or eight onion rings at a time, maybe just two of the fish fillets. Watch the oil's temperature, adjusting the heat accordingly. The moment you get things in the pan, the temperature drops. Raise the heat a bit, then once the oil gets back to 365°F, lower the heat perhaps to medium to maintain an even 365°F.

After one side has turned golden brown, turn with a large metal spatula or tongs, taking extreme care not to dislodge the crust.

All of this means you'll be doing double or triple duty as you fry quick-cookers like shrimp and onion rings: dipping some, watching the temperature, turning, coating more, almost all at once. Stay calm and focused.

Timing here is a matter of the food cooked:

shrimp, onion rings, zucchini rounds, broccoli or cauliflower florets: about
    2 minutes
scallops, mozzarella sticks: about 3 minutes
fish fillets: about 5 minutes
pork chops: about 16 minutes
chicken: about 18 minutes

If you notice that the chicken or pork starts to burn, lower the oil's temperature a bit, perhaps to 340°F. If you're at all in doubt about something being done, lift it gently out of the oil and take its internal temperature with an instant-read meat thermometer: pork should be at 160°F; chicken, about 165°F.

Use a large metal spatula to transfer the fried food to a large wire rack—never a plate lined with paper towels. Cover the counter under the rack with paper towels or wax paper to make clean-up easier, but hot fried food sitting directly on paper towels means soggy crusts where the food has sat and steamed. A wire rack assures good air circulation.

There is one trick to extra-crispy fried foods. Once everything's out of the oil and on the rack, raise the heat to high and bring the oil's temperature up to 390°F. If there are bits of coating and such in the oil, skim them off with a metal, slotted spoon because they can burn at this higher temperature—or begin now with a second skillet of fresh oil, bringing it up to the higher temperature. Once 390°F is reached, slip all the fried ingredients into this very hot oil until very dark and crunchy, perhaps 2 minutes, turning once. Transfer everything back to the wire rack.

Finally, salt the hot food just out of the oil. Yes, there was a lot of salt in the coating, but fried foods eat up sodium because of a complex relationship among the chemical compounds formed. You've come this far; just give in.

Just a little sprinkle of salt and Lemon-Pepper Fried Chicken is good to go.

Recipes for Pan-Frying

	Lemon-Pepper Fried Chicken	Cajun Fried Fish	Best-Ever Onion Rings	Southwest Fried Shrimp
1. Heat to 365°F	About 6 cups peanut oil	About 6 cups peanut oil	About 6 cups peanut oil	About 6 cups peanut oil
2. Prepare three bowls for the coating process	½ cup all-purpose flour 3 large egg whites whisked with ½ cup water until foamy 2 cups cornmeal mixed with 1 Tbs lemon pepper seasoning (page 355), 1 Tbs mild paprika, and 2 tsp salt	½ cup all-purpose flour 3 large egg whites whisked with ½ cup water until foamy 2 cups cornmeal mixed with 1 Tbs mild paprika, 2 tsp dried thyme, 1 tsp ground cumin, 1 tsp cayenne, and 2 tsp salt—or just 2 Tbs purchased Cajun seasoning mix	½ cup all-purpose flour 3 large egg whites whisked with ½ cup water until foamy 2 cups dried bread crumbs mixed with 1 Tbs dried thyme, 2 tsp onion powder, ½ tsp garlic powder and 2 tsp salt	½ cup all-purpose flour 3 large egg whites whisked with ½ cup water until foamy 1 cup cornmeal and 1 cup dried bread crumbs mixed with 1 Tbs pure ancho chile powder, 2 tsp ground cumin, 2 tsp dried oregano, 1 tsp ground cinnamon, 1 tsp dried thyme, and 2 tsp salt
3. Coat and fry, turning once or twice; transfer to a rack and season	One 4-pound chicken, cut into 9 pieces Salt to taste	Four 6-ounce skinless thin white-fleshed fish fillets Salt to taste	2 large onions, cut into ½-inch-thick slices and the various rings in each layer divided Salt to taste	2 pounds medium shrimp, peeled but with the final tail section intact, deveined, and then butterflied (see page 238)

	Southern Fried Pork Chops	Fried Scallops	Curried Mozzarella Sticks	Crunchy Broccoli and Cauliflower
1. Heat to 365°F	About 6 cups peanut oil	About 6 cups peanut oil	About 6 cups peanut oil	About 6 cups peanut oil
2. Prepare three bowls for the coating process	½ cup all-purpose flour 3 large egg whites whisked with ½ cup water until foamy 2 cups cornmeal mixed with 2 Tbs mild paprika, 2 tsp ground black pepper, and 2 tsp salt	½ cup all-purpose flour 3 large egg whites whisked with ½ cup water until foamy 2 cups dried bread crumbs mixed with 1 Tbs minced dried lemon peel, 1 Tbs minced parsley, 2 tsp salt, 1 tsp celery seeds, and 1 tsp ground black pepper	½ cup all-purpose flour 3 large egg whites whisked with ½ cup water until foamy 2 cups dried bread crumbs mixed with 2 Tbs curry powder (see page 113) and 2 tsp salt	½ cup all-purpose flour 3 large egg whites whisked with ½ cup water until foamy 1 cup cornmeal and 1 cup dried bread crumbs mixed with 1 Tbs crumbled dried rosemary, 2 tsp dried oregano, 2 tsp dried thyme, and 2 tsp salt
3. Coat and fry, turning once; transfer to a rack and season	Four 8-ounce bone-in pork chops Salt to taste	2 pounds sea scallops Salt to taste	1½ pounds semi-firm mozzarella, cut into ½-inch sticks and frozen Salt to taste	1 pound broccoli florets and 1 pound cauliflower florets Salt to taste

Pasta in a Cream Sauce

There's nothing better than pasta in a delicate if slightly decadent cream sauce—and nothing worse than noodles drowned in cream. Reduce the cream well and use good cooking know-how to build a sophisticated sauce with grated cheese as well as a dry fortified wine, some liquor, or a little broth. • MAKES 4 SMALL SERVINGS, SUITABLE FOR A FIRST COURSE—OR 2 HEARTY MAIN-COURSE SERVINGS

• **STEP 1** Cook and drain 8 ounces dried or 12 ounces fresh pasta. Use enough water so the noodles dance in the boil. Go for about 3 quarts of water here—and a pot large enough to hold it and the pasta comfortably.

Although soft, fresh pasta often works better in simple cream sauces, the noodles may not have the tensile strength to hold up to lots of other ingredients. If your sauce will be well stocked, consider sturdier dried pasta.

There's an old Italian axiom that tubes hold cream, noodles carry tomatoes. In reality, either will do. The dictates of culinary authenticity may be unforgiving, but they're also overrated on most weeknights.

Drain the cooked pasta in a colander in the sink. Do not rinse: the sticky, starchy coating will later hold the sauce on the noodles.

• **STEP 2** Heat 1 or 2 tablespoons fat in a large sauté pan or skillet set over medium-high heat. There are two choices:

> **unsalted butter,** the traditional mate to cream
> **olive oil,** a decidedly cleaner taste

However, olive oil may also fall out of suspension as the cream reduces. Don't worry: it will coat the noodles when they're added in step 6.

Over the years, we've again and again reduced the amount of added fat in a cream sauce—not for health reasons (heaven forfend), but because the dish tastes best when most of its fat comes from the cream.

One final note: use a large pan, preferably a 12-inch high-sided sauté pan or perhaps a 14-inch skillet. The pan's got to hold the sautéed ingredients, the pasta, and the sauce comfortably; a 10-inch skillet is simply too small.

Onions

Why have onions and their kin become the basis of most of the world's cuisine? Most plants store air, not water, in their leaves. Some leafy greens are as much as 70% air by volume. Thus, they shrink dramatically over the heat without much sizzle—which is why most recipes ask you to put spinach and the like in the pan with some rinsing water still adhering to the leaves; the water helps break down the fibers in the absence of much natural moisture.

Onions, by contrast, don't immediately shrink because they hold mostly water. Their many inner layers are actually the water-engorged base of the leaves (you can see them coming right out of a scallion or a leek). The leaves die off in the winter, leaving the bulb behind so that it can flower and seed the following year. All that water (and attendant carbohydrates) means that an onion adds rich, nutrient-laced, flavor-packed juices to a soup, sauce, braise, stir-fry, or curry.

For the best-tasting cream sauce, first sauté the vegetables and aromatics to soften them without much caramelization—then add the liquid.

The added broth or wine has been reduced to a glaze: a line scraped through the liquid will hold its shape for a few seconds before any liquid flows back in place.

• **STEP 3** Sauté up to 3 cups prepared vegetable, protein, a combination of both, or even of several. The sauté should be simple, just a few ingredients—and all prepared (that is, diced or minced, maybe even seared or parboiled) so they can be finished off quickly in the sauce. There's no reason to add the full amount, especially if you want to keep the sauce light.

Use a diced onion as part of the base when you have a hearty base like meat or nuts. Thinly sliced leeks offer a lighter taste; scallions, a little zip, better when paired with other vegetables. Shallots, a less sweet alternative if also a softer vegetable, should also be diced, not chopped. The point is to get as much flavor out of the vegetables as quickly as possible; if browned, they will darken the sauce—not the worst thing, except in terms of aesthetics. Of course, some very light or simple sauces—peas and carrots, garlic and frizzled bacon—don't need any aromatics at all.

All meats should be trimmed. The fat's in the cream; rendered animal fat will just skim the dish. Chicken skin and any fat underneath should be removed; the breasts, cut into thin strips. Turkey, veal, and beef are also best cut into thin strips like tiny scaloppine (see page 325) so they'll cook quickly. Dark-meat chicken and pork should be cubed. Remove sausage meat from its casings.

Shrimp should be peeled and deveined; large ones, cut in half. Scallops impart a briny flavor quickly, but large ones need to be cut crosswise into two disks. Fresh or frozen lump crabmeat and canned clams are, of course, ready without any preparation.

Many fish fillets flake into ridiculous threads in a sauté. To solve the problem, use a firm-flesh fish, such as cod or halibut, cut into 1-inch chunks.

In a vegetarian sauce, sweet root vegetables are wonderful with the cream. Since they take a while over the heat to get tender, they need to be diced quite small—or consider shredding carrots, peeled kohlrabi, or sweet potatoes through the large holes of a box grater. Or try slightly later chunks, about ¾ inch each, but parboiled in a pan of boiling water for 5 to 7 minutes until they're on the verge of being tender. Easier choices are spring and summer vegetables like asparagus and broccoli, although both need to be cut into small bits; broccoli stems should not be wasted but instead sliced into matchsticks.

Although peas cook in no time, the dish is even easier if you use frozen peas. Indeed, any frozen vegetable, thawed and drained, will work. A bag of frozen, mixed vegetables with some noodles and a little cream make a hearty meal in minutes.

When this step is completed, the main ingredients should be

slightly undercooked. They're going to continue cooking with the flavorings and the cream in steps 4 and 5, but only for a couple minutes. Make sure they're close to being done.

• STEP 4 Add a little minced herbs or dried spices and about ¼ cup broth, dry fortified wine, or liquor; reduce to a glaze. A pasta in cream sauce is not about the cream; it's actually about the layers of flavor that the cream enhances. So the choices are manifold: a pinch of ground ginger with shrimp; some snipped chives with cubed, skinless turkey breast and sliced pears; or even smoked paprika with pork loin and thinly sliced onions.

Cream sauces also need a secondary liquid to balance the flavors. Use broth (chicken, vegetable, fish, or beef) or clam juice, depending on the main ingredient. But use only ¼ cup. This is no braise.

White wine is masked by the cream to come; red wine, never used because of its staining color. Instead, dry vermouth, dry Marsala, or dry Madeira make excellent foils. But no red vermouth or port—too sweet, more like dessert.

Or other liquors can be added like vodka, Calvados, or Armagnac. But be forewarned: liquors can ignite over the heat. Follow these safety rules:

1. Remove the skillet or pan from the heat before adding the liquor.
2. Turn off the exhaust vent—it can suck up the flames.
3. If the mixture ignites, don't grab the pan. Cover it and remove it from the heat. Wait at least 20 seconds for the fire to go out.
4. Always have a box of baking soda nearby to douse any flames on the counter.
5. Make sure your kitchen fire extinguisher is charged up.

This additional liquid should boil just until it becomes a glaze, no more than 30 seconds, maybe even less.

• STEP 5 Pour in about 1 cup heavy cream and bring to a full simmer. Like reverb at a rock concert, the cream's purpose is to amplify; too much is annoying. It should boil vigorously at the edges of the pan and start to roil in the center—no more than 2 minutes for a good reduction, probably just 1 minute if the cream's at room temperature and the pan's hot.

If you'd like to make a cream sauce without the cream, try using whole milk, goat's milk, soy milk, or rice milk. Each needs to be modified. Stir in whole milk and goat's milk at this point, mix well,

The secret to a good cream sauce? Use less cream than you might expect.

Cream is only the base of this cream sauce; cheese adds body and flavor.

The sauce has been reduced enough that it clings to the noodles with just a little extra in the skillet.

then scoop up about ½ cup of the simmering sauce and whisk it vigorously and quickly into a small bowl with a well-beaten, large egg yolk. Stir this mixture back into the sauce, keeping the skillet over the heat and stirring constantly just until the mixture thickens, about 10 seconds and not a second more. Remove the skillet from the heat to complete step 6.

If you're using soy and rice milk, you'll have to prepare the sauce for their addition. Add 1 teaspoon all-purpose flour to the pan once the sauté is completed in the middle of step 4, before the broth is poured in. Cook for 30 seconds, then add the broth and reduce as directed, whisking all the while to dissolve the flour. Finally, pour in the soy or rice milk at this stage, stirring constantly until the dissolved flour thickens it slightly.

• **STEP 6** Add the cooked pasta and about ¼ cup grated or shredded cheese (about 2 ounces); season lightly with salt and freshly ground pepper, then toss gently. Add the cheese last, along with the cooked pasta, while the pan's over the heat. Toss gently with tongs to loosen up the pasta, then remove from the heat.

One last note on appearance: ground white pepper will leave no unattractive black flecks in the sauce. But white pepper has a different taste, more sour and piquant. Go easy until you get the hang of it—or just use black pepper and say "hang it" to appearances.

Recipes for Pasta in Cream Sauces

	Bowtie Pasta with Crab in a Mustard Cream Sauce	Ziti with Mushrooms in a Marsala Cream Sauce	Linguine Nogada	Rigatoni with Chicken and Apples
1. Cook and drain	8 ounces dried bowtie pasta	8 ounces dried ziti	12 ounces fresh linguine	8 ounces dried rigatoni
2. Heat	2 Tbs unsalted butter	2 Tbs olive oil	2 Tbs unsalted butter	1 Tbs unsalted butter
3. Sauté	12 ounces lump crabmeat, picked over for shell and cartilage 1 celery rib, thinly sliced	¾ pound cremini mushrooms, cleaned and thinly sliced	1 medium yellow onion, diced 2 garlic cloves, minced 1½ cups chopped walnut pieces	6 to 8 ounces boneless skinless chicken breasts, cut into thin strips 2 medium apples, peeled, cored, and chopped
4. Add and reduce	1 Tbs Dijon mustard 2 tsp minced dill ¼ cup fish broth or clam juice	2 tsp stemmed thyme ¼ cup dry Marsala	2 tsp chili powder 1 tsp stemmed thyme ½ tsp ground cumin ¼ cup vegetable broth	1 Tbs minced tarragon ¼ cup brandy
5. Pour in and simmer	1 cup cream	1 cup cream	1 cup cream	1 cup cream
6. Toss in the cooked pasta and cheese; salt and pepper to taste	¼ cup finely grated Parmesan	¼ cup finely grated Parmesan	¼ cup crumbled Oaxaca cheese or Queso Blanco	¼ cup grated Gruyère

	Penne à la Vodka	Spaghetti Prima Vera	Noodles with a Carrot Curry Cream Sauce	Fettuccini with Clams in a Garlic Cream Sauce
1. Cook and drain	8 ounces dried penne	12 ounces fresh spaghetti	12 ounces fresh thin noodles	8 ounces dried fettuccini
2. Heat	1 Tbs unsalted butter	2 Tbs unsalted butter	1 Tbs almond oil	2 Tbs unsalted butter
3. Sauté	1 medium yellow onion, diced 8 Roma or plum tomatoes, seeded and chopped	2½ cups peas, thinly sliced carrots, thinly sliced asparagus, and small broccoli florets; or 2½ cups frozen mixed vegetables, thawed	¾ pound carrots, shredded through the large holes of a box grater 1 Tbs minced peeled fresh ginger	12 ounces canned minced clams, drained 4 garlic cloves, minced
4. Add and reduce	2 tsp minced oregano 1 tsp stemmed thyme ¼ tsp red pepper flakes ¼ cup vodka	2 Tbs shredded basil ¼ cup vegetable broth	1 Tbs curry powder (see page 113) ¼ cup dry vermouth	2 tsp minced oregano ¼ cup clam juice
5. Pour in and simmer	1 cup cream	1 cup cream	1 cup cream	1 cup cream
6. Toss in the cooked pasta and cheese; salt and pepper to taste	¼ cup finely grated Pecorino	¼ cup finely grated Parmesan	¼ cup crumbled soft goat cheese (chèvre)	¼ cup finely grated Parmesan

Asian Picadillo served in lettuce leaves

Picadillo

This Latin American, Cuban, Mexican, or Caribbean ground beef mélange of aromatics, spices, and vinegar is an easy way to have lunch in the house when company arrives—just tear a head of lettuce into leaves, then fill each of these lettuce "cups" with a little picadillo. Roll them up and eat like little wraps. Picadillo is also an easy filling for tacos, burritos, or even Enchiladas (page 118)—and a great filling for Omelets (page 213). In Cuba, it's often served over rice and beans; but it can also be spooned over mashed potatoes (see page 21), baked sweet potatoes, or steamed plantains. • MAKES 4 SERVINGS

• **STEP 1** Heat about 2 tablespoons oil in a large saucepan over medium heat. Consider almost any oil, from olive to walnut, canola to almond, even toasted sesame to mustard seed. Simply latch the tastes of that oil onto the other ingredients: olive oil with Mediterranean flavors, toasted sesame with Asian, mustard seed with East Indian, canola with almost anything. Avoid toasted oils and most solid fats like lard or duck fat.

Although picadillo is generally considered a dish from the Americas, you can skew the flavors this way and that at will. In fact, there's no reason not to use unsalted butter in a French-inspired picadillo with ground veal, dried cherries, minced tarragon, chopped shallots, and red wine. Whimsical, yes—but definitely diverting, particularly in lettuce-leaf cups some summer evening alongside a glass of crisp, sweet Riesling.

• **STEP 2** Stir in about 1 cup diced aromatics and accents; cook, stirring constantly, until softened. Picadillo is all about aromatics— here and again in step 4. These should be a canvas for the other flavors. Consider the base aromatics to be

> **thinly sliced leeks,** white and pale green parts only, halved
>   lengthwise and washed to remove sand
> **diced onions,** red or yellow
> **minced scallions**
> **diced shallots**

and the accents to be

> **minced garlic cloves**
> **minced garlic scapes**
> **minced peeled fresh ginger**
> **minced ramps**

For a balanced picadillo, the ground meat and aromatics are cooked until they're ready to eat before the secondary aromatics and flavorings are added, thus allowing these latter to be more present, more fragrant in the overall dish.

For the best taste, use them in pairings like shallots and garlic, onions and garlic scapes, leeks and ginger. These should all be diced or minced quite small so that everything's about the size of the ground meat to come.

• **STEP 3** Add 1 pound ground meat; cook until it begins to brown, stirring often, about 5 minutes. Any ground meat will do: veal, beef, chicken, turkey, pork, buffalo, ostrich, even textured soy protein, so long as it's the "ground beef flavor" variety. Or use a combination, particularly ground beef or buffalo with ground pork. However, seek out lean ground beef, preferably 93% lean or so. The fat's not going anywhere except in the mixture itself, so less is better.

For the best taste, grind the meat yourself. Buy sirloin or bottom round, then grind it at home with a meat grinder or the grinder attachment on your stand mixer. Or simply ask the butcher to grind it for you right at the market. You'll have leaner ground beef; plus, it won't be a mixture of trimmings from the cow's butchering. Indeed, you can ask the butcher to grind any cut you select: pork shoulder, turkey breast cutlet, lamb stew meat, or even boneless skinless chicken breasts.

One last note on the ground meat: you can reduce its amount to ½ pound or so and add a diced vegetable like a seeded bell pepper or a very dark-skinned plantain.

Picadillo is enhanced with some dried fruit and a secondary aromatic: on left from top, dried nectarines, raisins, dried apricots, and candied ginger; on right, a green chile, a jarred roasted red pepper, roasted garlic cloves, and caper berries.

• **STEP 4** Stir in ¼ cup diced dried fruit, up to ¼ cup minced secondary aromatic, and one or two minced fresh herbs or ground spices. All dried fruit must be diced so as to avoid pulpy bits in the mix. Consider:

> **dried apples**
> **dried cherries**
> **dried currants**
> **dried mango**
> **dried nectarines**
> **dried pears**
> **dried pineapple**
> **raisins**, golden or otherwise

Or skip the fruit altogether and add ¼ cup chopped candied ginger, a sweet/savory spark.

For that secondary aromatic, think antipasto and aromatic items from a salad bar, including

> **diced marinated artichoke hearts**
> **diced caper berries**
> **diced pitted green or black olives, or even stuffed olives**
> **minced anchovies**
> **minced drained capers**
> **minced jarred pimientos or roasted red peppers**

minced roasted garlic (provided no garlic has been used earlier)
minced seeded fresh chiles
minced seeded pickled jalapeños
thinly sliced sun-dried tomatoes

All should be cut into small bits so they'll meld quickly. But practice good culinary balance: you don't need as much minced anchovy as, say, diced olive or sun-dried tomatoes—or no more than 1 tablespoon minced capers. Or consider mixing two secondary aromatics: roasted garlic and chopped caper berries, minced pimientos and jalapeños, or chopped olives and a seeded minced serrano chile.

Cilantro or parsley is probably the most authentic herb for Latin American picadillos, but you also could use basil, mint, thyme, or tarragon. Plan on about 2 tablespoons, then either add a little ground spice (cinnamon, nutmeg, coriander) or use chile powder or a flavorful spice blend as a complement. For the difference between herbs and spices, see page 230.

• **STEP 5** Pour in ¾ cup liquid and 2 tablespoons vinegar or acidic citrus juice; cook uncovered, stirring often, until the liquid has been reduced to a glaze and almost absorbed, about 5 minutes. Season with hot red pepper sauce, salt, and freshly ground black pepper to taste. The ground meat is cooked through at this point; this step is just about getting more aromatic flavor into the dish.

Although the liquid can be broth, wine, or a dry fortified wine, it can also include tomato sauce. In the end, the liquid's probably best if it's a combination like ½ cup beef broth and ¼ cup dry sherry or ½ cup dry white wine and ¼ cup tomato sauce.

Don't neglect fish sauce (see page 388) and/or soy sauce, but use no more than 2 tablespoons of either or both in the mix of liquids. An excellent Asian pairing would be to start the dish with toasted sesame oil and then finish it here with ½ cup shaoxing (see page 374) or dry sherry, 2 tablespoons soy sauce, and 2 tablespoons fish sauce.

You can also use coconut milk—although preferably mixed 50/50 with broth or wine. Avoid cream and milk since you will be adding acid at the same time, acid which will curdle them. If you really want the taste of dairy in the picadillo, consider using ¼ cup yogurt as part of your liquid.

Concerning that acid, almost any vinegar will do, from low-acid rice vinegar to apple cider vinegar, sweet balsamic to even sweeter white balsamic, although white or red wine vinegar is perhaps the easiest and most accessible choice. But do stay away from flavored vinegars (fig, raspberry, and the like) as well as seasoned rice vinegars, full of sugar. What about lemon or lime juice, a nice spark in this otherwise light dish?

The picadillo may or may not need salt at this stage, depending on if you've added olives, capers, soy sauce, fish sauce, and the like. However, it will almost certainly need freshly ground black pepper to give it one last quick layer of flavor.

Recipes for Picadillos

	Cuban Picadillo	Asian Picadillo	Hawaiian Picadillo	Argentinean Picadillo
1. Heat	2 Tbs olive oil	2 Tbs toasted sesame oil	2 Tbs canola oil	2 Tbs olive oil
2. Stir in and soften	1 small yellow onion, diced 3 garlic cloves, minced	5 medium whole scallions, diced 2 garlic cloves, minced	1 small yellow onion, diced 1 garlic clove, minced 1 Tbs minced peeled fresh ginger	1 small yellow onion, diced 3 garlic cloves, minced
3. Add and brown	8 ounces lean ground beef 8 ounces ground pork	10 ounces ground pork 6 ounces lean ground beef	1 pound lean ground beef	1 pound lean ground beef
4. Stir in	¼ cup chopped dried mango ¼ cup chopped green olives 2 Tbs minced cilantro 1 tsp ground cumin	¼ cup chopped dried currants 2 Tbs chopped crystallized ginger 1 minced seeded serrano chile 2 Tbs minced cilantro ½ tsp five-spice powder (see page 149)	¼ cup chopped dried pineapple 2 Tbs chopped caper berries 1 anchovy fillet, minced 1 Tbs minced mint 2 Tbs minced parsley	¼ cup chopped raisins 1 hard-boiled egg, chopped ¼ cup chopped pitted green olives 2 Tbs minced parsley ¼ tsp ground cloves
5. Pour in and reduce before seasoning	½ cup beef broth ¼ cup tomato sauce 2 Tbs red wine vinegar Several dashes hot red pepper sauce Salt and pepper to taste	½ cup plus 2 Tbs chicken broth 2 Tbs soy sauce 2 Tbs rice vinegar Pepper to taste	½ cup chicken broth 3 Tbs unsweetened pineapple juice 1 Tbs soy sauce Pepper to taste	½ cup beef broth ¼ cup red wine 2 Tbs red wine vinegar Several dashes hot red pepper sauce Salt and pepper to taste

	Turkey Picadillo	Italian-Style Picadillo	Vietnamese Picadillo	Caribbean Picadillo
1. Heat	2 Tbs almond oil	2 Tbs olive oil	2 Tbs peanut oil	2 Tbs canola oil
2. Stir in and soften	1 medium leek, white and green parts only, halved lengthwise, washed carefully, and thinly sliced 1 garlic clove, minced	1 small yellow onion, diced ¼ cup chopped, seeded, jarred Italian peperoncini 3 garlic cloves, minced	3 medium whole scallions, diced 4 ounces shallots, minced 2 Tbs minced peeled fresh ginger	1 small yellow onion, diced ½ cup minced seeded green bell pepper 3 garlic cloves, minced 1 Tbs minced peeled fresh ginger
3. Add and brown	1 pound ground turkey	8 ounces ground pork 8 ounces ground veal	8 ounces lean ground beef 8 ounces ground pork	8 ounces ground chicken 1 small very ripe yellow plantain, peeled and diced
4. Stir in	¼ cup chopped dried cranberries ¼ cup minced, peeled, and seeded pear 2 Tbs minced parsley 1 Tbs stemmed thyme 2 tsp minced sage	¼ cup toasted pine nuts ¼ cup diced sun-dried tomatoes 2 Tbs minced basil 1 tsp minced rosemary 1 tsp stemmed thyme	¼ cup chopped golden raisins ¼ cup minced radishes 2 Tbs minced cilantro 2 Tbs minced mint	¼ cup chopped dried mango 2 Tbs minced sun-dried tomatoes 1 fresh jalapeño chile, seeded and chopped 2 Tbs minced parsley ¼ tsp grated nutmeg ¼ tsp ground cloves
5. Pour in and reduce before seasoning	½ cup dry vermouth ¼ cup unsweetened apple juice 2 Tbs dry white wine Salt and pepper to taste	½ cup dry Marsala ¼ cup tomato sauce 2 Tbs balsamic vinegar Salt and pepper to taste	½ cup dry sherry 2 Tbs soy sauce 2 Tbs fish sauce (see page 388) 2 Tbs lime juice Pepper to taste	½ cup chicken broth ¼ cup coconut milk 2 Tbs cider vinegar Salt and pepper to taste

Fish Fillets with Cream and Tarragon

Poached Fish Fillets

Here's a wonderful way to cook thicker fish fillets: hake, cod, grouper, and the like—or even snapper fillets, provided they're at least 1 inch thick. With slow oven-poaching, the fish stays moist, nestled into an aromatic broth that then becomes the sauce, ladled into individual bowls. • MAKES 4 SERVINGS

• **STEP 1** Preheat the oven to 400°F. Lay 1½ pounds skinless, thick-fleshed fish fillet(s) in a 12-inch, oven-safe sauté pan, then pour in enough broth, an enhanced broth, or a range of appropriate liquids to come about halfway up the fish fillets. (Do not yet set the pan over the heat.) For tips on removing the skin, see page 124—or have your fishmonger do it for you.

The fillets should be fairly thick so they hold up to the poaching. Snapper, sole, orange roughy, and the like would disintegrate as they poach. Tuna steaks, best rare or medium-rare, should be saved for the grill; here, they will be almost cooked through, the flesh an unappetizing, dry gray (at best).

Either leave the chosen fillets whole or cut them into 4 servings before returning the fish to the pan. Some fillets, like halibut and cod, may be large enough to come as a single piece; others, like scrod or pollock, will come in several pieces to make up the required weight.

In terms of the liquid, use as your base

> **broth**—specifically vegetable broth or fish stock/clam juice
>
> **wine**—dry white wine or occasionally red wine
>
> **a broth/wine combo**—50/50 perhaps (although it's hard to tell exactly since you'll be eyeing the amounts in the pan), or weighted slightly one way or the other, more savory (more broth) or more sweet (more wine), depending on the other aromatics to be added
>
> **unsweetened apple cider**—whether alone or in combination with broth or wine
>
> **canned tomato sauce**—usually in a 50/50 combo with white wine
>
> **beer**—a sweet, sticky braising liquid that needs to be balanced by lots of aromatics and perhaps some vegetable broth so it isn't quite so heavy
>
> **soy sauce and shaoxing** (see page 374)—for Asian pairings, neither should be more than ¼ cup, the remainder of the necessary liquid filled out with broth

To poach fish fillets, you have to eyeball the right amount of liquid—pour it in until it comes about halfway up the fillets in the pan.

The amount used is difficult to predict because one batch of fillets may well be thicker or thinner than another, depending on the type you've chosen. Keep this in mind: poach the fish; do not boil it. In general, for a fillet about 1½ inches thick, you'll need about 1½ cups liquid.

• **STEP 2** Use a wide spatula to transfer the raw fish from the pan to a large cutting board. Add up to 6 tablespoons minced aromatics to the liquid in the pan and bring to a simmer over medium-high heat. Start to build the sauce—but keep in mind that this is not a stew or a sauté. Use a mixed batch of aromatics, no one predominant, perhaps two, three, or even four types. The amounts are small because everything's simply about flavoring that liquid in the pan. Begin with minced or thinly sliced aromatics so you can get several in a spoonful with each bite of fish:

Once the fillets have been poached, the leftover liquid, now the base of the sauce, can be enhanced with aromatics and any number of enrichers—here, heavy cream.

onion

shallot

leek, white and pale green parts only, halved lengthwise and
    carefully washed to remove sand

ramps

scallions

fresh chiles

peeled fresh ginger

garlic cloves

garlic scapes

lemongrass, very tender white end only, crushed

fresh herbs

dried herbs, in moderation and particularly their whole versions like
    crushed cumin seeds, a cinnamon stick, or a star anise pod

sun-dried tomatoes

chopped pitted olives

drained capers

Thai curry paste (page 386), no more than 1 teaspoon or so

vindaloo paste (page 395), no more than 1 teaspoon or so

As usual, a combination of aromatics might well be best: onion and garlic, scallions and lemongrass. Or try minced tarragon with shallots and white wine; caraway seeds with garlic and beer; oregano, rosemary, or thyme with an onion and red wine; a cinnamon stick and a few crushed whole peppercorns with tomato sauce and red wine.

• **STEP 3** (optional): Add 1½ cups chopped or thinly sliced vegetables; cover tightly, reduce the heat to very low, and simmer slowly until the vegetables are crisp-tender. This step is sometimes optional, although not often, since a few vegetables give the sauce body. These vegetables are to flavor the liquid, not to make a well-stocked stew, so the best are those that are the most aromatic:

chopped zucchini

peeled and roughly chopped cucumber

quartered cherry tomatoes

thinly sliced celery

thinly sliced mushrooms, particularly shiitake caps

trimmed, thinly sliced fennel

thinly sliced and then diced carrots

thinly sliced and then diced parsnips

peeled and diced sweet potatoes

peeled and diced parsley root

peeled and diced celeriac

peeled, seeded, and diced winter squash, such as butternut
    or acorn squash

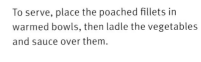

To serve, place the poached fillets in warmed bowls, then ladle the vegetables and sauce over them.

These all cook at about the same rate, provided the roots and winter squash are indeed diced into ¼-inch pieces. Thus, this step is all about your knife technique. Needless to say, you won't use all of a celeriac or a winter squash; less is more in this simple preparation. Save the remainder for another use. For now, add everything to the pan, cover, reduce the heat so that the liquid simmers slowly, and cook the vegetables just until crisp-tender.

Missing from the list are vegetables that wouldn't leach much flavor: turnips, rutabaga, and peas, to name a few. That said, peeled white or yellow-fleshed potatoes can make a nice addition since they so readily absorb other flavors. You'll also need to cook diced potatoes a few minutes longer, just to make sure they're tender. One note: do not use russets; their starch can cloud the sauce.

Also missing from the list are vegetables that would turn to mush during the poaching: broccoli and cauliflower florets, string beans, asparagus, and such. And of course, no leafy greens.

• **STEP 4** Partially submerge the fish fillets in the liquid, bring it back to a simmer, cover, and place in the oven for 7 minutes for every inch of thickness. The fish is cooked when you can stick a flatware knife into the thickest part, hold it there for 5 seconds, and then touch the flat side of the knife to your lips and feel warmth—not any chill, not even ambient room temperature, but also certainly not excessive heat.

• **STEP 5** Transfer the cooked fish to individual serving bowls. Set the pan back over medium-high heat, bring the liquid to a low simmer, and enrich and/or thicken it. Season with salt and freshly ground black pepper. Then divide the sauce among the fillets in the bowls. If you haven't cut the fish into four individual servings, do so now in the pan before you transfer the pieces to the individual bowls. By the way, these bowls can be slightly warmed in a very low-heat oven so they keep the fish warm—but the bowls should be just warmed, certainly not at all hot, because they'll continue to cook the fish and can render the fillets dry and overly flakey.

This step is the most dramatic in terms of what you can do with the dish. Here's a list of enrichers (some will thicken, too) with proposed amounts:

About ¼ cup cream

About ¼ cup coconut milk

About ¼ cup plain regular, low-fat or fat-free yogurt

3 tablespoons puréed cooked or canned vegetables such as asparagus, green beans, or white beans

About 3 tablespoons mashed roasted garlic (see page 333 for instructions on how to roast a head)

2 tablespoons aioli (see page 197)

2 tablespoons peanut butter or other nut butter

1½ tablespoons tomato paste

If Asian flavors are abundant in the dish and soy sauce hasn't already been used as part of the poaching liquid, consider forgoing the salt and pepper and seasoning the dish now with a splash or two of soy sauce, then thickening it with 1 tablespoon hoisin sauce, Chinese bean sauce, oyster sauce, or even plum sauce.

Or skip the enrichers and thicken the sauce with one of these three methods:

1. Make a beurre manié (see page 209) of 1 tablespoon unsalted butter, softened to room temperature, and 1 tablespoon all-purpose flour. Whisk it into the liquid in five or six additions, each fully incorporated before adding the next.
2. Whisk 1 large egg yolk until foamy in a medium bowl, then whisk in about ½ cup of the simmering liquid from the pan in a slow, steady stream until smooth; whisk this combined mixture back into the pan.
3. Whisk 1½ teaspoons cornstarch or potato starch with 1 tablespoon water until smooth in a small bowl, then add this slurry into the pan and whisk while simmering until slightly thickened.

Although the enrichers and thickeners tend to be mutually exclusive categories, cream and a beurre manié can be used in combination. You can also mix a couple of the enrichers, like peanut butter and coconut milk.

• **STEP 6** (optional): Garnish the individual servings. Once the thickened sauce is in the bowls and over the fish, consider adding a little garnish over each serving. For each serving, consider at least one, perhaps two of the following:

2 tablespoons minced seeded tomato (if there is no tomato in the sauce)

½ tablespoon minced herb, particularly basil, parsley, oregano, or tarragon

1 teaspoon aromatic olive oil

1 teaspoon toasted walnut oil

1 teaspoon toasted sesame oil

1 teaspoon lemon or lime juice

Recipes for Poached Fish Fillets

	Fish Fillets with Coconut Curry	Fish Fillets with Cream and Tarragon	Southeast Asian Poached Fish Fillets	Fish Fillets Poached with Fennel
1. Preheat the oven; pour in enough liquid to come halfway up the fillet(s)	About 1½ cups dry white wine	About 1½ cups dry white wine	About 1½ cups fish stock or clam juice	About 1½ cups rosé wine
2. Remove fish, then add and bring to a simmer	2 medium whole scallions, minced 1½ Tbs minced peeled fresh ginger 1 tsp Thai yellow curry paste (see page 386)	2 ounces shallots, minced 2 garlic cloves, minced	1 medium whole scallion, diced 2 Tbs minced peeled ginger One 4-inch piece lemongrass, white part only, crushed (discard before serving) 2 Thai hot chiles, thinly sliced	3 ounces shallots, diced 1 Tbs minced rosemary 2 tsp stemmed thyme
3. (optional) Add, reduce the heat, and simmer until crisp-tender	6 ounces shiitake mushrooms, stems removed and discarded, the caps thinly sliced	2 celery ribs, thinly sliced 2 medium carrots, thinly sliced	Omit	1 medium fennel bulb, trimmed and thinly sliced ¼ cup sliced pitted black olives
4. Partially submerge, cover, place in the oven, and poach	1½ pounds skinless thick-fleshed fish fillet(s)	1½ pounds skinless thick-fleshed fish fillet(s)	1½ pounds skinless thick-fleshed fish fillet(s)	1½ pounds skinless thick-fleshed fish fillet(s)
5. Transfer the fish, enrich and/or thicken the sauce, and season to taste	¼ cup coconut milk Soy sauce to taste	¼ cup cream Beurre manié (see page 209) Salt and pepper to taste	2 Tbs peanut butter	3 Tbs mashed roasted garlic (see page 333)
6. (optional) Garnish	½ Tbs minced basil per serving	Omit	1 teaspoon fish sauce (see page 388) and 1 teaspoon lime juice per serving	1 teaspoon aromatic olive oil per serving

	Chowder-Style Poached Fish Fillets	Spanish-Inspired Poached Fish Fillets	Japanese-Inspired Poached Fish Fillets	Shanghai-Style Poached Fish Fillets
1. Preheat the oven; pour in enough liquid to come halfway up the fillet(s)	1 cup milk Enough dry white wine to make up the difference	About 1½ cups red wine	¼ cup mirin[1] Enough fish stock or clam juice to make up the difference	¼ cup soy sauce ¼ cup shaoxing (see page 374) or dry sherry Enough vegetable broth to make up the difference
2. Remove fish, then add and bring to a simmer	1 small yellow onion, diced 1 Tbs minced dill 2 tsp stemmed thyme	½ small red onion, diced 2 garlic cloves, minced 2 tsp minced oregano ¼ tsp saffron One 4-inch cinnamon stick (discard before serving)	3 medium whole scallions, diced ¼ cup shredded daikon radish 2 Tbs minced peeled fresh ginger	1 medium whole scallion, thinly sliced 2 Tbs minced peeled fresh ginger 2 garlic cloves, minced Up to 10 dried Chinese red chiles One 4-inch cinnamon stick One star anise pod (discard the whole spices before serving)
3. (optional) Add, reduce the heat, and simmer until crisp-tender	1 celery rib, thinly sliced 1 medium carrot, thinly sliced ½ cup fresh or frozen corn kernels	½ cup canned chickpeas, drained ¼ cup sliced pitted black olives	6 ounces mitake mushrooms, thinly sliced; or shiitake mushrooms, the stems removed and discarded, the caps thinly sliced	6 ounces shiitake mushrooms, stems removed and discarded, the caps thinly sliced
4. Partially submerge, cover, place in the oven, and poach	1½ pounds skinless thick-fleshed fish fillet(s)	1½ pounds skinless thick-fleshed fish fillet(s)	1½ pounds skinless thick-fleshed fish fillet(s)	1½ pounds skinless thick-fleshed fish fillet(s)
5. Transfer the fish; enrich and/or thicken the sauce	¼ cup cream Also thickened with an egg yolk (see page 000)	3 Tbs puréed jarred roasted red peppers or pimientos	2 Tbs purchased miso paste	1½ tsp cornstarch dissolved with 1 Tbs water
6. (optional) Garnish	½ Tbs minced parsley per serving	½ Tbs minced cilantro per serving	¼ tsp toasted sesame oil per serving	¼ tsp toasted sesame oil per serving

[1]Mirin is a sweetened, low-alcohol Japanese cooking wine made from rice. It is available in most stores in the Asian aisle—or always from online Asian markets.

The queen of comfort food, a pot pie is a retro treat, a good make-ahead for after the movies or the soccer game. The only real trick? Good knife technique. The vegetables should be diced into ¼-inch cubes so they fully flavor the sauce. • MAKES 8 SERVINGS

• **STEP 1** Preheat the oven to 350°F. Meanwhile, heat 3 tablespoons fat in a large saucepan or small Dutch oven set over medium heat. Because a pot pie is comfort food, stay away from complex fats like olive, sesame, or almond oil. Yes, walnut oil would add a nutty note, but it's largely wasted in the casserole, more distraction than enhancement. Instead, stick with unsalted butter, the usual favorite; or skip its slight tang and wash out the initial palette with any of the neutral vegetable oils from corn to canola.

You'll need a fairly large pot. Ahead, you'll be adding at least 3 cups of aromatics, lots of meat, 4 cups diced vegetables, and 2 cups liquid—a minimum of 3 quarts, maybe more. In most cases for cooking (but not for baking), work in a pan larger than you might think you need. A good stir should bring nothing to the lip.

• **STEP 2** Add 3 to 3½ cups chopped, mixed aromatics, preferably some variation of a mirepoix (see page 57); cook, stirring often, until softened. The traditional filling for a pot pie verges toward the sweet; use up to 2 cups diced onion as the base and then add other vegetables to the mix—for example, thinly sliced celery and carrots for a classic mirepoix.

Or consider substitutes for the onion: leeks and shallots. But avoid scallions: too bright and overwhelming for American comfort food. Instead, consider peeled pearl onions—or if you don't want to peel them, use frozen pearl onions right out of the freezer.

Skip the carrot if you like and simply use 2 or 3 celery ribs instead of the one. Or substitute diced trimmed fennel, one diced seeded fresh chile, or even some diced peeled celeriac—all more fussy but welcome nonetheless. Basically, you want an aromatic match to the onion or its substitute. The only trick is that everything should be diced into small bits or cubes. (For the definitions of "dice," "chop," and such, see page 180.)

• **STEP 3** Add 1½ pounds boneless meat, trimmed and chopped into ½-inch pieces; cook, stirring often, just until the meat loses its raw color. The meat will shrink as it cooks, but the pieces should still be slightly larger than the vegetables for the traditional American look. Nonetheless, before you cut the meat into these small pieces, trim it well, taking off fat and connective tissue that will weigh the mixture down. There's no point in a pot pie being full of rendered fat; the richness comes from the sauce and the vegetable medley.

Consider these your choices:

boneless skinless dark meat turkey
boneless skinless turkey breast
boneless skinless chicken thighs
boneless skinless chicken breasts
trimmed pork loin
trimmed beef or buffalo sirloin

Other meats may be too difficult to work with for such quick comfort. Yes, you can use various kinds of stew meat—lamb, beef, or veal—but you need to dice them quite finely, into ¼-inch pieces. What about lamb loin? Too expensive for this homey concoction. The same goes for pork or beef tenderloin. And ground beef? Too rubbery when long-cooked, an unappealing texture. However, you can have good success by buying economical turkey legs, skinning them, and chopping up the meat; removing all the tendons makes the preparation a bit of a chore, but the meat itself is moist and heavenly in the final dish.

If you want to make a vegetable pot pie, skip this step entirely and add 8 cups prepared vegetables in step 6.

If you want to make a shrimp or seafood pot pie, skip this step, then stir 1½ pounds peeled and deveined medium shrimp (about 30 per pound) or 1½ pounds cubed halibut or cod into the stew just before you pour it into the baking dish in step 6. If desired, roughly chop the shrimp so they are in bite-sized pieces. Or use thawed cold-water salad shrimp (sometimes incorrectly called "baby" shrimp).

An egg crust starts by cutting shortening into flour until the mixture resembles very coarse sand.

Roll out the egg crust on a well-floured surface, flouring the dough and your pin as well so nothing sticks.

By rolling in several directions, you can create a rectangle slightly larger than the baking dish.

Gently roll up the dough, then unroll it on top of the baking dish, filled with the pot pie mixture (here, the hearty-but-healthy mixture for Vegetable Pot Pie).

Just before baking, crimp the crust closed, sealing the filling into the baking dish.

If you don't want to go to the trouble of an egg crust, drop a biscuit crust over the pot pie—an easier and perhaps homier alternative.

• **STEP 4** Stir in ¼ cup all-purpose flour as well as up to 2 tablespoons dried herbs, dried spices, and/or other flavorings; stir over the heat until all the vegetables and meat are evenly coated, then cook, stirring constantly, for 1 minute. Do not substitute any other flour here—whole wheat, self-rising, or cake. You need the right glutens to thicken the stew. That said, if you have wheat allergies, try ground oat flour. The texture will be gummier, but it's a better substitute than cornstarch, which makes the stew too gelatinous.

Economical as pot pie is, it makes sense to use dried herbs; they soften and mellow without the aromatic spark of their fresh kin. Consider thyme, parsley, and sage, as well as marjoram and rosemary in lesser portions. Or mix a few of these herbs together: parsley and tarragon; rosemary, oregano, and thyme. All of which brings up the question of a spice mix: a Southwestern mélange of ground cumin, dried oregano, and chili powder; or a French-inspired mixture of dry mustard, dried tarragon, and thyme. Any of these will work, so long as your expectations are in line with what you are creating. If you're trying to replicate the flavors of some frozen pot pie you remember from childhood, you'll be disappointed with one of these spice blends. Better to go for a little dried parsley, maybe with thyme in the mix.

Other flavorings that can be stirred in at this point include Dijon mustard and Worcestershire sauce, either the original or any of its new-fangled permutations. Mango chutney is particularly appealing in a pork pot pie, with or without a curry blend (see page 113). If you've used chiles as part of your aromatic mélange, balance them now with a little apricot all-fruit spread. Tomatoes will add too much moisture; instead, consider tomato paste or chopped sun-dried tomatoes.

Cook the mixture for 1 minute, stirring constantly, so the flour loses its raw taste and thoroughly coats the meat and aromatics. In no case let it brown; it should be a pale color, not white, a little beige, but in no sense deeply colored, if really colored at all.

• **STEP 5** Pour in 2 cups broth or enhanced broth and scrape up any browned bits on the pot's bottom. Match the broth to the meat: chicken with chicken or turkey, beef with beef, and just about anything with pork. Vegetable broth makes a much lighter sauce, one better suited to warmer weather.

Once you've chosen the broth as the base, enhance it in any number of ways: white or red wine, dry vermouth, dry sherry, beer, cream, or even coconut milk for some sort of Thai version. In general, avoid juices and tomato sauce: both too sweet. Use at least ½ cup of the enhancement—or even up to 1 cup for a richer sauce.

• **STEP 6** Stir in 4 cups prepared, diced vegetables and bring to a simmer; cover, reduce the heat to low, and simmer until the vegetables are almost tender, between 10 and 20 minutes. Then pour the filling mixture into a 9 x 13-inch baking dish; season with salt and freshly ground black pepper to taste. And now for a reversal of usual cooking methods: the vegetables go in after the liquid, not before. Yes, you could have added them after the meat in step 3, but they tend to overcook and turn squishy. Adding them now assures that they'll end up with a little tooth when the dish comes out of the oven.

Frozen vegetables are, of course, typical here, a '50s convenience that rarely deters the dish's success. Buy a frozen vegetable medley and enhance it with a little chopped fresh vegetables, roots, or tubers, or even another type of frozen vegetable—say, a bag of mixed vegetables paired with a small bag of frozen lima beans.

That said, almost any fresh vegetable will work: cauliflower florets to asparagus, acorn squash to peas, green beans to Chinese long beans, potatoes to celery. Everything must be seeded and peeled, then if necessary diced into ¼-inch cubes. The only thing we'd avoid? Leafy greens, which turn too mushy, waggling unattractively off the spoon.

If you've added roots, tubers, winter squash, or other hard vegetables, the stew needs to simmer slowly for about 20 minutes. Everything should be almost tender when you pour it into the baking dish.

Pot pies love salt, sure, but especially ground black pepper. Be generous with your fresh grindings to flavor the vegetables and season the meat. How do you know when you've got the seasoning right? Taste the stew. It should be bright and mouthwatering. Start with ½ teaspoon salt and work your way up from there in small increments.

• **STEP 7** Prepare a topping, place over the filling in the baking dish (there must be holes for steam to escape), and then bake until lightly browned and bubbling, about 45 minutes. Dropped biscuit topping or a rolled crust? A biscuit topping is made by placing tablespoonfuls onto the crust, almost sealing it closed but leaving little gaps for steam. A rolled crust is treated like a pie crust: stretched under the rolling pin on a floured work surface. Here are three:

1. Parmesan Biscuit Topping
   Whisk 1½ cups all-purpose flour, 2 tablespoons finely grated Parmigiano-Reggiano, 2 teaspoons baking powder, ¼ teaspoon grated nutmeg, and ¼ teaspoon salt in a large bowl. Stir in 6 tablespoons unsalted butter, melted and cooled, and about ½ cup heavy or whipping cream until a wet dough forms. Drop by heaping tablespoonfuls onto the top of the pot pie filling.

2. Sour Cream Biscuit Topping
   Whisk 1½ cups all-purpose flour, 2 teaspoons baking soda, 1 teaspoon dry mustard, and ½ teaspoon salt in a large bowl. Stir in ½ cup milk, ¼ cup sour cream, and 2 tablespoons unsalted butter, melted and cooled, until a wet dough forms. Drop by heaping tablespoonfuls onto the top of the pot pie filling.

3. Egg Crust
   Cut ½ cup solid vegetable shortening or unsalted butter into 2 cups all-purpose flour and 1 teaspoon salt using a pastry cutter or a fork. Stir in 1 large egg, well beaten, and 6 to 9 tablespoons milk until a soft dough forms. Flour a large work surface, place the dough on top, and flour it as well. Roll the dough into a 10 x 14-inch rectangle. Gently fold the dough so it's easy to transfer to the top of the casserole. Unfold over the filling and tuck in the sides, then cut a few vent slits across the crust.

Or forgo this fandango and use a purchased pie crust or even frozen puffed pastry. Thaw either according to the package's instructions. You'll probably need two purchased crusts to cover the baking dish and you'll have to trim any circles into squares; use the trimmings to plug holes. Some frozen pie crusts are sold in a pie tin; these must fully thaw before they can be removed.

Once baked, remove the pot pie and let it cool on a wire rack for at least 5 minutes before serving. The filling will stay quite hot but the taste will be markedly improved with a little time off the heat.

Recipes for Pot Pies

	Classic Turkey Pot Pie	Chicken Pot Pie	Curried Pork Pot Pie	Southwestern Pork Pot Pie
1. Preheat the oven; heat	3 Tbs unsalted butter	3 Tbs unsalted butter	3 Tbs canola oil	3 Tbs canola oil
2. Add and cook	2 cups frozen pearl onions 2 celery ribs, thinly sliced	1 medium yellow onion, diced 2 celery ribs, thinly sliced	6 ounces shallots, diced	4 ounces shallots, diced 1 celery rib, thinly sliced
3. Add and cook	3 pounds turkey legs, bones and tendons removed and discarded, the meat chopped	1½ pounds boneless skinless chicken breasts, cubed	1½ pounds pork loin, trimmed and chopped	1½ pounds pork loin, trimmed and chopped
4. Stir in and cook 1 minute, stirring constantly	¼ cup all-purpose flour 1 Tbs Dijon mustard 1 Tbs Worcestershire sauce 1 tsp dried sage 1 tsp dried thyme	¼ cup all-purpose flour ¼ cup chopped sun-dried tomatoes 1 Tbs dried tarragon 1 Tbs dried thyme ¼ tsp grated nutmeg	¼ cup all-purpose flour 2 Tbs mango chutney 1 Tbs curry powder (see page 113) 1 tsp ground cinnamon ½ tsp red pepper flakes	¼ cup all-purpose flour 2 Tbs apricot all-fruit spread 1 Tbs chili powder 1 tsp ground cinnamon 1 or 2 fresh jalapeño chiles, seeded and minced
5. Pour in	2 cups chicken broth	1½ cups chicken broth ½ cup cream	1½ cups vegetable broth ½ cup coconut milk	2 cups chicken broth
6. Stir in and simmer, covered—then pour into a 9 x 13-inch baking dish and season	4 cups frozen mixed vegetables Salt and pepper to taste	2 cups frozen lima beans 2 cups fresh or frozen corn kernels Salt and pepper to taste	6 ounces snow peas, chopped 2 cups canned sliced water chestnuts Salt and pepper to taste	4 medium fresh tomatillos, hulled and chopped 2 medium yellow-fleshed potatoes such as Yukon Golds, diced Salt and pepper to taste
7. Make the topping, assemble and bake	Egg Crust (see step 7 above)	Sour Cream Biscuit Topping (see step 7 above)	Egg Crust (see step 7 above)	Sour Cream Biscuit Topping (see step 7 above)

	Vegetable Pot Pie	Shrimp Pot Pie	Lobster Pot Pie	Meat-and-Potato Pot Pie
1. Preheat the oven; heat	3 Tbs unsalted butter	3 Tbs unsalted butter	3 Tbs unsalted butter	3 Tbs canola oil
2. Add and cook	1 medium yellow onion, diced 1 medium carrot, thinly sliced 1 celery rib, thinly sliced	1 medium yellow onion, diced 1 medium carrot, thinly sliced	1 large leek, white and pale green parts only, halved lengthwise, washed carefully, and thinly sliced 2 celery ribs, halved lengthwise and thinly sliced 2 garlic cloves, minced	4 ounces shallots, minced 1 small green bell pepper, seeded and diced
3. Add and cook	Omit	Omit	Omit	1½ pounds beef sirloin, trimmed and chopped
4. Stir in and cook 1 minute, stirring constantly	¼ cup all-purpose flour 1 Tbs Worcestershire sauce 1 Tbs dried parsley 1 Tbs dried thyme	¼ cup all-purpose flour 1 Tbs Worcestershire sauce 1 Tbs dried tarragon ½ tsp red pepper flakes	¼ cup all-purpose flour 2 Tbs Dijon mustard 1 Tbs Worcestershire sauce 1 Tbs dried tarragon	¼ cup all-purpose flour 1 Tbs Worcestershire sauce 1 Tbs tomato paste 2 tsp ground coriander 1 tsp ground cumin 2 garlic cloves, minced
5. Pour in	2 cups vegetable broth	2 cups vegetable broth	1½ cups fish stock or clam juice ½ cup cream	1½ cups beef broth ½ cup red wine
6. Stir in and simmer, covered—then pour into a 9 x 13-inch baking dish and season	2 cups fresh or frozen corn kernels 1 medium red bell pepper, seeded and chopped 1 small sweet potato, peeled and diced very small 2 cups frozen lima beans 2 cups fresh shelled or frozen peas Salt and pepper to taste	1 medium fennel bulb, trimmed and diced 2 cups sliced frozen sliced okra 1½ pounds medium shrimp, peeled, deveined, and roughly chopped Salt and pepper to taste	2 medium yellow-fleshed potatoes, such as Yukon Golds, peeled and diced 1 large red bell pepper, seeded and diced 1 cup fresh shelled or frozen peas 2 pounds frozen lobster tails, shelled and the meat chopped Salt and pepper to taste	3 medium yellow-fleshed potatoes, such as Yukon Golds, peeled and diced 1 cup fresh shelled or frozen peas Salt and pepper to taste
7. Make the topping, assemble, and bake	Parmesan Biscuit Topping (see step 7 above)	Egg Crust (see step 7 above)	Egg Crust (see step 7 above)	Parmesan Biscuit Topping (see step 7 above)

Sunday dinner any night of the week—a Burgundian Pot Roast with its own pan sauce

Who makes pot roast anymore? Well, we do, unabashed fans of braised, delectable chuck or brisket as we are. Let's face it: it's not a Wednesday night dinner (unless you've got the day off). But it's certainly a Saturday night one. Or a holiday feast. • MAKES 8 SERVINGS

• **STEP 1** Heat ¼ cup oil in a large Dutch oven set over medium heat. Here's the chance to use that enormous, heavy Dutch oven you bought at the outlet mall. There's really no other possible equipment, except for a large, heavy-duty, enamel-coated, flame-safe casserole. In the end, you need a pot big enough to hold all this meat, lots of vegetables, and the liquid.

We're adding a fair amount of oil here because we're going to add a fair amount of meat for 8 servings. Use a neutral-flavored or untoasted nut oil on its own or in combination with unsalted butter. The perfect fit: 2 tablespoons untoasted walnut oil and 2 tablespoons unsalted butter.

Don't use toasted nut or seed oils—and steer clear of olive oil, generally too floral for this deep braise. That said, an Italian-style pot roast with fennel, potatoes, tomatoes, and leeks would be nicely complemented by a 50/50 combo of olive oil and butter.

• **STEP 2** Brown a 4- to 4½-pound boneless trimmed pot roast or brisket; transfer to a plate. This braise starts with a relatively cheap cut of meat, a little tough, with lots of connective tissue that melts and tenderizes over time and heat. A beef chuck roast is the classic. If you can lay your hands on a boneless beef chuck roast, even better. Ask the butcher at your market for one. He or she will probably also take you for a true carnivore and your service may markedly improve. The boneless roast should be tied into a log; either ask the butcher to do this for you or roll it up yourself and tie it around its tubular circumference in several places with butcher's twine.

That said, any cut from the cow's chuck (the front shoulder and legs) makes a fine pot roast: arm roast, boneless arm roast, boneless arm shoulder roast, boneless chuck shoulder roast, chuck eye roast, or cross-rib roast. Perhaps the most tender cut is the old-fashioned 7-blade pot roast, named because the cut bone in the meat looks like the number 7. In all cases, if the bone remains in the meat, compensate for its weight by adding another ½ pound or so to the total weight.

If you can't get one 4- to 4½-pound roast, try two roasts, one set on top of the other. You'll need to switch their places several times during the long oven stay, but the cooking time will work out about right with the added thickness of the two cuts on top of each other.

And then there's beef brisket, which runs down the cow's chest below the short ribs: the bacon of a cow, as it were. A brisket is actually quite tough, but the sheer amount of connective tissue in the thing turns it moist in a slow braise. A whole brisket is 8 to 11 pounds, so you'll want a section for this technique. The so-called

Although a pot roast can be made with a variety of tough cuts of beef, none should lard up the sauce. Here, the overlying layer of fat is trimmed from a beef brisket.

Thicker cuts like this boneless chuck roast need to be tied to hold their shape. Begin by wrapping butcher's twine around the meat, its cut side pointed toward and/or away from you.

Then secure the twine without pulling so tight that the meat bunches up. Two or three more loops will do it for this roast.

"flat cut" or "first cut" is less fatty, without the overhanging chuck-like flap (or "cap" or "deckel") over the meat (which also turns irresistibly tender when braised). The "point cut" (or "nose cut" or "thick cut") is cheaper and fattier, the cap (or deckel) in place over the meat.

In either case, trim off the brisket's outer layer of fat, usually ¼ to even ½ inch over the meat. Run a sharp, thin knife along the meat's surface plane, angling the blade to take off the fat without cutting into the meat. (Or have your butcher trim the brisket for you.) If you're working with a point cut, you'll need to get in under the cap (or deckel) to get out some of the fat.

Brown the meat well, as much as 5 minutes per side, working in batches if you've got more than one roast. No one's going to eat it rare anyway. You're not so much adding to the meat's flavor as you are building caramelization on its external surface and the bottom of the pot, flavoring that will later enhance the sauce.

• **STEP 3** With the meat out of the pot, add 3 cups thinly sliced aromatics; cook, stirring often, until softened, about 5 minutes. Onions, leeks, and shallots are the choices. Scallions are too bright; ginger, just plain wrong unless you're making a Shanghai-style braise. Make very thin slices. Over long braising, the aromatics need to soften and melt into the sauce, sweetening it considerably and giving it a slightly thicker texture. The slices, even very thin ones, will hold up longer, flavoring the stew completely before they dissolve.

• **STEP 4** Toss in some minced garlic, herbs, spices, or flavorings; cook until aromatic, about 20 seconds. Feel free to use dried herbs. They'll soften considerably over time. However, do crumble them between your fingers first. More surface area exposed means more flavor in the sauce.

Other flavorings include things like Dijon mustard, Worcestershire sauce, minced and seeded chipotles canned in adobo sauce, minced anchovies, or chopped sun-dried tomatoes (do not use the ones packed in oil). A very sweet/savory pot roast can be made by stirring 1 or 2 tablespoons prepared horseradish into the pot at this point. It will actually sweeten during braising, its vinegary base barely present, its nose-spanking flavor all gone.

Go nuts; add lots of flavor. The braise will blend and complement most additions. Try these over-the-top combinations: Dijon mustard, Worcestershire sauce, a few bay leaves, a cinnamon stick, some ground cumin, and dried oregano; or rinsed capers, minced anchovies, chopped black olives, chopped sun-dried tomatoes, dried oregano, mint, and dill.

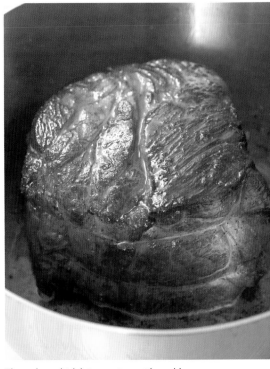

The only real trick to a pot roast is making sure the meat is well browned on all sides before it is braised.

- **STEP 5** Pour in about 2½ cups liquid, a part of which can be canned diced tomatoes; scrape up any browned bits on the pot's bottom; and return the meat and any accumulated juices around it to the pot. Bring to a simmer, cover, reduce the heat to low, and simmer very slowly for 1½ hours. Use broth or wine, red or white. Dry fortified wines like dry Madeira should be used in combination with broth—as should canned diced tomatoes, no more than 1¼ cups of the total liquid amount.

- **STEP 6** Stir in about 8 cups sliced, chopped, or cubed vegetables; cover and continue simmering until the meat is very tender, 1½ to 2½ additional hours. Remove the meat and vegetables to a platter, skim the sauce, and season with salt and freshly ground black pepper to taste. Long-cooked vegetables are what's called for, in 1- to 1½-inch cubes: seeded and peeled winter squash, seeded bell peppers, carrots, sunchokes, and potatoes, as well as peeled celeriac, kohlrabi, parsnips, sweet potatoes, turnips, and rutabagas. Even peeled and chopped beets can be thrown in, provided you don't mind an eerie cast to the sauce.

If you want a green vegetable in the mix, consider Brussels sprouts or cabbage. Cut off the stem end of the sprouts, then halve or quarter them—or shred them by making thin slices through the heads. Or cut the cabbage in half, remove its "core" (the triangular stem running up into the head), and roughly chop it, separating the leaves. Celery will unappealingly melt into threads; peeled celeriac (or celery root) is a better option.

Now it's just a matter of the meat's getting tender. We once braised three 4-pound briskets for a magazine article and they took 3, 3½, and 5 hours respectively, all

Shape vs. Weight

In almost any braise, the meat's mass and shape are more important than its weight. A 3-pound, 3-inch-thick piece of meat will take longer to cook than a 3-pound, 2-inch-thick piece of meat. And even more telling, a 2-pound, 1-inch-thick cut will cook more quickly than a 1-pound, 2-inch cut. Outside of a microwave and other fancy kitchen devices, meat cooks outside to inside. The more mass, the longer it needs to tenderize from those outside planes in.

Meat is sliced "against the grain"—
that is, against the grain of the
fibers in the cut, much like the
grain in wood. Sometimes, you
can see the fibers at the surface.
Slice 90 degrees to their direction.
If you can't immediately see them,
run your fingers along the surface
to see which way the fibers run.
Again, slice 90 degrees from their
direction. And if all else fails, slice
a small piece off the end and look
at the fibers inside.

When done, the meat can be carved into
slices against the grain. Notice how they
then stay together without shredding or
sharding.

other factors the same. Suffice it to say that beef is tough because
of a variety of factors: how much the cow used the muscle, how
stressed the cow was in its life, how stressed it was at slaughter, its
overall health, even the temperature and humidity when it was
raised as a calf. So be patient. Sit back, pop open a bottle of red
wine, and let the meat get incredibly tender.

After you take the meat and vegetables out of the pot, skim
the sauce. Tilt the pot up on one side and remove the glistening
layer of melted fat sitting on top. Don't stir or jar the pot. In fact,
it helps to set the pot aside for 5 minutes before you do this. And
even better, make the dish the day before; refrigerate the meat/veg-
etables and the sauce separately, then pull off the congealed sauce
on top of the sauce before reheating everything in a large Dutch
oven over medium heat.

When salting the dish, think about the other things you've
added. Dijon mustard, olives, capers, anchovies, Worcestershire
sauce? These are all quite salty. Taste the sauce and go sparingly,
adding more salt in small increments, perhaps just ¼ teaspoon at
a time.

• **STEP 7** Thicken the sauce. While the meat and vegetables rest
out of the pot, bring the sauce to a full simmer by raising the heat
under the pot to medium-high. Whisk 1 or 2 tablespoons arrowroot, potato starch, or cornstarch with 2 tablespoons water, broth,
vinegar, lemon juice, cognac, brandy, dry sherry, or unsweetened
apple, cranberry, or pomegranate juice. Whisk this mixture into
the simmering sauce, then continue whisking until thickened,
usually about 30 seconds. Immediately remove the pot from the
heat.

Or thicken the sauce with a beurre manié (see page 209)
made of 2 tablespoons all-purpose flour and 2 tablespoons room-
temperature unsalted butter. Drop by nine or ten additions into
the stew, one at a time, whisking all the while, incorporating each
fully before adding the next.

Recipes for Pot Roasts

	The "New Classic" Pot Roast	Italian-Style Pot Roast	Southwestern Brisket	Jewish Brisket
1. Heat	¼ cup canola oil	2 Tbs olive oil 2 Tbs unsalted butter	¼ cup canola oil	¼ cup canola oil
2. Brown and remove	One 4-pound boneless beef chuck roast, trimmed and tied into a log	One 4½-pound 7-blade chuck roast, trimmed	One 4½-pound brisket, trimmed	One 4½-pound brisket, trimmed
3. Add and cook	2 medium yellow onions, halved and thinly sliced	2 medium yellow onions, halved and thinly sliced	2 medium yellow onions, halved and thinly sliced	2 medium yellow onions, halved and thinly sliced
4. Toss in	2 garlic cloves, minced 2 Tbs prepared horseradish 1 Tbs dried thyme 1 Tbs dried parsley 2 bay leaves (discard before serving)	2 garlic cloves, minced 1 whole rosemary sprig tied together with 6 to 8 thyme sprigs and 4 parsley sprigs ¼ cup chopped pitted black olives 2 Tbs chopped golden raisins 1 tsp fennel seeds	3 garlic cloves, minced 1 or 2 chipotle chiles, canned in adobo sauce, stemmed and chopped 1 Tbs Worcestershire sauce 2 tsp mild paprika 1 tsp ground cumin 1 tsp dried oregano One 4-inch cinnamon stick (discard before serving)	3 garlic cloves, minced 1 Tbs mild paprika ½ tsp ground allspice 4 dried figs, chopped 3 bay leaves (discard before serving)
5. Return meat to pot and pour in	2 cups beef broth ½ cup dry white wine	1½ cups chicken broth 1 cup canned diced tomatoes	2 cups beef broth ½ cup dry red wine	2½ cups beef broth
6. Add and continue cooking, then remove meat and vegetables	2 medium parsnips, peeled and sliced 2 medium kohlrabi, peeled and chopped 2 medium sweet potatoes, peeled and cut into 1-inch-thick rings	5 medium carrots, sliced 3 medium fennel bulbs, trimmed and sliced	1 large butternut squash, halved, seeded, peeled, and chopped 2 medium bell peppers, seeded and chopped	20 small red-skinned potatoes, halved 3 medium carrots, sliced
7. Thicken	2 Tbs arrowroot whisked into 2 Tbs dry sherry	2 Tbs tomato paste (First, remove the bundle of herbs.)	2 Tbs arrowroot whisked into 2 Tbs apple cider vinegar	2 Tbs potato starch whisked into 2 Tbs water

	Brisket with Mushrooms and Figs	Shanghai-Style Pot Roast	Burgundian Pot Roast	Winter Sunday Pot Roast
1. Heat	¼ cup canola oil	¼ cup canola oil	2 Tbs untoasted walnut oil 2 Tbs unsalted butter	¼ cup peanut oil
2. Brown and remove	One 4½-pound beef brisket, trimmed	One 4-pound boneless chuck roast, trimmed and tied into a log	One 4-pound boneless beef chuck roast, trimmed and tied into a log	One 4-pound arm or shoulder roast, trimmed
3. Add and cook	2 large leeks, white and pale green parts only, halved lengthwise, washed carefully, and thinly sliced	2 medium yellow onions, halved and thinly sliced	6 ounces shallots, thinly sliced	2 medium onions, halved and thinly sliced
4. Toss in	4 garlic cloves, minced 1 Tbs dried thyme 1 Tbs dried sage 2 bay leaves (discard before serving)	6 garlic cloves, minced 3 Tbs minced peeled fresh ginger 2 Tbs finely grated orange zest Two 4-inch cinnamon sticks 2 star anise pods 2 bay leaves (discard the whole spices before serving)	1 Tbs dried tarragon 1 Tbs dried thyme 1 Tbs Dijon mustard 1 Tbs Worcestershire sauce 8 sun-dried tomatoes, sliced 4 allspice berries 2 bay leaves (discard before serving)	4 garlic cloves, minced ¼ cup chopped dried cranberries 1 Tbs Dijon mustard 2 tsp dried thyme 2 bay leaves (discard before serving)
5. Return meat to pot and pour in	2¼ cups beef broth ¼ cup red wine vinegar	1½ cups beef broth ½ cup soy sauce ½ cup shaoxing (see page 374) or dry sherry	1½ cups beef broth 1 cup dry red wine	1 cup beef broth 1 cup canned diced tomatoes ½ cup dry Madeira
6. Add and continue cooking, then remove meat and vegetables	12 dried whole figs 2 large portobello mushroom caps, thinly sliced 12 shiitake mushroom caps, thinly sliced ½ ounce dried porcini, crumbled	4 medium carrots, thickly sliced 4 medium white-fleshed boiling potatoes, peeled and cut into 2-inch pieces 2 cups jarred roasted whole chestnuts	2 medium celeriacs, peeled and cubed 2 medium turnips, peeled and cubed 2 medium carrots, sliced	2 medium sweet potatoes, peeled and cubed 1 medium Russet potato, peeled and cubed 2 medium carrots, sliced 1 medium bell pepper, seeded and chopped
7. Thicken	2 Tbs potato starch whisked into 2 Tbs water	2 Tbs cornstarch whisked into 2 Tbs rice vinegar	2 Tbs potato starch whisked into 2 Tbs red wine vinegar	2 Tbs arrowroot whisked in 2 Tbs water

Rack of Lamb

A rack of lamb is the lamb version of a standing rib roast, the bones arching out of the perfect rounds of loin; the taste, a fusion of mild, sweet meat and deeply seared bone—all in all, incredibly delicious. While we give instructions here for frenching and trimming the rack, you can always ask the butcher to do those things for you. For more servings, double or triple the recipe at will, using more lamb racks. • MAKES 2 SERVINGS (CAN BE DOUBLED OR TRIPLED)

• **STEP 1** Preheat the oven to 375°F; french and trim an 8-bone, 1½-pound rack of lamb. A rack of lamb is a set of lamb loin chops that have not been sliced apart—technically, bones 6 through 12, the lamb usually processed around 6 to 8 months of age. However, most racks sold in North America have 8 bones, not 7, an extra bone added to make an even number of chops on the rack.

The USDA grades lamb in several categories: "prime," "choice," and "good" are most often available in the supermarket; "utility" and "cull" grades are mostly ground. As with all USDA-graded meat, prime is heavily marbled; choice, less so, slightly chewier but less fatty—perhaps a better choice for health reasons. Indeed, the key difference between "prime" and "choice" by USDA standards is the higher fat content of the former designation.

A "frenched" rack has the fat and tendons removed from between the rib bones so that each is cleaned and visible, arching out of the round (or oblong) loin below. There's no difference in taste, per se, between the frenched and unfrenched—you're simply removing very tough collagen and connective tissue that will not get tender during the rack's short time in the oven. Plus, the presentation will be more dramatic, the bones sticking out of the meat.

You'll need a sharp boning knife (slightly thinner than a chef's knife) for this task. Position the rack of lamb on a cutting board with the bones arching down and lifting the meat up slightly. Note the loin, the tube of meat at one end of the bones. About an inch or so above that loin along the ribs, score the fat and meat, cutting down to the bones without cutting through or into the bones themselves. Scrape the fat, tendon, and some meat off the bones, pulling the knife along the bones and away from the loin. Scrape a few times to get rid of most of whatever is covering the bones' surface.

One note before you continue: a classically trained chef might take off the meat, tendons, and fat all the way down to the loin (sometimes called the "eye"), leaving nothing else. However,

HOMEMADE BREAD CRUMBS

To make your own, save stale pieces of French, Italian, or other crunchy bread until they are quite hard, way beyond toasting. Remove the crusts and grind the slices into crumbs in a food processor. Either spread them on a large baking sheet and bake in a preheated 300°F oven, tossing occasionally, until lightly browned, then cool to room temperature— or simply spread them on a large baking sheet and set them aside at room temperature for a day or two until they are very dry and hard. In either case, seal the bread crumbs in a small plastic container for up to 5 days, checking occasionally to make sure they haven't gotten moldy. Or freeze in a sealed container indefinitely, using them right out of cold storage.

TO FRENCH A RACK OF LAMB: First, slice down between the tender eye (at right) and the fattier connective tissue lying on the bones.

Then scrape and peel this fattier layer off the bones, pulling it away from the eye. Either take it right down to the loin—or leave a little meat and fat for nibbling.

Finally, scrape between the bones to remove any fat or tissue, thereby cleaning them and leaving them fairly bare.

there's good flavor in some of that meat and fat just above the eye and so we counsel you to leave about an inch or so of it for nibbling after roasting. Should you want a more elegant presentation, by all means french the thing right down to the loin itself, leaving a small amount of fat just at the loin to protect it. But why be a carnivore if you don't intend to pick at the bone?

Starting at that line you scored in the meat, slice between the bones and away from the loin, moving up each side of each rib and thereby removing more meat, tendon, and fat from between the bones, along their inside surfaces. Cut the material or flap nearest the loin between the bones to remove whatever has been scraped off the bones.

Turn the rack over and use your knife to scrape and clean the bones, working around the ribs in all directions, removing the rubbery membranes and any connective tissue.

Now that the rack's been frenched, also remove much of the fat from off the loin itself, cutting along the surface planes to slice off thick layers. You needn't be obsessive—fat protects the meat—but there's no reason to have blobby veins of it over the loin. Besides, the coating you'll build in the next step will protect the meat in the oven as well.

• **STEP 2** Use a double coating on the lamb loin: first 1 to 2 tablespoons of a wet coating, then about ½ cup of a seasoned dry coating. Smear any of the following pasty condiments or sauces—or more choices at your whim—onto the loin at the base of the ribs, coating it without getting any on the exposed bones:

Roll the coated eye through chopped herbs or spices gathered together on a cutting board.

Rest the bones on the roasting pan's lip so they arch up and lift the eye a little out of what will become a pool of rendered fat.

When perfectly cooked, slice through the bones of a rack of lamb, thereby removing the chops one at a time.

2 tablespoons barbecue sauce

2 tablespoons Chinese bean paste

2 tablespoons chutney

2 tablespoons hoisin or chouhee sauce

2 tablespoons honey mustard

2 tablespoons prepared or Dijon mustard

1 to 2 tablespoons jerk seasoning paste (see page 50)

1 to 2 tablespoons Thai curry paste (see page 386)

1 to 2 tablespoons vindaloo paste (see page 395)

1 to 2 tablespoons wasabi paste

You want a thick condiment with some savory heft—not applesauce or any jam. Instead of tomato sauce, use pizza sauce, bottled chili sauce, or even ketchup; instead of aioli or mayonnaise, try pesto or a sun-dried tomato spread.

To make a dry exterior coating, start with one of these:

½ cup dried unseasoned bread crumbs

½ cup finely ground nuts

or ½ cup of a combination of the two

Any of these dry coatings should then be seasoned with about 1 teaspoon salt and ½ teaspoon freshly ground black pepper (or to taste) as well as one of the following:

dried mushrooms, perhaps ¼ ounce, finely ground in a spice grinder

one or two stemmed and seeded dried chiles, finely ground in a spice grinder

pure chili powder (that is, ground dried chiles without oregano and cumin in the mix)

powdered green tea

a selection of dried herbs, perhaps 1 tablespoon of the more present stuff like rosemary or tarragon, up to 2 tablespoons of the more subtle additions like sage or thyme

Don't use chiles as a seasoning if there's already hot stuff in the pasty, smeared-on condiment. And be careful of oversalting or overpeppering the coating, particularly if the wet mixture first applied was salty (like hoisin sauce) or spicy (like Thai curry paste). The best way to season the dry coating is to put everything in a mini food processor or a spice grinder and give it a whir until well blended, maybe just 2 or 3 seconds, so as not to grind the bread crumbs or nuts to dust.

Spread the seasoned bread crumbs and/or dried nuts on a cutting board in a pile about the length of the loin, then set the loin end of the coated rack bone side down into the mixture. Roll the meat so it's completely coated, pressing and patting the dry mixture in place as necessary. It's unnecessary for any of the dry coating to stick to the bones.

● **STEP 3** Set in a roasting pan and roast until an instant-read thermometer inserted into the thickest part of the loin registers 135°F (our choice) or 145°F (the USDA recommendation). Let stand 5 minutes before carving. Set the coated rack so the bones arc underneath the meat, thereby gently lifting it up in the middle. We find it's best to set the bones against the side of the pan, sticking over the edge by about ½ inch, so that they rest on the pan's rim and lift the meat farther out of what will be rendered fat.

There's a disparity between our notions of "done" and the USDA's. We feel a pink, rosy center is best for lamb, still tender without being too rare—that is, 135°F, about 25 minutes if the rack was close to room temperature and the oven was adequately preheated. If you prefer it rarer still, roast to 130°F, about 22 minutes. The USDA always makes a strict bid for safety and thus recommends 145°F as their medium-rare—little pink left, maybe just at the very center; it may take about 35 minutes to get to this higher temperature. Higher yet—and not recommended by us—are the USDA's recommendations for medium (160°F) and well-done (170°F). At such temperatures, perhaps you were instead thinking of a pair of Italian lamb-skin loafers?

Walnut and Herb-Crusted Rack of Lamb

Recipes for Racks of Lamb

	French-Inspired Rack of Lamb	Chinese-Inspired Rack of Lamb	Green-Tea Rack of Lamb	Walnut and Herb-Crusted Rack of Lamb
1. Preheat the oven; french and trim	One 1½-pound, 8-bone rack of lamb	One 1½-pound, 8-bone rack of lamb	One 1½-pound, 8-bone rack of lamb	One 1½-pound, 8-bone rack of lamb
2. Coat the rack with	2 Tbs Dijon mustard ¼ cup dried bread crumbs and ¼ cup ground walnuts mixed with 1 Tbs dried tarragon and 1 minced garlic clove as well as salt and pepper to taste	2 Tbs Chinese black bean sauce ½ cup dried bread crumbs lightly ground with 1 minced medium scallion, 2 tsp minced peeled fresh ginger, and ½ tsp five-spice powder (see page 149) as well as salt and pepper to taste	2 Tbs chutney 6 Tbs dried bread crumbs combined with 2 Tbs powdered green tea as well as salt and pepper to taste	2 Tbs Dijon mustard ½ cup ground walnuts mixed with 2 tsp dried parsley, 2 tsp dried thyme, 1 tsp dried rosemary, and 1 tsp dried oregano as well as salt and pepper to taste
3. Roast to an internal temperature of	135°F or 145°F, about 25 or 35 minutes	135°F or 145°F, about 25 or 35 minutes	135°F or 145°F, about 25 or 35 minutes	135°F or 145°F, about 25 or 35 minutes

	Thai Rack of Lamb	Oven-Barbecued Rack of Lamb	Mushroom-and-Herb-Rubbed Rack of Lamb	Jerk Rack of Lamb
1. Preheat the oven; french and trim	One 1½-pound, 8-bone rack of lamb	One 1½-pound, 8-bone rack of lamb	One 1½-pound, 8-bone rack of lamb	One 1½-pound, 8-bone rack of lamb
2. Coat the rack with	2 Tbs bottled Thai peanut sauce ½ cup ground walnuts combined with 2 Tbs dried bread crumbs, 2 tsp ground lemongrass, and 1 tsp ground ginger as well as salt and pepper very moderately	2 Tbs barbecue sauce ¼ cup dried bread crumbs and ¼ cup ground pecans, mixed with 2 tsp chili powder, 1 tsp dried oregano, and ¼ tsp garlic powder as well as salt and pepper to taste	2 Tbs Dijon mustard 6 Tbs dried bread crumbs mixed with 2 Tbs ground-to-a-powder dried mushrooms, ½ tsp ground cinnamon, and ¼ tsp grated nutmeg as well as salt and pepper to taste	2 Tbs jerk seasoning paste (see page 50) ½ cup dried bread crumbs as well as salt and pepper to taste
3. Roast to an internal temperature of	135°F or 145°F, about 25 or 35 minutes	135°F or 145°F, about 25 or 35 minutes	135°F or 145°F, about 25 or 35 minutes	135°F or 145°F, about 25 or 35 minutes

Ribs

Nothing beats pork ribs—but indoors, not on the grill? Indeed, you can make perfect ribs every time in the oven provided you have 1) patience, 2) patience, 3) patience, and 4) a good rub. This technique is a two-step process: steam the ribs, then roast them. The steam begins to melt the ample fat and connective tissue, then the oven's slower, drier ambient temperature melts the collagen and melds the rub with the surface juices. • MAKES ONE RACK (CAN BE DOUBLED, TRIPLED, OR EVEN QUADRUPLED)

• **STEP 1** Use high heat to bring about 1 inch water to a boil in a wok fitted with a steaming rack or in another jury-rigged steaming contraption. Trim a 2½-pound rack of pork ribs, then set on the rack, cover tightly, and steam for 30 minutes. Remove the ribs from the steamer; cool for 10 minutes. This technique is designed for most kinds of pork ribs. However, do not use "country-style" pork ribs, cut from the loin's fatty blade end, often boneless and heavily marbled. Rather, you want the real thing, the perfect bone-and-meat combo. To that end, you have three choices:

1. **Spare ribs.** Taken from the belly, just above the breast, these are the quintessence of ribs to most Americans, a higher ratio of bone to meat, with a knuckle-like rib tip at the end.
2. **Saint Louis–style ribs.** This version of spare ribs has the knuckly, cartilage-laced rib tips removed.
3. **Baby back ribs.** Taken from just below the loin, these have more meat than bone—and are also less fatty. Use two 1¼-pound racks of baby back ribs for this recipe. A Scandinavian specialty, baby backs were ground to feed in the United States until the marketing campaigns of several chain restaurants made them a barbecue staple.

The three types of pork ribs: from left, spare ribs, Saint Louis-style ribs, and baby back ribs.

Most racks must be trimmed. Begin by taking off the translucent membrane that runs along the inside curve of the bones, a membrane almost always missing from baby backs but almost always present on spare ribs. Taking care not to poke or slice the meat, use a paring knife and pry the membrane off one corner, much like opening one corner of a well-sealed envelope's flap. Once the corner is lifted up, hold the membrane flap in one hand and the rack itself in the other (holding both with paper towels helps) and peel the membrane off the rack, gently but forcefully prying the two apart. Should the membrane tear, pry off the little fragments and threads left against the bones and meat with a paring knife.

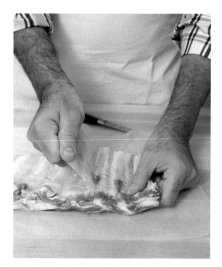

Before the rib rack is steamed, the translucent membrane should be peeled off its meatless side; in the heat, this membrane will go taut and cause the rack to curl up.

Once steamed, make a small cut at the base of each rib to assure that the rack doesn't curl up in the oven. Note how the meat has begun to pull back from the bones.

Next, use that paring knife to remove most of the fat (perhaps 70 to 80%) that lies along the outside curve of the meat. You certainly can't get it all, but carefully slice off the large hunks and veins. However, leave the fat that lies between the ribs so that it can protect the thin coating of meat that lies between the bones.

Will this technique work with a 2½-pound rack of veal or a 3-pound rack of beef ribs, bones that are loaded with meat, familiar from a bone-in standing rib roast? Yes, but the ribs themselves will have to be cut into 3-rib sections to fit on the steaming rack, and they will take longer than pork ribs to get tender: 15 extra minutes in the steamer, up to 1 extra hour in the oven.

Equipment

A wok with a steaming rack is the easiest way to cook a single rack of ribs. If you want to cook more racks or don't have a steaming rack for your wok, you'll need to improvise: perhaps a wire cooling rack in a large roasting pan that can then be covered tightly with aluminum foil; a very large vegetable steamer set in a Dutch oven with a tight-fitting lid; or a thin, narrow rack in a long fish poacher, lifted up out of any simmering water. None of these racks can have rubber feet, which will melt in the heat. If you use a metal cooling rack, such as one you'd use to cool cookies just out of the oven, give it a good spray with nonstick spray so nothing sticks to it; consider cutting a potato into 2-inch rings and setting these under its feet, the better to lift it out of the water.

Cutting between the rib bones, you can slice the rack to fit the contraption you've got. If you must stack ribs on top of each other to fit, switch them around with tongs a couple times during steaming.

You'll also have to check the water level a couple times, making sure it hasn't boiled away. No high boil here—just a good simmer under a tight-fitting lid to get the ribs super-hot so the fat and connective tissue starts to melt.

• **STEP 2** Preheat the oven to 300°F. Coat the steamed ribs with about 3 tablespoons purchased or homemade dry barbecue rub, then roast in the oven on a rack in a large roasting or broiler pan until tender, about 1½ hours. Use tongs to transfer the racks to a cutting board. They are most likely gray and unappealing, the meat having perhaps balled up, especially if you didn't peel off every speck of that pesky membrane. If the rib rack itself has curled, its ends bending around toward each other, cut through the curved fat and some of the meat between some of the ribs without separating them so that the rack lies flat again. The glistening rack, once cooled, needs no additional liquid for the rub to stick.

Of course, there are bottled dry rubs aplenty for ribs. But you can make your own, following these steps:

1. Start out with 2 teaspoons packed light brown sugar, 2 teaspoons mild smoked paprika, and 1 teaspoon kosher salt. Smoked paprika will add the necessary smokiness, something a grill can do naturally but that an oven cannot do without help. If you don't want a smoky taste on the ribs, substitute the more traditional mild (or "sweet") paprika, familiar from our great aunt's deviled eggs. But do not use a sugar substitute instead of the brown sugar. The brown sugar will melt as it heats, sealing the rub to the meat.

2. Fill out the remaining 4 teaspoons of the rub with dried herbs (in greater quantities) and dried spices (in lesser quantities). Applicable herbs might be sage, oregano, or thyme; dried spices can be ground cinnamon, cumin, ginger, coriander, or pure chili powder, as well as garlic powder, ground black pepper, cayenne, or dry mustard. Consider this a good gauge: 1 teaspoon each of two dried herbs, then 2 teaspoons total of 3 or 4 dried spices. Make sure you make notes in the margin of this book so you know what you used in the rub you made.

Pat the spice rub evenly over the ribs before roasting. Note that here they are set up on a wire rack over a baking sheet, so they will not rest in any fat that melts off during cooking.

The ribs are done when the bones wiggle freely. Stick a fork in the meat between the ribs; the intermediary connective tissue should be quite tender, soft and luxurious. The ribs also taste best if they sit at room temperature for up to 10 minutes before serving. They'll also cut better between the bones when you slice them up with a heavy chef's knife or cleaver.

A little patience and voilà: Classic Oven-Roasted Ribs

Recipes for Ribs

	Pepper-Rubbed Ribs	Jerk Oven-Roasted Ribs	Cajun Oven-Roasted Ribs	Classic Oven-Roasted Ribs
1. Steam	One 2½-pound pork rib rack, trimmed; or two 1¼-pound baby back rib racks, trimmed	One 2½-pound pork rib rack, trimmed; or two 1¼-pound baby back rib racks, trimmed	One 2½-pound pork rib rack, trimmed; or two 1¼-pound baby back rib racks, trimmed	One 2½-pound pork rib rack, trimmed; or two 1¼-pound baby back rib racks, trimmed
2. Preheat the oven; coat the ribs and roast	2 tsp packed light brown sugar 2 tsp smoked paprika 1 tsp kosher salt 3 tsp (1 Tbs) black peppercorns, cracked in a mortar with a pestle or in a small, sealed plastic bag with the bottom of a heavy pot 1 tsp garlic powder	2 tsp packed light brown sugar 2 tsp smoked paprika 1 tsp kosher salt 1 tsp dried thyme 1 tsp onion powder 1 tsp ground allspice 1 tsp cayenne ½ tsp ground cinnamon	2 tsp packed light brown sugar 2 tsp smoked paprika 1 tsp kosher salt 1 tsp dried parsley 1 tsp dried sage 1 tsp ground cumin ½ tsp ground celery seeds ½ tsp cayenne ¼ tsp garlic powder	2 tsp packed light brown sugar 2 tsp smoked paprika 1 tsp kosher salt 1 tsp dried oregano 1 tsp ground cumin 1 tsp dry mustard ½ tsp onion powder ½ tsp ground black pepper ¼ tsp ground cinnamon ¼ tsp garlic powder

	Mole-Rubbed Oven-Roasted Ribs	Lemon-Pepper Oven-Roasted Ribs	Chinese-Inspired Oven-Roasted Ribs	Chili-Rubbed Oven-Roasted Ribs
1. Steam	One 2½-pound pork rib rack, trimmed; or two 1¼-pound baby back rib racks, trimmed	One 2½-pound pork rib rack, trimmed; or two 1¼-pound baby back rib racks, trimmed	One 2½-pound pork rib rack, trimmed; or two 1¼-pound baby back rib racks, trimmed	One 2½-pound pork rib rack, trimmed; or two 1¼-pound baby back rib racks, trimmed
2. Preheat the oven; coat the ribs and roast	2 tsp packed light brown sugar 2 tsp smoked paprika 1 tsp kosher salt 1 tsp unsweetened cocoa powder 1 tsp crushed sesame seeds 1 tsp ground cumin 1 tsp dried oregano	2 tsp packed light brown sugar 2 tsp smoked paprika 1 tsp kosher salt 4 tsp lemon pepper seasoning (see page 355)	2 tsp packed light brown sugar 2 tsp smoked paprika 1 tsp kosher salt 2 tsp five-spice powder (see page 149) 1 tsp ground coriander 1 tsp ground sesame seeds	2 tsp packed light brown sugar 2 tsp smoked paprika 1 tsp kosher salt 2 tsp pure ancho chili powder 1 tsp dried oregano 1 tsp ground cumin 1 tsp ground black pepper

Risotto

There's no more legendary technique—simply stated: "stir, stir, stir." But if you Zen out and get into the motion, there's absolutely nothing to this classic dish except patience. Serve it as a side dish, or on its own as a first course, perhaps as a replacement for pasta in Italian meals. Or stock it full and offer it as a main course, a tossed salad on the side. • MAKES 6 SERVINGS AS A SIDE DISH OR A FIRST COURSE

• **STEP 1** Warm 7 cups broth and perhaps a few seasonings in a large saucepan over very low heat. Do not simmer. Risotto is all about the broth, maybe even more so than the rice. The rice will slowly thicken that broth, which will have a long time to concentrate over the heat. In essence, you're reducing and reducing the broth, perhaps fivefold. Thus, it must be the best-tasting broth imaginable. Better to buy frozen demi-glace and reconstitute it according to the package's instructions than to have your hard work wrecked by some bland, watery broth.

Before you start adding the warmed stock in small amounts, the Arborio grains are cooked until they turn translucent with an opaque, white core.

Warming that broth really has nothing to do with the spices. Sure, it's nice to infuse the broth with some extra flavor, but the point is to warm the broth so that it doesn't shock the rice later when it's added.

Don't use fresh herbs—except for rosemary, which needs time over the heat to soften. For the rest, keep them out of this step and sprinkle them, minced, over individual servings later so their taste will be more present, less dulled by the heat.

At this stage use no more than 1 teaspoon dried spices: celery seeds, fennel seeds, ground cumin (very untraditional but intriguing), grated nutmeg, dry mustard, or perhaps saffron—although 1 teaspoon of any of the latter three will be far too much; consider their addition to be no more than ¼ teaspoon. Still, you needn't use any. Are you preparing risotto as a bed for a slice of roast beef (see page 306) or a piece of roasted chicken (see page 290)? Then keep the broth simple and the dried spices on the shelf.

• **STEP 2** Heat 3 tablespoons oil in a 11- to 12-inch, 4-quart sauté pan or risotto pan set over medium heat. Olive oil or unsalted butter are, of course, the customary fats. However, many other oils and fats, all untraditional, will offer a pleasing taste and variety. Risotto with walnut or almond oil is a treat indeed. Or a risotto that begins with 2 tablespoons unsalted butter and 1 tablespoon olive oil will be meltingly silky and irresistible. Just stay away from toasted nut and seed oils. Neutral oils won't do much for the taste, but perhaps they also won't get in the way of other ingredients you'll add to the dish, especially if you intend to stock the pan with other vegetables.

• **STEP 3** Add 1½ cups chopped aromatics and cook, stirring often, until softened, perhaps 3 to 5 minutes. A large chopped yellow onion is traditional, but feel free to substitute thinly sliced or chopped shallots; halved, cleaned, and thinly sliced leeks (white and pale green parts only); or even a diced red onion. Minced garlic is often added to this mixture—but minced, peeled fresh ginger? Well, why shouldn't you want to make a spiky, interesting side dish to a roasted duck? Although risotto is an Italian dish, it can also be Italian-*inspired,* a diverting pairing of international flavors. However, keep any and all changes to a minimum. Sure, a little ginger and later some cubed peeled and seeded butternut squash will make an innovative side dish, but you want to add no more than all that, keeping risotto, well, itself. Too much innovation and the dish loses its roots to become just a heap of dolled-up rice.

• **STEP 4** (optional): Stir in 2 cups sliced, shredded, or cubed prepared vegetables; cook, stirring constantly, until the vegetables begin to soften or give off their liquid. There's no need to add any vegetables, but you can at will. In general, consider how long the rice will be over the heat (at least another 45 minutes). So choose long-cooking vegetables: sweet potatoes, winter squash, roots, even rutabaga. All must be peeled (and seeded if necessary). Keep the cubes small—about ½ inch. They should melt in the sauce as the rice cooks. If you want to add fresh spring vegetables or greens—asparagus, peas, Swiss chard, and the like—save these until step 8.

• **STEP 5** Add 1½ cups Arborio rice; cook, stirring constantly, until translucent at the edges of the grains, about 30 seconds. Risotto must be made with Arborio rice, a medium-grained, pearl-colored, fairly squat-kernelled rice. (To learn about rice starch, see page 23). Arborio is named for an Italian town about halfway between Turin and Milan, on the Pó River, one of the most flooding, punishing waterways on the continent—and terrific for rice production. That said, Arborio is now grown in California and several other locales.

What Arborio has in abundance is soluble starch on the grains' outer surfaces. Do not substitute other rices. Some chefs make risotto from other rices, but they grind raw Arborio to a powder and stir it into the dish during the last 5 minutes of cooking—a cheat, for sure, and not exactly fit fare for this Italian tradition.

The Arborio kernels will begin to turn translucent over the heat—but the core will remain very white, a little dot in the translucence.

• **STEP 6** Pour in ½ cup white wine or a dry fortified wine. Cook, stirring constantly, until the wine has reduced to a glaze. Steer clear of dry fortified wines that add too much flavor: 10-year Madeira, for example, or port of any variety. Yes, you can make Sicilian-inspired risotto with dry Marsala, but the dish will have a pronounced taste, more center of the plate than side. In general, go for white wine or dry vermouth.

A Sauté Pan

Sometimes called a *sauteuse* (French, soh-TOOS), it's like a skillet but with a flat bottom and straight sides, higher than those of a skillet, perhaps 4 inches or so. A sauté pan provides even heating, eschewing the sloping sides of a skillet that allow for some cooling toward their edges.

A specialty risotto pan is about like a sauté pan without a handle—or with a handle that clips on and arches over the pan so you can cart it to the table.

Add more warmed broth or other liquids in very small quantities. You want to abrade as much starch into the broth as possible without waterlogging the grains.

Stir, stir, stir—the secret of risotto. Over low heat, keep stirring until the skillet is almost dry after each addition of stock.

When almost done, the risotto can be mounded in the pan, the rice grains now opaque and the surrounding sauce quite creamy.

Stir constantly with a wooden spoon until the wine has been reduced to a thick glaze. When you pull your spoon through the mixture, liquid should not immediately flow back into the dry mark you just made.

● STEP 7 Reduce the heat to low and stir in the warmed broth in ⅓-cup increments, stirring each over the heat until almost fully absorbed before adding more. Continue adding similar amounts of warm broth and stirring over the heat until the rice is creamy and al dente, about 45 minutes to 1 hour. Season with salt and freshly ground black pepper. As food scientist Harold McGee has pointed out, risotto is all about turning rice into a sauce. As you stir, you gently abrade the kernels and thus take off microscopic bits of softened, soluble starch. You're not really stirring to get the broth into the rice. Rather, you're stirring to get the rice into the broth—or at least the rice starch.

There's no need to be exact about how much liquid you add each time, but ⅓ cup is about right, never more, maybe even less. Here are four tips for success:

1. The broth in its own saucepan and indeed the broth in the sauté or risotto pan with the Arborio should never come to a boil. It may barely simmer at times in the sauté pan; at that point, you want to lower the heat so that it steams more than it bubbles but still is hot enough to dissolve the rice starch. Plan on adjusting the heat many times. This whole process should go slowly—never quickly—and so it is perhaps a true moment of counterculture in our fast-paced, digital age. It should take at least 45 minutes, maybe 1 hour, to get through those 7 cups of broth—that is, ⅓ cup every 2 or 3 minutes.

2. After each addition of broth, keep stirring until the line you make in the pot doesn't immediately refill with liquid. If you pull your spoon through the mixture, there should be noticeable borders. The moment there are, add more broth and keep stirring. If you add broth and it immediately cooks down to this stage, the heat is too high; turn it down so that the broth has more time to catch the abraded rice starch.

3. Don't stir vigorously. Slow, steady, and constant—that's how the soluble starch begins to come off the kernels and thicken the broth. But do not let the rice stick to the pan without any broth around it. Should you notice it's sticking, lower the heat further, add more broth, and stir more.

4. After about 40 minutes, the rice will have turned opaque again, mostly because you've begun to rub off the soluble layers. The mixture will thicken considerably and can be mounded when spooned into a corner. Keep stirring and adding little bits of broth, perhaps no more than 2 tablespoons—you're very close to done.

That moment of being done is, nonetheless, hard to predict. If the rice has been sitting on the store shelf and is dried out, the whole process may take a bit longer. Although 7 cups broth should do the trick, it's sometimes helpful—and less stressful—to have a cup or so of extra broth on hand just in case the rice is still a bit hard after those first 7 cups have been fully incorporated. If you've bought 2 quarts, you'll automatically have the extra cup you may need.

Once you notice the kernels have turned opaque again, start tasting the rice. It should be tender with just a little chew at the core (al dente). Mushy, soft rice does not make for successful risotto. Besides, the rice will continue to soften as it comes off the stove and you pull the rest of the meal together.

Do not season the dish with salt until the last minute. Salt will otherwise retard that soluble fiber from relaxing and thickening the risotto. If you're passing on to the next two steps, wait and season the dish after either or both.

• **STEP 8** (optional): **During the last 5 or 10 minutes of cooking, stir in some chopped and stemmed quick-cooking greens or green vegetables.** As you see the kernels turning opaque and taste them getting tender, stir in stemmed and chopped chard, baby spinach, broccoli florets, chopped sugar snaps or snow peas, or any other leafy or spring green vegetable: asparagus, peas, or chopped green beans. Avoid kale and celery, which will take too long to soften.

• **STEP 9** (optional): **Remove from the heat and stir in 6 tablespoons unsalted butter, heavy cream, and/or grated hard Italian cheese.** Here's a final finish, utterly optional. Although grated Parmigiano-Reggiano is a traditional garnish, also consider grated Pecorino, aged Asiago, Ricotta Salata, aged Boerenkaas, or an aged hard goat cheese.

The risotto is now ready to be served—and fairly quickly, at that. You can cover it and set it off the heat for perhaps 10 minutes, but it will begin to firm up, all that starch finally coming into its own in the sauce.

Recipes for Risottos

	Classic Risotto	Mushroom Risotto	Swiss Chard Risotto	Butternut Squash Risotto
1. Warm	7 cups chicken broth	7 cups chicken broth ½ tsp fennel seeds ¼ tsp saffron	7 cups chicken broth 2 Tbs minced rosemary ½ tsp grated nutmeg	7 cups chicken broth ½ tsp celery seeds ¼ tsp grated nutmeg
2. Heat	3 Tbs olive oil	3 Tbs olive oil	2 Tbs olive oil 1 Tbs unsalted butter	2 Tbs olive oil 1 Tbs unsalted butter
3. Add and cook	1 large yellow onion, chopped 1 garlic clove, minced	1 large yellow onion, chopped 2 garlic cloves, minced	1 large leek, white and pale green parts only, halved lengthwise, washed carefully, and thinly sliced 6 garlic cloves, minced	6 ounces shallots, peeled and chopped
4. (optional) Stir in and cook	Omit	8 ounces (½ pound) cremini mushrooms, cleaned and thinly sliced	½ cup chopped sun-dried tomatoes	1 small butternut squash, peeled, seeded, and diced
5. Add	1½ cups Arborio rice	1½ cups Arborio rice	1½ cups Arborio rice	1½ cups Arborio rice
6. Pour in and reduce	½ cup dry white wine	½ cup dry vermouth	½ cup dry vermouth	½ cup dry white wine
7. Add, stirring all the while, and season with salt and pepper	The warmed broth in ⅓-cup increments	The warmed broth mixture in ⅓-cup increments	The warmed broth mixture in ⅓-cup increments	The warmed broth mixture in ⅓-cup increments
8. (optional) Stir in	Omit	Omit	4 cups chopped, stemmed chard leaves	Omit
9. (optional) Stir in	Up to 6 Tbs unsalted butter	6 Tbs finely grated Parmigiano-Reggiano Garnish with stemmed thyme	6 Tbs finely grated Parmigiano-Reggiano	6 Tbs finely grated Parmigiano-Reggiano

	Prima Vera Risotto	Curried Vegetable Risotto	Spinach and Mushroom Risotto	Lobster and Asparagus Risotto
1. Warm	7 cups chicken broth ¼ tsp saffron	7 cups chicken broth 2 Tbs curry powder (see page 113) ¼ tsp saffron	7 cups chicken broth ½ tsp ground mace	4 cups (1 quart) fish broth 3 cups vegetable broth ½ tsp fennel seeds ¼ tsp saffron
2. Heat	2 Tbs unsalted butter 1 Tbs olive oil	3 Tbs olive oil	3 Tbs olive oil	3 Tbs unsalted butter
3. Add and cook	1 large yellow onion, chopped 2 garlic cloves, minced	1 large yellow onion, chopped 2 Tbs minced peeled fresh ginger 1 garlic clove, minced	1 large yellow onion, chopped	1 large leek, white and pale green parts only, halved lengthwise, washed carefully, and thinly sliced
4. (optional) Stir in and cook	1 medium carrot, diced 1 small fennel bulb, trimmed and diced	12 ounces cauliflower florets ½ cup canned chickpeas, drained and rinsed	6 ounces shiitake mushrooms, stems discarded, the caps thinly sliced	Omit
5. Add	1½ cups Arborio rice	1½ cups Arborio rice	1½ cups Arborio rice	1½ cups Arborio rice
6. Pour in and reduce	½ cup dry sherry	½ cup dry sherry	½ cup dry vermouth	½ cup rosé wine
7. Add, stirring all the while, and season with salt and pepper	The warmed broth mixture in ⅓-cup increments	The warmed broth mixture in ⅓-cup increments	The warmed broth mixture in ⅓-cup increments	The warmed broth mixture in ⅓-cup increments
8. (optional) Stir in	1 cup shelled fresh or frozen peas 6 pencil-thin asparagus spears, cut into 1-inch sections	Omit	4 ounces baby spinach leaves	1 pound pencil-thin asparagus spears, cut into 1-inch segments 1 pound frozen lobster tail meat, thawed and shelled, then chopped
9. (optional) Stir in	6 Tbs heavy or whipping cream	Up to 6 Tbs unsalted butter Garnish with minced cilantro	6 Tbs finely grated aged goat cheese Garnish with stemmed thyme	6 Tbs grated Pecorino

Roasted Birds 1: Under 4½ Pounds Each

Who doesn't love roasted chicken or its feathery kith and kin? Maybe it was eating them at your grandmother's or maybe it was discovering them as an adult and wishing you'd eaten them at your grandmother's—but chances are, you want to know how to make the best bird imaginable. So here it is: a French-inspired, classic, two-phase process: first on the stove, then in the oven. We give the amounts for four servings, but this recipe can be prepared for more people by getting more birds in more skillets over more burners. • MAKES 4 SERVINGS

• **STEP 1** Set the rack in the oven's center and preheat the oven to 375°F; truss the bird(s) and season with salt and freshly ground black pepper.

Suitable birds

Small chickens under 4½ pounds. Although the USDA recognizes three classes of chicken, only the first, "broiler/fryers" (2½ to 4½ pounds), is suitable for this technique. The second, "roasters" (5 to 7 pounds), needs prolonged, dry-heat cooking (see page 296). And the third, "stewers" (5 pounds or more but up to 1½ years old), is tough enough to require a slow braise, usually cut into pieces for dishes like Cacciatora (page 69) or Chicken Soup (page 83). For 4 servings: roast one broiler/fryer chicken and offer a side vegetable or salad.

Pintades or guinea fowl. These ground-nesting birds (French, pen-TAHD) are originally from Africa but are now primarily associated with French cuisine. Ready for flight, they are 100% deeply oxygenated, dark meat. For 4 servings: roast one with several sides for small eaters; get two if we're coming over.

Game hens. "Cornish game hens" is a poor moniker, more marketing than reality; these birds are actually a cross between two small domesticated chickens. Some can weigh up to 3 pounds; others are quite small, about 1 pound. For 4 servings: try one large game hen with plenty of side dishes or two to three smaller ones.

Pheasants. These game birds were brought to North America in the eighteenth century by wealthy lay-abouts who needed something else to hunt if only to kill time. Apparently, they had less time than they thought, because the birds now run wild across many parts of the country. The meat is rich and flavorful, slightly gamy but less richly dark than pintades. Small birds, especially, pheasants, often come with the inner organs still hanging in the body cavity; remove these before trussing (see below). For 4 servings: plan on two 1-pound birds.

Poussins. Pronounced even in the plural poo-SEN, these are small, 4- to 6-week-old chickens, sometimes called "squab chickens" (but not squabs—see below). They're very sweet, quite juicy. For 4 servings: use four bony 1-pound birds.

Squabs. Young domesticated pigeons, these birds have a rich, oily gaminess, a decided treat with a glass of hearty red wine. For 4 servings: cook four 1-pound birds.

Partridges and Scottish or Continental pigeons. These game birds are now making a run for the American market thanks to high-end suppliers. The meat is red, quite rich, and a little chewy. For 4 servings: since they run a little over ½ pound each with lots of meat, use four birds.

Quail. With its sweet, irresistible meat and excellent bone-to-meat ratio, quail are a fancy dinner party favorite. If you've bought butterflied ones, round them back up like a miniature chicken for trussing (see below). For 4 generous servings: plan on eight 5-ounce quail.

Selecting and storing birds

When you're at the market shopping for birds, looks for supple, pliable, intact skin with a pink hue. Dating on poultry packaging is without government enforcement and left to the discretion of producers, butchers, and supermarkets. Indeed, a small-shop butcher rarely dates meat because she or he knows what's good to sell. But without enforced standards, all labels are not equal: note the differences among "sell by," "best if used by," and "use by." But do not rely solely on any of these. Also rely on your nose. A fresh bird should be almost odorless, certainly without any sulfurous tang. When in doubt, ask the butcher to open the package.

Once home, remove any inner organs and the neck from inside both cavities, back and front; cook the bird(s) within one or two days of purchase—or unwrap the raw bird(s), place one (or two if they're small) in a zip-closed plastic bag, squeeze out the air, seal, and freeze for up to 4 months. Freezing birds in their supermarket containers is a bad idea; the Styrofoam bottom is porous, permitting cross-contamination; and air pockets under the plastic wrap can promote freezer burn.

To thaw, place any of these birds on a large plate to catch drips and set in the refrigerator for 18 to 36 hours. Room-temperature thawing allows the skin to defrost long before the meat, so the skin rests at an unsafe temperature for too long. Never refreeze a thawed bird.

Do not remove the skin! It will protect and baste the meat while roasting. If you have diet concerns, remove the skin before serving but not before cooking. If, however, you like crisp skin, set the bird(s) on a plate unwrapped in the refrigerator for 24 hours so that the skin dries out before cooking, thereby turning crunchier in the oven.

Trussing

Partly to preserve the bird's appearance for presentation, but mostly to assure even cooking, truss it—that is, tie it together to hold its shape. Even split-open quail should be rounded like a Lilliputian chicken and then trussed.

Start with dye-free, food-safe butcher's twine, available in kitchenware stores, online outlets, and some high-end supermarkets. Cut off and discard the birds' wing tips (those flapper thirds at the end of each wing) by inserting a knife's tip into the joint's center and prying back before slicing off each tip.

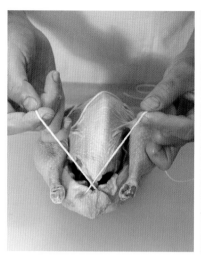 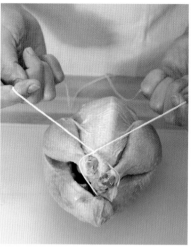 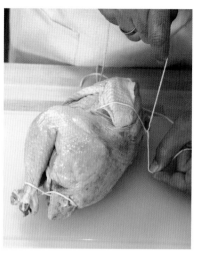

TO TRUSS A SMALL BIRD: First, set the bird (here, a pheasant) breast side up on your work surface, then wrap butcher's twine around the little "tail" below the large opening.

Wrap the twine up and around the legs, securing them together.

Next, secure the wings in place by wrapping the twine over the thighs and around the body.

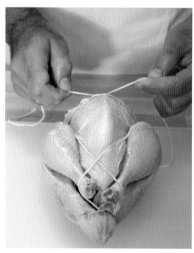

Finally, knot the twine right on top of the breast bone before snipping off any excess.

There are two basic methods for trussing:

1. **French.** Set the bird on a cutting board breast up, legs toward you. Start with a piece of twine about 5 times longer than the bird. Set the middle of the twine under the little tail, the triangular piece of meat below the large opening, wrap it around this little tail once, pull both ends of the twine up, and wrap each around the end of the nearest leg. Now pull the two ends of the twine up and cross them over each other before pulling fairly tight. Lay each side of the twine in the crevasse along the thighs at the breast, wrap both sides under the bird's back, and then draw them up and around the breast, pulling the twine tight and also pulling the wings up onto the top of the breast, thereby holding them in place. Once the twine is wrapped around the body, make a tight knot and cut off any excess twine.

2. **Rustic.** Pull the wings close to breast, then tie them in place by wrapping and knotting the twine around the bird's body. Tie the legs together over the large opening, crossing them over each other and winding the twine around the ends before knotting it, thereby mostly closing the large opening.

When you're done trussing the birds, wash your hands with soap under very warm water for twenty seconds, about the time it takes to sing a verse and chorus of "Jingle Bells." When the bird or birds go into the oven, wash all equipment and utensils with hot, soapy water, preferably in the dishwasher. Disinfect laminate countertops, granite, concrete, marble, stainless or porous materials with approved cleaners.

• **STEP 2** Heat 3 tablespoons fat in a large, oven-safe skillet over medium heat. Olive oil offers a clean finish; untoasted walnut oil, an earthy aroma; and almond oil, a bright sweetness. A neutral oil, while certainly usable, offers nothing to the bird itself, providing only a blank canvas for the sauce to come.

The best bet is a combination of 2 tablespoons unsalted butter and 1 tablespoon oil. Do not use all butter—a little oil will keep the milk solids from burning as the bird browns on top of the stove. And avoid any toasted or smoky oils or fats, both of which simply mask the taste of the meat.

Use a high-sided, 10- or 12-inch, oven-safe skillet—not a sauté pan with straight sides, but rather a skillet, the sides of which are a rounded curve off the bottom. That rounded well will allow you to collect the fat by tipping the pan to the side, the better to baste the bird.

If you're working with several birds, you may need to use more skillets to accommodate them, each set over a separate burner. Use the requisite amount of fat in each skillet.

• **STEP 3** Add the bird(s) breast side down and brown, turning occasionally and basting often. Because of the way the breast bone rounds under the meat, the bird may well lean to one side—a problem you'll remedy in a minute. For now, tilt the pan, spoon up some of the fat, and drizzle it over the bird(s). Brown well, basting once or twice; turn the bird(s) to the other side of the breast and continue browning and basting. Then set it or them on their sides, doing the same operation.

To brown thoroughly, small chickens and large game hens will take about 10 minutes; pintades and pheasants, about 8 minutes; and the rest, 5 to 6 minutes. When done, the skin should be golden brown, somewhat stiff, and glistening with juice.

One note: if you're working with several birds, you may have to brown them in batches—or work in two skillets set over two burners. If so, have extra fat on hand to add to the pan should you notice it's running dry.

• **STEP 4** Turn the bird(s) breast side up, place the skillet in the oven, and roast, basting often, until an instant-read meat thermometer inserted into the thickest part of the thigh without touching bone registers 165°F. Things have changed at the USDA. Time was, the government recommended cooking almost all birds to

The birds are first browned and basted almost continually with the fat in the skillet.

The only way to tell if the bird is done? Take its temperature right in the thickest part of the thigh.

175°F, even 180°F—almost incinerated, shardy and ridiculously dry. The bureaucrats have since come around to a more sensible recommendation: 165°F. Salmonella is well gone at this lower temperature; the meat is juicy and tender, just the barest hint of pink at the bone.

To take the bird's temperature, insert an instant-read meat thermometer into the thigh at the end farthest away from the legs' tips, back by the wings, holding the probe parallel with the skillet's bottom. Make sure the probe gets into the center of the meat without touching bone.

When will the right temperature be reached? It's a hard call, determined by the bird's age, its health, its moisture content, your oven's accuracy, and the weight of the skillet. Plan on

50 to 60 minutes for a small chicken
35 to 45 minutes for large game hens, pintades, and pheasants
20 to 25 minutes for squab, regular game hens, and poussins
15 minutes for partridges and pigeons
8 minutes for quail

Baste larger birds every 10 to 15 minutes, tilting the hot skillet to the side to spoon up the juices; baste smaller birds just once or twice during roasting.

Once the birds are properly roasted, make an easy pan sauce, no more than some herbs along with broth, cream, and/or wine, just to nap over the meat.

• **STEP 5** Transfer the bird(s) to a cutting board and make a simple pan sauce with any internal juices, a minced fresh herb, and ¼ cup liquid. Pick up the bird or birds one at a time with tongs, holding it over the skillet large-cavity opening facing down so the juices will pour out. Transfer to a cutting board to rest for 5 to 10 minutes. The meat will relax and the juices will reincorporate among the fibers.

Return the skillet to medium heat. Watch out: that skillet is burning hot! Add some broth, wine, dry fortified wine, unsweetened apple cider, or cream—or perhaps a combination like 3 tablespoons cream and 1 tablespoon dry Madeira. Also add one minced, leafy, green herb: rosemary, parsley, thyme, and the like. If you haven't added cream, you can enrich the sauce by whisking in 1 or 2 tablespoons unsalted butter—an at-will richness. In any case, whisk over the heat until reduced by half, picking up anything on the skillet's bottom to enrich the sauce. Taste for salt before serving.

To carve chickens and large game hens, use the method for carving large birds (see page 300). All other birds except quail should by cut in half, tip to tail, large opening to small—and then perhaps each half cut in half the short way, thereby making four quarters. Quail can be left whole or opened up along the backbone.

Recipes for Roasted Birds Under 4½ Pounds Each

	Roasted Chicken	Roasted Pintades	Roasted Game Hens	Roasted Pheasants
1. Preheat the oven; truss and season with salt and pepper	One 3½ pound small chicken	Two 2½-pound pintades or guinea fowl	Two 1½-pound game hens	Two 2½-pound pheasants
2. Heat	2 Tbs unsalted butter 1 Tbs olive oil	2 Tbs olive oil 1 Tbs unsalted butter	2 Tbs unsalted butter 1 Tbs olive oil	2 Tbs unsalted butter 1 Tbs canola oil
3. Brown	The bird	The birds	The birds	The birds
4. Bake	About 55 minutes	About 45 minutes	About 20 minutes	About 45 minutes
5. Remove bird(s); make a pan sauce	¼ cup dry white wine 1 Tbs stemmed thyme 1 Tbs unsalted butter	¼ cup red wine 1 Tbs minced oregano	¼ cup dry vermouth 2 Tbs minced sage 1 Tbs unsalted butter	3 Tbs heavy or whipping cream 1 Tbs Grand Marnier 1 Tbs stemmed thyme

	Roasted Poussins	Roasted Squabs	Roasted Partridges	Roasted Quail
1. Preheat the oven; truss and season with salt and pepper	Four 1-pound poussins	Four 1-pound squabs	Four 1-pound partridges	Eight 5-ounce quail
2. Heat	2 Tbs unsalted butter 1 Tbs canola oil	2 Tbs olive oil 1 Tbs unsalted butter	2 Tbs canola oil 1 Tbs unsalted butter	2 Tbs unsalted butter 1 Tbs canola oil
3. Brown	The birds	The birds	The birds	The birds
4. Bake	About 20 minutes	About 20 minutes	About 15 minutes	About 8 minutes
5. Remove bird(s); make a pan sauce	¼ cup dry vermouth 2 Tbs chopped chives 1 Tbs unsalted butter	¼ cup unsweetened apple cider 1 Tbs minced sage 1 Tbs unsalted butter	3 Tbs heavy or whipping cream 1 Tbs dry Madeira 1 Tbs minced oregano	¼ cup port 2 Tbs minced basil 2 Tbs unsalted butter

Roasted Birds 2: Over 4½ Pounds Each

As with many of the roasting techniques in this book, the yield is a range, rather than an amount, depending on what you choose: here, a 5-pound chicken with several sides will serve 6; an 8-pound capon, definitely 6, maybe 7; a 14-pound turkey, 12 at your holiday feast. For the technique to roast duck and goose, see page 365. • MAKES 6 TO 12 SERVINGS

• **STEP 1** Position the rack in the middle of the oven or at the highest setting it can go that will still accommodate the bird with a couple inches to spare at the top of the oven; preheat the oven to 375°F. Make pockets under the skin of the breast and the thighs of a large chicken, a capon, or a turkey; fill these pockets with aromatic herbs an/or whole dried spices, then season the large cavity with salt and freshly ground black pepper and fill it with various aromatics.

The three basic large birds

1. Chickens over 5 pounds are technically labeled "roasters" by the USDA and are fit for this technique since they have quite a bit of subcutaneous fat that protects the meat in the oven. Moreover, much of that fat would not render off in a quick-cooking method, such as that used for smaller birds (see page 290). Read the label carefully to get a bird that hasn't been doped with saline solution, broth, or preservatives. A careful roasting technique takes away the need for fancy additives that only mask the meat's taste.
2. A capon is a gelded rooster, one unnecessary for the coop and unwanted by the producer. Like any castrato, it plumps up considerably. In the end, a capon is a wonderful cross between a chicken and a turkey, the meat quite rich but also a little firmer, not quite as soft as a chicken's.
3. Most turkeys sold today are the domesticated, dim-witted, white-feathered kin of their more irascible, wild counterparts, the ones that Benjamin Franklin wanted to make the national bird. Domesticated turkeys are sold either "minimally processed," which means there are no additives to the meat; or "processed," which means the meat has been injected with broth, water, a saline solution, MSG, sodium erythorbate (a preservative), or several of these. Read the label. So-called "self-basting" birds have almost always been doped. Once again, a good roasting technique will make you swear off anything but minimally-processed turkeys, which are both less altered and better tasting.

Frozen turkeys—and indeed, all birds—should be thawed in the refrigerator, about 1 day for every 4 pounds. A frozen bird can also be wrapped tightly in a large plastic bag and defrosted, completely submerged, in a large bowl of cold water at room temperature, changing the water every 30 minutes to assure it stays cold. A 10-pound bird should take about 4 hours.

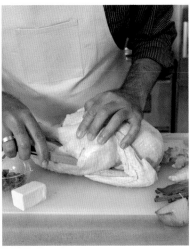

TO PREPARE A LARGE BIRD FOR ROASTING: First, open a pocket between the skin and the breast so you can push in some aromatics and/or herbs.

Keep enlarging that pocket over the breast as you add more aromatics or herbs.

Cut a small hole between the skin and meat over one of the thighs to create a pocket between the two.

Preparing the bird

Before you begin, check both openings, large and small, to remove any giblets or other parts left inside. Save these for making gravy (see page 299).

To make a pocket over the breast meat, set the bird on a cutting board. Beginning at the point of meat on either side of the large opening, lift up the skin and run a finger between it and the meat, thereby releasing its sticky adherence from the meat and creating a little pocket, first on one side of the breast bone, then on the other. Enlarge these pockets by running your finger, then several fingers, between the

Fill these pockets over the thighs with the same sort of aromatics and/or herbs used for the breast.

Don't neglect the cavity. It should be filled with some large aromatics like celery chunks, quartered onion, or cut-up lemons.

skin and meat (without stretching the skin into something resembling your favorite has-been actress' neck).

Once a pocket has been created on either side, add some chopped leafy herbs. Best with chicken and capon are tarragon, parsley, rosemary, or oregano; with turkey, sage, thyme, oregano, and marjoram—although in reality almost any leafy herb will work for any large bird. You can also use a combination of perhaps two: rosemary and oregano, tarragon and parsley. But there's no accounting for amounts here: add just enough herbs that they lightly cover the meat without causing unsightly bulges under the skin.

To make a pocket over a thigh, turn the bird on its side and use a knife to make a slit in the skin between the knee joint and the back of the thigh. Run your finger inside the skin and over the meat, thereby loosening the skin without stretching it. Add some more of the same chopped herbs you used for the breast. Repeat with the other thigh.

Set the bird back breast side up on the cutting board, large opening toward you. Season the inside of the cavity with a little salt and some freshly ground black pepper, then push in a few aromatics: a quartered onion, several sliced celery ribs, a sliced carrot or two, a quartered lemon, and/or a thickly sliced fennel bulb. For an interesting twist, consider some whole dried spices: a cinnamon stick or two, a couple bay leaves, a few whole cloves, a small handful of juniper berries, or maybe even some allspice berries.

The prepared bird starts out in the oven breast side down on the rack set in the roasting pan.

• **STEP 2** Truss the bird, then coat the skin with 2 to 4 tablespoons fat. For a discussion of the two ways to truss a bird so that it won't flatten out in the oven's heat, see page 292.

Almost any oil will do, so long as it's not a toasted nut or seed oil. That said, neutral-flavored oils like canola and corn will add nothing to the roasted flavor. Instead, try olive, untoasted walnut, or untoasted almond oil. Or use unsalted butter, softened to room temperature. You'll need to smear it evenly over the bird, coating the legs and wings as well as the breast and thighs. Do not use melted butter, which will then brown too quickly in the oven and turn bitter on the skin. In all cases, use 2 tablespoons for a 5- to 7-pound bird; 3 for an 8 to 10 pounder; ¼ cup for the rest.

Must you add fat? In fact, no. But it certainly helps to crisp the skin in the oven's ambient heat, making for a more luscious dinner.

And one final note on larding up the bird: many classic techniques also ask you to spread the same fat under the skin and thus over the meat where the herbs are. There's no reason to add this much fat, given modern poultry production and the resulting fat layer bred into birds. Yes, birds from 50 years ago needed protection in the heat; today, that added fat is a silly (if indeed luscious) excess.

• **STEP 3** Season the skin with salt and freshly ground black pepper, set the bird breast side down on a rack in a large roasting pan, and roast for 1 hour. Turn breast side up and continue roasting until an instant-read meat thermometer inserted into the thickest part of the thigh without its touching bone registers 165°F, between 1 hour 15 minutes and 3 hours 45 minutes, depending on size. You'll need a heavy-duty roasting pan and a rack that can lift the bird out of the rendered fat, preferably a rack that forms a wide, flattened "X" when opened and secured, the bird resting in the top crook of that "X." A heavy-duty roasting pan will reflect the heat and allow for even browning. Failing either the pan or the roasting rack, use a broiler pan and a footed wire rack, often the one that comes with the broiler pan, or perhaps a metal wire rack with metal feet (no rubber), the kind usually used to cool cookies and such.

Season the bird well by massaging salt, preferably kosher salt, and pepper over its skin, about 2 teaspoons for every 5 pounds. It's easiest to begin with the bird on the cutting board, seasoning its breast (the large oval lobes that run from the large opening back over the bird), wings, and upper legs; then transfer it to the rack breast side down and season the underside and the thighs.

Why kosher salt? It has a bright, mineral-like taste, thanks to its lack of iodine, often added to other versions of table salt. Kosher salt—called "koshering salt" in Great Britain and "coarse cooking salt" in many others parts of the world—also has larger grains that will not melt and slide off the juicy bird in the oven. But one warning: if you've bought a kosher chicken, turkey, or capon, you'll want to cut down on the salt dramatically because these birds have already been salted at processing.

To turn the bird on the rack after it has roasted for 1 hour, use silicon gloves, a new-fangled invention that allows you to grab a hot bird and turn it by hand. Failing that, use large tongs in one hand with a metal spatula in the other for balance. But in any case, remember that the bird's cavities are filling with hot juices that can spill out and cause a nasty burn. Don't turn the bird so that the large or small opening ever lies on the vertical; instead, rotate it as on a rotisserie rod so that its axis remains parallel with the oven floor. Still, watch out for those heated juices.

Now continue roasting the bird, basting occasionally with pan drippings to protect the breast meat from the oven's heat and to continue to crisp the skin.

There are three markers to tell when the bird is done:

1. When the thigh is pricked, the juices run clear.
2. The skin is well browned, golden or a little deeper.
3. The internal temperature of the thigh registers 165°F.

Indeed, that last method is the only sure one, even if you have a bird with a built-in pop-up timer. Turn the bird so the large opening faces away from you and insert the probe straight into the thickest part of the thigh without touching

GIBLET GRAVY

While the bird is roasting, place the heart, gizzard, and neck as well as 2 cut-up celery ribs, 1 cut-up medium carrot, and 1 bay leaf in a small saucepan with 2 cups chicken broth and 2 cups water. Set the pan over medium-high heat and bring to a simmer. Cover, reduce the heat to low, and simmer until the gizzard is tender, about 1 hour. Add the liver and continue simmering for 20 minutes. Drain in a colander set in the sink over a large bowl, thereby catching and reserving 2 cups juice. Discard the celery, bay leaves, and peppercorns; dice the heart, gizzard, and liver as well as any available meat from the neck. Set the reserved liquid and the diced innards aside separately, in the refrigerator if they're to be at room temperature for more than 20 minutes.

After the bird comes out of the oven, skim the pan drippings of surface fat, using either a fat separator available at cookware stores or a large spoon against the side of the pan; you should have about ½ cup liquid left in the roasting pan. If desired, add 2 or 3 tablespoons broth, set the roasting pan over the medium heat (if the pan is flame-safe, that is), bring to a simmer, and scrape up any browned bits on its bottom.

Melt 3 tablespoons unsalted butter in a large skillet, then sprinkle 3 tablespoons all-purpose flour over it. Wait for 10 seconds, then stir well and cook until beige, about 1 minute. Whisk in several small amounts of the reserved giblet broth, just a couple of tablespoons at a time, slowly dissolving the flour mixture into the broth. Continue whisking in the broth, then stir in the reserved, skimmed pan liquid. The moment the mixture comes to a low simmer, remove it from the heat and stir in the diced giblet meat. Season with salt and freshly ground black pepper.

TO CARVE THE BIRD: First wiggle the thigh-and-leg quarter loose, then slice down through the joint that connects it to the body.

After you've taken off the leg, slice the meat off the thigh bone in fairly large chunks.

Next, wiggle the wings free and slice them off the breast, carving right down through the joint.

Finally, slice the meat off the breast, using long, even, steady strokes to get thin, tender slices.

bone, holding the probe parallel to the oven's floor. For safety, also insert the probe into the breast right at the thickest part above where you took the thigh's temperature, again holding the probe parallel to the oven's floor. In a very large bird, the breast may take longer to cook than the thighs, which can withstand lots more cooking anyway.

In general, plan on 15 to 17 minutes per pound, but do not rely on atmospherics or the clock to determine if the bird is done. That said, just as a rough guideline, a 6-pound chicken takes about 1 hour 40 minutes; an 8-pound capon, about 2 hours 10 minutes; and a 14-pound turkey, about 3 hours 30 minutes. However, a bird's getting done is dependent on a range of factors: its temperature when it went into the oven (some people let them stand at room temperature for up to 1 hour—not safe, but the cooking time will be reduced by as much as 15%), the thickness of the skin, any hot spots in the oven, and the amount of heat the roasting pan reflects. Here's the best plan for a dinner party: make a simple roasted tomato soup for a first-course, open a bottle of wine, and plan on a rough approximation of when the bird will be done.

Should a very large bird brown too much, moving well beyond mahogany, tent it loosely with foil to protect the meat as it continues to cook. Uncover when the internal meat temperature reaches 160°F to crisp up the skin for the final minutes of roasting.

Once out of the oven, let the bird rest at room temperature for 10 minutes.

Recipes for Roasted Birds Over 4½ Pounds Each

	French Country Roast Chicken	Italian-Inspired Roast Chicken	Country Capon	Thanksgiving Turkey	Greek-Inspired Roast Turkey
1. Preheat the oven; herb, stuff, and season the bird	One 5- to 5½-pound roasting chicken Minced tarragon for the breast and thighs 2 quartered medium onions and 1 quartered lemon for the large cavity Salt and pepper to taste	One 5- to 5½-pound roasting chicken Minced rosemary, oregano, and lemon zest for the breast and thighs 4 quartered shallots and 1 thickly sliced medium fennel bulb for the large cavity Salt and pepper to taste	One 8-pound capon Minced sage and stemmed thyme for the breast and thighs 1 quartered medium onion, 2 thickly sliced celery ribs, 2 thickly sliced medium carrots, and 1 bay leaf for the large cavity Salt and pepper to taste	One 12-pound turkey Minced sage for the breast and thighs 2 quartered medium yellow onions, 2 sliced celery ribs, 2 sliced parsnips, two 4-inch cinnamon sticks, and 6 allspice berries for the large cavity Salt and pepper to taste	One 10-pound turkey Minced dill and oregano for the breast and thighs 2 quartered lemons, 3 quartered shallots, 2 whole garlic heads, upper third sliced off and discarded, and 3 bay leaves for the large cavity Salt and pepper to taste
2. Truss, then coat	2 Tbs unsalted butter, at room temperature	2 Tbs olive oil	3 Tbs walnut oil	4 Tbs (½ stick) unsalted butter, at room temperature	¼ cup olive oil
3. Season and roast to an internal temperature of	Kosher salt and pepper to taste 165°F, about 1 hour 20 minutes	Kosher salt and pepper to taste 165°F, about 1 hour 20 minutes	Kosher salt and pepper to taste 165°F, about 2 hours 10 minutes	Kosher salt and pepper to taste 165°F, about 3 hours 20 minutes	Kosher salt and pepper to taste 165°F, about 2 hours 45 minutes

Roasted Fish on a Bed of Mixed Vegetables

Roasted Fish

Roasted over a bed of sliced vegetables, a whole fish is a one-pan meal. The vegetables pick up some of the flavors, caramelizing in the natural juices. • MAKES 4 SERVINGS

• **STEP 1** Preheat the oven to 375°F. Place 6 to 8 cups sliced roots or long-cooking vegetables in a 14-inch rectangular roasting pan or a 14-inch cast-iron skillet, drizzle in ¼ cup oil, and bake until partially tender, about 40 minutes to 1 hour. You'll want rings or slices about ½ inch thick. Consider these:

> **peeled halved medium rutabagas**
> **peeled large sweet potatoes**
> **medium yellow onions**
> **trimmed large fennel bulbs**
> **peeled large beets**
> **peeled large turnips**
> **large yellow-fleshed potatoes,** such as Yukon Golds
> **peeled large carrots**
> **peeled large parsnips**
> **Brussels sprouts,** the thick stems removed

Or mix and match the vegetables: onions and turnips, carrots and fennel, potatoes and parsnips. The only roasting vegetable we wouldn't recommend are beets—and that's only for aesthetics. If you'd don't mind their staining what's around them, they're a fine mix with more bitter turnips or more aromatic fennel.

Lay the vegetables in the baking pan, perhaps in slightly overlapping rows. They will eventually form a bed for the fish. Drizzle the oil over them: olive oil, an untoasted nut oil, or a neutral-oil like corn or vegetable oil. For Asian-inspired preparations, use canola or another neutral oil—or even untoasted sesame oil. In all cases, avoid toasted oils, esoteric seed oils, unsalted butter, and rendered animal fat.

Start out by filling a roasting pan with sliced root vegetables (here, carrots and parsnips) and stuff the fish with herbs and aromatics.

Sliced onion and fennel will be partially cooked in 30 minutes; the other roots, in 40 minutes—but in truth, the onion and fennel can go longer, particularly if they're mixed with the other vegetables. None should be soft, but they should all have begun to soften and perhaps brown lightly at the edges.

• **STEP 2** Stuff the body cavity of two scaled, cleaned, 1½-pound whole fish with various herbs, whole dried spices, aromatics, and/or flavorings. For a discussion of how to choose a fresh fish, see page 135. Use any whole fish that's fresh at the market: snapper, bass, drum, parrotfish, wreckfish, or tilapia.

After stuffing the body cavity with some herbs and/or aromatics, trim the tail so the fish will fit in the roasting pan.

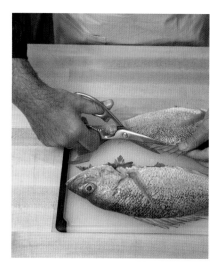

Trim the dorsal fins as well, taking care not to cut into the skin or flesh.

The only exception is trout, generally smaller than what's called for. Buy three or four and stuff them as directed, doubling the amount of whole dried spices to compensate for the increased number of fish. The cooking time must also be adjusted: roast the vegetables about 1 hour, then roast the trout on top of them for another 20 minutes.

Fresh, leafy herbs are a natural here: rosemary or tarragon stems, parsley or cilantro leaves. Pair them if you will with sun-dried tomatoes, fennel fronds, olives, marinated artichoke hearts, or other salad-bar favorites.

There's no compelling need to use onion or even most aromatics inside the fish's body, but do consider scallions or roasted garlic (see page 333—or simply bought off the salad bar at the supermarket) as well as minced peeled fresh ginger and feathery celery leaves (rather than the stalks).

Avoid ground dried spices but do consider any whole version of a dried spice—peppercorns, star anise, allspice berries, cinnamon sticks—so long as it's not placed in combination with too many other flavors. A star anise pod, some minced peeled ginger, and cilantro sprigs give the fish an Asian-inspired flavor.

• **STEP 3** Lightly oil and season the outside of the fish, then set it atop the vegetables in the pan and roast until the meat flakes with a fork and the vegetables are quite tender, about 30 to 40 minutes. Rub a little of the same oil you used for the vegetables over both sides of the fish, about 2 teaspoons per side, not forgetting the head and tail. Or if desired, drizzle the fish with a toasted nut or seed oil before it goes in the oven, a complementary fat if you've used a neutral oil in this step.

In general, salt and pepper the fish on both sides, using kosher salt and several grinds of black pepper. You might also consider crushed pink peppercorns for a more nosy aroma or ground white pepper for a lightly more sour seasoning. Or skip the salt and pepper altogether and use soy sauce, fish sauce (page 388), or Worcestershire sauce, all very salty but a nice complement to Asian herbs.

The only real way to tell if a whole fish is done is to pull some of the meat back from thick section of the belly; see if it flakes or is gelatinous. But don't worry: assuming you haven't let it roast for hours, a roasted fish is fairly forgiving, the skin keeping the meat moist in the oven.

Use a wide spatula to transfer the fish to a cutting or carving board. Be careful: it's delicate and can chip and break. Support it along the length of its body. For carving instructions, see page 360. Serve the fish with the roasted vegetables.

Recipes for Roasted Fish

	Roasted Fish on a Bed of Fennel	Roasted Fish on a Bed of Turnips	Roasted Fish on a Bed of Mixed Vegetables	Asian Roasted Fish
1. Preheat the oven; bake	4 large fennel bulbs, trimmed and cut into ½-inch slices ¼ cup olive oil	6 medium turnips, peeled and cut into ½-inch slices ¼ cup walnut oil	4 large carrots, peeled and cut into ½-inch slices 4 large parsnips, peeled and cut into ½-inch slices ¼ cup almond oil	12 whole medium scallions, cut into thirds 1 large fresh bamboo shoot, peeled and thinly sliced ¼ cup sesame oil
2. Stuff	Two 1½-pound whole fish, cleaned and scaled 2 to 4 rosemary sprigs 4 to 6 oregano sprigs 3 to 6 parsley sprigs 2 tsp finely grated lemon zest	Two 1½-pound whole fish, cleaned and scaled 6 to 8 tarragon sprigs 2 small lemons, thinly sliced	Two 1½-pound whole fish, cleaned and scaled 4 to 6 parsley sprigs 4 to 6 cilantro sprigs 4 garlic cloves, minced	Two 1½-pound whole fish, cleaned and scaled Two 2-inch pieces ginger, peeled and cut into thin rings 8 to 10 cilantro sprigs 2 star anise pods
3. Oil and season, then roast	Olive oil Salt and pepper to taste	Walnut oil Salt and pepper to taste	Almond oil Salt and pepper to taste	Sesame oil Soy sauce to taste

	Roasted Fish on a Bed of Beets	Roasted Fish and Potatoes	Greek-Inspired Roasted Fish	Caribbean Roasted Fish
1. Preheat the oven; bake	4 large beets, peeled and cut into ½-inch slices 1 medium onion, peeled and cut into ½-inch slices ¼ cup walnut oil	2 large yellow-fleshed potatoes, cut into ½-inch rings 10 large Brussels sprouts, stemmed and sliced 1 Tbs minced rosemary ¼ cup olive oil	3 medium yellow onions, peeled and cut into ½-inch rings ½ cup sliced pitted black olives 1 Tbs drained and rinsed capers ¼ cup olive oil	4 medium cassava, peeled and sliced into ½-inch rings ¼ cup canola oil
2. Stuff	Two 1½-pound whole fish, cleaned and scaled 8 to 10 parsley sprigs Two 4-inch cinnamon sticks	Two 1½-pound whole fish, cleaned and scaled 6 roasted garlic cloves 6 Tbs chopped celery leaves	Two 1½-pound whole fish, cleaned and scaled 6 to 8 oregano sprigs 4 to 6 dill sprigs 4 tsp finely grated lemon zest 2 tsp red pepper flakes	Two 1½-pound whole fish, cleaned and scaled 4 to 6 Tbs jerk seasoning paste (see page 50)
3. Oil and season, then roast	Walnut oil Salt and pepper to taste	Olive oil Worcestershire sauce to taste	Olive oil Salt and pepper to taste	Canola oil Salt and pepper to taste

Roasted Meat

Nothing looks more impressive yet takes as little effort as a rib roast, a leg of lamb, or a pork loin. In keeping with the simple elegance of one of these roasts, this technique is basically just "season and shove," as in "I'm going to season this and shove it in the oven." Why complicate perfection? • MAKES BETWEEN 4 AND 10 SERVINGS, DEPENDING ON THE CUT CHOSEN

• **STEP 1** Preheat the oven to 375°F. If desired, french a bone-in roast, then tie any kind of roast with butcher's twine to hold its shape in the heat. For the roasts you can use with this technique, consider this list, divided between those that have the bone still attached and those that are boneless:

AN HERB CRUST

Any loin or tenderloin can benefit from this simple crust—once the meat is out of the oven. While it rests at room temperature, mix about ½ cup chopped, mixed herbs on a plate (for example, chives, tarragon, and parsley; or parsley, rosemary, and oregano; or parsley and thyme). Spread about 2 tablespoons Dijon mustard over the meat, then roll it in the fresh herbs just before slicing.

Oven Calibration

Ovens, like pianos, go out of whack over time. Invest in a small oven thermometer, hang it from the middle rack, and see if its reading matches what you've set the oven to. If not, compensate with the dial or call out a repair person to recalibrate your oven. Most ovens have hot spots; rotate the roasting pan a half turn once to assure even cooking.

bone-in rib and other roasts

beef rib roast, 3 to 4 bones, 4½ to 7 pounds
veal rib roast ("rack of veal"), 6 ribs, 4 to 5 pounds
buffalo rib roast, 4 bones, 6½ to 8 pounds
venison rib roast, 6 to 8 ribs, 3 to 4 pounds
pork rib roast, 8 bones, 4 to 5 pounds
bone-in leg of lamb, 5 to 6 pounds
bone-in fresh ham, about 7 to 10 pounds

boneless roasts, tenderloins, and loins

boneless beef rib roast, 5 to 6 pounds
beef tenderloin, 4 pounds
veal tenderloin, 4 pounds
buffalo tenderloin, 4½ to 5 pounds
venison tenderloin, 4 to 5 pounds
venison loin, 5 to 6 pounds
elk tenderloin, about 3 pounds
elk loin, about 4 pounds
pork loin, 3½ to 6½ pounds
boneless fresh ham (not smoked), 5 to 7 pounds

Rib roasts

A beef, veal, buffalo, or venison rib roast is the loin (not the tenderloin) with the ribs still attached. (For a discussion of the various USDA grades of beef, see page 351.)

The animals' ribs are numbered, starting nearest the hip, farthest from the shoulder. Bones 1 through 4 are the meatiest; bones 2 and above have an increasingly large arc of meat above the center eye with an increasingly large honeycomb of fat between the two—

more pronounced in cows, less so in buffalo and veal. Above bone 4, the oblong eye itself starts to break apart with blobs of fat.

For the best beef or buffalo rib roast, ask for bones 1 through 3 or 4. Ask the butcher to slice off the back bone if it's still attached, but never let him or her slice the center eye of meat (the loin) off the bones and tie it back on. You want the bones to cradle the meat and infuse it with flavor as it roasts.

That said, a veal, pork, or venison rib roast is indeed smaller and so usually not sliced into 3-bone sections but instead sold with most or all of the ribs still together—perhaps bones 1 through 6, maybe even through 8. These roasts often lack the distinct inner marbling of beef but also have a thick layer of fat over the center eye.

Tenderloins and loins

A tenderloin is a luxurious and quite tender muscle; it forms the smaller side of T-bone and Porterhouse steaks (see page 355). When sliced into rounds, these are "filets mignons" (see page 129). Either buy the whole tenderloin or buy a center-cut tenderloin, the long tube of meat minus 1) the thicker end (which is sold as the Chateaubriand in some butcher shops), 2) the thinner tail, and 3) the small rope of meat running underneath. If you do buy a whole beef or buffalo tenderloin, it will be quite long—best to cut it in half the short way in the middle so it's easier to handle in and out of the oven. That said, the thinner end will roast more quickly than the thicker one, so you'll have to take a temperature reading fairly often to ascertain where things stand—or roast it whole, following the tips to tie it as stated below.

A beef or buffalo tenderloin often needs to be peeled—that is, the silver skin, a translucent membrane running over the meat's surface, must be sliced off and removed. Use a thin knife to shear it off the surface planes without gouging the meat. While you're doing that, also remove any surface fat. Or ask the butcher to "peel and trim" the tenderloin for you.

Don't confuse a tenderloin with the loin—the round eye under the rib roast. Pork, venison, and elk loins are different from their tenderloins: chewier, meatier, less meltingly tender. In fact, pork tenderloins don't make this list for roasting. They are small, no more than 1½ pounds at the outside limit. To roast them is to gray them—they will not have enough time in the oven using this method. Cook pork tenderloins using the technique for boneless steaks (page 350): sear them in a cast-iron skillet on top of the stove, then place them in a preheated 450°F oven until an instant-read meat thermometer inserted into the thickest part of the meat registers 160°F, about 15 minutes, maybe less depending on its thickness.

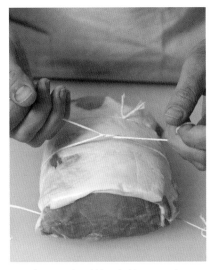

A pork roast should be tied in several places around its middle, so it doesn't flatten and spread out during cooking.

Tie a rib roast in several places around the center eye, looping the butcher's twine between the bones.

What's perfect on a rib roast? Lots of kosher salt and freshly ground black pepper.

Ham

The best bone-in hams are "shank-end hams," cut closer to the shin. You'll need to take off some of the external fat—but not all, leaving perhaps half the thickness. A fresh ham will take a long time in the oven; it thus needs that fat for protection. If the fat bothers you, cut it off later on your plate. Do not use a smoked or cured ham for this technique.

Leg of lamb

Trim the leg of lamb of almost all visible, surface fat; there's plenty of inner marbling. While a bone-in leg of lamb is a perfect "season and shove" cut, a rack of lamb is another matter entirely. Yes, it is technically the same thing as a rib roast—the loin, the ribs—but it's more delicate and requires its own technique (see page 273).

Preparing the roast

Remove large surface planes of fat that lie along the cut's surface. But don't go nuts. There's no need to remove every speck of fat. In fact, you shouldn't. Some fat keeps the roast juicy.

To trim the fat, use a thin boning knife to slice under the fat and carve it away from the meat without nicking or gouging the meat itself. Never cut down into inner veins or clefts; leave these inner pockets and chambers alone, the fat in place. It's tricky work—and you can ask the butcher to do it for you—but it's also a good time to assess the meat's fibers: see which way they're running for later when you carve the roast.

All rib roasts can be frenched, using the same technique as that used for Rack of Lamb (page 273). If you don't want to go to the trouble or are squeamish about such procedures, your butcher will gladly do it for you.

Once you've got the cut trimmed and frenched (if desired), tie it with butcher's twine. Almost all roasts flatten as they cook; tenderloins and loins can curl. Tying assures even cooking as well as an elegant presentation.

For rib roasts, loop the butcher's twine between the bones and around the meat, creating a circle that will hold the eye (or loin) in place. Make as many circles as there are spaces between the bones.

Tenderloins and loins are quite easy to tie: simply wrap the string in circles around the roast every 2 or 3 inches. Do not pull too tight; keep the string taut against the meat's surface. If you're working with a whole beef, buffalo, or veal tenderloin, fold the thinner end under the roast and tie it in place so that this section is as thick as the thicker section. This way, the whole tenderloin will roast evenly.

Tie a bone-in ham by wrapping the circles of twine around the meat while circumnavigating the bone, if it's still in place. Make each circle exact and tight, thereby holding the meat together and possibly onto the bone.

The only exception here is a leg of lamb, which doesn't need to be tied because it doesn't spread as easily, thanks to the way the planes of meat lie against the bone.

• **STEP 2** Oil and season the roast. Without a doubt, the best seasoning is the simplest: olive oil, walnut oil, or unsalted butter; kosher salt; and freshly ground black pepper. For every pound of meat, use 2 teaspoons fat, 1 teaspoon kosher salt, and ½ teaspoon freshly ground black pepper.

That said, all meat indeed takes to other herbs and spices. Here's a list of the best choices, the proportions per pound of meat and in addition to the fat, salt, and pepper:

beef and buffalo: 1 minced garlic clove, 1 teaspoon dried thyme, and/or 1 teaspoon chili powder

veal: 1 minced garlic clove and/or 1 teaspoon red pepper flakes as well as 1 teaspoon minced tarragon, dill, chervil, or thyme

venison and elk: 1 teaspoon packed light brown sugar, 1 minced garlic clove, and/or 1 teaspoon red pepper flakes as well as 1 teaspoon dried rosemary, oregano, or sage

pork (except for ham): 1 minced garlic clove, 1 teaspoon fennel seeds, 1 teaspoon finely grated lemon zest, and/or ½ teaspoon ground cumin. If you didn't use ground cumin, you may also add 1 teaspoon dried rosemary, oregano, sage, or marjoram.

ham: 1 minced garlic clove, 1 teaspoon finely grated orange zest, and/or 1 teaspoon red pepper flakes as well as 1 teaspoon ground cumin, ½ teaspoon ground cinnamon, and ¼ teaspoon grated nutmeg

lamb: 1 minced garlic clove and 1 teaspoon finely grated lemon zest as well as a combination of 1 teaspoon dried mint, rosemary, oregano, or dill

Any meat, rubbed with the spices, should be left at room temperature for 15 to 20 minutes while the oven preheats, so the spices begin to infuse the surface as the salt breaks down the exterior cells.

Still, elk and venison, particularly if wild, may need to be marinated before being rubbed with spices because they can be quite gamy and are thus a better match to more complex flavors. Here's a basic marinade: 2 cups red wine or unsweetened apple cider, 3 tablespoons red wine vinegar, 2 tablespoons crushed juniper berries, 1 tablespoon stemmed thyme, 1 tablespoon chopped fresh rosemary, ½ teaspoon ground allspice, and 4 bay leaves. Place the rack, loin, or tenderloin in the marinade in a large baking pan, cover, and refrigerate overnight, turning and basting occasionally.

▶ **STEP 3** Place the roast on a rack in a large roasting pan and roast until an instant-read meat thermometer inserted into the thickest part of the roast registers a degree of doneness to your satisfaction. Let stand at room temperature for 10 minutes, then carve. All

The Roasting Temperature

There's a vast culinary divide with regard to the correct temperature for roasting meat. Some insist on incinerating meat at 500°F, an inferno that supposedly sears the outside and keeps the inside juicy. It's adequate for blue, maybe for rare; but the roast burns like Judas Iscariot in hell if you prefer medium-rare or a higher internal temperature, the outer inch or more getting well done long before the center eye sets.

Others prefer a lower temperature—around 300°F, even as low as 250°F. While it is true that the roast stays moist and juicy, even to the edges, it never develops a crunchy crust, the salt never melding with the fat to create that irresistible crunch. Yes, high-end chefs roast meats this way; but then they put it under an 800°F salamander for a few minutes to get a crust. That's a tool most of us don't have at home. Plus, at 250°F, you'll have dinner on the table in, oh, 7 or 8 hours—not really an option, even on a Saturday night.

This moderate-heat technique splits the difference: the outside crusts while the inside warms. Yes, even at an internal temperature for rare, there's a little arc of medium-done meat around the outside of a rib roast, but it's a trade-off for a perfectly set eye and a crunchy outer wall.

that's left is to wait while the meat and the heat do the work. Baste all roasts occasionally with pan juices, just to make sure the outer edge stays moist. But other than that, resist opening the oven door; the heat dips and then must return to a stable temperature. Consistency may be the hobgoblin of small minds, Mr. Emerson; but it's the bliss of roasts.

For rosy lamb, pink veal, moist pork, and medium-rare beef and other meats, the timing at 375°F is as follows:

beef rib roast: 17 to 18 minutes per pound
veal rib roast: 18 to 20 minutes per pound
buffalo and venison rib roast: 16 to 17 minutes per pound
pork rib roast: 25 to 30 minutes per pound
leg of lamb: 17 to 18 minutes per pound
pork loin: 25 to 30 minutes per pound
beef tenderloin: 12 to 15 minutes per pound
veal tenderloin: 14 to 16 minutes per pound
buffalo, venison, and elk tenderloins: 11 to 13 minutes per pound
venison and elk loin: 14 to 16 minutes per pound
pork loin: 20 to 25 minutes per pound
fresh ham: 25 to 30 minutes per pound

These are approximations for medium-rare or like-mannered degrees of doneness; for medium, you'll need to add several minutes per pound; for blue or rare, shave off a couple minutes per pound. If the roast is to be in the oven longer than 2 to 2½ hours—ham, leg of lamb—tent it with foil should it begin to brown too deeply.

Begin checking the internal temperature about halfway through the suggested roasting time, just so you always know where you stand. Insert an instant-read meat thermometer into the thickest part of the roast without the probe's touching bone.

If the bone-in cut is more than 3 pounds or the boneless cut more than 4 pounds, consider taking the meat out of the oven 5°F below the optimal temperature because it will continue to rise as the meat rests. Smaller cuts, however, are not hefty enough to have the temperature rise by more than a degree or two as it rests.

And rest it should. Every cut of meat benefits from standing at room temperature about 10 minutes before carved. The cellular fibers relax, allowing the juice, now lying in planes through the cut, to reincorporate off those planes and between the fibers.

Carving a roast

Loins and tenderloins are easy to carve: just slice off rounds.

Rib roasts require a bit more work. Stand the roast so its bones are pointing straight up and oriented to the right for a right-handed person or to the left for a left-handed person. Hold the meat in place with a meat fork inserted into the center eye. Use a thin carving knife to slice along and around the inside arc of the bones, thereby removing the eye in one piece as the bones fall off. Do not carve too close to the bones; leave some meat for those who like to gnaw. Slice between the bones to separate them. Stand the eye cut side down on the carving board, hold it in place with a meat fork, and slice down, starting with one of the ends to create a thin slice and then carving off more as you move along the roast. We prefer steak-like ½-inch-thick slices.

To carve a leg of lamb, set it bone side down and cut thin slices, starting at the top and slicing off a piece at a 45-degree angle diagonal down toward the exposed bone (never cut parallel to the bone). When you've cut off several slices, turn the leg over and slice more pieces off, always cutting horizontally from the thickest part down to the exposed bone.

To carve a bone-in fresh ham, follow the directions for a leg of lamb, taking into account that the bone is much smaller and much less of a guide without a few cuts to tell where things stand. To carve a boneless fresh ham, carve thin slices on an angle against the grain (see page 270), this time cutting down through where the bone should have been. There's no avoiding that some pieces will end as chunks, given the various chambers of meat that lie inside the roast.

Always pass extra salt and ground black pepper on the side when you serve roasted meat so everyone can season the pieces to their liking.

You must have a meat thermometer to tell if a roast is done. Insert it into the center of the thickest part of the cut without the probe's touching bone.

TO CARVE A RIB ROAST: First, slice along the curvature of the bones to remove the round eye, thereby removing the bones in one piece.

Then slice between the bones to create roasted beef ribs, perfect for those who like to gnaw.

Finally, cut the eye into thick slices. The end slices will be slightly more done than those in the middle.

Recipes for Roasted Meats

	Standing Beef Rib Roast	Roasted Rack of Veal	Roasted Venison Rack	Roasted Bone-In Pork Roast
1. Preheat the oven; french if necessary and tie	One 2- to 4-bone, 3- to 7-pound beef rib roast, trimmed, frenched, and tied	One 6-bone, 5-pound veal rib roast, trimmed, frenched, and tied	One 8-bone, 4-pound venison rib roast, trimmed, frenched, and tied	One 8-bone, 5-pound pork rib roast, trimmed, frenched, and tied
2. Season with	Up to ¼ cup plus 2 tsp olive oil Up to 7 tsp kosher salt Up to 3½ tsp ground black pepper	3 Tbs plus 1 tsp unsalted butter, melted 5 tsp minced tarragon 5 tsp kosher salt 2½ tsp ground black pepper 5 minced garlic cloves	2 Tbs plus 2 tsp walnut oil 4 tsp minced oregano 4 tsp packed light brown sugar 4 tsp red pepper flakes 4 tsp kosher salt 2 tsp ground black pepper	3 Tbs plus 1 tsp olive oil 5 tsp fennel seeds 5 tsp minced rosemary 5 tsp minced oregano 5 tsp kosher salt 2½ tsp ground black pepper
3. Roast	About 1 to 2 hours, to 125°F for medium-rare	About 1½ hours, to 140°F for medium-rare	About 1 hour 10 minutes, to 125°F for medium-rare	About 1 hour 20 minutes, to 160°F

	Roasted Leg of Lamb	Roasted Beef Tenderloin	Roasted Pork Loin	Roasted Fresh Ham
1. Preheat the oven; french if necessary and tie	One 6-pound bone-in leg of lamb, trimmed	One 2½ pound beef tenderloin, trimmed and tied	One 4-pound pork loin, trimmed and tied	One 8-pound bone-in fresh ham, trimmed and tied
2. Season with	2 Tbs olive oil 2 Tbs minced mint 2 Tbs minced dill 2 Tbs finely grated lemon zest 2 Tbs kosher salt 1 Tbs ground black pepper 4 minced garlic cloves	3 tsp unsalted butter, melted 2 tsp olive oil 2½ tsp kosher salt 1¼ tsp ground black pepper	2 Tbs plus 2 tsp olive oil 4 tsp minced oregano 4 tsp minced rosemary 4 tsp finely minced lemon zest 4 tsp kosher salt 2 tsp ground black pepper 4 minced garlic cloves	3 Tbs unsalted butter 2 Tbs plus 1 tsp olive oil 2 Tbs plus 2 tsp finely minced grated orange zest 2 Tbs plus 2 tsp red pepper flakes 4 tsp ground cumin 2 Tbs plus 2 tsp kosher salt 4 tsp ground black pepper
3. Roast	About 1 hour 40 minutes, to 135°F for rosé	About 33 minutes, to 125°F for medium-rare	About 1 hour 40 minutes, to 160°F	About 2 hours 40 minutes, to 160°F

Roasted Shrimp

This technique is such an easy way to prepare North America's favorite seafood that we're surprised more people don't do it—and more often, too. This is great buffet and company-supper fare; for crowds, double or even triple the recipe by making a second or even a third 9 x 13-inch baking dish at the same time. • MAKES 4 SERVINGS

• **STEP 1** Pour ¼ cup fat in a 9 x 13-inch baking dish or a similarly sized roasting pan. Olive oil provides the best, fruit-filled, aromatic balance to the sweet shrimp. Untoasted almond or walnut oil will offer a nutty taste, more elegant perhaps but also out of the norm. Sesame oil, however, will man-handle the shrimp, beating it senseless. Also avoid neutral oils and refined peanut oil, all of which add nothing—unless there's a heavy concentration of chiles and such in the dish, in which case they won't get in the way of these more powerful flavors. But for sure skip any toasted oils and any animal fats like butter that will simply scorch, frying the shrimp into a bitter mess. If you really want the taste of butter, use ghee (see page 25).

• **STEP 2** Add a handful of one kind or several kinds of whole herbs, whole dried spices, or aromatics to the baking dish. Set the dish in the oven, then heat the oven to 450°F for 15 to 20 minutes. Turn the oven on only after you have placed the filled baking dish in it. As the oven heats, the oil will slowly come up to the proper temperature, those herbs and spices releasing their flavors over time.

Use whole herbs on their stems: thyme, rosemary, parsley, tarragon, or mint sprigs, for example. This is not a dish for dried herbs, nor even for minced ones.

That said, a dried spice or two can perk things up, but always use whole spices, never ground—allspice berries, cardamom pods, juniper berries, cloves, or cinnamon sticks, to name a few. These and seeds of all varieties (fennel, cumin, and celery, for example) benefit from being lightly crushed in a mortar with a pestle; failing that, in a small, sealed plastic bag with the bottom of a heavy saucepan. Peppercorns—black, red, green, pink, white, even Szechwan, all fruits or seeds of various vines and trees—should be crushed as well. The one exception: never use a whole nutmeg.

Don't neglect pitted olives, whole garlic cloves, drained capers, roughly chopped anchovies, thickly sliced sun-dried tomatoes, or even fresh or dried chiles, all able to flavor the oil and turn it into a simple sauce. None of these is to be eaten. Yes, you can sop up some of the olive pieces with crunchy bread; but by and large, these various flavorings are meant simply to season the oil itself.

ROASTED SCALLOPS

We've tried this technique with scallops to good results. Scallops are not as firm as shrimp, so you must be very careful when tossing them in the dish. Use 2 pounds large sea scallops, each cut into 2 disks; or 2 pounds bay scallops. They'll need about 5 minutes in the oven's heat before they're ready. Relatively mild, scallops should be more delicately flavored than shrimp; so go easy on the herbs, using perhaps two-thirds of what you'd use for the same amount of shrimp.

• STEP 3 Lay about 2 pounds peeled and deveined shrimp over the herbs or spices, then roast until pink and firm, about 8 minutes for medium shrimp, 10 for large shrimp, and 13 for jumbo ones, tossing gently two or three more times.

Buying shrimp

Shrimp are North America's favorite seafood; around a billion pounds a year are fried, baked, grilled, steamed, barbecued, stir-fried, or even eaten as sushi in the United States alone! Still, all labelings—"jumbo," "large," "medium"—are mere window dressing with no enforced value.

To avoid confusion, buy shrimp the way your market does: by determining how many make a pound. It takes between 30 and 35 medium shrimp to make a pound, around 20 or even 15 large ones to do the same. There are even monsters of the deep, U-5s and U-2s: fewer than (that is, "U" for "under") 5 and even 2 required to make a pound. These will take considerably longer to roast, maybe up to 20 minutes. In any event, do not use small salad or "baby" shrimp—actually, full-grown, cold-water shrimp from frigid places like Newfoundland. These small shrimp will cook too quickly, never really taking on the taste of the herbs and oil.

The shrimp lying on the ice at your market may look fresh; chances are, they aren't. Almost all sold in North America are flash-frozen on the trawler, perhaps not the best move for romantic aesthetics but a good step for preservation. Your market most likely buys them frozen in boxes and thaws them for display.

Beat them at their game. Go back to the frozen food section of your supermarket and buy your own—or ask your fishmonger to sell you a frozen bag or box from his stash. Look for an "IQF" label: "individual quick frozen." In other words, they're

TO PEEL SHRIMP: First pry the shell loose along the seam in the underbelly, between the little legs. . . .

Then grasp the feathery bits of the tail and pull the meat free with a firm but steady pressure.

TO DEVEIN SHRIMP: Cut along the convex curve of the back, the little legs pointing down toward the cutting board, so you can expose and remove the black, green, or gray vein in the meat.

not a mass locked in a block of ice. Take out as many as you need and thaw them overnight in a bowl in the refrigerator, dumping out the ice melt occasionally.

If you buy the shrimp on the ice at your market, they should smell sweet and fresh, never briny, with absolutely no odor of gasoline (the trawler leaked fuel) or chlorine (they've been washed in it to kill bacteria, a legal but unsavory process). Your fishmonger may take you for a crank, but don't be afraid to ask "Can I smell those?"

The USDA permits two additives. Exposed to the air, the shelled meat will dehydrate; bathing it in sodium tripolyphosphate puts a thin, gelatinous, moisture-sealing coating on the meat. If you're leery of such chemistry, or are on a low-sodium diet, buy shrimp in their shells and peel them yourself.

Sodium bisulfite, the second additive, puts to rest black spot (aka melanosis), a natural condition caused by an enzyme running amok in the processed meat. Black spot is not harmful, just unsavory—and a sure indication the shrimp have been mishandled. Those with sulfite allergies should beware.

Roast the shrimp by layering them over the heated oil that has been infused with plenty of fresh herbs.

Peeling and deveining shrimp

To peel a shrimp (that is, to remove its shell), turn the body over so that the small legs are facing you. Use your thumbs to gently pry the shell loose, starting in the middle of the body and pulling out. The shell should come loose, attached just at the small end. Grasp this end of the tail as its farthest corner with your fingertips and pull gently, releasing the meat from those little fins.

All shrimp have a so-called "vein" that runs down the meat's outer curve. This "vein" is actually the digestive track, often full of sand and other impurities. (Deveining a shrimp is actually "de-intestining" it.) If the vein is sticking out at the larger end, hold the shrimp in one hand and gently pull it out. If the vein does not come out easily or completely, or if it's not visible, use scissors or a sharp paring knife to cut through the back curve of the shell (opposite the little legs) to a shallow depth of about ⅛ inch. Start at the fleshy end and stop cutting just before you reach the last tail segment. Pry the slit open and run the meat under cold water while you remove the vein.

All that said, you don't have to peel the shrimp at all (but devein them for sure, particularly if they're over about 30 per pound). Yes, the shells add a little more weight, so buy two additional medium or one large shrimp to compensate. You'll gain lots more shrimp flavor, but the meal will also be messier because you'll have to peel the shrimp as you eat them. Have lots of napkins on hand.

Once roasted, a little vinegar, wine, juice, or other acid will perk up the oil, making an easy "sauce" right in the baking dish.

Toss it all together right before you serve it.

The shrimp are done when the meat is pale pink and firm—quicker than you think. Tossing them a few times helps get the hot, aromatic oil all over the meat, thereby cooking them more quickly. Don't worry about being pretty. If the herbs get all jumbled up as you toss the shrimp, so much the better.

- **STEP 4** Remove the baking dish from the oven and stir in 2 or 3 tablespoons wine, juice, or acid, plus 1 teaspoon salt and about ½ teaspoon ground black pepper. The added liquid will sputter and spit. Stand back and pour close to the pan. Pouring from a height encourages sputtering and splashing.

Use this as a rule: the sharper the liquid, the less you use. Thus, you'd use 2 tablespoons white wine vinegar but 3 tablespoons white wine.

White or red wine? Your call. Just nothing too sweet: no Riesling, no late-harvest anything, no white Zinfandel. Wine offers a mild taste, fairly neutral, just a little sweetness. For more flavor, try any unseasoned vinegar: apple cider, white wine, red wine, balsamic, and the like. But avoid flavored vinegars or seasoned Asian rice vinegars, all of which contain lots of sugar. The shrimp are already sweet; there's no point in a double hit.

Or try lemon juice, a nice spark—or even orange juice, particularly thawed orange juice concentrate, a more potent flavoring. Basically, you're making a dressing, so you want a present flavor to make a good sauce for the shrimp.

Finally, you can add liquor, but be careful of its flaming in the hot baking dish. Simple liquors are best: tequila, brandy, cognac, and the like. Some flavored liqueurs are fine, so long as they're naturally flavored like Grand Marnier or Cointreau. Never use overly sweet liquors like raspberry vodka, Kahlúa, or Frangelico, all of which would turn this thing into some macabre shrimp dessert. If the sauce flames, cover the baking dish with one or two large lids until the fire is extinguished.

Stir in some salt (preferably kosher salt) and pepper (provided peppercorns are not already in the mix), then dish the whole thing up with a large spoon. The oil and natural shrimp juices will combine with the other liquid to make an instant sauce. Leave as many of the herbs or spices behind in the baking dish as you can—and be careful: if you've left the shells on the shrimp, some oil has gotten under them and is still superheated, like the cheese on hot pizza. In this case, it's best to let the shrimp sit for 5 minutes to be safe.

Rosemary Roasted Shrimp

Recipes for Roasted Shrimp

	Rosemary Roasted Shrimp	Thyme Roasted Shrimp	Italian-Inspired Roasted Shrimp	Szechwan-Style Roasted Shrimp
1. Pour in	¼ cup olive oil	¼ cup olive oil	¼ cup olive oil	¼ cup unrefined peanut oil
2. Add and heat	5 rosemary sprigs	12 thyme sprigs 2 peeled whole garlic cloves	4 rosemary sprigs 6 roughly chopped sun-dried tomatoes 4 peeled whole garlic cloves 2 roughly chopped anchovy fillets	1 Tbs Szechwan peppercorns 1 star anise pod 2 whole cloves 1 tsp fennel seeds 1 to 2 tsp red pepper flakes
3. Lay on top and roast, stirring occasionally	2 pounds medium shrimp (about 30 per pound), peeled and deveined	2 pounds large shrimp (about 18 per pound), peeled and deveined	2 pounds medium shrimp (about 30 per pound), peeled and deveined	2 pounds medium shrimp (about 30 per pound), peeled and deveined
4. Remove from the oven and stir in	2 Tbs white wine vinegar 1 tsp salt ½ tsp ground black pepper	2 Tbs balsamic vinegar 1 tsp salt ½ tsp ground black pepper	2 Tbs balsamic vinegar 1 tsp salt ½ tsp ground black pepper	3 Tbs rice vinegar 1 tsp salt ½ tsp ground black pepper

	French-Inspired Roasted Shrimp	Jerk Roasted Shrimp	Tex-Mex Roasted Shrimp	Greek-Inspired Roasted Shrimp
1. Pour in	¼ cup untoasted walnut oil	¼ cup canola oil	¼ cup olive oil	¼ cup olive oil
2. Add and heat	6 tarragon sprigs 6 allspice berries, crushed	8 cilantro sprigs 1 to 2 Tbs jerk seasoning (see page 50)	6 cilantro sprigs 1 fresh jalapeño, seeded and sliced One 4-inch cinnamon stick 1 Tbs cumin seeds, crushed	6 oregano sprigs 6 dill sprigs 4 mint sprigs 4 parsley sprigs 1 Tbs drained and rinsed capers 1 tsp red pepper flakes
3. Lay on top and roast, stirring occasionally	2 pounds medium shrimp (about 30 per pound), peeled and deveined	2 pounds medium shrimp (about 30 per pound), peeled and deveined	2 pounds medium shrimp (about 30 per pound), peeled and deveined	2 pounds medium shrimp (about 30 per pound), peeled and deveined
4. Remove from the oven and stir in	3 Tbs red wine 1 tsp salt ½ tsp ground black pepper	2 Tbs lime juice ½ tsp salt	2 Tbs white wine vinegar 1 tsp salt ½ tsp ground black pepper	3 Tbs retsina or floral white wine 1 tsp salt ½ tsp ground black pepper

Scallops or Shrimp with a Pan Sauce

If you buy the shrimp already peeled and deveined, here's a main course that can be ready in 15 minutes—or 20 if you dawdle. Have cooked rice at the ready to round out the meal, or make a company dinner with Gratin (page 159) as an elegant side dish. • MAKES 4 LARGE SERVINGS

• **STEP 1** Heat 3 tablespoons fat in a 14-inch skillet or sauté pan over medium heat. Use almost any fat you prefer—with the exception of strong-tasting toasted nut and seed oils or rendered bacon fat. Olive oil, walnut oil, unsalted butter—all these will be quite delicious with the sweet shrimp or scallops. However, unsalted butter may begin to burn, turning quite brown, as the shellfish cooks. If so, lower the heat to medium-low until the vegetables get into the pan.

• **STEP 2** Place 1½ pounds sea scallops, bay scallops, or peeled and deveined medium shrimp (about 30 per pound) in one layer in the skillet or pan, working in batches as necessary; cook just until opaque, about 2 minutes, turning once. Transfer to a large plate. Scallops of any ilk should be placed flat side down, then turned once after a minute or so, just so both their flat sides caramelize a little.

Sea scallops are often quite large, sometimes up to 5 ounces each for some of the monsters currently harvested. If you prefer the plate to look a little fuller, consider buying smaller sea scallops so that you have a few more per serving. Or search out bay scallops, very small scallops, found mostly along the Atlantic seaboard of North and South America. Despite their name, they don't necessarily live in bays but in shallow water, particularly in fields of eelgrass. It may take up to 15 to 20 of these tiny scallops to make a pound.

For a discussion of shrimp and how to peel and devein them, see page 314. You may want to use larger shrimp for this dish, perhaps those that weigh in at about 20 per pound, perhaps even 15 per pound. They are meatier and make a nice presentation with the vegetables. They will need at least 3 minutes in the skillet to be partially cooked—pink and just starting to firm up.

In fact, all these shellfish should still be a little gelatinous at their centers. They will continue to steam on the plate outside of the skillet and they will cook when they return to the heat for the final minute or so. Plan on about 1 minute for bay scallops, 2 minutes for medium shrimp, and 3 for large sea scallops and larger shrimp, all turned once during cooking. Do not crowd the skillet; do this task in batches. Use a large spatula to scoop the shellfish out of the skillet so as to leave as much fat behind as possible.

A perfectly seared scallop (left) and shrimp, both ready for an easy pan sauté.

A good sauté often involves a well-stocked skillet.

In most cases, herbs and spices are added after the aromatics and vegetables in a quick sauté to help preserve their nosy fragrance. (In contrast, herbs and spices are often added between the aromatics and vegetables in a braise or soup to mellow their flavors over the heat.)

• **STEP 3** Add another 1½ tablespoons fat, then 4 to 5 cups chopped or sliced aromatics and/or quick-cooking vegetables, and finally a good bit of minced herbs and/or a small amount of a dried spice. Cook, stirring often, until somewhat softened. As a rule, use the same fat you used in step 1. However, if you sautéed the shrimp or scallops in olive or walnut oil in step 1, it's very sophisticated to add unsalted butter now.

The vegetables are largely a matter of preference, so long as they all are quick-cookers: peas, asparagus, broccoli or cauliflower florets, celery, thinly sliced carrot, or even some frozen mixed vegetables. (For a more complete list of spring and quick-cooking vegetables, see page 26.) An aromatic like a thinly sliced shallot or a diced scallion or two is welcome but not necessary.

That said, you can add long-cookers so long as you parboil—that is, precook—them. Potatoes, preferably a yellow-fleshed variety like Yukon Golds, are particularly appealing with tomatoes in a shrimp sauté. Bring a large pot of water to a boil over high heat, then peel and dice the potatoes into ½-inch squares. Drop them into the water and boil until almost tender, perhaps 6 to 10 minutes depending on their residual moisture. Drain in a colander set in the sink, then refresh under warm water so as not to chill them down.

Timing here is a matter of the vegetables chosen: sliced pencil-thin asparagus spears will take no more than 3 minutes; diced onion and cubed zucchini, perhaps 4 minutes; sliced mushrooms, perhaps 8 minutes to soften and give off their liquid that must be partially evaporated; thinly sliced fennel, up to 10 minutes. Choose vegetables that can cook together—an onion, shallot, or scallions will work with almost anything since they only sweeten further the longer they're cooked. But asparagus and fennel would be a bad match since the asparagus would turn soggy long before the fennel was cooked.

For herbs and spices, consider a couple tablespoons your outer limit for minced fresh herbs and perhaps just ½ teaspoon for dried spices like cinnamon, red pepper flakes, or nutmeg—or even less, just a smidgen to flavor the sauce.

Add garlic now, too, but certainly no more than 3 minced cloves, usually less. Keep the delicacy and sweetness of the dish first and foremost in your mind. Think spring or summer even if you're in the dead of winter.

Keep in mind that the 1½ cups liquid will get poured into the skillet in the next step and must be reduced to a glaze. Do not overcook the vegetables now. They should still be crisp, just on the verge of tender, when you proceed to the next step. The only way to tell? Taste, of course.

- **STEP 4** Pour in 1½ cups broth, wine, cream, canned diced tomatoes, an enhanced version of any, or a combination; raise the heat to high and boil until the liquid has been reduced to a glaze, about 2 to 4 minutes. As stated, the base liquids are broth, wine, or canned diced tomatoes. You can also mix these three among themselves in varying quantities or enhance broth or canned tomatoes with a dry fortified wine like dry Marsala or dry Madeira. Use either red or white wine, depending on the flavor depth of the sauce—and enhance any three of the base with cream, perhaps up to ½ cup of the total volume.

- **STEP 5** Stir in 1½ tablespoons brightener, then return the scallops or shrimp to the skillet. Cook just until firm, 1 to 2 minutes. Season with salt and freshly ground black pepper. A brightener is any liquid that can enliven the basic flavors of the stew, such as

> **vinegar of any stripe except flavored vinegars**
> **soy sauce** (in which case omit salting the dish at the end)
> **Dijon mustard**
> **pomegranate molasses, red currant jelly, or another sweet/tart**
> **condiment**
> **a citrus juice, preferably lemon,** although lime, orange, and
> grapefruit are not out of the question
> **a liquor such as brandy, cognac, or whisky,** particularly if
> you've used cream in the sauce

These can be used alone or in classic combinations like soy sauce and rice vinegar or brandy and lemon juice. Never use vinegar or a citrus acid if there's cream in the sauce.

One warning: the sauce is hot; if using liquor, pour it quickly into the center of the pan, blending the alcohol before it has a chance to flame. Should it flame, quickly cover the skillet and set it aside off the heat until the fire goes out, perhaps 20 seconds.

Return the scallops or shrimp and any juices on the plate to the skillet, nestling everything into the sauce as well as you can. Now let the sauce cook for just 1 or 2 minutes, just to reheat the shellfish and cook them through, just until the shrimp turn pink and firm, until the scallops turn firm and opaque. The only real way to tell is to cut one open and see that the insides have set but are not stringy or dry.

Taste the sauce and season with salt and freshly ground black pepper, perhaps 1 teaspoon salt and ½ teaspoon pepper. Remember that with only rare exceptions, all shrimp and scallops came from salt water and are therefore salty in and of themselves.

Reduced to a glaze

A glaze is not so reduced as you might think. When you pull a wooden spoon through the mixture, the resulting line, exposing the skillet's surface, should stay intact for a second or two before the liquid flows back into place. Perhaps it's just a small hesitation, but the sauce holds its shape, even momentarily. A glaze does not mean that the liquid has been reduced until it lacquers the ingredients.

Once the sauce is built, nestle the scallops or shrimp back into the skillet, just to heat them through in the last minute or two of the suace's reduction.

Recipes for Scallops or Shrimp

	Scallops Puttanesca	Scallops with Zucchini, Lemon, and Almonds	Scallops with Cauliflower and Capers	Moroccan-Style Scallops
1. Heat	3 Tbs olive oil	3 Tbs olive oil	3 Tbs olive oil	3 Tbs canola oil
2. Sauté and transfer	1½ pounds sea scallops	1½ pounds sea scallops	1½ pounds sea scallops	1½ pounds bay scallops
3. Add and cook	1½ Tbs olive oil 1 small yellow onion, thinly sliced 1 medium fennel bulb, trimmed and thinly sliced 1 medium red bell pepper, seeded and chopped ½ cup chopped pitted olives 2 Tbs drained capers 2 minced anchovy fillets 3 garlic cloves, minced	1½ Tbs olive oil 4 ounces shallots, thinly sliced 2 celery ribs, thinly sliced 1 medium zucchini, diced ¼ cup slivered almonds 2 Tbs drained capers 2 Tbs minced grated lemon zest 1 Tbs minced oregano 2 garlic cloves, minced	1½ Tbs unsalted butter 1 small onion, thinly sliced 12 ounces cauliflower florets ¼ cup chopped golden raisins 2 Tbs chopped drained capers 2 tsp stemmed thyme 2 garlic cloves, minced	1½ Tbs canola oil 1 medium yellow onion, diced 2 jarred roasted red peppers or pimientos, thinly sliced 2 cups canned chickpeas, drained and rinsed 2 Tbs minced cilantro 2 Tbs minced peeled fresh ginger 1 tsp ground cumin ½ tsp ground cinnamon ⅛ tsp saffron
4. Pour in and reduce	1½ cups canned diced tomatoes	1 cup dry white wine ½ cup vegetable broth	1 cup fish broth or clam juice ½ cup dry vermouth	1 cup canned diced tomatoes ½ cup dry white wine
5. Stir in, return the shellfish, and season	1½ Tbs red wine vinegar Salt and pepper to taste	1½ Tbs Dijon mustard Salt and pepper to taste	1½ Tbs white wine vinegar Salt and pepper to taste	1½ Tbs pomegranate molasses Salt and pepper to taste

	Shrimp, Asparagus, and Tomato Sauté	Shrimp with Apples, Leeks, and White Wine	Sautéed Shrimp, Scampi-Style	Shrimp Nogada
1. Heat	3 Tbs olive oil	3 Tbs walnut oil	3 Tbs olive oil	3 Tbs canola oil
2. Sauté and transfer	1½ pounds medium shrimp, about 30 per pound, peeled and deveined	1½ pounds large shrimp, about 20 per pound, peeled and deveined	1½ pounds large shrimp, about 20 per pound, peeled and deveined	1½ pounds large shrimp, about 20 per pound, peeled and deveined
3. Add and cook	1½ Tbs olive oil 1 pound pencil-thin asparagus spears, thinly sliced 2 Tbs minced basil 2 Tbs minced chives ½ tsp red pepper flakes 3 garlic cloves, minced	1½ Tbs unsalted butter 2 large leeks, white and pale green parts only, halved lengthwise, washed carefully, and thinly sliced 1 medium tart green apple, peeled, cored, and diced 1 Tbs stemmed thyme 1 Tbs minced tarragon 2 garlic cloves, minced	1½ Tbs unsalted butter 8 ounces broccoli rabe, chopped 4 ounces shallots, diced 1 Tbs minced rosemary ½ tsp grated nutmeg ½ tsp red pepper flakes	1½ Tbs unsalted butter 1 poblano chile, seeded and diced 1 cup walnut pieces ⅓ cup chopped raisins ½ cup pomegranate seeds 1 Tbs minced oregano ½ tsp ground cinnamon
4. Pour in and reduce	1½ cups canned diced tomatoes	1½ cups dry white wine	1½ cups dry white wine	1 cup vegetable broth ½ cup cream
5. Stir in, return the shellfish, and season	1½ Tbs balsamic vinegar Salt and pepper to taste	1 Tbs lemon marmalade Salt and pepper to taste	1 Tbs balsamic vinegar Salt and pepper to taste	1½ Tbs pomegranate molasses Salt and pepper to taste

An elegant dinner in no time: Veal Scaloppine with Tomatoes and Capers

Scaloppine

With a wide range of meats—veal, turkey, pork, or even boneless skinless chicken breasts—you can make this Italian favorite in less than 10 minutes once you've prepped the ingredients. The fried strips of meat and their sauce are best over buttered noodles, brown rice, roasted roots, or mashed potatoes (see page 21).

• MAKES 4 SERVINGS

• **STEP 1** Flatten about 1 pound scaloppine to ⅛ inch thick on a cutting board between sheets of wax paper or plastic wrap. Just how do you spell the name of this dish? It's "scaloppine" (and a plural noun to boot) in Italy but "scaloppini" (or even "scallopini"—and a singular noun as in "The scaloppini is good") on the menus of Italian restaurants in America. Why the difference? Menu-Italian stateside caters to a movie stereotype—thus, the Scorcese-induced preference for "i's" (and "o's," too—but none here).

Scaloppine come in several varieties:

Don't be shy—pound the scaloppine meat until it's quite thin, just ⅛ inch thick or so.

1. **Veal.** The most tender choice and often sold presliced, these can be cut with a fork and have a mild, delicate taste.
2. **Turkey.** A lower-fat alternative, these are also often sold presliced. Or you can buy a turkey London broil, then slice it into very thin strips. You'll need a sharp chef's knife and a steady hand. Or ask the butcher to slice it into scaloppine for you.
3. **Pork.** Trim a 1-pound pork loin of surface fat, then cut it into two or three tubular sections. Slice these lengthwise into ¼-inch-thick strips—although they will be pounded thinner. The taste will also be a little heavier than veal or turkey.
4. **Chicken.** Boneless skinless chicken breasts should be cut into ¼-inch-thick strips. Avoid mushy chicken tenders, the thin tubes of muscle running under the breasts.

Although you may have purchased ready-to-go veal or turkey scaloppine, it's probably still not thin enough for this quick sauté. The slices should be around ⅛ inch thick, considerably thinner than those generally sold in the supermarket.

To pound, place the slices of any of these meats between sheets of wax paper or plastic wrap; then use the bottom of a large saucepan, the smooth side of a meat mallet, or the side of a heavy cleaver to flatten them, working along their length as you pound, thereby keeping them long rather than just spreading them out wide. However, there's no doubt they'll spread a bit—space them about 2 inches apart before you set in with the saucepan or mallet. And don't press; whack—gently and determinedly, not wildly. The cut should be evenly flattened with no holes.

A skillet of scalloppine cooks in minutes. Have everything ready to go before you start.

• **STEP 2** **Heat about 2 tablespoons fat in a large heavy skillet (have more fat at the ready).** Although veal, chicken, turkey, and pork have different flavors and textures, when pounded thin, floured, and fried, their common characteristics override any differences. Thus, the fat used is integral to the sauce to come, not necessarily to the meat.

Avoid more esoteric fats like almond oil or duck fat. This is a quick dish—the more complex flavors will not have time to meld sufficiently. Instead, stick with the two traditional choices: unsalted butter or olive oil. Consider butter for bitter, sweet, sour, or heavier flavors; olive oil, for lighter tastes, simpler combinations. Think ahead to what's going in the pan in step 6. Butter and lemon juice or butter and cream are classics, decidedly delectable. But what of olive oil and white wine, or olive oil and Grand Marnier? In any case, have more butter or olive oil on hand. The coating on the scallopine will eat it up.

• **STEP 3** **Place about 1 cup seasoned all-purpose flour on a plate, then dredge the scaloppine in this mixture; slip into the skillet in batches and cook until lightly browned, about 1½ to 2 minutes per side, adding more fat as necessary. Transfer to a plate.** Use about 1 teaspoon salt and 1 teaspoon freshly ground black pepper to season the flour (see page 51). There's no need for other herbs; save these for the sauce itself.

Gently press the pounded strips in the seasoned flour, coating both sides and shaking off any excess; then slip them into the pan in batches, perhaps three or four at a time. Turn with tongs to avoid pricking.

The scaloppine may not brown much. This technique is not about crusting the meat; rather, it's about the skillet sauce napped over these delicate strips. Light beige is fine, provided the meat has cooked through. Lower-fat cuts like turkey and chicken may crimp at the edges.

If you're working in batches, transfer the cooked strips to a plate, then add a little more fat to the skillet if need be, perhaps just 1 tablespoon. Wait a few seconds for the butter or oil to get hot, then slip in more coated slices.

• **STEP 4** **Create a simple sauté with easily cooked vegetables, just until warmed through.** If the skillet is dry, add another tablespoon or two of fat, just to coat its bottom.

Once all the strips are fried and on the plate, speed is of the essence. Save winter squash, potatoes, Brussels sprouts, and other hard vegetables for longer-cooking dishes.

A finely chopped shallot or onion is a fine base on its own—or add some thinly sliced celery, seeded and diced bell pepper, or thinly sliced mushrooms for a slightly more complicated sauté. You needn't necessarily add the onion first to soften it—but that said, if the onion is the hardest vegetable in the grouping, it will need a little head start, perhaps just 1 minute if finely chopped.

In the end, this sauté requires vegetables easily cooked or just warmed through. A good choice, therefore, includes frozen vegetables like artichoke hearts, corn, peas, and lima beans. Or go the super-easy route: dump a 10- to 16-ounce bag of your favorite frozen mixed vegetables in the pan and warm them through.

Don't neglect nuts and fruit, dried or fresh. Berries add a lovely acidity to the sauté, even with that bag of frozen veggies; walnuts, a nice crunch. Quartered prunes offer sweet accents; quartered dried apricots, sour ones.

Classic combinations include artichoke hearts and lemon, shallots and berries, or mushrooms and garlic. Try zucchini, tomatoes, summer squash, green beans, peas, or shelled edamame for summer takes on this classic dish.

Finally, add an herb if desired, but there's no reason you have to. Thyme and oregano are traditional; tarragon, a nice twist; rosemary, rather heavy-handed.

• **STEP 5** Pour in about ¾ cup wine or broth, raise the heat to medium-high, and cook until reduced by half, about 3 minutes. The taste of scaloppine is light on the tongue, quite bright; the sauce, therefore, is traditionally built with white wine, port, or a dry fortified wine like dry vermouth. Wine adds a delicate sweet/sour taste, a better balance to sweet (berries, shallots, onions, orange zest), earthy (mushrooms, artichokes), or bitter (greens, celery) components.

But also consider chicken, vegetable, or beef broth. Broth makes a silkier sauce, more the taste of a thin stew.

• **STEP 6** Add a simple enhancer like a sour spark, a sweet accent, or a light pour of cream. Now's your chance to balance the flavors and take the dish to a level not usually attained in quick sautés. For a sweet accent, try tomato paste, maple syrup, pomegranate molasses, fruit chutney, or thawed orange juice concentrate. For a sour spark, consider lemon juice, prepared mustard, or a range of vinegars: balsamic, white balsamic, sherry, red or white wine.

In general, add a sweet accent with strong-tasting ingredients like shallots, onions, greens, or nuts; add a sour spark with duller flavors like mushrooms, peas, or cauliflower. A little goes a long way: 2 tablespoons is the outside limit. Maple syrup with walnuts in the sauté? Just 2 teaspoons, maybe less. If you're adding cream, consider ⅓ cup. You needn't measure; just don't douse the pan.

• **STEP 7** Return the scaloppine to the pan and warm through before adding salt and freshly ground black pepper to taste. This step should take about 1 minute; then check for seasoning, remembering that there's salt in the coating that's fallen off into the sauce.

Scaloppine are a canvas for a quick sauce.

Recipes for Scaloppine

	Veal Scaloppine with Artichokes and Green Peppercorns	Veal Scaloppine with Mushrooms and Marsala	Veal Scaloppine with Tomatoes and Capers	Pork Scaloppine with Peppers
1. Pound	1 pound veal scaloppine	1 pound veal scaloppine	1 pound veal scaloppine	1 pound pork scaloppine
2. Heat	2 Tbs olive oil	2 Tbs unsalted butter	2 Tbs olive oil	2 Tbs olive oil
3. Dredge, brown, and transfer	1 cup all-purpose flour 1 tsp salt 1 tsp ground black pepper	1 cup all-purpose flour 1 tsp salt 1 tsp ground black pepper	1 cup all-purpose flour 1 tsp salt 1 tsp ground black pepper	1 cup all-purpose flour 1 tsp salt 1 tsp ground black pepper
4. Sauté	One 10-ounce package frozen quartered artichoke hearts, thawed 2 Tbs toasted pine nuts 1 tsp green peppercorns 2 minced garlic cloves	8 ounces white button or cremini mushrooms, cleaned and thinly sliced 2 tsp stemmed thyme	4 or 5 Roma or plum tomatoes, seeded and chopped 2 Tbs chopped drained capers 2 tsp chopped rosemary	2 cubanels or Italian frying peppers, seeded and thinly sliced 2 garlic cloves, minced 1 Tbs chopped oregano
5. Pour in and reduce	¾ cup dry vermouth	¾ cup dry Marsala	¾ cup beef broth	¾ cup dry vermouth
6. Stir in	2 Tbs Worcestershire sauce	⅓ cup heavy or whipping cream	1 Tbs sweet vermouth	2 Tbs white wine vinegar
7. Return, reheat, and season	Salt and pepper to taste	Salt and pepper to taste	Salt and pepper to taste	Salt and pepper to taste

	Creamy Turkey Scaloppine	Turkey Scaloppine Puttanesca	Chicken Scaloppine with Peas	Curried Chicken Scaloppine
1. Pound	1 pound turkey scaloppine	1 pound turkey scaloppine	1 pound chicken scaloppine	1 pound chicken scaloppine
2. Heat	2 Tbs unsalted butter	2 Tbs olive oil	2 Tbs unsalted butter	2 Tbs canola oil
3. Dredge, brown, and transfer	1 cup all-purpose flour 1 tsp salt 1 tsp ground black pepper	1 cup all-purpose flour 1 tsp salt 1 tsp ground black pepper	1 cup all-purpose flour 1 tsp salt 1 tsp ground black pepper	1 cup all-purpose flour 1 tsp salt 1 tsp ground black pepper
4. Sauté	4 ounces shallots, diced ½ pound yellow summer squash, sliced ½ tsp caraway seeds	1 small yellow onion, diced 2 large tomatoes, seeded and finely chopped 2 Tbs drained capers 1 chopped anchovy fillet	6 ounces white button or cremini mushrooms, cleaned and thinly sliced ½ cup fresh shelled or frozen peas 2 tsp stemmed thyme ¼ tsp grated nutmeg	1 medium yellow onion, diced ½ cup frozen lima beans, thawed 2 minced garlic cloves 1 Tbs minced peeled ginger 2 tsp curry powder (see page 113)
5. Pour in and reduce	¾ cup white wine	¾ cup chicken broth	¾ cup chicken broth	¾ cup white wine
6. Stir in	⅓ cup heavy or whipping cream	2 Tbs tomato paste	⅓ cup heavy or whipping cream	1 Tbs fruit chutney
7. Return, reheat, and season	Salt and pepper to taste	Salt and pepper to taste	Salt and pepper to taste	Salt and pepper to taste

Shanks and Bones

We make lamb shanks, osso buco, and the rest whenever we get the chance—sometimes for company, sometimes because it's a Sunday night and there's a movie we've been meaning to watch. The bones slowly melt their marrow into the stew—plus, there's all that rich connective tissue in the meat. If you've got plans to sit down at 8:00 pm exactly, make this braise earlier in the day (or the day before), then refrigerate it so you can reheat it, covered, in a preheated 350°F oven for 30 minutes before serving. As a plus, you'll be able to skim some of the fat off the sauce before reheating. • MAKES 4 SERVINGS

• **STEP 1** Preheat the oven to 350°F. Heat 3 tablespoons fat in a very large Dutch oven or heavy oven casserole over medium heat. The size and the weight of the pan are of uncompromising importance. The Dutch oven or oven casserole should hold at least 8 quarts, preferably 10, maybe even 12 if you have brontosaurus-style lamb shanks. It should be a heavy pot, a good conductor of heat, with a tight-fitting lid—all the usual braise stuff except more so: the meat needs lots of help getting tender at the bone.

The majority of the flavor here will come from the cured and/or smoked meat, the shanks or bones themselves, and the vegetables. A toasted oil would be overkill in that heavy mix. Use some of the mid-range fats (see page 17)—that is, unsalted butter or any untoasted oil: olive, walnut, almond, canola, or corn, to name a few. Even sesame oil can form the base of an Asian-style braise.

• **STEP 2** (optional); Crisp 6 ounces chopped smoked and/or cured pork product or its substitute (see page 18); transfer to a bowl. As with many braises, this step is utterly optional but sometimes of supreme importance. The taste of the meat on these shanks and bones can be powerful: a little gamy, sometimes with a mineral tang, and quite rich. Bacon, pancetta, and their ilk cut the richness exceptionally well, making this dish oddly lighter while nonetheless increasing the overall fat.

How does that work? The jury's still out; satiety studies are ongoing with unsure results, one person's experience only approximating another's. However, it may have to do with the way we experience taste: multiple layers may indeed produce a more satisfying meal. If you eat too much of any one thing—or any one kind of taste—the brain may well signal that you're full, a safeguard against eating too much in case something's gone bad. Eat only a heaping portion of fried chicken at an outdoor picnic and you'll feel sick or headachey within minutes, but oddly hungry an hour later.

• **STEP 3** Working in batches, brown 4 to 6 pounds shanks or bones or 8 pounds oxtails in the pot, about 8 minutes per batch, turning once. Transfer to the same bowl you used in step 2. You're working with big cuts, thanks mostly to the bones. They'll need to be browned in batches to avoid overcrowding. You simply cannot get all the meat into contact with the heat at once. Again, you're building a sauce here—not cooking the meat, the caramelization therefore enhancing what's to come more than it's helping the meat (see page 45 for an explanation of browning in a braise). Consider these your options:

Four 1¼-pound beef shanks
Four 1-pound lamb shanks
Four 1-pound beef shin sections
Four 1-pound veal shanks, cross-cut (aka, osso buco in Italian— oh-soh BOO-coh, "pierced bone")
Four 1-pound pork shin sections, skin removed
6 pounds bone-in beef short ribs
8 pounds oxtails

Beef shanks and osso buco need to be tied, despite the fact that the meat adheres to the bone. Tie them around their circumferences with butcher's twine to help hold their shape. Over time in the braise, the meat will loosen and flatten, all that connective tissue that holds it to the bone dissolving into the sauce.

Sometimes, it takes a pantry to make a good braise—here, the ingredients for Spanish-Inspired Osso Buco.

• **STEP 4** Pour off all but 2 tablespoons fat and add about 1 cup diced basic aromatics; cook, stirring often, until softened. Either use one of the basic aromatics—onions, shallots, leeks, or scallions—or use a mirepoix of onions, celery, and carrot or the like (see page 57). The amount is not much here; a little goes a long way. Dice—even mince—everything so that it will melt in the oven.

• **STEP 5** Stir in about 6 cups roughly chopped, long-cooking vegetables; cook, stirring often, until lightly browned or wilted, about 5 minutes. Steer clear of quick-cooking vegetables with the exception of peas (their skins help them hold up in the braise). Otherwise, go for long-cookers: roots like parsnips, tubers like yellow-fleshed potatoes, or winter squash like red kuri. All must be prepped: peeled, seeded if necessary, and cut into 1½- to 2-inch pieces. Unlike the basic aromatics, these pieces needn't melt and should be left large enough to counterbalance the hearty meat.

Thickly sliced mushrooms add an earthy touch, but cook them long enough that they release their moisture and it breaks down to a glaze.

Don't forget tomatoes, canned or fresh. If canned, use whole tomatoes and drain them well. You need no extra liquid, just rich flavor. Avoid any canned varieties that include other seasonings.

GREMOLATA

This aromatic mix is often sprinkled over cooked osso buco: 2 tablespoons minced parsley, 1 tablespoon finely minced lemon zest, and 1 minced garlic clove. Simply mix everything together in a small bowl; plan on about a little more than 2 teaspoons per serving. Double or even triple at will. (It's also great mixed with mayonnaise as a sandwich spread.)

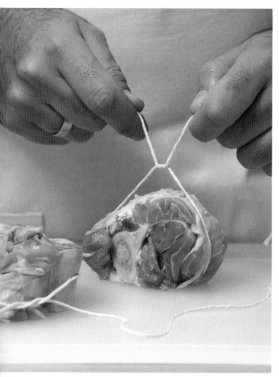

Beef and veal shanks should be tied so they'll hold their shape in the intense, moist heat of the long braise.

Or use hearty greens like kale or cored cabbage, roughly chopped, as part of the mixture. Greens cook down dramatically, so use double the amount necessary to fill the quota.

• STEP 6 Stir in any flavorings, minced garlic, spices, or dried herbs until aromatic. Now's your chance to create a dish that reflects your taste. First, consider flavorings like sun-dried tomatoes (if there are no tomatoes already added), chopped pitted olives, or chopped dried fruit. And perhaps stir in Dijon mustard, prepared horseradish, or even ketchup for a layered depth. Avoid barbecue sauce; add a smoky note with smoked paprika.

Dried herbs actually work better than fresh, which can be too present and fragrant. This broth must develop over time; there's no point in having little pockets of deep fragrance in the overall canvas. Better to have a well-balanced sauce stocked with lots of flavors.

Bay leaves and cinnamon sticks add lots of flavor without clouding the sauce. Of course, they must be removed before serving. Small whole spices—cloves, allspice berries, cumin or mustard seeds in particular—can get lost in the braise only to become an unwanted crunch when served. Consider putting them in a mesh tea ball so that you can fish them out at the end.

If desired, add heat now: perhaps a seeded and chopped dried chile or two, a seeded chipotle canned in adobo sauce, or some red pepper flakes. These need time to develop and mellow in the broth. This dish is no nose-spanker, no tongue-piercer.

In like manner, add a generous amount of ground black pepper now, not later. This stew, despite its richness, is all about subtlety. Black pepper can override the carefully developed flavors. Adding it now will assure that it melds into the sauce, a subtle match to sweeter spices and herbs.

• STEP 7 Stir in 3 cups broth or enhanced broth, all the browned and frizzled meat, and any accumulated juices. Bring to a full simmer, then cover and place in the oven until the meat is meltingly tender, about 2½ to 3½ hours. Season with salt when done. Although beef broth may seem the no-brainer here, it needn't be. If you've made a lighter stew—say, with lots of canned tomatoes, saffron, and chickpeas—consider chicken or even vegetable broth, both more aromatic alternatives. Veal shanks and even lamb shanks, of course, take to veal stock—not an everyday thing in our supermarkets. Search out veal demi-glace, available frozen, sometimes in concentrate at high-end markets; water it down to the package-prescribed amount to be used as stock. Failing that, chicken broth is a better foil to the veal: lighter, more in keeping with the tender meat.

Also consider enhancing the broth with another liquid: white or red wine, a dry fortified wine, or beer. These, while aromatic, will sweeten considerably as they stew. Use them judiciously, just an accent to the broth, not more than 1 cup of the total. Stay away from cream—too drenching—but do try 1 cup coconut milk in an Asian-inspired dish. Also stay away from fruit juices and tomato sauce—get these flavors into the pot earlier on, as dried fruit or tomatoes themselves.

Timing here is, as usual for a braise, difficult to predict, despite the predilection for most food writers to state some sort of definite marker. The connective tissue and the meat itself may have varying amounts of moisture, varying amounts of fibrous tendons. Oxtails may well be done in 2 hours; plan on 3 hours for everything else but start checking at the 2½-hour mark, prodding the meat occasionally with a fork to see if it's close to falling off the bone, tender and juicy. Do not raise the oven's temperature; instead, be patient and open another bottle of wine.

The well-browned shanks are nestled back into the sauce, ready for the oven.

• **STEP 8** (optional): **Place the meat and vegetables in individual, warmed serving bowls; set the pot over medium-high heat, bring the sauce to a simmer, and thicken it.** The sauce is quite rich; consider skimming its top layer of fat before you proceed. Thicken using one of these seven procedures:

1. Whisk a beurre manié of 1 or 2 tablespoons unsalted butter and 1 or 2 tablespoons all-purpose flour (see page 209) in several increments into the simmering sauce, whisking each until fully incorporated before adding the next.
2. Whisk 2 teaspoons arrowroot or potato starch with ½ cup of the hot sauce from the pot, then whisk this mixture back into the simmering sauce until thickened.
3. While the shanks or bones braise in the oven, cut the top quarter off a head of garlic, exposing the cloves inside; wrap the head in aluminum foil; and roast until soft, about 1 hour. Cool to room temperature, then squeeze the garlic cloves into a small bowl and mash into a purée. Whisk this into the simmering sauce.
4. Whisk 2 or 3 tablespoons tomato paste into the simmering sauce.
5. Whisk 2 to 3 tablespoons yellow cornmeal into the simmering sauce. The texture will be grainier but the flavor will be sweeter.
6. Place 1½ cups vegetables from the pot and sauce in a large blender or food processor fitted with the chopping blade; blend or process until smooth, scraping down the canister's sides as necessary. Whisk this purée back into the sauce over the heat.
7. For Asian flavorings, whisk 2 or 3 tablespoons peanut or almond butter into the simmering sauce until melted.

A well-cooked shank shows the meltingly tender meat pulling away from but still adhering to the bone. The butcher's twine should be snipped off just before the shank is served.

Recipes for Shanks and Bones

	Classic Osso Buco	Spanish-Inspired Osso Buco	Beef Short Ribs with Mushrooms and Wine	Southwestern Oxtails
1. Preheat the oven; heat	2 Tbs olive oil 1 Tbs unsalted butter	3 Tbs olive oil	3 Tbs olive oil	3 Tbs canola oil
2. (optional) Crisp and transfer	Omit	6 ounces dried Spanish mild chorizo, chopped	6 ounces bacon, chopped	6 ounces bacon, chopped
3. Brown and transfer	Four 12- to 16-ounce cross-cut veal shanks (osso buco)	Four 12- to 16-ounce cross-cut veal shanks (osso buco)	6 pounds bone-in beef short ribs	8 pounds beef oxtails
4. Add and cook	1 small yellow onion, diced 1 celery rib, thinly sliced	4 ounces shallots, minced 1 small red bell pepper, seeded and diced	1 medium yellow onion, diced	1 medium yellow onion, minced
5. Stir in and cook	1 medium carrot, sliced 1 medium fennel bulb, trimmed and thinly sliced 3 cups canned tomatoes, drained and chopped	2 medium carrots, sliced 2 cups canned chickpeas, drained and rinsed 3 Roma or plum tomatoes, diced	1½ pounds mushrooms, preferably a mix of types, thickly sliced (discard shiitake and portobello stems) ½ ounce dried porcinis, crumbled	4 Roma or plum tomatoes, diced 2 medium carrots, sliced 2 medium parsnips, sliced 1 cup frozen lima beans
6. Stir in	1 Tbs dried parsley 1 Tbs dried oregano 2 tsp dried thyme 1 tsp ground black pepper 2 bay leaves (discard before serving) 2 garlic cloves, minced	3 Tbs chopped pitted black olives 2 Tbs red wine vinegar 1 Tbs dried oregano 1 Tbs dried cilantro 1 tsp smoked paprika ¼ tsp saffron 3 garlic cloves, minced	¼ cup chopped pitted green olives 2 Tbs dried thyme 1 Tbs crumbled dried rosemary ½ tsp ground black pepper 1 garlic clove, slivered	2 Tbs chili powder 1 Tbs dried oregano 1 Tbs honey 1 tsp ground cumin 1 tsp ground cinnamon ½ tsp ground black pepper 1 or 2 pickled jalapeños, stemmed, seeded, and minced 2 bay leaves (discard before serving)
7. Stir in, simmer, cover, and bake— then season	3 cups beef broth The veal shanks and any accumulated juices Salt to taste	2 cups beef broth 1 cup red wine The veal shanks, chorizo, and any accumulated juices Salt to taste	2 cups red wine 1 cup beef broth The short ribs, bacon, and any accumulated juices Salt to taste	2 cups beef broth 1 cup dry sherry The oxtails, bacon, and any accumulated juices Salt to taste
8. (optional) Enrich	Puréed vegetables (see step 8 above)	3 Tbs tomato paste	A beurre manié (see step 8 above)	1 head roasted garlic, puréed (see step 8 above)

	Beef Short Ribs in Mexican Chili Sauce	Beef Shanks with Mushrooms and Cabbage	Lamb Shanks with White Beans and Lemon	Lamb Shanks with Artichokes and Dill
1. Preheat the oven; heat	3 Tbs canola oil	3 Tbs olive oil	3 Tbs olive oil	3 Tbs olive oil
2. (optional) Crisp and transfer	6 ounces Mexican chorizo, chopped	6 ounces bacon, chopped	Omit	6 ounces pancetta, chopped
3. Brown and transfer	6 pounds bone-in beef short ribs	Four 1-pound beef shanks	Four 1-pound lamb shanks	Four 1-pound lamb shanks
4. Add and cook	1 medium yellow onion, diced	1 medium yellow onion, diced	4 ounces shallots, minced	1 small red onion, diced 1 celery rib, thinly sliced
5. Stir in and cook	3 Russet potatoes, peeled and cubed 4 New Mexican red chiles and 2 dried ancho chiles, seeded and finely chopped	1 pound cremini or white button mushrooms, cleaned and thickly sliced 1 small cabbage head, halved, cored, and shredded	4 cups canned white beans, drained and rinsed 1 medium fennel bulb, trimmed and chopped	12 baby artichokes, halved 4 Roma or plum tomatoes, diced
6. Stir in	6 dried figs, quartered 3 garlic cloves, minced 1 Tbs dried oregano 1 Tbs dried thyme 2 bay leaves One 4-inch cinnamon stick (discard before serving)	1 Tbs Dijon mustard 1 Tbs prepared horseradish 1 tsp dried sage ½ tsp caraway seeds ½ tsp ground allspice ½ tsp ground black pepper	1 Tbs dried rosemary 1 Tbs dried thyme 1 Tbs finely grated lemon zest 1 tsp ground black pepper 2 bay leaves (discard before serving) 2 garlic cloves, minced	1 Tbs drained capers 1 Tbs dried dill 2 tsp dried oregano 2 tsp finely grated lemon zest 1 tsp ground black pepper One 4-inch cinnamon stick (discard before serving)
7. Stir in, simmer, cover, and bake— then season	1½ cup beef broth One 12-ounce bottle of beer The short ribs, chorizo, and any accumulated juices Salt to taste	3 cups beef broth The beef shanks, bacon, and any accumulated juices Salt to taste	2 cups chicken broth 1 cup dry white wine The lamb shanks and any accumulated juices Salt to taste	2 cups vegetable broth 1 cup dry white wine The lamb shanks, pancetta, and any accumulated juices Salt to taste
8. (optional) Enrich	Puréed vegetables (see step 8 above)	2 tsp potato starch dissolved in ½ cup sauce	1 head roasted garlic, puréed (see step 8 above)	2 Tbs tomato paste

Korean Beef Skewers

No more bottled marinades! There are a few tricks to making your own. You'll need to start these skewers earlier in the day so the marinade has plenty of time to infuse the meat. • MAKES 8 SKEWERS

• **STEP 1** Cut 1½ pounds meat into thin strips. Choose meat that's fairly lean, that can be cooked quickly, and that itself does not have an overly pronounced flavor, better to absorb and complement the marinade.

All cuts must be trimmed of excess surface fat. Duck breasts should be skinned as well, but fully half the weight of a duck breast lies in its skin and fat. So buy 3 pounds to get 1½ pounds meat after you skin and de-fat them.

Chicken and duck can be cut into thin strips: lay the meat with the thin ends to your left and right on a cutting board, then position your knife at an angle, tilted at about 45 degrees from the meat itself. Draw the blade down and through the meat, thereby cutting wide, thin strips, about ¼ inch thick.

Any version of purchased scaloppine is ready to use except you need to cut them into ½-inch-wide strips the length of the scaloppine itself.

To slice beef sirloin, place it on your cutting board and run your fingers across its surface to determine which way the grain lies, little fibrous strips running through the cut like the grain of wood. Position your knife at a right angle to these strips and make long thin cuts, again angling the blade back (rather than cutting straight down) to produce the widest strips.

A beef tenderloin doesn't have as pronounced a grain and so should be cut into 4-inch tubular chunks, these then thinly sliced along their length. If some of the strips are too wide, cut them in half lengthwise. In like manner, pork and lamb loins should be cut into 3 or 4 pieces, each of these pieces sliced the long way into ¼-inch-thick strips.

You can also use peeled and deveined shrimp, particularly larger shrimp (about 15 to 20 per pound) as well as whole sea scallops—but you won't cut these into strips; simply use them whole.

• **STEP 2** Whisk together a marinade in a large bowl, add the meat, and toss well. Cover and refrigerate for 3 to 8 hours. The best marinade is not very wet. Rather, there should be just enough liquid that the spices shine through without drowning

Among the cuts, consider:

boneless skinless chicken breasts
boneless skinless chicken thighs
boneless duck breasts
turkey scaloppine
veal scaloppine
beef sirloin or tenderloin
lamb loin

Everything's ready to go for beef skewers.

Although you want thin strips, always slice the meat against the grain. Slicing this piece of sirloin the long way will result in strips that are little more than loosely held together shards.

The marinated meat is threaded onto the skewers the long way, so it bunches up like material on a curtain rod.

the meat. In fact, when you take the strips out of the bowl after they've been marinated, there may be almost no marinade left. Consider your proportions to be up to ¼ cup liquid and/or oil and up to 3 tablespoons herbs, spices, and minced aromatics as well as perhaps some salt and freshly ground black pepper.

Always go with a mix of liquids. Start with almost any oil: canola, olive, sesame, even toasted oils, which work wonders against beef, pork, or lamb—the oil, about half the total liquid amount.

From there, add other flavors with other liquids. Broth or red or white wine is perhaps the simplest base, a ready canvas for herbs and other flavorings. Unsweetened juices, too, will work, provided you steer clear of lemon or lime juice (too tart and overwhelming) and fresh pineapple juice (it contains an enzyme that actually digests meat—but canned pineapple juice will work fine, the enzyme neutralized by the canning process). Other choices would include dry fortified wines like dry vermouth or dry Madeira; fish sauce (see page 388); liquid smoke; orange juice, particularly undiluted frozen orange juice concentrate; pomegranate molasses; soy sauce; tomato paste; or Worcestershire sauce.

Use good judgment to ascertain the right balance. Worcestershire sauce and liquid smoke are merely flavoring agents, best used in combination with canola oil or broth. Unsweetened apple cider on its own will get very sweet; balance it with a toasted nut oil, a little more bitter. Indeed, taste the marinade before adding the meat. If you don't like what you've got, better to start again than to waste the meat.

The choices of the spices are manifold. Particularly appealing minced herbs include rosemary, mint, oregano, and dill—all quite strong and fully able to withstand a little time sitting in the marinade without losing their punch. Dried spices also work wonders: ground cumin, cinnamon, or allspice, as well as grated nutmeg. Crushed fennel seeds complement pork. Consider using Szechwan peppercorns, cayenne, or red pepper flakes for heat rather than a vinegar-based bottled hot sauce.

And don't forget aromatics: minced scallions, minced peeled fresh ginger, minced garlic cloves, seeded minced fresh chiles, or finely grated citrus zest. Set any of these on your cutting board and rock a heavy knife through them, back and forth and back and forth, until they're quite finely minced. No one wants a big hunk of garlic on the cooked meat.

What's missing? Vinegar and its kin. The marinade is put onto thin strips that would cook in the presence of so much acid. To brighten the flavors, sprinkle the cooked skewers with rice or balsamic vinegar before serving.

Finally, add about 1 teaspoon salt and ½ teaspoon or so freshly ground black pepper—but only if you haven't used a salty condiment like Worcestershire sauce or soy sauce. There's also no reason to use ground black pepper if you've loaded the marinade with cayenne or other hot stuff.

● **STEP 3** Thread 8 bamboo skewers with the meat and up to 6 cups very roughly chopped spring or summer vegetables. Heat a large grill pan or griddle over medium-high heat until smoking, grease lightly, and grill the skewers until done, about 7 minutes, turning once. To thread the meat onto the skewers, stretch out the long strips, then crimp them up, much like crimping cloth. This will allow the pieces of meat to have many folds, the better to catch the heat and caramelize while still holding on to a little of the marinade. Don't think satay, long strips of meat on skewers; rather, take the strip and crimp it to bite-size.

Thread shrimp back and forth at least twice onto the skewers so they don't fall off; set the scallops one flat side down on a cutting board and skewer them through their sides, the skewer parallel to the cutting board.

The vegetables should be cut to about the same size as the crimped-up pieces of meat. If the vegetable slices or chunks are too large, the meat will never touch the grill pan's hot surface and so will do nothing but gray and steam above the heat. Make sure that everything on the skewer can come in contact with the pan's hot surface.

Consider a range of spring and summer vegetables including zucchini, yellow summer squash, red and yellow onions, hot chiles, corn, bell peppers, cherry tomatoes, various mushrooms, and broccoli or cauliflower florets. Indeed, a satisfying skewer can be made with turkey meat, marinated simply in canola oil, white wine, curry powder (see page 113), and minced peeled fresh ginger, then skewered with cauliflower florets and pieces of green bell pepper. Thread these ingredients onto the skewers in alternating patterns so two pieces of the same ingredient are never next to each other.

To grease a hot grill pan or griddle, grasp a wadded-up piece of paper towel with a pair of tongs, soak the paper towel with a little oil, and then rub it quickly over the grill so that the paper doesn't ignite. There's no need for a fancy oil here: vegetable oil will do the trick. The flavor of any other oil would be almost instantly burned away.

Set the skewers on the hot surface and cook, turning about every 2 minutes, until well browned and hot. The meat is so thin, it will cook almost instantly; the vegetables should simply be crisp-tender.

To serve, either pull everything off the skewers in the kitchen, mounding it all in a large serving bowl; or place individual skewers on plates and let everyone slip the meat and vegetables off on their own. But the skewers are hot and their ends, sharp—don't leave children unattended.

Recipes for Skewers

	Veal Satay	Pomegranate Duck Skewers	Asian-Style Pork Skewers	Jerk-Style Chicken Skewers
1. Slice into thin strips	1½ pounds veal scaloppine	3 pounds duck breast, skin and fat removed	1½ pounds pork tenderloin, trimmed	1½ pounds boneless skinless chicken breasts
2. Mix together and add the meat	2 Tbs coconut milk 1 Tbs toasted sesame oil 1 Tbs peanut oil 2 Tbs minced cilantro 1 Tbs curry powder (see page 113) 1 Tbs minced peeled fresh ginger 2 garlic cloves, minced	3 Tbs minced rosemary 2 Tbs pomegranate molasses 2 Tbs walnut oil 1 tsp salt ½ tsp ground black pepper	1 medium scallion, minced 2 Tbs soy sauce 2 Tbs toasted sesame oil 1 Tbs finely grated orange zest 1 Tbs minced peeled fresh ginger 2 garlic cloves, minced	2 medium scallions, minced 2 Tbs canola oil 1 Tbs stemmed thyme ½ tsp ground allspice ½ tsp ground cinnamon ½ tsp grated nutmeg ½ tsp cayenne 1 tsp salt 2 garlic cloves, minced
3. Skewer with the meat and cook	4 medium scallions, white and pale green parts only, cut into 1-inch sections 2 cups fresh pineapple chunks, peeled and cored 1 medium red bell pepper, seeded and cut into 1-inch strips	3 medium yellow summer squash, cut into chunks 4 hot red cherry peppers, seeded and quartered	12 ounces whole cremini mushrooms, cleaned 2 cups broccoli florets	2 very ripe plantains, cut into 1-inch rounds 2 medium red bell peppers, seeded and cut into 1-inch strips

	Moroccan-Inspired Chicken Skewers	Szechwan-Inspired Lamb Skewers	Korean Beef Skewers	Barbecued Beef Skewers
1. Slice into thin strips	1½ pounds boneless skinless chicken thighs	1½ pounds lamb loin, trimmed	1½ pounds beef sirloin, trimmed	1½ pounds beef sirloin, trimmed
2. Mix together and add the meat	¼ cup canola oil 2 tsp ground cumin 2 tsp ground ginger 1 tsp turmeric 1 tsp ground cinnamon 1 tsp salt ½ tsp ground black pepper ¼ tsp ground coriander	2 Tbs soy sauce 2 Tbs toasted sesame oil 2 Tbs sesame seeds 1 Tbs five-spice powder (see page 149) 2 tsp Szechwan peppercorns ½ tsp red pepper flakes 2 garlic cloves, minced	1 medium whole scallion, minced 2 Tbs toasted sesame oil 1 Tbs sesame seeds 2 Tbs soy sauce 1 Tbs honey 4 garlic cloves, minced	3 Tbs canola oil 1 Tbs tomato paste 2 Tbs chili powder 2 Tbs minced oregano 1 Tbs ground cumin 2 tsp liquid smoke 1 tsp light brown sugar 1 tsp salt ½ tsp ground cinnamon ½ tsp ground black pepper
3. Skewer with the meat and cook	2 large red onions, cut into wedges 16 cherry tomatoes 1 cup dried apricots, preferably California apricots	2 corn ears, halved lengthwise and cut into 1-inch thick half-moons 2 cups shiitake mushroom caps, halved	2 medium red onions, cut into thin wedges 1 medium yellow bell pepper, seeded and cut into small chunks	3 medium zucchini, cut into chunks 2 medium red bell peppers, seeded and cut into small chunks

A sophisticated brunch or lunch—or an easy dinner: Chard Soufflé

Soufflé

Like Risotto (page 284), this is one of those storied techniques, often spoken about in whispers, the voice trailing off: "Once, I had this great shrimp soufflé, but I'd never try to make. . . ." Fear not! As long as you follow some basic rules, a soufflé puffs every time: a dramatic dinner of eggs, sauce, and intense flavors, light as air, economical, too—golden brown and stunning. • MAKES 4 SERVINGS

• **STEP 1** Preheat the oven to 400°F; lightly grease and coat the inside of a 2-quart (8-cup) round soufflé dish. The soufflé will be baked at 375°F, but preheat the oven to 400°F. When you open the oven door to put the soufflé in, the temperature will drop, thanks to escaping heat. Preheating to a higher temperature assures a more even heat when the soufflé first gets into the oven, the most crucial moment for building its structure.

Preparing the soufflé dish or charlotte mold

As a general rule, use the same type of fat for greasing the dish or mold that you will use to build the roux in the next step: unsalted butter, olive oil, walnut oil, or even rendered bacon fat. Think through the soufflé you will build. Olives, sun-dried tomatoes, and grated cheese? Then use olive oil in the baking dish. Caramelized shallots and minced garlic? Then use unsalted butter. Artichoke hearts and crumbled, crisp bacon? Then use perhaps some of the cooled, rendered bacon fat in the pan. Dab whichever fat on a piece of wax paper or a paper towel, then use either to grease the inside of the soufflé dish; you're assured the fat will get into the seam between the dish's wall and bottom, because your fingers will glide around the dish in all directions, coating everything.

Here's a properly buttered soufflé dish, coated with grated cheese.

Once you've greased the inside of the soufflé dish, coat it with about 3 tablespoons of one of the following:

> **hard cheese like Parmigiano-Reggiano or aged Asiago,**
> finely grated
> **nuts,** finely ground in a mini food processor or a spice grinder
> **unseasoned dried bread crumbs**

Tilt the baking dish on its side and spoon the required amount into the well where the wall meets the bottom, thereby keeping the bits of cheese or whatever from sticking across the dish's bottom before they've had a chance to coat its walls. Now tip the dish fully onto its side, spill the grated cheese or whatever up the interior walls, and rotate the dish, tilting and jostling until the sides are well coated. Set the baking dish upright (bottom side down) and rap it once or twice against the coun-

The Soufflé Dish

The requirements are specific and exacting: round, with 3- to 4-inch tall straight sides that come down perpendicular to their bottoms, no curving or bowing. There may be fancy fluting on the outside of the dish, but never on the inside. Invest in the proper baking dish; a soufflé can only be made with the right tool. Besides, a soufflé dish of this size is multi-purposed: great as well for pudding, casseroles, or even Macaroni and Cheese (page 173).

That all said, Julia Child and her co-writers in *Mastering The Art of French Cooking* suggest using a charlotte mold: an old-fashioned, straight-sided dessert mold, usually made of metal, with very high sides, now available mostly in high-end kitchenware stores and from online outlets. To make this version of a soufflé, the mold would need sides at least 4 inches high and a bottom about 6 inches in diameter. Because it's a metal pan—not ceramic, as most soufflé dishes—the stated baking time may be a little off, reduced by perhaps 5 minutes.

Then again, baking and roasting times are always hints, never rules. Your oven may not be calibrated the same as ours, the eggs you use may be slightly cooler or warmer than ours, and your atmospherics may well be different from ours (the humidity, temperature, and your general mood when you whap what you whap with the whisk).

ter, just to knock any excess coating off the sides, giving you more to work with across the bottom. Tilt and jostle the dish until the bottom is also coated. You can now see if there are any spots you've missed. Dab bare patches with fat and add a pinch more ground nuts or whatever you've used to coat them.

• **STEP 2** Make a modified blond roux of 4½ tablespoons fat and 3½ tablespoons all-purpose flour in a large saucepan over medium-low heat. A soufflé is basically a puffed-up sauce. You make a roux, then whisk in liquid to create one of two classic sauces: a velouté (French, vel-oo-TAY, a roux with broth or wine added) or a béchamel (French, besh-MEL, a roux with milk or cream added).

Sounds complicated? Indeed, no. Start by making a modified roux, more fat than flour compared to the classic proportions. For a discussion of roux, see page 57—and of blond roux, page 58. Whisk the fat and flour over medium-low heat just until the flour is fully dissolved, until the mixture is no longer grainy. Then continue whisking as it bubbles for about 20 seconds—no browning, just so the flour loses its raw, unpleasant taste.

Which brings up the question of the tool you use. Look for a balloon-shaped whisk about 5 inches across, large enough to stir the ingredients in the saucepan but not so large as to miss what's lurking in the corners.

The traditional fat for the roux is unsalted butter. There may be little point in kicking against the goads, but there's also no reason to be bound by culinary scholasticism. Perhaps walnut or olive oil? You could also use a neutral-flavored oil, canola and the like, although you'll be adding no taste whatsoever to the concoction and so must then rely solely on what will fill the soufflé, whether it be cheese, herbs, or chopped, cooked bacon. Rendered bacon or duck fat are both stunning indulgences, worth every life-shortening bite.

• **STEP 3** Whisk in 1½ cups broth, milk, wine, or a combination in a slow, steady stream; continue whisking until the mixture comes to a simmer and thickens, about like a velvety cream soup. Remove the pan from the heat. Basically, use

broth, of any variety depending on the protein or vegetables to be added in step 5

milk, of any variety: whole, low-fat, or even fat-free

wine, white only, no staining reds

dry vermouth

coconut milk, regular or low-fat

Or best of all, use various combinations of these—say, ¾ cup beef broth and ¾ cup low-fat milk; 1 cup dry white wine and ½ cup chicken broth; or 1 cup chicken broth and ½ cup coconut milk.

True, many traditional chefs would balk at the notion of anything except milk in a soufflé—and only whole milk at that. But other liquids provide various canvasses, some better with savory ingredients. What about wine and broth with spinach and garlic laced into the eggs? Or even unadulterated broth with a heartier breakfast soufflé of sautéed sausage meat and chopped jarred roasted red peppers?

• **STEP 4** Whisk in 6 large egg yolks one at a time. First, divide the eggs, letting the 6 yolks fall into a separate bowl from the 8 whites you'll use in a bit.

With the saucepan off the heat, tilt the bowl with the yolks over it, letting one yolk at a time drop in, whisking constantly after each has been added, creating a smooth mixture before you let the next slide in. Don't beat the mixture to death, but do keep whisking to avoid scrambling the eggs in the still-hot sauce.

• **STEP 5** Stir in 1½ cups diced ready-to-eat protein or quick-cooking vegetables, some herbs, spices, and freshly ground black pepper, and, if desired, about 2 tablespoons finely grated cheese. Whatever goes into a soufflé batter must be ready to eat: purchased lump crabmeat; thinly sliced celery; or frozen quartered artichoke hearts. Sliced mushrooms must be first sautéed in butter, olive oil, or what have you; ground beef must be cooked through, whether in the microwave or on the stove; and chopped pancetta or bacon must be cooked until crispy in a skillet with oil or butter over medium heat.

Everything should be in small bits. A soufflé needs heft, the egg whites' rising up from trapped steam; they can't be weighed down by ham hunks. If you're, say, using meat from a purchased rotisserie chicken or a package of smoked trout, make sure you've diced it into small cubes, about ¼-inch pieces. Nuts, too, should be finely chopped.

At this stage, avoid long-cooking vegetables: butternut squash, parsnips, and the like. They must be thoroughly cooked. However, you can make an excellent soufflé with a thawed package of winter squash purée, mixed with some sautéed, diced onion, ground cinnamon, and grated nutmeg. Or stir in a carrot shredded through the large holes of a box grater, mixed with a little curry powder (page 113).

All of which brings up the question of the herbs and spices. There's a wide range here, although traditional chefs insist every soufflé embrace ¼ teaspoon grated

The best way to separate an egg? Through your clean fingers.

Separating Eggs

Dividing eggs can be cause for alarm among some cooks. Never fear—just don't use the egg shells, the one place where residual salmonella most likely lurks. Instead, use a purchased egg separator, available at cookware stores; or use a cleaned hand. Crack the egg into the cup of your palm, then slowly tilt your hand so the egg white slips between your fingers while the yolk stays put—which you then plop into a separate bowl. Yes, it's a little gross, especially if you were never one for mud pies as a child. Just wash your hands well afterward.

The egg whites have been beaten to the proper consistency: soft, droopy peaks without any dry, grainy, or rough patches.

nutmeg as well as perhaps ⅛ teaspoon cayenne. There's no gainsaying their contribution, but a savory soufflé can be made with a vast variety of minced herbs and dried spices—so long as you don't go overboard. Consider a few teaspoons herbs or perhaps ½ teaspoon dried spices the outer limit. With some play, of course. You can forgo the protein and vegetables altogether and simply make a soufflé of eggs and lots of minced, fresh herbs, perhaps ¼ cup of a mixture from the market or your garden.

Which brings up yet another "that said"—the one about a cheese soufflé. To make perhaps the most basic savory soufflé, stir in 1 cup finely grated semi-hard or hard cheese: Gruyère, Emmental, Parmigiano-Reggiano, or Pecorino, to name a few. If so, go with the classic spices, that grated nutmeg and cayenne, in accordance with traditional praxis and a terrific match to the cheese. But never use pregrated cheese. If you're going to the trouble to make a soufflé, don't dare use anything but the best. Would you double-date with the Queen in your blue jeans?

• **STEP 6** Beat 8 large egg whites and ¼ teaspoon salt in a large bowl until stiff but not dry; fold the beaten egg whites and egg yolk mixture together. Beaten egg whites are a foam held together by proteins. For the best height, the eggs should be between 65°F and 75°F, called "room temperature" in cookbook parlance, but perhaps a little chillier than you keep your house. Set the egg whites in the bowl on the counter for 15 to 20 minutes or take the whole, in-shell eggs for a 3- to 5-minute dunk in a bowl of warm (never hot) water. In this temperature range, the protein chains are elongated and ready to form a lattice-work structure. (This is all in direct contrast to whipped cream, which is a foam held together with fat, the bits as close together as possible to trap air—and thus, cold cream whips higher than room-temperature cream.)

Although it's a bad idea to salt scrambled or fried eggs before they come off the heat (salt indeed toughens eggs before they're set), here its grains help shred the whites under the beaters or whisk, allowing them to incorporate air more quickly.

Because of various chemical interactions, egg whites will not whip to peaks in the presence of one speck of egg yolk, water, or oil. Make sure the bowl into which the whites are dropped as well as the whisk or electric beaters are all scrupulously cleaned and dried before you begin. There's no reason to get this far into a soufflé and have to back out because the whites won't inflate.

Go at the whites with a large balloon whisk or an electric mixer at high speed. If beating by hand, use even, rounded strokes, whipping the whites around the bowl with lots of wrist and forearm action. If you're using your shoulder, you're beating too vigorously and you'll tire out quickly. Try a lighter, faster action at the elbow.

The whites should increase about eightfold in volume and be smooth and shiny.

When you grab up a little with the whisk or the turned-off beaters and invert it or them into the air, the whites should form a droopy peak about like some '50s rock-star's hair. It's easy to overbeat the whites, especially if you're using an electric mixer. They begin to look dull and grainy, even lumpy. But it's also easy to correct the problem: add another large room-temperature egg white and beat again until those droopy, shiny, velvety peaks appear. An extra egg white will not affect the soufflé's perfection.

Folding the whites into the sauce mixture is only a matter of not deflating all that air you've worked into the whites. Now and only now, drop the whisk; it would break apart the delicate structure you've built. Use a flat rubber spatula to fold about a third of the egg whites into the sauce mixture, working in slow, steady arcs to make sure everything's incorporated without losing its precious volume. Then fold this combined mixture back into the remaining egg whites, lifting the spatula through the combined mixture in even arcs, turning the spatula's flat face as you arc it through the mixture so that much of the sauce gets turned over and onto the whites. However, don't go too far: better some streaks of undissolved white than losing all the volume you worked so hard to create.

Add the beaten egg whites to the sauce in batches, about a third at a time.

• **STEP 7** Spoon the soufflé mixture into the prepared baking dish; place the filled dish in the oven, turn the temperature down to 375°F, and bake absolutely undisturbed until browned and set, about 35 to 40 minutes. Don't pour—the weight of the mixture on top will mash down on the protein-laced air structure below. Instead, spoon the mixture into the prepared dish, taking care to fill it evenly and thoroughly—no gaps or airholes. Press down gently to fill any.

Set the soufflé in the oven, close the door, and immediately decrease the temperature to 375°F. Then leave the soufflé alone. These first few moments are critical: the top needs to firm up so that it can trap the steam inside, thus forcing the whole thing to rise up, filled with hot air but crusty on top.

Fold in gentle arcs to keep the beaten egg whites fluffy.

After perhaps 30 minutes, the soufflé will be set but the insides will still be a bit creamy, perhaps undercooked. If you like loose-set scrambled eggs, consider taking the thing out now. However, a few more minutes will certainly not hurt the soufflé and the internal structure will become more set and airy. But be careful: too long in the oven and the thing dries out inexorably.

Serve within minutes of its coming out of the oven. It will begin to deflate almost immediately, the steam losing its punch under the dome. Serve by scooping up portions with a large spoon, thereby puncturing the soufflé but also making sure that everyone gets some of the browned bits across the top and down the sides.

Recipes for Soufflés

	Cheese Soufflé	Bacon and Artichoke Soufflé	Broccoli Cheddar Soufflé	Winter Squash Soufflé
1. Preheat the oven; grease and coat an 8-cup soufflé dish	Unsalted butter 3 Tbs grated Parmigiano-Reggiano	Nonstick spray 3 Tbs grated Parmigiano-Reggiano	Unsalted butter 3 Tbs grated Parmigiano-Reggiano	Unsalted butter 3 Tbs ground walnuts
2. Whisk into a blond roux over the heat	4½ Tbs unsalted butter 3½ Tbs all-purpose flour	4½ Tbs cooled, rendered bacon fat 3½ Tbs all-purpose flour	4½ Tbs unsalted butter 3½ Tbs all-purpose flour	4½ Tbs unsalted butter 3½ Tbs all-purpose flour
3. Whisk in until thickened and simmering	1½ cups milk	¾ cup beef broth ¾ cup milk	1½ cups milk	1 cup milk ½ cup dry white wine
4. Whisk in	6 large egg yolks, one at a time	6 large egg yolks, one at a time	6 large egg yolks, one at a time	6 large egg yolks, one at a time
5. Stir in	½ cup grated Gruyère[1] ½ cup grated Parmigiano-Reggiano ¼ tsp grated nutmeg ⅛ tsp cayenne	10 ounces frozen artichoke quarters, thawed and squeezed of excess moisture 4 ounces cooked bacon, crumbled 2 tsp minced dill ½ tsp ground black pepper ¼ tsp grated nutmeg	¾ cup grated Cheddar One 10-ounce package frozen chopped broccoli, thawed and squeezed of excess moisture 2 tsp stemmed thyme ¼ tsp grated nutmeg ⅛ tsp cayenne	One and a half 10-ounce packages frozen winter squash purée, thawed ½ tsp ground cinnamon ¼ tsp grated nutmeg
6. Beat to stiff peaks and fold in	8 large egg whites, at room temperature ¼ tsp salt	8 large egg whites, at room temperature ¼ tsp salt	8 large egg whites, at room temperature ¼ tsp salt	8 large egg whites, at room temperature ¼ tsp salt
7. Spoon into the prepared bowl and bake	35 to 40 minutes	35 to 40 minutes	35 to 40 minutes	35 to 40 minutes

[1]For hard, semi-firm, or semi-soft cheeses, the general rule is that 1 ounce = 2 grated tablespoons—and thus 4 ounces = ½ cup and 8 ounces = 1 cup.

	Crab Soufflé	Chard Soufflé	Curried Cauliflower Soufflé	Smoked Trout Soufflé
1. Preheat the oven; grease and coat an 8-cup soufflé dish	Olive oil 3 Tbs dried bread crumbs	Unsalted butter 3 Tbs dried bread crumbs	Walnut oil 3 Tbs dried bread crumbs	Olive oil 3 Tbs dried bread crumbs
2. Whisk into a blond roux over the heat	4½ Tbs olive oil 3½ Tbs all-purpose flour	4½ Tbs unsalted butter 3½ Tbs all-purpose flour	4½ Tbs unsalted butter 3½ Tbs all-purpose flour	4½ Tbs olive oil 3½ Tbs all-purpose flour
3. Whisk in until thickened and simmering	1 cup dry white wine ½ cup milk	1 cup dry white wine ½ cup vegetable broth	1 cup milk ½ cup dry white wine	1 cup milk ½ cup vegetable broth
4. Whisk in	6 large egg yolks, one at a time	6 large egg yolks, one at a time	6 large egg yolks, one at a time	6 large egg yolks, one at a time
5. Stir in	1½ cups purchased lump crabmeat, picked over for shell and cartilage 2 tsp minced tarragon 1 tsp stemmed thyme ¼ tsp cayenne	8 ounces Swiss chard leaves, cored, chopped, and cooked with 1 tablespoon butter in a large skillet ¼ cup finely chopped pecans 2 Tbs finely grated Parmigiano-Reggiano ½ tsp ground black pepper ¼ tsp grated nutmeg	12 ounces cauliflower florets, steamed until tender 1 Tbs curry powder (page 113) 2 tsp finely grated lemon zest ½ tsp ground black pepper	1 smoked trout fillet, skinned and crumbled ¼ cup chopped sun-dried tomatoes 2 tsp Dijon mustard ½ tsp ground black pepper
6. Beat to stiff peaks and fold in	8 large egg whites, at room temperature ¼ tsp salt	8 large egg whites, at room temperature ¼ tsp salt	8 large egg whites, at room temperature ¼ tsp salt	8 large egg whites, at room temperature ¼ tsp salt
7. Spoon into the prepared bowl and bake	35 to 40 minutes	35 to 40 minutes	35 to 40 minutes	35 to 40 minutes

Steaks 1: Strip and Other Boneless Steaks with a Compound Butter

You'll need a large cast-iron skillet to make boneless steaks indoors—well, that and good ventilation. Save your nonstick skillet for Omelets (page 213); the coating may not withstand these high temperatures. • MAKES 4 SERVINGS

• **STEP 1** Make a compound butter. Steak and butter: Dante and Beatrice, a match made in heaven—but not without some help. A better alternative to a pat of butter on a steak is a compound butter, made with herbs, spices, ground nuts, and/or seasonings.

For about 5 tablespoons compound butter, follow these steps:

Cast-Iron Cookware

Cast iron is an excellent conductor of heat—and superbly nonstick once seasoned. Its surface is full of infinitesimal gashes that must be filled with fat (the so-called "seasoning"). To get a new cast-iron skillet ready for the heat, coat it lightly with vegetable or canola oil and set it in a preheated 300°F oven for 1 hour. Cool to room temperature, do not wipe out, and repeat twice. Once seasoned, a cast-iron skillet must never be scrubbed or washed with detergent (which will dissolve the fats trapped in those gashes). To clean, pour about 2 tablespoons kosher or coarse-grained salt into a cooled skillet, then add a little hot water and wipe with a wad of paper towels, using the salt's graininess to remove any baked on bits. Once smooth, rinse off any salt and set the skillet over high heat until smoking.

1. Start with 4 tablespoons (that is, ¼ cup or ½ stick) unsalted butter, at room temperature. Do not melt the butter; it will be too soft and oily, the milk solids' falling out of suspension. Instead, leave it on the counter in a small bowl until it's quite spreadable, perhaps a couple hours.
2. Stir in 1 teaspoon oil, whether olive, walnut (toasted or not), sesame, canola, or any number of flavors depending on the palette you wish to build. Butter is a little sour; the oil will balance it with sweet, savory, or floral accents.
3. Next, add 2 or 3 teaspoons (in total) of one or two flavorings: minced herbs, ground toasted nuts, minced garlic or fresh ginger, dried spices (ground cinnamon, grated nutmeg, and the like), a flavoring like minced olives or capers—or perhaps a combination like smoked paprika and a minced garlic clove, stemmed thyme and finely grated lemon zest, minced tarragon and sun-dried tomato, or minced rosemary and pitted black olives.
4. Finally, stir in ¼ teaspoon salt. Why start with unsalted butter and then add salt? Salted butter is just too darn salty without much of the actual mineral taste of salt.

Set the compound butter aside at room temperature to meld the flavors while you prepare the steaks.

• **STEP 2** Preheat the oven to 450°F and turn the vent on high or open a kitchen window. Set a seasoned cast-iron skillet over high heat until smoking, about 5 minutes. Then oil four 8- to 10-ounce strip steaks and season them with salt and freshly ground black pepper; slip them into the pan and leave undisturbed for 4 minutes. A 14-

inch cast-iron skillet should do the trick. You want enough surface area so that the skillet holds all the steaks. Plus, you want extra room so that any juice released from the steaks is immediately boiled off, the skillet fairly dry so the steaks don't steam or stew. If your skillet is not large enough, use two, each set over its own burner.

The steaks

Almost all strip steaks are taken from the top loin, a lean strip of the short loin, about at the mid-point of a cow's back between the ribs and the sirloin. Most of the United States calls this cut a "New York strip"—except for Kansas City butchers who often refer to it as a "Texas strip" and New York City butchers who sometimes call it a "Kansas City strip." Confused? Rightly so. Ask your butcher for beef strip steaks cut from the top loin. Trim off any fat that rings the cut. Strip steaks sometimes have a "tail"—a little piece of meat that curves around one end. For even cooking, trim this off as well.

If you don't want to use a strip steak, you have four choices. For a more economical preparation, use sirloin, particularly top sirloin. It will be slightly tougher than a strip but just as tasty. When cooked and before serving, slice thinly against the grain to compensate for its more pronounced fibers (see page 270).

Top blade steaks, also called "flat iron steaks," have gained in popularity recently and are now difficult to find outside of specialty markets and butcher shops. The steak, heavily marbled, is taken from the bony top blade roast, a shoulder roast; the connective tissue (and bones, of course) are removed to produce two steaks from each roast. Like a sirloin, these should be sliced against the grain into thin strips after cooking.

Or use Delmonico steaks—that is, rib-eyes without the bone. Flavorful and fatty, these should never be cooked to more than medium-rare or the juices will escape without the collagen having broken down to provide any other moisture. At an internal temperature of 145°F or (God forbid) more, they're an unappetizing lot.

Finally, forgo strips for hanger steaks, a bistro classic, sometimes called *onglets* (French, AHWNG-lay) or "butcher's steaks." A hanger steak actually "hangs" from the diaphragm, attached to the last rib and the kidneys. It cooks fast: just 2 minutes over high heat before you turn it with tongs and place it in the oven. A fibrous cut, it can be tough. Consider marinating it overnight in the refrigerator in red wine to help break down the stringiness. If you've bought a whole hanger steak, it's in two lobes, which must be separated into two, long tubes of steak. One lobe is larger than the other and can be cut in half—

To make a compound (that is, flavored) butter, a little oil balances the butter's sour taste, the better to complement the other spices or flavorings.

Beef Grades

All beef sold in the United States is graded by the USDA. Of the eight categories, the top three are "prime," "choice," and "select." From there, the demarcations continue through such unsavory designations as "utility" and "canner." Prime, of course, is tops, well marbled and fatty; in the United States, over 80% of it goes to restaurants. Which is fine because choice cuts are less fatty, a little more chewy, and full of the taste of beef, rather than beef-laced fat.

Set the steaks in a very hot cast-iron skillet—and leave them undisturbed with the vent going at full blower.

Turn the steaks only after they have crusted and gotten a deep caramelization.

you'll then have three steaks from one whole, two-lobed hanger. Once cooked, thinly slice the steaks against the grain (widthwise) for the most tender pieces.

Oiling, seasoning, and cooking the steaks

Before they go into the hot skillet, the steaks need a quick coating of some oil, preferably a neutral oil with a high smoke point like canola or grapeseed oils, as well as refined safflower, corn, soybean, or peanut oils. You'll add more flavor later with the compound butter; there's no point in overdoing the flavors now. Simply rub ½ teaspoon into each side of each steak before seasoning it with salt and pepper.

Kosher salt makes the best crust, a little mineral crunch on the outside of the steaks.

Never use preground black pepper. If you're going to the trouble to make steaks at home, grind fresh black peppercorns to order. To make a steak au poivre, crush ¼ cup whole black peppercorns in a mortar with a pestle or grind lightly in a spice grinder, just until very grainy. Press these into the steaks with the kosher salt.

Over high heat, the steaks will get crusty yet incredibly flavorful. The exact chemistry of this appetizing incineration is still a bit of a food-science mystery; suffice it to say that the natural sugars and proteins break apart and realign to form new, irresistible flavor molecules. Yes, the outside of the steak is quite dry, thanks to the heat. But don't worry—you'll hardly notice it except with your knife. Salivary glands go into overdrive for these chemical compounds. In other words, you mistake desiccated dryness for juiciness because of sheer appetite.

• **STEP 3** Turn with tongs, set the skillet in the oven, and roast to the desired internal temperature, determined by an instant-read meat thermometer inserted into the center of one steak. Transfer the steaks to plates, let rest for 5 minutes, and then top each steak with 1½ tablespoons compound butter. For strips and the like, we recommend three temperatures: 120°F for rare, 125°F for medium-rare—and, if pressed, 145°F for medium. Of course, the USDA only recommends the latter and calls it "medium rare" with escalating temperatures above that (see page 130 for a comprehensive list).

Insert an instant-read meat thermometer on the diagonal into the thick center of one of the steaks after 3 minutes in the oven. If you've let them come near room temperature before cooking, they'll be almost done. Once the steaks are out of the oven, let them rest before adding the compound butter so that it doesn't simply run all over the plate.

Recipes for Strip and Loin Steaks

	Strip Steaks with Parsley Thyme Butter	Strip Steaks with Garlic Lemon Butter	Strip Steaks with Smoked Paprika Butter	Delmonico Steaks with Fragrant East-Indian Butter
1. Stir together	4 Tbs unsalted butter, at room temperature 1 tsp olive oil 3 Tbs minced parsley 1 Tbs stemmed thyme ¼ tsp salt	4 Tbs unsalted butter, at room temperature 1 tsp olive oil 1 Tbs grated lemon zest 1 tsp lemon juice 2 garlic cloves, finely minced ¼ tsp salt	4 Tbs unsalted butter, at room temperature 1 tsp olive oil 2 tsp smoked paprika 1 tsp ground cinnamon ½ tsp grated nutmeg ¼ tsp salt	4 Tbs unsalted butter 1 tsp mustard seed oil 1 Tbs minced cilantro 2 tsp garam masala (see page 27)
2. Preheat the oven and the skillet; season and sear	Four 8- to 10-ounce strip steaks, trimmed Olive oil Kosher salt and ground black pepper to taste	Four 8- to 10-ounce strip steaks, trimmed Olive oil Kosher salt and ground black pepper to taste	Four 8- to 10-ounce strip steaks, trimmed Olive oil Kosher salt and ground black pepper to taste	Four 10-ounce Delmonico steaks Canola oil Kosher salt and ground black pepper to taste
3. Turn and roast in the oven, then top with the prepared compound butter	To 120°F for rare, 125°F for medium-rare, and 145°F for medium, about 3 to 6 minutes	To 120°F for rare, 125°F for medium-rare, and 145°F for medium, about 3 to 6 minutes	To 120°F for rare, 125°F for medium-rare, and 145°F for medium, about 3 to 6 minutes	To 120°F for rare, 125°F for medium-rare, and 145°F for medium, about 3 to 6 minutes

	Delmonico Steaks with Chile Butter	Black Pepper Sirloin	Sirloin Steaks with Wasabi Butter	Hanger Steak with Walnut Butter
1. Stir together	4 Tbs unsalted butter, at room temperature 1 tsp olive oil 1 Tbs chili powder 2 tsp minced oregano ¼ tsp salt	4 Tbs unsalted butter, at room temperature 1 tsp olive oil 1 Tbs cracked black peppercorns 2 tsp minced rosemary ¼ tsp salt	4 Tbs unsalted butter, at room temperature 1 tsp toasted sesame oil 1 tsp wasabi powder ½ tsp soy sauce	4 Tbs unsalted butter, at room temperature 1 tsp toasted walnut oil 1 Tbs finely minced toasted walnut pieces ¼ tsp salt
2. Preheat the oven and the skillet; season and sear	Four 10-ounce Delmonico steaks Olive oil Kosher salt and ground black pepper to taste	Four 8-ounce top sirloin steaks, trimmed Canola oil Kosher salt	Four 8-ounce top sirloin steaks, trimmed Peanut oil Kosher salt	One 1½-pound hanger steak, cut into two lobes and trimmed Canola oil Kosher salt and ground black pepper to taste
3. Turn and roast in the oven, then top with the prepared compound butter	To 120°F for rare, 125°F for medium-rare, and 145°F for medium, about 3 to 6 minutes	To 120°F for rare, 125°F for medium-rare, and 145°F for medium, about 3 to 6 minutes	To 120°F for rare, 125°F for medium-rare, and 145°F for medium, about 3 to 6 minutes	To 120°F for rare, 125°F for medium-rare, and 145°F for medium, about 3 to 6 minutes

Steaks 2: Rib-Eyes, T-Bones, Veal Chops, and Other Bone-In Steaks

You can't get a good crust on the outside of a bone-in steak if you cook it in a skillet. The bone stays in contact with the hot surface while the meat pulls up. The only solution? A preheated broiler and a little patience with the clean-up.

• MAKES 4 SERVINGS

• **STEP 1** Mix together 2 tablespoons plus 2 teaspoons (that is, 8 teaspoons) dried spice rub. A dried spice rub is simply a mixture of spices, suitable to massage into meat. Fresh herbs have no place. Instead, use their dried versions (dried oregano and rubbed sage, for example) as well as a host of other spices: ground cinnamon, grated nutmeg, ground chiles, chili powder, red pepper flakes, ground allspice, and the like. Many ground dried spices are quite powerful; use less than you might expect: little more than ¼ teaspoon at a time.

That said, all spices must be ground: fennel, celery, and cumin seeds; dried lemon peel or dried lavender; whole pink, green, and/or black peppercorns. Use a spice grinder to turn them into a fine powder, one that matches any dried spices you've chosen.

In like manner, use only the dried version of traditionally wet ingredients. Onion powder, garlic powder, granulated garlic, and ground ginger take the place of onions, garlic, and ginger. But be careful: these are powerful additions, a concentrated punch. Also, rather than using a citrus zest, seek out ground dried lemon and orange peel in the spice aisle; these are pleasant, zesty additions, perfect with veal chops. Use more of these than you would onion powder—perhaps up to 1 teaspoon of the total amount.

So armed with these criteria, here's how to build 2 tablespoons plus 2 teaspoons—that is, 8 teaspoons—of a dry rub.

1. Start with 2 teaspoons kosher salt. Kosher salt is coarse-grained and will thus yield a nice crust. For a fancier touch, forgo kosher salt and use a coarse-grained sea salt. But do not use one that's too coarse, too much like grains of very coarse sand; if so, grind it with any other whole spices in the spice grinder or in a mortar with a pestle. All that said, if you use common table salt, realize that it tastes about twice as salty as kosher or sea salt. Perhaps cut it down to 1 teaspoon.

2a. Fill out the remainder of the necessary rub with a premade or purchased blend like chili powder, curry powder (page 113) or garam masala (page 27). Be careful of purchased spice blends that are more chile than flavor. Also, if a purchased blend includes salt, reduce the amount of salt used. Add 4 teaspoons of any of these blends, then doctor the mix with 2 teaspoons of other dried or ground spices. Add more floral taste with dried lavender, more herbal taste with dried herbs, and more sweetness with ground allspice, cinnamon, nutmeg, cloves, or mace. With bottled chili powder, try 2 teaspoons dried thyme, and 1 teaspoon each ground cinnamon and dried oregano; with bottled yellow curry powder, 2 teaspoons ground coriander as well as dribs and drabs of ground cumin, ginger, allspice, and cayenne.

2b. Or build your own rub from scratch. After the salt, start with a base flavor: say 2 teaspoons ground coriander, pure ancho chile powder, or finely crumbled dried rosemary. Then add 4 teaspoons dried spices that match the base. For example, if you started with dried rosemary, add ground fennel seeds, dried oregano, ground dried lemon peel, and garlic powder; if you started with pure ancho chile powder, add ground cumin, dried oregano, dried thyme, and onion powder for a Southwestern flare. Think along these overgeneralized but helpful lines: Italian seasonings traditionally include rosemary, oregano, and thyme; Provençal, thyme, basil, and lavender; Moroccan, coriander, cumin, ginger, cinnamon, and orange peel; and French bistro, tarragon, thyme, parsley, and garlic.

The best rub for bone-in steaks is made with a dried spice mixture. Here's the mélange for Cowboy Rib-Eyes.

● **STEP 2** Set four bone-in steaks on a cutting board, rub 1 teaspoon oil, acid, or liquor onto each side of the steaks, then rub each side with 1 teaspoon dry rub. Set aside while the broiler preheats, or cover and refrigerate for perhaps 1 hour.

The steaks

Twelve- to 16-ounce steaks would be best, but these are admittedly old-fashioned amounts per serving. If you're eating less meat these days or would like smaller portions, cut this recipe in half, serving each person half a steak. You'll then need only 1 tablespoon plus 1 teaspoon rub (that is, 4 teaspoons)—of which only 1 teaspoon should be kosher salt.

Among your choices for the steaks, consider:

1. **Rib-eye steaks.** A rib steak is taken from the same ribs as a rib roast—except the bones are cut apart to form individual steaks. That said, rib-eyes are not usually cut from the leanest bones (numbers 1 through 3, see page 306), but from more bones farther on, the meat more fatty and also more cartilaginous.

2. **Porterhouse and T-bone steaks**. These steaks are cut through the bone (shaped like a "T") running in the short loin. On one side, there's a strip steak; on the other, the tenderloin (or

TO APPLY A DRY RUB: First, oil the steak so the dry rub will stick.

Then sprinkle the spice mixture evenly over the steak.

Finally, massage the spice mixture into the meat.

filet). As a general rule, a Porterhouse has a larger piece of the tenderloin than a T-bone.

3. **Club steaks.** A top-loin steak with the bone—essentially a bone-in strip steak. Extremely tender, they are a rarity these days, but sometimes found in big-box retailers as well as specialty markets.

4. **Veal chops.** There are two varieties suitable for this technique: loin or rib chops. The loin chop is roughly the equivalent of a beef Porterhouse; the rib, a beef rib-eye. Do not use veal shoulder chops, in need of a long braise.

5. **Game versions:** buffalo, venison, elk, and the like. Like beef steaks but often smaller, all are butchered with rib-eyes, T-bones, and Porterhouses in the mix. Search out these erstwhile staples and now exotics from online suppliers or order them at high-end butcher counters.

To trim or not to trim? The fat will enhance the flavor, but it will not protect the meat as it cooks in the broiler. Trim off any fat around the steaks' perimeters but leave any internal veins in place.

Seasoning the steaks

The prepared rub sticks by rubbing the steaks with some sort of liquid:

oil—olive, an untoasted nut oil, or a neutral oil like safflower (on the mild end of the fat spectrum—see page 17)

acid—lemon juice or a vinegar of some sort (forgetting about flavored vinegars, of course)

liquor or dry fortified wine—cognac, brandy, whisky, or dry vermouth (but forgetting about any sweet liqueurs or cordials)

Once the steaks have been moistened, rub about 1 teaspoon dry rub onto each side, taking care to massage it into the meat without pressing so hard the rub balls up. Steady, gentle pressure is best; this is not deep-tissue work.

Now the steaks need to rest—either at room temperature while the broiler pre-heats or in the refrigerator for any duration longer than 10 minutes. If you've used an acid like lemon juice, it will begin to color and break down the meat's fibers; do not let steaks coated with an acid rest for more than 20 minutes. If you've used oil or a liquor, you have more time, up to an hour.

• STEP 3 Position the broiler pan or a lipped baking sheet 4 inches from the broiler element; preheat the broiler for 10 minutes. Place the steaks in the pan or the baking sheet; broil until browned, then turn and continue broiling until the steaks reach the desired internal temperature, taken with an instant-read meat thermometer inserted into the center of one of the steaks. If the steaks have been in the refrigerator, let them stand at room temperature while the broiler heats.

The broiler pan or a heavy-duty baking sheet needs to get very hot as it sits under the element before the steaks are added. There should be a good sizzle once the meat is placed on the tray or sheet. But be careful: either is very hot, having sat under an intense element for a good while. Use sturdy cookware; flimsy pans will warp.

The steaks can be left alone for about 4 minutes per inch of thickness, until well browned; then turn them with tongs. There'll be lots of popping and hissing, the juices exploding off the hot surface. Make sure the vent is on high—or open a window.

Once turned, the steak will take less time to cook (that bottom side was sitting against the hot pan). Check the internal temperature with an instant-read meat thermometer after 2 minutes if you like them rare, 3 minutes for medium-rare. We actually don't recommend rib-eyes rare: the cartilage has not yet softened and the meat can be too chewy. See page 130 for a discussion of beef's doneness.

Properly cooked veal should have a pink, warm center at a slightly higher temperature than that for medium-rare beef—about 140°F (although the USDA recommends 145°F). To reach the proper temperature, the veal chops may take 4 or 5 minutes after turning—but watch them carefully: because of internal fat stores and low cartilage, their internal temperature rises precipitously the longer they're over the heat. In no circumstance should a veal chop be cooked to a higher temperature than those recommended; it will dry out and become tasteless.

If people at your table like steaks done to differing degrees, take the rare steaks out, tent with foil, and put the pan or sheet back in the oven with the remaining steaks, removing them as they get done to each person's liking. The rare steaks, unfortunately, will not be as hot as the others since they'll have been out of the oven the longest. But all steaks should be set aside to rest before serving. Beef fibers need 5 minutes to relax and let the juices flow back between the cell layers. No, dinner won't peel the roof of your mouth off. But the steaks will be tender and juicy every time.

Although there's plenty of salt in that dry rub mix, some of it may have slipped off with the juices in the pan. Always have extra salt and pepper to pass at the table.

Recipes for Rib-Eyes, T-Bones, and Other Bone-In Steaks

	Cowboy Rib-Eyes	Herb-Rubbed Rib-Eyes	Jerk Rib-Eyes	Tuscan T-Bones
1. Mix	2 tsp kosher salt 2 tsp pure ancho chili powder 1 tsp ground cinnamon 1 tsp dried thyme 1 tsp dried oregano ½ tsp ground allspice ½ tsp ground cumin	2 tsp kosher salt 2 tsp dried basil 1 tsp dried marjoram 1 tsp dried thyme 1 tsp rubbed sage 1 tsp ground dried lemon peel	2 tsp kosher salt 1 tsp ground coriander 1 tsp dried thyme 1 tsp ground ginger 1 tsp cayenne ½ tsp ground allspice ½ tsp grated nutmeg ½ tsp onion powder ½ tsp garlic powder	2 tsp kosher salt 2 tsp ground dried lemon peel 2 tsp ground dried rosemary 1 tsp dried oregano ½ tsp dried thyme ½ tsp garlic powder
2. Coat and prepare	Four 12-ounce rib-eye steaks 8 tsp canola oil	Four 12-ounce rib-eye steaks 8 tsp olive oil	Four 12-ounce rib-eye steaks 8 tsp red wine vinegar	Four 16-ounce T-bone steaks 8 tsp olive oil
3. Preheat the broiler—then broil the steaks or chops to the desired doneness, turning once	Our guide: 125°F for medium-rare	Our guide: 125°F for medium-rare	Our guide: 125°F for medium-rare	Our guide: 120°F for rare or 125°F for medium-rare

	Four-Pepper Porterhouses	Classic Herbed Veal Chops	Orange Pepper Veal Chops	Indonesian-Inspired Veal Chops
1. Mix	2 tsp kosher salt 2 tsp cracked black peppercorns 1 tsp cracked white peppercorns 1 tsp cracked green peppercorns 1 tsp cracked pink peppercorns 1 tsp dried thyme	2 tsp kosher salt 2 tsp dried tarragon 1 tsp ground dried lemon peel 1 tsp ground fennel seeds 1 tsp ground celery seeds 1 tsp ground black pepper	2 tsp kosher salt 1 Tbs ground dried orange peel 2 tsp ground black pepper 1 tsp rubbed sage	2 tsp kosher salt 1 tsp light brown sugar 1 tsp ground ginger 1 tsp ground coriander 1 tsp ancho chile powder ½ tsp ground fenugreek ½ tsp ground dried lemon peel ½ tsp onion powder ½ tsp garlic powder
2. Coat and prepare	Four 16-ounce Porterhouse steaks 8 tsp lemon juice	Four 12-ounce veal loin chops 8 tsp olive oil	Four 12-ounce veal loin chops 8 tsp orange juice	Four 12-ounce veal rib chops 8 tsp ginger juice
3. Preheat the broiler—then broil the steaks or chops to the desired doneness, turning once	Our guide: 120°F for rare and 125°F for medium-rare	Our guide: 140°F for medium-rare	Our guide: 140°F for medium-rare	Our guide: 140°F for medium-rare

Steamed Whole Fish

A steamed whole fish is a light, tasty dinner any night of the week. Plan on two fish for four eaters; if you double the recipe, use a second steamer. • MAKES 4 SERVINGS

• **STEP 1** **Stuff the body cavities of two 1½- to 2-pound whole fish with sliced or diced aromatics, dried whole spices, and/or fresh herb sprigs; season the outside of the fish.** First things first. Measure how thick the fish is at its fattest point below the head. You'll need this information later to determine the cooking time.

The kind of fish you steam depends on what's at the market. Don't go in just looking for trout or snapper; go with what's fresh.

But don't be fooled. Whole fish lying fresh on the ice at your market are not necessarily fresh. (And if your market offers only whole fish in sealed, cellophane-wrapped packages, go elsewhere.) It always helps to know when the fish deliveries are made or when a wholesale fish market in your city or region is open. Closed on Saturdays and Sundays? Then the fish on Monday morning has probably been there since Friday night.

When selecting a whole fish, take into account these factors:

1. The scales are firm, flat, and prickly, not loose and soft.
2. The eyes are mounded and protrude slightly.
3. The gills are red without a white film.
4. The tail is full, not curled or otherwise desiccated.
5. The fish itself smells fresh.

Once you know what's fresh, you're free to choose among many kinds, including

> pink, gold, black, or any variety snapper
> black, striped, spotted, large-mouth, or fresh-water bass
> any variety of drum
> tilapia
> rockfish
> tilefish
> wreckfish

Bountiful Oceans?

Consider the ethics of your fish choice. Although film strips and movies in grade school may have taught us that the oceans provide a limitless bounty, they are quickly being depleted, many types of fish disappearing from the wild with alarming rapidity. Species themselves also come in and out of sustainability, depending on various governments' and commissions' regulations. Check government and sustainability Web sites for the latest updates.

For this technique, avoid flat fish (flounder, fluke) and small fish (sardines, smelts), all not easily stuffed. Also avoid large whole fish (halibut, salmon) because they will not fit in most home steamers. If you want to steam fresh-water or sea trout, buy four 12-ounce trout, one per serving.

Whole fish are usually sold with the scales still attached, and occasionally with the guts intact, too. Have your market's fishmonger scale and gut the fish for you— but do check her or his work, even right there at the counter. We've come home

TO DEBONE A COOKED FISH: First, cut off the head and tail, then pull out the dorsal fins that lie along the back.

After that, make a long, shallow cut right along the backbone.

To steam a whole fish, the body cavity should be stuffed with all sorts of spices and flavorings, the fish placed on a bed of aromatics.

many a time only to take a knife to the fish because of left-on scales, scraping them off around the head and tail. Some unscrupulous markets won't scale anywhere near the heads or tails because if the fish isn't fresh, both can snap off.

Do not remove the skin. Even if you're not a fan of fish skin, it will protect the meat during steaming, keeping it from getting water-logged. You can remove it on your plate.

The body cavities can be stuffed with simple aromatics like sliced scallions or shallots, minced peeled fresh ginger, bay leaves, or fresh herbs on their stems like basil, mint, thyme, rosemary, oregano, or a mixture of several. Crushed mustard, cumin, celery, and fennel seeds add lots of flavor; star anise pods or whole cloves, a powerful punch to be used judiciously.

Close the fish over the aromatics, then season the outside with some ground black pepper and a little salt or one of its substitutes: soy sauce, fish sauce (see page 388), or Worcestershire sauce.

You can also use this technique to steam a very large, 3- to 3½-pound whole fish. The steaming contraption will need to be larger to accommodate the fish—and you may have to use the full amount of herbs for two smaller fish in this one larger one. Furthermore, the timing will have to be increased proportionately—plan on about 14 minutes per inch of unstuffed thickness.

• **STEP 2** Prepare the steamer rack with a bed of fresh herbs, thinly sliced citrus, and/or aromatic vegetables. The prepared fish should lie on a bed of mixed aromatics including various herb sprigs, citrus

Next, use a fork to peel off the exposed skin.

Then use a large spatula or cake server to take one fillet off the spine and ribs.

Slip a knife under the backbone and remove it and its ribs in one pull. Now the bottom fillet can be easily lifted off its skin on the cutting board.

slices (lemon, lime, or orange), sliced leeks, peeled rounds of fresh ginger, shaved fennel, spinach leaves, celery fronds, and the like. Do not repeat a spice used inside the body. The easiest bed involves a few leaves of Napa cabbage, sprinkled with some minced fresh herbs. However, you can dress the bed to your liking: fresh bay leaves, leafy mint sprigs, or a handful of cleaned ramps, to name a few choices.

Since neither the fish nor their bed of aromatics can rest in the simmering water, there are several contraptions for steaming a whole fish:

1. **A wok with a steamer rack.** The wok must be large enough to accommodate both fish at once. If the rack's slats are far apart, you'll have to build a bed that includes herb sprigs and the like, so smaller aromatics don't fall through.

2. **A fish poacher with a rack.** Many poachers come with a small rack that allows the fish to sit off the heat but still rest in the simmering liquid. However, steaming is not poaching; the rack may not be high enough to lift the fish out of the bubbling liquid. Modify it by standing it on small, upside-down ramekins or on 1- or 2-inch columnar sections of a large potato.

3. **Large, covered bamboo steamers** that fit over a large saucepan. The steamers should be about 12 to 14 inches in diameter and fit securely over the pan, resting on its lip. You may need to slice off the tail to make the fish fit. Use two steamers (plus the cover), two beds of aromatics, and one fish per steamer, stacked so that the fish are positioned perpendicular to each other for even cooking.

4. **A large sauté pan and a small baking rack.** Lift the rack up as you would the rack in a fish poacher, using perhaps rounds cut from a raw potato. Make sure the sauté pan's lid is tight-fitting so the liquid does not boil away. Also make sure the rack's feet are not rubberized or coated in a material that will melt over the heat.

SERVING SUGGESTIONS

Serve the fish over cooked rice, Risotto (page 284), cooked lentils, sautéed or steamed greens, steamed asparagus spears, roasted or grilled lettuce, roasted or braised leeks, mashed potatoes (see page 21), baked sweet potatoes, or steamed, mashed plantains.

• **STEP 3** Once the aromatic bed and its racks or steamers are in place, add liquid to the pan or wok until it comes about ½ inch below the rack's bed; bring the liquid to a simmer over high heat. Place the stuffed fish on the rack(s) or in the steamers, cover, reduce the heat to medium, and steam for about 12 minutes per inch of unstuffed thickness. The amount of liquid, of course, depends on the contraption you've used—perhaps as little as ½ cup in a rigged-up fish poacher; perhaps more than 1 cup in a wok with a steaming rack.

White wine, vegetable broth, or clam juice are the obvious choices, but also consider unsweetened apple or pineapple juice, a dry fortified wine mixed with broth, or even a little brandy mixed with broth. If you've used wine or broth alone, consider spiking it with 1 to 2 tablespoons white wine vinegar for balance.

How do you know when the fish is done? Two ways:

1. Insert a flatware knife into the thickest part of the meat without going through to the cavity, hold it there for 5 seconds, then touch the flat of the blade to your lips. If it's warm, not cool or even room temperature, the fish is done.
2. More commonly, use a fork to pull a little bit of the meat back just at the center of the body. The meat should flake into defined shards.

Remove the fish from the rack or racks with a large, flat spatula, preferably one designed for turning fish. A too-small spatula is a recipe for a fish broken in half or chipped into pieces. Transfer the fish to a cutting board and carve as follows:

1. Cut off (and reserve) the head. There are good tidbits in the cheeks and just under the skin.
2. To remove the dorsal fin at the top of the back, pull it out with your fingers. If the fish is too hot to handle, let it rest another 2 or 3 minutes and try again.
3. Use a fish knife, a wedge-shaped cake server, or a flatware knife to make a cut straight along the back where that fin was, head to tail; cut through the skin but not far into the meat and certainly not down to the bone.
4. Prick the skin just below the head on the side facing you with a fork, then peel off the skin by pulling the fork up and over the fish.
5. Slide a fish knife or cake server under the part of the meat nearest the head and lift up, gently pulling the knife down the fish's body and thereby dislodging the fillet from the bones underneath. Transfer to a plate.
6. Run the knife or the cake server under the backbone, lift up, peel away, and discard it.
7. Slide the knife or cake server between the bottom fillet and the skin lying against the cutting board; lift up and peel the fillet gently off the skin. Transfer this second fillet to a plate.

Recipes for Steamed Whole Fish

	Asian-Inspired Steamed Fish	Steamed Fish with Mixed Herbs	Greek-Style Steamed Fish	Japanese-Style Steamed Fish
1. Stuff and season	Two 1½-pound whole fish, cleaned and scaled 8 medium whole scallions, minced 2 Tbs minced peeled fresh ginger Soy sauce to taste	Two 1½-pound whole fish, cleaned and scaled Garlic cloves Rosemary, oregano, and thyme sprigs Celery seeds, crushed Salt to taste	Two 1½-pound whole fish, cleaned and scaled Garlic cloves Dill fronds Chopped black olives Thin lemon slices Salt to taste	Two 1½-pound whole fish, cleaned and scaled Pickled ginger Shredded daikon A little prepared wasabi paste Soy sauce to taste
2. Prepare the rack by making a bed with	Cilantro sprigs	Sliced leeks	Sliced fennel bulb and its fronds	Dried wakame seaweed soaked in boiling water to soften
3. Pour in, bring to a simmer, and steam	White wine 1 Tbs rice vinegar	White wine	Chicken broth 1 Tbs white wine vinegar	Sake

	Southwest Steamed Fish	Puttanesca-Style Steamed Fish	Steamed Whole Fish with Lemon and Herbs	Steamed Whole Fish with Red Onions and Oranges
1. Season and stuff	Two 1½-pound whole fish, cleaned and scaled Jarred roasted red peppers Roasted garlic Lime slices Chile powder Cumin seeds, crushed Lime juice Salt to taste	Two 1½-pound whole fish, cleaned and scaled Chopped pitted black olives Drained capers Jarred roasted red peppers Fennel seeds, crushed Balsamic vinegar Salt to taste	Two 1½-pound whole fish, cleaned and scaled 2 lemons, very thinly sliced Fennel seeds Salt to taste	Two 1½-pound whole fish, cleaned and scaled 2 oranges, thinly sliced Green peppercorns, crushed Salt to taste
2. Prepare the rack by making a bed with	Cilantro sprigs	Flat-leaf parsley sprigs	Mint and flat-leaf parsley sprigs	Sliced red onion on cabbage leaves
3. Pour in, bring to a simmer, and steam	Beer	Red wine	Vegetable broth	Red wine One 4-inch cinnamon stick

Roasted Duck with Plums, Cranberries, and Cinnamon

Steam-Roasted Stuffed Duck or Goose

Duck and goose have plenty of subcutaneous fat, not to protect them from cold water as is commonly reported, but to aid buoyancy. Unfortunately, that fat can get in the way of a crisp bird, turning both the skin and the meat soggy and unappetizing. To deal with it, steam the bird first to render off most of that fat, then roast the bird until crispy and irresistible. • MAKES 4 OR 8 SERVINGS

• **STEP 1** Start with the stuffing. For a duck, simmer 1½ cups chopped dried fruit and 1 cup broth or an enhanced broth in a large saucepan, covered, until the liquid has been almost all absorbed. Double these amounts for a goose. Set aside off the heat. A dried fruit stuffing will absorb some of the fat and turn into a luscious side dish, a perfect complement to the water fowl. By contrast, a bread-crumb stuffing would get too boggy; a meat stuffing, too pudding-like.

The kind of dried fruit you use is a matter of personal choice: raisins, dried pineapple, mango, currants, and raspberries, to name a few. When shopping for dried fruit, use the same criteria you use for fresh: plump, good aroma, and good color (although admittedly duller than its fresh kin). For this stuffing, it's best to use a blend, particularly a sweet/tart combination: cranberries and plums or raisins and apricots. That said, a single dried fruit and a single herb (added in step 3) will make an elegant pairing, well suited to a holiday meal: dried apricots and rosemary, for example; or prunes and mint.

In any event, chop the fruit, even raisins, into small pieces, about ½ inch or smaller. Whole dried fruit plumps in the heat to become unpleasant little balls of explosive hot sugar.

For the liquid, use broth, preferably chicken or maybe vegetable, which can be enhanced with smaller amounts of wine, unsweetened juice, dry fortified wine, brandy, or cognac. Be careful of using too much unsweetened fruit juice, which can turn the whole thing into a dessert stuffing, too sweet and rather bleak. Never use cream or anything too sweet like port or a dessert wine.

You'll need some aromatics, spices, and softened dried fruit to make a stuffing for a duck or goose.

• **STEP 2** For a duck, cook about 1½ cups diced aromatics or a modified mirepoix (see page 57) with 2 tablespoons fat in a second large saucepan over medium heat until softened. Again, double these amounts for a goose. In general, use unsalted butter, an untoasted nut oil, or a neutral-flavored oil like corn or safflower. Do not use olive oil: too perfumy. And do not use toasted nut or seed oils as well as other animal fats: too difficult to tame.

Spoon the cooled stuffing mixture into the duck's or goose's large cavity before trussing the bird.

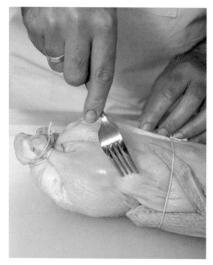

Prick a duck's or goose's skin all over with a fork so much of the subcutaneous fat melts away as the bird steams.

Although a mirepoix is a mixture of onions, celery, and carrots, you needn't adhere to the classic proportions. Sure, a diced onion or a few shallots are the easiest way to start—just a little savory accent to the fruit. But you can also add a few minced garlic cloves or two tablespoons of minced, peeled fresh ginger to the mix for a light accent. In any event, all the vegetables should be diced into pieces that match the bits of fruit.

In terms of other vegetables, don't use roots or tubers—with the exceptions of carrots, which should be cut into long matchsticks or shredded through the large holes of a box grater; celeriac, which should be peeled and finely diced; or sweet potatoes, likewise peeled and finely diced. As a general rule, stick with quick-cooking vegetables as your accents like fennel, fresh tomatillos, peas, celery, or a seeded bell pepper. Avoid tomatoes—too wet and easily overpowered by the dried fruit. But do consider chopped sun-dried tomatoes as well as chopped, pitted olives. Also avoid the standard mush-up vegetables: asparagus, green beans, broccoli florets—although thick broccoli stems can certainly be diced for an interesting, rather grassy twist in the filling with, say, golden raisins.

- **STEP 3** Stir in some minced fresh herbs or dried spices as well as ½ teaspoon salt; mix in the cooked fruit and set aside to cool to room temperature. Don't get carried away—the dried fruit is the predominant flavor. Keep the herbs and spices to simplicity, one or two. Dried herbs offer a more subtle taste, but fresh will give the stuffing an unmistakable spark, less heavy and perhaps more satisfying.

Again, remember that you're making a double batch for a goose, so adjust the herbs or spices accordingly. The salt, however, is just an accent and should not be doubled.

- **STEP 4** Stuff a 5- to 6-pound duck or a 10- to 12-pound goose with the stuffing. Truss the bird closed and prick it all over with a fork. If possible, search out and roast a moulard duck, a French specialty, larger than the standard North American fare. If you can only find a Pekin (also called a "Long Island" duck), it must be a large specimen, the body cavity large enough to hold the stuffing without packing it in. For Pekins, the best choice is a so-called "roaster ducking," usually around 6 pounds. By USDA standards, a duckling must be less than 16 weeks old and does not yet have a hardened bill. Older ducks are often very tough and stringy, not a good match for this simple technique because they're in need of a long, slow braise.

Although a "gosling" sounds tender, the term is often used to indicate weight (under 8 pounds) rather than age. Better to go for a "young goose," one whose bones have not become too heavy—the meat is still tender and supple.

Either a duck or a goose may still have pin feathers and remnants of quills attached, particularly in the fleshy joints between the legs. Remove any feathers or quills with a pair of sterilized tweezers.

Spoon the cooled stuffing into the bird's large cavity (making sure, of course, that any giblets and the neck have been removed); then truss with butcher's twine, using the same technique as used for a roasted chicken or turkey (see page 291).

And finally, use a dinner fork to prick the skin, beginning at the large opening and working your way back across the whole bird. Be assiduous, paying special attention to the fatty deposits around the breast and thighs. Do not prick down and into the meat; rather, poke through the skin and fat—often and exactly. These holes will let the rendered fat seep out as the bird steams.

Set the bird on a steamer rack, ready to go into a large, flame-safe roasting pan for steaming.

• **STEP 5** Steam on a rack over 1 inch of simmering water in a large roasting or steaming pan, 45 minutes for a duck or 1 hour for a goose. There are large, oval roasters designed for this technique; but you can improvise with a large roasting pan and a wire rack, provided you have lots of aluminum foil to cover it and make a tight seal so no steam escapes.

Fill the pan with about 1 inch of water; add a metal rack, one with feet that raise it above the water. (The feet must have no coating on them that can melt in the heat.) Bring the water to a boil over high heat, then add the bird breast side up. Cover tightly, reduce the heat to medium-low, and steam away the fat, checking occasionally to make sure the water has not evaporated.

• **STEP 6** Preheat the oven to 375°F. Set the bird on its rack in a second, large roasting pan, season with salt and freshly ground black pepper, and roast uncovered until an instant-read meat thermometer inserted into the thickest part of the thigh without touching bone registers 165°F, about 1 hour for a duck or 1½ to 2 hours for a goose. Cool for 10 minutes on a cutting board before carving. You'll now need a second large roasting pan—or you'll have to wash the one you've used to steam the bird. In either case, the bird should be again breast up on the rack. It's easiest to lift the rack and bird together out of the one pan and transfer it to the other. Be especially careful of melted fat sitting in little pools just inside the body.

As the bird roasts, baste it occasionally with the pan juices, if desired. The easiest way to do this is with a bulb baster: slurp up some of the juices, then squirt them over the duck or goose.

Once roasted, take the bird's temperature by following the same procedure as that for a large chicken or turkey (see page 299), taking care not to hit bone and not to poke through to the stuffing.

Once steamed, the bird is ready to be roasted on a rack to golden perfection.

PAN JUICES

Pour all the juices in the pan into a fat separator (available at cookware stores)—or failing that, into a glass bowl.

Wait 5 minutes for the fat to separate, then pour off the juices underneath the layer of the fat in the separator or skim off and discard the fat on top with a large spoon.

If the roasting pan is flame-safe, set it over medium heat—perhaps over two burners for a large pan—and add ¾ cup chicken broth. Bring to a simmer, scraping up any browned bits on the pan's bottom. Continue simmering until the liquid in the pan is half the amount you started with. Pour the juices out from under the fat in the separator into the roasting pan; or stick a bulb baster into the juices below the fat in a glass bowl, draw them up, and squirt them into the roasting pan. Continue simmering until just slightly thickened, perhaps another 2 minutes. Check for salt and pepper before serving.

Once out of the oven, you're ready to carve. Your tools are a meat fork and a thin carving knife, the better to get down inside the joints. Follow these rules:

1. Spoon out the stuffing and place it on a large platter or in a serving bowl.
2. Cut the skin and some of the meat that lies between the breast and the thigh-and leg quarter, running your knife closer to the breast side as you cut down. Once loosened, the thigh can be wiggled to reveal its ball-and-socket joint. Slice through this joint, then set this thigh-and-leg quarter aside and repeat on the other side of the bird.
3. Wiggle the drumstick and thigh, revealing the joint between them. Slice through the joint, removing the drumstick. Repeat with the other thigh quarter. If desired, slice the thigh meat off the bone at a diagonal to yield the largest chunks.
4. Do that same wiggling operation to discover the wing joints, then slice through them to remove the wings. If desired, crack the wing into the drumlet and the winglet by bending them open at the opposite position from their natural angle until you hear the joint pop. Once revealed, slice through the joint.
5. Finally, hold the breast with the meat fork at the top of the concave ridge of breastbone. Begin at the outside of the breast (farthest from the bone) and draw the knife slowly through the meat in long, controlled movements to produce thin slices of meat. Discard the carcass and serve the meat and fruit stuffing at once.

Recipes for Ducks and Geese

	Roasted Duck with Raisins, Pineapple, and Fennel	Roasted Duck with Plums, Cranberries, and Cinnamon	Roasted Duck with Cherries and Cognac	Asian-Inspired Roasted Duck with Mango, Garlic, and Ginger
1. Simmer	1 cup chopped golden raisins ½ cup chopped dried pineapple 1 cup dry white wine	1 cup diced pitted prunes ½ cup chopped dried cranberries 1 cup red wine	1½ cups chopped dried cherries 1 cup cognac or brandy	1 cup chopped dried mango ½ cup chopped dried pineapple 1 cup dry sherry
2. Cook	1 small yellow onion, diced 1 small fennel bulb, trimmed and diced 2 garlic cloves, minced	3 ounces shallots, diced 1 small green bell pepper, seeded and diced 1 celery rib, diced	1 small yellow onion, diced 2 celery ribs, thinly sliced	3 medium whole scallions, minced 1 medium carrot, shredded through the large holes of a box grater 2 garlic cloves, minced 1 Tbs minced peeled fresh ginger
3. Stir in and cool	1 Tbs chopped rosemary ½ tsp salt	1 tsp ground cinnamon ¼ tsp grated nutmeg ½ tsp salt	1 Tbs stemmed thyme ½ tsp salt	2 tsp five-spice powder (see page 149) ½ tsp salt
4. Stuff	One 5- to 6-pound duck, giblets and neck removed	One 5- to 6-pound duck, giblets and neck removed	One 5- to 6-pound duck, giblets and neck removed	One 5- to 6-pound duck, giblets and neck removed
5. Steam	Over 1 inch of simmering water for 45 minutes	Over 1 inch of simmering water for 45 minutes	Over 1 inch of simmering water for 45 minutes	Over 1 inch of simmering water for 45 minutes
6. Season and roast	Salt and pepper About 1 hour, to 165°F	Salt and pepper About 1 hour, to 165°F	Salt and pepper About 1 hour, to 165°F	Salt and pepper About 1 hour, to 165°F

	Thanksgiving Goose	Christmas Goose	Roast Goose with Apricots and Rosemary	Roast Goose with Dried Berries
1. Simmer	2 cups chopped dried cranberries 1 cup chopped dried golden raisins 1 cup red wine 1 cup chicken broth	1 cup chopped raisins ½ cup chopped dried cranberries ½ cup chopped dried apricots ½ cup chopped glacéed citron ½ cup chopped candied ginger 1 cup port 1 cup chicken broth	2 cups chopped dried apricots 1 cup chopped dried cherries 2 cups dry vermouth	1 cup chopped dried blueberries 1 cup chopped dried raspberries 1 cup chopped dried cranberries 1 cup dry white wine 1 cup chicken broth
2. Cook	6 ounces shallots, minced 2 celery ribs, thinly sliced 1 medium carrot, thinly sliced	6 ounces shallots, diced 2 celery ribs, thinly sliced 1 small fennel bulb, trimmed and diced	1 medium yellow onion, diced 1 medium red bell pepper, seeded and diced 1 celery rib, thinly sliced	4 ounces shallots, thinly sliced 1 medium fennel bulb, trimmed and diced 1 medium green bell pepper, seeded and diced
3. Stir in and cool	2 Tbs minced sage 2 tsp stemmed thyme ½ tsp salt	1 Tbs stemmed thyme 1 Tbs minced rosemary ½ tsp ground cinnamon ¼ tsp grated nutmeg ¼ tsp ground cloves ½ tsp salt	2 Tbs minced rosemary ½ tsp salt	1 Tbs minced tarragon 1 Tbs minced parsley 1 tsp stemmed thyme ½ tsp salt
4. Stuff	One 10- to 12-pound goose, giblets and neck removed	One 10- to 12-pound goose, giblets and neck removed	One 10- to 12-pound goose, giblets and neck removed	One 10- to 12-pound goose, giblets and neck removed
5. Steam	Over 1 inch of simmering water for 1 hour	Over 1 inch of simmering water for 1 hour	Over 1 inch of simmering water for 1 hour	Over 1 inch of simmering water for 1 hour
6. Season and roast	Salt and pepper About 2 hours to 165°F	Salt and pepper About 2 hours to 165°F	Salt and pepper About 2 hours to 165°F	Salt and pepper About 2 hours to 165°F

Stir-Frying

Stir-frying is now a global technique, once solely associated with Asia and still particularly suited to a wok. There are hundreds of varieties, Hunan to Szechwan, Cantonese to American take-out—even Korean, East Indian, and Peruvian varieties these days. But you needn't get all hung up on authenticity (unless you want to). A good stir-fry is simply a solid technique: first good knife skills, then good cooking ones. • MAKES 4 SERVINGS WITH RICE

• **STEP 1** Heat a large wok over medium-high heat; swirl in 2 tablespoons oil. Peanut and/or untoasted sesame oil are perhaps the base of most stir-fries, but you can also use neutral oils like sunflower or vegetable oils. Do not use olive, nut, or especially any toasted nut or seed oil—and, heaven forfend, stay away from unsalted butter. Once the wok is heated until it just starts to smoke, pour the oil around the top rim, letting it flow down to the center, swirling the wok to make sure its interior is mostly coated.

• **STEP 2** Add a few diced or minced aromatics; stir-fry just until fragrant, about 30 seconds. These are the three rules of stir-frying:

1. All the ingredients should be cut up, prepared, and in little containers beside the stove before you start cooking. To put it another way, have your mise-en-place done (French, meez-on-PLAHS, "set in place"). Most chefs and food writers today reduce this standard culinary phraseology to "mise" (meez), as in "I've done my mise and am now ready to stir-fry."
2. Don't dally. Until the liquids for the sauce are poured in, never stop tossing and stirring the ingredients over the heat. Once the wok's hot and at a go, you be, too. Use two flat-surface, wooden paddles—or failing those, two heat-safe, silicon spatulas or even two wooden spoons. Grab the ingredients out of the wok's bottom and gently toss it up on and onto the sides, thereby pushing other things down into the well over the heat.
3. Keep kids and pets away so you can concentrate. This is cooking with major heat—and the goal is to soften and cook the various ingredients without caramelizing their external proteins and sugars. Stay calm but have fun with it.

For a stir-fry, everything is prepped so it will cook as quickly as possible. Here, the meat is sliced against the grain into long, thin strips.

The list of Chinese aromatics is slightly different from that of Western ones. For the most part, onions, bell peppers, celery, and carrots are not aromatics in traditional Chinese cooking—no mirepoix here. Rather, these vegetables are treated as, well, vegetables, and added later.

For the aromatics, choose three or four among these:

up to 1 cup dried Chinese red chiles—little firecrackers you don't eat but that flavor the sauce—or up to 1 tablespoon red pepper flakes

up to 4 ounces shallots, diced

up to 7 medium whole scallions, diced

up to ¼ cup orange zest, thinly sliced, or peeled off with a vegetable peeler and cut into long strips

up to ¼ cup seeded and minced fresh chiles, perhaps green ones like serranos or jalapeños or red ones like overwhelming Thai hots

up to 3 tablespoons minced garlic cloves, or maybe a little more for a garlic sauce

up to 2 tablespoons minced peeled fresh ginger

up to 1 tablespoon sesame seeds

up to 2 teaspoons Szechwan peppercorns, a member of the citrus family, a little sour and hot, with a strange, tongue-numbing property

For the appropriate taste, balance hot with sweet (chiles with orange zest or scallions) or even sweet with sour (orange zest with Szechwan peppercorns or ginger).

Most of these aromatics must be diced. Hold a chef's knife securely in one hand, the sharp edge straight down and resting lightly on the cutting board. Curl the fingers of your other hand into your palm, then use these turned-under fingers to hold the item against the cutting board and push it slowly under the knife as you rock the blade up and down, never removing its tip from the cutting board. Move the food to be diced toward the knife, not the knife toward the food.

Cook the meat just until it loses its raw, red color.

For a traditional stir-fry, make sure there are plenty more vegetables than protein.

A stir-fry is all about technique over the heat: toss and stir the ingredients constantly, rarely letting them rest in the hot pan.

• **STEP 3** Add 1 pound shredded or diced protein; stir-fry until almost cooked through. Everything must be shredded or diced so that it cooks quickly. Again, good knife technique is important, making even cuts so that the protein is in similarly sized pieces as it hits the wok.

Choose quick-cooking meats—never long-stewers or cheap cuts:

> **boneless skinless chicken breasts and/or chicken thighs**
>
> **boneless skinless turkey London broil or breast cutlet,** diced
>
> **pork tenderloin or loin,** cut into ¼-inch-thick rounds and then these into ¼-inch matchsticks
>
> **ground pork or turkey** (but almost never ground beef)
>
> **lamb tenderloin,** cut just like the pork
>
> **beef sirloin,** cut against the grain (see page 270) into long, thin strips
>
> **shrimp,** preferably medium (about 30 per pound), peeled and deveined—any larger than this should be roughly chopped into bite-sized bits
>
> **scallops,** roughly chopped
>
> **lobster tail meat,** roughly chopped
>
> **pressed or dried tofu** (see page 147), thinly sliced and cut into ¼-inch matchsticks

Everything should be tossed repeatedly over the heat until it's almost ready to eat—about 1 to 1½ minutes for shellfish and tofu; 2 to 3 minutes for the other proteins.

And now a truth—or a confession, if you will. In a bid for health, we've actually dropped a step or two from this technique. By and large, the protein is always first pan- or deep-fried before it is stir-fried. This "twice-frying" allows the meat to have some crunch in the final dish but also adds quite a bit of fat. Still, it may be worth a whirl once in a while. You'll have to work with the protein long before you build the stir-fry. Mix the diced or shredded meat with 1 tablespoon cornstarch, 1 tablespoon soy sauce, 1 tablespoon shaoxing (see page 374) or dry sherry, and 1 teaspoon sugar in a large bowl; set aside while about ½ cup peanut oil heats in a large wok over medium-high heat until the oil is glistening with little waggles across its surface. Stir the meat in its marinade one more time, then drop the pieces into the wok. Be careful: the splattering is intense, thanks to that soy sauce and shaoxing. Stir-fry until crisp, about 1 minute; then transfer to a large bowl using a slotted spoon, pour the oil out of the wok, and start this stir-fry technique from the top, taking into account that the meat is already partially cooked and so should be added *after* the vegetables have been stir-fried in the next step.

The Wok

A good one is sturdy and heavy, with a deep well into which ingredients can fall back to the heat from the sloping sides. Those sides are key since you can move food up onto them to keep the items from burning or simply getting overcooked.

A flat-bottomed wok is preferable to one with a curved bottom—unless you've got an open fire pit in your stovetop. You can set a flat-bottomed wok right on the burner; curved-bottom ones have to be lifted up on a ring, thereby lifting the surface too far from the heat and cooling it a bit. (Stir-frying is all about cooking with lots of heat.)

There are few substitutes for a wok—but you can search out so-called "chef's pans," round-bottomed pans with sloping sides, a little shallower than a traditional wok. That said, a high-sided sauté pan can do in a pinch with its wide space for evaporation and lots of contact for heat—but the ingredients can singe with so little room to move them out of the heat.

• **STEP 4 Add about 4 cups chopped or sliced quick-cooking vegetables; stir-fry until crisp-tender, about 2 minutes.** The vegetables should actually be cut and sliced a little larger than the protein; for one thing, they need to stay crisp in the heat. Again, pay attention to the knife technique. You're not dicing; instead, you're chopping and slicing. Lift and reposition the knife often to get the most even pieces from the vegetables.

Liquids are just flavorings, added at the end and reduced to a glaze.

Shaoxing

Shaoxing is a salted Chinese cooking wine made from rice, sometimes also called "Chinese sherry." The word can also be spelled "Shao Shing" or "Shaoh-sing" or even "Huo Tiao"—that last translated as "carved flower," a reference to the urns in which the wine was once stored. Interestingly, about 1000 years ago, grapes were cultivated for wine in China, but rice eventually won over. Do not substitute sake, a Japanese rice wine. In a pinch substitute dry sherry instead. If you don't want alcohol in the stir-fry, substitute vegetable or chicken broth.

Any quick-cooking vegetable will do, preferably a mix: broccoli florets, zucchini, and bamboo shoots; or snow peas, shredded carrots, and thinly sliced mushrooms. Don't forget that thinly sliced onions, carrots, celery, and seeded bell peppers count as vegetables in most Chinese cooking. For a list of other, suitable vegetables, see those for Lo Mein (page 165).

For an authentic taste, include in the mix up to ¼ cup canned Chinese preserved vegetables, among them snow peas, mustard greens, radishes, turnips and/or their greens, cabbage, and even bamboo shoots. Chinese preserved vegetables are quite salty; Szechwan bottlings are, of course, spicy. All in all, it's a musky and pungent product that mellows only somewhat over the heat.

Or use preserved Chinese black beans as some of the total amount of vegetables. These are a salty, rich variety of preserved soy beans, usually flavored with ginger, garlic, and perhaps chiles. A favorite in southern China, they should be used sparingly, perhaps just ¼ cup or so.

That all said, potatoes are making a splash in China, now the world's largest producer. If you'd like to make a potato stir-fry, you'll have to work with them before you start the dish. First, shred the potatoes through the large holes of a box grater or shred them into large threads using a turning slicer, a Japanese tool for making little threads of vegetables, like that familiar garnish of carrots and/or daikon on plates of sushi. You can often find this tool at high-end cookware stores or from Asian cookware outlets on the Web. Soak the shreds or potato threads in a large bowl of cool water for 15 minutes, then drain and add them in this step, stir-frying until crisp-tender. If you find the wok runs dry (potatoes absorb moisture like crazy), add a little more oil to compensate and to keep them from sticking.

And now for another truth (or confession): vegetables in a stir-fry are endlessly variable—and endlessly optional. Four cups of sliced vegetables will give you 4 servings—and so the recipes at the end of this section have been so designated, not necessarily for authenticity, but simply to get a well-rounded meal on the table. However, in much Chinese cooking, the meat and vegetable dishes would be separate, complementary but distinct. Indeed, you might consider making one meat or protein stir-fry with few vegetables, and then another vegetable stir-fry, perhaps hotter or sweeter to balance what you did with the meat. More complicated and time-consuming, sure, but an interesting mix nonetheless.

The meat, the vegetables, the aromatics—they're all giving off quite a bit of steam by this point. Keep everything moving, grabbing it out of the well and gently tossing it up onto the sides of the wok, making sure everything's searing without poaching in the accumulating liquid at the bottom—and making sure that the liquid has a chance to simmer and condense into a sauce.

• **STEP 5** Finish the sauce with 2 tablespoons soy sauce, 2 tablespoons thick Chinese condiment, 1 tablespoon vinegar or acid, 1 tablespoon shaoxing or dry sherry, and if desired, up to 2 teaspoons hot chile paste or chile oil. Bring to a simmer, stir-frying constantly. For both a discussion of soy sauce and a list of thick Chinese condiments, see page 168.

For the vinegar or acid, there's a wide range. All these will change the basic flavorings of the dish—and are often added at the end of Western dishes as well to brighten the flavors at the last moment. Look at the schema this way:

low acid with much sweetness: balsamic vinegar, orange juice
low acid but with little sweetness: rice vinegar
moderately high in acid but also sweeter: white balsamic vinegar, Chinese black vinegar, Chinese red rice vinegar
moderately high in acid but less sweet: red wine vinegar, white wine vinegar, apple cider vinegar
high in acid: lime juice, lemon juice, white vinegar

In general, stir-fries use vinegars in the second and third categories: rice wine or Chinese black vinegar, for example. But there's no reason to limit your choices by tradition. Add the vinegar that best balances the other things in the wok. If there's already sour ginger, go for a lower-acid vinegar; if there are sweeter vegetables like snow peas and carrots, go for a higher-acid one. In all cases, avoid any flavored vinegars or *seasoned* rice vinegar that has been laced with sugar.

These proportions are simply guidelines, barely enforced. A sweet-and-sour dish would have perhaps 3 tablespoons vinegar; it would also have a little sugar added at this point—as would the favorite General Tsao's Chicken (or Shrimp, or whatever). You should feel free to play with these amounts, using them as not as speed limits but as a mere basic course in driver's ed. There is no one way to stir-fry; the technique—and the dish that ensues—is as varied and manifold as the cooks in the world.

HOMEMADE CHILE OIL

To make your own chile oil, heat 1 cup peanut oil in a large saucepan over high heat until the surface ripples and waggles. Toss in 1½ cups chopped dried red chiles and if desired, 2 tablespoons Szechwan peppercorns. Reduce the heat to low, stir for 1 minute, then cover and set aside to cool to room temperature. Strain the oil into a glass container and store in a cool, dark place for up to 1 month.

A stir-fry is often thickened at the last minute with a little cornstarch whisked into water.

Finally, here's the last moment to add some heat with a Chinese chile condiment. The best are bean pastes laced with chiles, salty and aromatic. Some can be quite mild; others, hellishly hot. Or use chile oil, an infusion of dried chiles into vegetable or peanut oil.

Chile-laced condiments are often added to the cooked dish tableside, not in the wok. However, we feel their spike can be overpowering, often at the expense of all your hard work over the heat. Best to add them now so they can mellow slightly and color the dish, rather than simply masking it.

• STEP 6 (optional): Thicken the sauce with 1 teaspoon cornstarch whisked in 2 teaspoons water until dissolved. A stir-fry needn't be thickened, particularly if the heat was high enough to have reduced the liquid as it simmered and also if the stir-frying itself was vigorous enough to keep most things from leaching their internal juices over the heat. However, many are indeed thickened, a common enough practice in North America that people have come to expect it. The mixture of cornstarch and water is called a "slurry"; whisk until the cornstarch is thoroughly dissolved in a small bowl, then push the ingredients out of the center of the wok, leaving any liquid in the deep well. Pour the slurry into this and begin stir-frying immediately. The moment the sauce returns to a simmer and thickens somewhat, it's ready. Too much cooking over the heat will certainly cause the cornstarch to lose its vaunted thickening properties.

A wok full of Orange Beef, ready to be spooned over rice.

Recipes for Stir-Frying

	Pork and Vegetable Stir-Fry	Shrimp in Hot Garlic Sauce	Szechwan Scallops	No-Fry Sweet-and-Sour Chicken
1. Heat a wok and swirl in	2 Tbs peanut oil	2 Tbs peanut oil	2 Tbs peanut oil	2 Tbs peanut oil
2. Add and stir-fry until fragrant	3 medium whole scallions, diced 2 Tbs minced peeled fresh ginger 2 tsp red pepper flakes 3 garlic cloves, minced	½ cup dried Chinese red chiles ⅓ cup diced scallions 2 Tbs minced peeled fresh ginger 6 garlic cloves, minced	3 medium whole scallions, diced 2 Tbs minced peeled fresh ginger 2 tsp Szechwan peppercorns 2 garlic cloves, minced	2 ounces shallots, diced 2 Tbs minced peeled fresh ginger 1 tsp red pepper flakes 1 garlic clove, minced
3. Add and stir-fry until almost cooked through	1 pound pork tenderloin, sliced into ¼-inch-thick rounds, then cut into matchsticks	1 pound medium shrimp, peeled and deveined	1 pound sea scallops, each cut into 2 disks (see page 208)	1 pound boneless skinless chicken breasts, cut into thin strips
4. Add and stir-fry until crisp-tender	1 medium red bell pepper, seeded and thinly sliced 1 medium zucchini, diced ¼ cup preserved Chinese bamboo shoots	1 medium onion, sliced into thin rings 1 pound broccoli florets	8 ounces bean sprouts 6 ounces snow peas, thinly sliced ¼ cup chopped canned preserved Szechwan vegetables	1 medium red bell pepper, seeded and thinly sliced 2 celery ribs, thinly sliced ½ cup fresh pineapple chunks or pineapple chunks canned in juice
5. Pour in and bring to a simmer	2 Tbs soy sauce 2 Tbs Chinese bean sauce 1 Tbs rice vinegar 1 Tbs shaoxing or dry sherry	2 Tbs soy sauce 2 Tbs Chinese black bean sauce 1 Tbs Chinese black vinegar 1 Tbs shaoxing or dry sherry 1 tsp chile oil	2 Tbs soy sauce 2 Tbs hot Chinese bean sauce 1 Tbs rice vinegar 1 Tbs shaoxing or dry sherry	2 Tbs soy sauce 2 Tbs hoisin sauce 3 Tbs rice vinegar 1 Tbs shaoxing or dry sherry 1 tsp sugar
6. (optional) Thicken with	1 tsp cornstarch whisked in a small bowl with 2 tsp water until dissolved	Omit	Omit	1 tsp cornstarch whisked in a small bowl with 2 tsp water until dissolved

	Chicken and Black Beans	Orange Beef	Shredded Pork Stir-Fried with Dried Tofu	Lobster Stir-Fried with Chinese Vegetables
1. Heat a wok and swirl in	2 Tbs sesame oil	2 Tbs peanut oil	2 Tbs peanut oil	2 Tbs peanut oil
2. Add and stir-fry until fragrant	6 medium whole scallions, diced 2 tsp red pepper flakes 4 garlic cloves, minced	4 medium whole scallions, diced 3 Tbs thinly sliced orange zest 1 Tbs minced peeled fresh ginger 2 tsp Szechwan peppercorns 6 dried Chinese red chiles 2 garlic cloves, minced	6 medium whole scallions, cut into 1-inch pieces 2 Tbs minced peeled fresh ginger	6 medium whole scallions, cut into 1-inch pieces 2 Tbs minced peeled fresh ginger 2 garlic cloves, slivered
3. Add and stir-fry until almost cooked through	1 pound boneless skinless chicken thighs, diced into small cubes	1 pound beef sirloin, sliced into thin strips against the grain	½ pound pork tenderloin, cut into thin rings and then into matchsticks ½ pound dried tofu, cut into matchsticks	Four ¼-pound frozen lobster tails, meat only, thawed and cut into 1-inch pieces
4. Add and stir-fry until crisp-tender	1 medium yellow onion, sliced into thin rings 1 cup carrots, shredded through the large holes of a box grater 3 ounces snow peas, thinly sliced ¼ cup preserved Chinese black beans, chopped ¼ cup roasted peanuts, chopped	1 large red bell pepper, seeded and cut into thin strips 1 cup canned drained water chestnuts 3 ounces snow peas, thinly sliced ¼ cup preserved Chinese vegetables, preferably Szechwan-style preserved vegetables	6 celery ribs, thinly sliced	½ cup canned bamboo shoots ½ cup jarred baby corn ½ cup sliced canned water chestnuts 1 small red bell pepper, seeded and thinly sliced
5. Pour in and bring to a simmer	2 Tbs soy sauce 2 Tbs Chinese barbecue sauce 1 Tbs rice vinegar 1 Tbs shaoxing or dry sherry	2 Tbs soy sauce 2 Tbs Chinese plum sauce 1 Tbs orange juice concentrate, thawed 1 Tbs shaoxing or dry sherry	2 Tbs soy sauce 2 Tbs chouhee sauce 1 Tbs Chinese black vinegar or ½ Tbs balsamic vinegar and ½ Tbs Worcestershire sauce 1 Tbs shaoxing or dry sherry 1 tsp toasted sesame oil	2 Tbs soy sauce 2 Tbs Chinese bean sauce 1 Tbs rice vinegar 1 Tbs shaoxing or dry sherry
6. (optional) Thicken with	Omit	1 tsp cornstarch whisked in a small bowl with 2 tsp water	1 tsp cornstarch whisked in a small bowl with 2 tsp water	1 tsp cornstarch whisked in a small bowl with 2 tsp water

As the Moroccan Jewish author Edmond Amran El Maleh writes, "A tagine is filled with mystery." Well, maybe for writers. But not really for cooks, because a tagine is a surprisingly easy stew, sweet and aromatic, full of the flavors of North Africa, particularly Morocco and Algeria. Bring the pot to the table, lift the lid, and let the aromas wrap everyone in warmth and comfort. No mystery for you—it's all for them. • MAKES 6 SERVINGS

• **STEP 1** Mix 2 tablespoons (6 teaspoons) Moroccan spice powder with 2½ pounds cubed chicken or lamb until well coated; set aside. As is true for curry powder, there is no one Moroccan blend; however, the individual ingredients are a bit more standardized. The blend should include ground coriander, ground ginger, ground cumin, ground cinnamon, ground black pepper, and probably saffron. Since you'll need 6 teaspoons, consider this the basic formula as follows:

2 teaspoons ground coriander
1 teaspoon ground ginger
1 teaspoon ground cinnamon
1 teaspoon freshly ground black pepper
¾ teaspoon ground cumin
¼ teaspoon saffron

Tweak this blend to your liking: a little more cinnamon, a little less ginger; a little more cumin, a little less black pepper. A Moroccan blend often includes garlic powder—and perhaps that fits your taste, too? A traditional blend can also include dried rose buds, available from spice suppliers on the Web. Grind the buds to a fine powder in a spice grinder; use no more than 1 teaspoon in the total mixture.

Chicken is one of the traditional meats: use cubed boneless skinless thighs; breasts will be overcooked.

Lamb is the other. For the easiest preparation, use lamb stew meat, trimmed a bit of external fat. Or cube a boneless leg of lamb for a more pronounced taste—and more pronounced cooking time, extended by up to 1 hour.

Beef is not traditional—although you could use a cubed chuck or arm roast and increase the cooking time to 3 or 3½ hours. Pork is unheard of, against religious laws.

Why add the spices to the meat rather than warming them later as you would in a Western dish? Partly, yes, because the spices were once used to cover up the smell of bad meat. But mostly because the meat itself needs to pick up their flavors, to be in-

What Is a Tagine?

A tagine is both the cooking vessel and the dish cooked in it. In terms of the vessel, it's a wide, shallow pan, sort of like a sauté pan but with sloping sides, covered by a tall, conical lid. The lid is the real secret: it turns the whole thing into a slow cooker, all moisture sealed inside, swirling above the food, condensing, and dripping back into the sauce. For this technique, the tagine itself must be flame-safe; be careful of ceramic ones with reactive dyes, no good if you add an acidic fruit or wine. A small Dutch oven is a fine (if a bit less effective) substitute.

For a proper tagine, the cubed meat is mixed with the dried spices until well coated.

Once the aromatics have softened and the meat has browned, the long-cooking vegetables are scattered over the top before the final round of cooking.

fused not just with its own caramelized taste, but with something more complex, more redolent.

If you'd like to make a root vegetable tagine, use peeled carrots, turnips, potatoes, sweet potatoes, and/or seeded winter squash such as butternut or acorn squash. You'll also need to use more than 2½ pounds because they shrink dramatically when cooked—maybe as much as 4 pounds. Since there are roots as this technique's base in step 5, you'll need to use other vegetables besides, perhaps vegetables like broccoli or cauliflower florets, green beans, or peas. Finally, add more liquid, about 1 cup, in step 6—perhaps ¾ cup broth and ¼ cup wine.

• **STEP 2** Heat 3 tablespoons oil in a 2½-quart tagine or a 3- or 4-quart Dutch oven over medium heat. Use a neutral oil (canola, corn, or safflower), peanut oil, or even olive oil, more fragrant, more tilted to the Mediterranean than to Africa. Some Moroccan cooks use unsalted butter, a rich addition and not really necessary to the success of the dish. Nut oils, toasted or not, as well as seed oils have no part here—partly because nuts will later be added to the dish.

• **STEP 3** Add 1½ cups thinly sliced aromatics and cook, stirring often, just until softened, about 3 minutes. Raise the heat to high and add the meat with all its spices; stir over the heat until it loses its raw color and browns slightly, about 5 minutes. Thinly sliced, the aromatics are a better foil to the stew, long threads that slowly melt into the broth, giving the stew more texture when served. And onion is the best bet, although you can certainly try shallots or even leeks, all of which can perhaps be spiked by minced peeled fresh ginger or garlic—but remember: a little of either goes a long way since one or even both may be in the dried spice blend coating the meat.

Cook the aromatics just until softened, no more than a few minutes. Do not let them brown. Then add the meat, stirring constantly to make sure the spices do not burn. There should be almost no bitter notes in a tagine.

To be honest, browning the meat is not traditional in a tagine. That caramelization we prize is not held in such high esteem in many other cultures. Most Chinese stews, for example, involve no browned ingredients. Still, a little browning is worth the compromise in authenticity, enriching the sauce and balancing the sweet ingredients in the next step.

• **STEP 4** Stir in ¾ cup chopped dried fruit, ¼ cup chopped nuts, and 1 tablespoon honey. Here's the final flavor in the sauce before it's left to its own devices. For dried fruit, consider not only raisins, dried cherries, dried cranberries, and chopped dried pineapple, but also pitted dates (do not use the sugared varieties or any glacéed fruit used in candy making) as well as sun-dried tomatoes (tomatoes are, after all, technically a fruit), pitted olives (another fruit, green or black), or sliced preserved lemon, perhaps the most traditional ingredient and available at Middle Eastern markets or near the olives or roasted red peppers in some supermarkets.

The nuts can range from walnuts to skinned hazelnuts (see page 217 for how to skin them), but almonds are the most traditional. Avoid peanuts (legumes anyway), cashews (fruit anyway), and any seed.

Finally, the quality of the honey has a direct impact on the quality of the dish. Search out aromatic varieties; pine tree, oak, or chestnut would be particularly stunning.

A traditional tagine lid creates a steam-pressure bath that tenderizes the meat while keeping every drop of juice for the sauce.

• **STEP 5** Scatter 3 cups canned, drained chickpeas and/or roughly chopped vegetables over the meat mixture. Lay all these over the top of the stew so they leach their flavors into the sauce without necessarily drowning in its flavors. In other words, they'll be more purely themselves, interesting flavor accents in the final dish.

For vegetables, consider roots first and foremost: carrots, parsnips, turnips, potatoes, or sweet potatoes. Any of these should be peeled and seeded, if necessary; then they should be cut into ½-inch pieces.

Or try slightly more international combinations like 2 cups canned, drained chickpeas and 1 medium sliced seeded green bell pepper. Or what about 1 cup chickpeas; 1 large carrot, sliced into ½-inch rounds; and 1½ cups frozen quartered artichoke halves? Keep in mind that winter squash, sweet potatoes, carrots, and rutabagas are quite sweet; there's already honey in the stew. Balance sweet vegetables with earthier notes: potatoes, celery, or quartered Brussels sprouts.

If you're making a root tagine, as suggested in step 1, use other vegetables here: perhaps celery, fennel, or sliced, seeded green bell peppers. None is really traditional—but a strictly root vegetable tagine is not all that traditional either.

• **STEP 6** Pour ¼ cup wine, broth, or an enhanced version of either. Cover, reduce the heat to very low, and cook until the meat is tender, between 1½ and 3 hours. Season with salt to taste. Very little liquid goes in a tagine because every ingredient will steam and/or braise, releasing its juices and creating a sauce. But a little liquid helps things get moving at the start.

Enhance the wine or broth, not with a dairy product or coconut milk, but with a dry fortified wine like dry sherry (perhaps 1 tablespoon of the total amount), dry Madeira, or even a tiny splash of orange-flower water or rose water.

Get that lid tightly in place and let the stew cook over very, very low heat, just the barest simmer so nothing falls apart and the liquid doesn't boil away. The chicken thighs will need about 1½ hours; the lamb, between 2 and 2½ hours. The only way to tell is it's done: Cut and taste a piece. If you've made a root tagine, check it after 1½ hours—it may well need a little more time.

Season with salt and check the sauce—which may be a little soupy. Some cooks prefer it this way, ladled over plain couscous. Or thicken it somewhat. Remove the lid and raise the heat to medium-high, bringing the sauce to a full simmer, even a low boil, without disturbing the vegetables on top. Cook just until slightly thickened, about 5 minutes. Tilt the pan one way or another to see how thick the sauce is at the bottom. Once it's slightly thickened, remove the pan from the heat and set the lid back in place; set aside for 5 minutes before serving.

Lamb Tagine with Cranberries and Pecans

Recipes for Tagines

1. Mix together	Chicken Tagine with Artichokes, Dates and Almonds	Chicken Tagine with Preserved Lemon and Walnuts	Lamb Tagine with Sweet Potatoes and Dried Apricots	Lamb Tagine with Brussels Sprouts and Pistachios
1. Mix together	2 tsp ground coriander 1 tsp ground ginger 1 tsp ground cinnamon 1 tsp ground black pepper ¾ tsp ground cumin ¼ tsp saffron 2½ pounds boneless skinless chicken thighs, cut into 2-inch pieces	2 tsp ground coriander 2 tsp ground cinnamon 1 tsp ground cumin ½ tsp ground black pepper ¼ tsp ground ginger ¼ tsp saffron 2½ pounds boneless skinless chicken thighs, cut into 2-inch pieces	2 tsp ground cinnamon 1½ tsp ground coriander 1 tsp ground ginger 1 tsp ground cumin ½ tsp ground black pepper ¼ tsp saffron 2½ pounds lamb stew meat, trimmed and cut into 2-inch pieces	2 tsp ground coriander 1½ tsp ground cumin 1 tsp ground cinnamon 1 tsp ground black pepper ¼ tsp ground ginger ¼ tsp saffron 2½ pounds lamb stew meat, trimmed and cut into 2-inch pieces
2. Heat	3 Tbs canola oil	3 Tbs canola oil	3 Tbs canola oil	3 Tbs canola oil
3. Add, cook, then stir in	1 large yellow onion, thinly sliced The spiced meat	1 large yellow onion, thinly sliced 2 garlic cloves, minced The spiced meat	2 large leeks, white and pale green parts only, halved lengthwise, washed carefully, and thinly sliced 1 Tbs minced peeled fresh ginger The spiced meat	1 large yellow onion, thinly sliced 2 garlic cloves, minced The spiced meat
4. Stir in	¾ cup chopped pitted dates ¼ cup chopped slivered almonds 1 Tbs honey	¾ cup chopped preserved lemon ¼ cup chopped walnut pieces 1 Tbs honey	¾ cup chopped dried apricots ¼ cup chopped slivered almonds 1 Tbs honey	¾ cup chopped dried mango ¼ cup unsalted pistachios 1 Tbs honey
5. Scatter over the top	1 medium carrot, sliced into ½-inch rounds 2 cups frozen quartered artichokes	2 medium parsnips, cut into ½-inch rounds 1 cup fresh shelled or frozen peas	2 medium sweet potatoes, peeled and cut into 1-inch cubes	1 pound small Brussels sprouts, stemmed
6. Pour in, cover, and cook—then season	¼ cup dry white wine Salt to taste	3 Tbs chicken broth 1 Tbs pomegranate molasses Salt to taste	3½ Tbs vegetable broth ½ Tbs orange-flower water Salt to taste	¼ cup dry white wine Salt to taste

	Veal Tagine with Golden Raisins and Butternut Squash	Beef Tagine with Carrots and Figs	Lamb Tagine with Cranberries and Pecans	Root Vegetable Tagine
1. Mix together	2 tsp ground cinnamon 1 tsp ground coriander 1 tsp ground ginger 1 tsp onion powder ¾ tsp ground black pepper ¼ tsp saffron 2½ pounds veal stew meat, trimmed and cut into 2-inch pieces	2 tsp ground coriander 1½ tsp ground cinnamon 1 tsp ground cumin 1 tsp ground ginger ¾ tsp ground cumin ¼ tsp saffron 2½ pounds beef stew meat, trimmed and cut into 2-inch pieces	2 tsp ground coriander 1 tsp ground ginger 1 tsp ground cumin 1 tsp ground cinnamon 1 tsp ground black pepper 2½ pounds lamb stew meat, trimmed and cut into 2-inch pieces	2 tsp ground cinnamon 1 tsp ground coriander 1 tsp ground ginger 1 tsp ground cumin ½ tsp grated nutmeg ¼ tsp garlic powder ¼ tsp saffron 2 medium yellow-fleshed potatoes, peeled and cut into 1½-inch pieces 2 medium parsnips, cut into 1-inch rounds 1 medium turnip, peeled and cut into 1-inch pieces 1 medium carrot, cut into 1-inch pieces
2. Heat	3 Tbs canola oil	3 Tbs canola oil	3 Tbs canola oil	3 Tbs olive oil
3. Add, cook, then stir in	1 large yellow onion, halved and very thinly sliced The spiced meat	1 large red onion, halved and very thinly sliced The spiced meat	4 ounces shallots, thinly sliced The spiced meat	6 ounces shallots, thinly sliced The spiced root vegetables
4. Stir in	¾ cup chopped golden raisins ¼ cup pine nuts 1 Tbs honey	¾ cup quartered dried figs ¼ cup chopped walnut pieces 1 Tbs honey	¾ cup chopped dried cranberries ¼ cup chopped pecan pieces 1 Tbs honey	¾ cup chopped dried apricots ¼ cup chopped walnut pieces 1 Tbs honey
5. Scatter over the top	1 small butternut squash, peeled, halved, seeded, and cut into small cubes	2 medium carrots, peeled and cut into 1-inch sections	2 medium sweet potatoes, peeled and diced	3 cups cauliflower florets
6. Pour in, cover, and cook—then season	¼ cup dry white wine 1 Tbs pomegranate molasses Salt to taste	¼ cup unsweetened apple cider Salt to taste	3 Tbs chicken broth 1 Tbs pomegranate molasses Salt to taste	¾ cup vegetable broth ¼ cup dry vermouth Salt to taste

Thai Curry

As endlessly adaptable as East Indian Curry (page 112), Thai Curry includes a wet spice paste, coconut milk, plenty of vegetables, and a traditional set of Thai condiments and seasonings. There are actually hundreds of regional versions, all made with different curry pastes and a wide variety of ingredients. Although some Thai curries are quite complicated, this technique is the boiled-down essence, more of an easy weeknight dinner. • MAKES 4 SERVINGS

• **STEP 1** Heat 1 tablespoon oil in a Dutch oven over medium heat. As usual, most spicy dishes should begin with a neutral oil. In Thai Curry, there's going to be so much flavor and heat that peanut, canola, safflower, vegetable, corn, or sunflower oil is the best choice—less interaction, more flavor simply carried unchanged by the fat.

• **STEP 2** Add 1 cup roughly chopped aromatics, about 3 tablespoons minced peeled fresh ginger, and up to 2 tablespoons Thai curry paste; cook, stirring often, until the vegetable has softened and the mélange is fragrant, about 3 minutes. Sliced scallions are the usual beginning of a Southeast Asian stew, but there's no reason not to use onions, shallots, or leeks—with this difference: think how scallions will appear in the dish, floating in the coconut milk. Perhaps cut into 1-inch strips then? In like manner, any aromatic should be roughly chopped, certainly not diced or minced. No, you don't want a 1-inch piece of leek; but you do want a little more chew than what would be in a run-of-the-mill braise. The aromatics in this curry will not melt; they will instead become part of the larger vegetable mixture.

Pre-minced ginger is available in the produce section of most supermarkets. Buy it in a clear jar so you can see what you're getting: pale beige, never browned, and not water-logged. Still, fresh ginger is best, more aromatic and certainly more flavorful. See page 150 for tips on peeling and mincing it.

The holy trinity of Thai cooking (clockwise from left): lime juice, fish sauce, and palm sugar—or brown sugar, its more accessible substitute.

Thai curry paste
Packaged blends, found in high-end and specialty food markets, can be ridiculously hot. Red and green varieties are on fire; yellow, only a little less so. Don't go crazy until you get the hang of it—consider using less than 1 tablespoon of the purchased stuff the first time you make this dish. And read the labels carefully; the first or second ingredient should be lemongrass. If it's mostly chiles, it will be lacerating; if mostly oil, tame and senseless.

THAI CURRY SPICE BLENDS

Green Thai Curry Paste: Two 2-inch pieces lemongrass, 5 stemmed serrano or Thai hot chiles, 3 quartered garlic cloves, 2 teaspoons whole black peppercorns, 2 tsp cumin seeds, and 1 teaspoon ground coriander.

Hanglay (Burmese-Style) Curry Paste: Two 2-inch pieces lemongrass, 2 quartered garlic cloves, 1 stemmed serrano or Thai hot chile, 1 tablespoon cumin seeds, 2 teaspoons ground coriander, 1 teaspoon turmeric, 1 teaspoon tamarind concentrate

Masaman Curry Paste: One 2-inch piece lemongrass, 2 quartered garlic cloves, 2 stemmed serrano chiles, 3 cardamom pods, 1 teaspoon ground cumin, 1 teaspoon ground cinnamon, ¼ teaspoon grated nutmeg

Penang Curry Paste: One 2-inch piece lemongrass, 1 stemmed serrano or Thai hot chile, 1 quartered garlic clove, 3 tablespoons cilantro leaves, 2 tablespoons unsalted roasted peanuts, 1 teaspoon ground coriander

Red Thai Curry Paste: One 2-inch piece lemongrass, 2 dried seeded New Mexican red chiles (toasted in a small skillet, then covered with boiling water for 15 minutes and drained), 4 quartered garlic cloves, 1 tablespoon lime zest

Yellow Thai Curry Paste: One 2-inch piece lemongrass, 1 seeded serrano or Thai hot chile, 1 quartered garlic clove, 2 whole cloves, 1 tablespoon cumin seeds, 1 teaspoon ground coriander, 1 teaspoon ground cinnamon

But why settle for someone else's blend? To build your own, you'll need a sturdy spice grinder—then follow these four steps.

1. Start with one or two 2-inch pieces of lemongrass, white part only. Crush them with a meat mallet or the bottom of a heavy pot, then place in the grinder.
2. Add some quartered garlic cloves and one or several stemmed, small chiles, preferably serranos or Thai hots, seeded or not at your discretion. Give all these a few-seconds' grind until finely chopped, a little pulpy.
3. Add small amounts (a teaspoon or two) of one or several of these spices: a few cardamom pods, some ground coriander, poppy seeds, sesame seeds, ground cinnamon (particularly Vietnamese cinnamon), and/or grated nutmeg.
4. Then add smaller amounts of these spices at your discretion: cumin seeds, ground allspice, cumin, mace, or celery seeds. Adding fenugreek or fennel will skew the dish toward India—not a bad thing, just a note. And dried herbs—thyme, tarragon, parsley—add a nice, nosy touch, good with complex vegetable medleys. But skip basil now; it will be added fresh in step 5. Once everything is in the grinder, give it all a good whirl until quite pasty and uniform.

Any of these will make more than you need. Store the rest in a small jar in the freezer for up to 3 months; allow it to come back to room temperature before using.

And finally, one addition, completely optional but key to authentic Southeast Asian cooking: shrimp paste (*kapi* in Thai, *mam tom* in Vietnamese, and *belacan* in Malay). It's available in most Asian markets and from online suppliers. Made from fermented shrimp, usually left out in the sun to liquefy and decay, shrimp paste is notoriously pungent, like old socks wrapped in seaweed, rotted and fishy. (Malaysian varieties are actually buried to ferment them further.) Thai varieties are often quite dark; Vietnamese, a bit lighter; those from Hong Kong, lighter still. Higher-quality products, by and large, have a less (if only slightly less) pungent smell. If you're adventurous, use shrimp paste in this recipe either by putting ½ to 1 teaspoon in the spice grinder with the other spices or by crumbling a like amount into a powder and adding it with a purchased Thai curry paste (provided the packaged product doesn't already have it in the mix—read the label).

• **STEP 3** Pour in 1¾ cups coconut milk and ½ cup secondary, complementary liquid; bring to a simmer and cook for 1 minute. Coconut milk is made by cooking coconut flesh in water, then straining out the solids. In general, stir it up before adding it to a dish so that any solids, fallen out of suspension, re-liquefy and turn smooth. Light coconut milk is simply the second (or further) pressing of the same solids, much of the fat having already been pressed out. Either will work here. Do not use cream of coconut, a sweetened concoction for cocktails.

The secondary or complementary liquid can be a range of clear liquids: broth, wine, dry vermouth, dry sherry, unsweetened apple juice, or unsweetened pineapple juice—in other words, a clear liquid that will somehow enhance the taste of the coconut milk.

• **STEP 4** Stir in 1¼ pounds cubed, sliced, or shredded protein and cook for 2 to 10 minutes, until almost cooked through. Nothing's browned, just added to the pan. Basically, chose anything you would choose for a stir-fry:

beef sirloin, cut into thin strips
boneless skinless chicken breasts, cut into thin strips
boneless skinless chicken thighs, trimmed and roughly chopped
clams (use 4 pounds and a bigger saucepan because of the shells), scrubbed
dried tofu (see page 147), cubed
fish, firm-fleshed like halibut or monkfish tail, cubed
lamb loin, cut into thin rounds
pork loin, trimmed, cut into thin rounds, and then these cut
     into matchsticks
scallops, bay or sea, the latter cut into two disks (see page 208)
shrimp, medium (about 30 per pound), peeled, deveined, and
     perhaps roughly chopped if larger than bite-size

The time it will cook will depend on what's used: shrimp and scallops, only a few minutes; pork loin, maybe up to 10 minutes, depending on the cut.

If you want to make a vegetarian stew, omit this step and add 8 cups vegetables in the next.

• **STEP 5** Add 4 cups cubed or prepared vegetables, ¼ cup chopped fresh basil, 1 tablespoon lime juice, 1 tablespoon grated palm sugar (or light brown sugar), and 1 tablespoon fish sauce. Bring to a simmer, stir well, cover, reduce the heat to low, and simmer slowly until the **vegetables are tender**, about 15 minutes. The easiest choices are the quick-cooking vegetables: peas, yellow squash, celery, mushrooms, bell peppers, snow peas, green beans, Chinese long beans, broccoli florets, and the like. If you use broccoli stems, make sure they are cut into small cubes. In like manner, pare down

Jarred Thai curry paste (left) is often drier and less cohesive than homemade. It also relies more heavily on chiles for its flavor.

A final squeeze of lime juice brightens up a pot of Thai Shrimp Curry.

winter squash, sweet potatoes, or regular spuds. Peel and chop them into ¼-inch cubes. They've only got 15 minutes or so over the heat; they need to be small to get tender.

If you can find Thai basil, purple and with a spicy, licorice-like taste, by all means add it here. Or if you find holy basil, a spicy East-Indian herb from the same family, flavored more with cinnamon and nutmeg, try that as well. But good old-fashioned Mediterranean basil will work wonders, an aromatic punch in this creamy braise.

You've probably heard of the various "holy trinities" of culinary lore: onions, celery, and carrots for the French; onions, celery, and green bell peppers the Cajuns. The holy trinity of Thai cooking is lime juice, sugar, and fish sauce.

Fish sauce—*nam pla* in Thai, *nuoc mom* in Vietnamese, *teuk trai* in Cambodian, and sometimes labeled "fish gravy" in Hong Kong bottlings—is a salty condiment, the soy sauce of Southeast Asia. By and large, Thai bottlings are more aromatic; Vietnamese, sweeter; and Chinese, milder—but there are as many types of fish sauce as there are regional and national enclaves. Higher-quality bottlings have a markedly more aromatic flavor, but all are made with fermented fish: most from fresh fish, a few from dried. The best include additional spices (ginger and other aromatics); the worst, just doused with MSG or soy sauce. While fish sauce smells pungent in the bottle, it mellows beautifully over the heat. If the idea of fish sauce bothers you, consider that there is a Western derivation, brought back to Europe during the British Raj in India: Worcestershire sauce, made from fermented, salted anchovies.

If you can find it, use finely grated palm sugar, a product of the sap of the flowering stalks of palm trees, boiled down in large kettles and then preserved in cakes. Thai varietals are by and large paler, silkier, and sweeter than Malaysian or Indonesian varietals. If you can lay your hands on this specialty product, usually available in hard cakes, by all means grate 1 tablespoon into the sauce. It's substitute, brown sugar, is not traditional, but rather a bow to the North American supermarket.

A good Thai curry should be served over a good rice. Jasmine, basmati, Texmati, or other fragrant long-grains come to mind, but don't neglect a short-grain, glutinous rice, often labeled as "sticky rice" or "sweet rice" in Asian markets. The sticky grains will hold the coconut sauce much as the starch on pasta holds a cream sauce.

Recipes for Thai Curries

	Thai Chicken Curry	Thai Shrimp Curry	Masaman Beef Curry	Penang Fish Curry
1. Heat	1 Tbs canola oil	1 Tbs peanut oil	1 Tbs peanut oil	1 Tbs peanut oil
2. Add and cook	1 medium onion, sliced into thin rings 3 Tbs minced peeled fresh ginger Up to 2 Tbs red or yellow Thai curry paste	4 medium whole scallions, thinly sliced 3 Tbs minced peeled fresh ginger Up to 2 Tbs yellow Thai curry paste	4 ounces shallots, chopped 3 Tbs minced peeled fresh ginger Up to 2 Tbs Masaman curry paste	1 medium onion, sliced into thin rings 3 Tbs minced peeled fresh ginger Up to 2 Tbs Penang curry paste
3. Pour in	1¾ cups coconut milk ½ cup dry white wine	1¾ cups coconut milk ½ cup dry vermouth	1¾ cups coconut milk ½ cup dry sherry	1¾ cups coconut milk ½ cup dry white wine
4. Stir in	1¼ pounds boneless skinless chicken breasts, cut into thin strips	1¼ pounds medium shrimp, peeled, deveined, and roughly chopped	1¼ pounds beef sirloin, thinly sliced	1¼ pounds monkfish, cubed
5. Add, cover, and simmer	1 medium red bell pepper, seeded and chopped 2 medium yellow summer squash, chopped ¼ cup chopped basil 1 Tbs lime juice 1 Tbs grated palm sugar or light brown sugar 1 Tbs fish sauce	6 ounces snow peas, roughly chopped 1 large tart green apple, peeled, seeded, and chopped 4 garlic scapes, roughly chopped ¼ cup chopped basil 1 Tbs lime juice 1 Tbs grated palm sugar or light brown sugar 1 Tbs fish sauce	1 pound green beans, sliced ¼ cup chopped basil 1 Tbs lime juice 1 Tbs grated palm sugar or light brown sugar 1 Tbs fish sauce	1 medium red bell pepper, seeded and chopped ½ pound sugar snap peas ¼ cup chopped basil 1 Tbs lime juice 1 Tbs grated palm sugar or light brown sugar 1 Tbs fish sauce

	Burmese Curry	Red Thai Curry	Green Thai Curry	Vegetarian Yellow Thai Curry
1. Heat	1 Tbs canola oil	1 Tbs canola oil	1 Tbs canola oil	1 Tbs canola oil
2. Add and cook	4 medium whole scallions, thinly sliced 3 Tbs minced peeled fresh ginger Up to 2 Tbs Hanglay curry paste	1 medium yellow onion, sliced into thin rings 3 Tbs minced peeled fresh ginger Up to 2 Tbs red Thai curry paste	4 ounces shallots, thinly sliced 3 Tbs minced peeled fresh ginger Up to 2 Tbs green Thai curry paste	1 medium yellow onion, sliced into thin rings 3 Tbs minced peeled fresh ginger Up to 2 Tbs yellow Thai curry paste
3. Pour in	1¾ cups coconut milk ½ cup fish broth or clam juice	1¾ cups coconut milk ½ cup chicken broth	1¾ cups coconut milk ½ cup unsweetened pineapple juice	1¾ cups coconut milk ½ cup dry sherry
4. Stir in	1¼ pounds medium shrimp, peeled, deveined, and chopped	1¼ pounds boneless skinless chicken thighs, roughly chopped	1¼ pounds dried tofu (see page 149), sliced into matchsticks	Omit
5. Add, cover, and simmer	1 cup drained, canned chickpeas 1 medium carrot, thinly sliced ½ small Napa cabbage head, cored and shredded ¼ cup chopped basil 1 Tbs lime juice 1 Tbs grated palm sugar or light brown sugar 1 Tbs fish sauce	2 medium yellow-fleshed potatoes, peeled and diced 12 ounces Chinese long beans, thinly sliced ¼ cup chopped basil 1 Tbs lime juice 1 Tbs grated palm sugar or light brown sugar 1 Tbs fish sauce	1 yellow bell pepper, seeded and chopped 1 cup roughly chopped jarred chestnuts 1 medium yellow summer squash, cubed ¼ cup chopped basil 1 Tbs lime juice 1 Tbs grated palm sugar or light brown sugar 1 Tbs fish sauce	1 medium butternut squash, peeled, halved, seeded, and chopped 8 ounces cremini mushrooms, thinly sliced 1 medium green bell pepper, seeded and chopped ¼ cup chopped basil 1 Tbs lime juice 1 Tbs grated palm sugar or light brown sugar 1 Tbs fish sauce

Veggie Burgers

The best way to make a veggie burger is with beans or lentils—and the best way to top it is with cole slaw, whether purchased or homemade, vinegar-based or mayonnaise-laced. Have other condiments on hand, too—and lots of napkins.

• MAKES 4 BURGER PATTIES

• **STEP 1** Cook 1 cup chopped aromatics with 1 tablespoon oil in a medium skillet until softened and very lightly browned, stirring often, about 4 minutes. Pour the contents of the skillet into a food processor fitted with the chopping blade. A good veggie burger starts with a solid base. A medium yellow onion is the natural here; but also consider shallots or cleaned and sliced leeks (white and pale green parts only). Yes, scallions will work, but they turn the mixture a depressingly neon green, tasty but none too appealing.

Add a minced garlic clove or perhaps two—but be careful: made with mild lentils or beans, veggie burgers are easily over-whelmed. (Indeed, this warning will become the mantra of this technique.) You don't want to make a garlic burger.

The same can be said for minced peeled fresh ginger. A little? Sure. But more than 2 teaspoons? Overkill. Besides, ginger would need to be balanced by more complex herbs in the next step—or by a blend like curry powder (page 113) or garam masala (page 27).

A food processor is essential for making Veggie Burgers at home.

• **STEP 2** Add 1¾ cups cooked or canned and drained beans, lentils, or chickpeas, ½ cup roughly chopped nuts, ½ cup rolled oats, 1 large egg, a little dried spice or minced herb, 1 teaspoon salt, and some freshly ground black pepper. Pulse until grainy but well combined. The amount of beans called for is about a 15-ounce can. Of course, you can make them from scratch, soaking about ¾ cup dried beans in water overnight, then boiling them in a large pot of water over low heat until tender, perhaps 1 hour or so. But this seems beyond the pale. After all, the beans will be ground in the food processor.

Still, for lentil burgers, you'll most likely have to cook your own. Place about 1 cup brown or green lentils in a large saucepan, cover with water to a depth of 3 inches, bring to a boil, reduce the heat to low, and simmer until tender, about 15 minutes. Drain them over the sink through a fine-mesh sieve. Do not use yellow or red lentils, Southeast Asian and East Indian favorites that would disintegrate into a mush before they could be properly processed in this dish.

Once processed, the mixture is quite grainy but lacks any chunks or hard bits.

Fry the veggie patties to a deep golden brown, a little texture on their outside to contrast with the creamy, soft insides.

That all said, check the salad bar at your market. There may be undressed, cooked lentils in the line-up. Indeed, the salad bar can be a fine place to shop for a recipe like this: there's that one rib of celery, that one carrot, that roasted garlic clove.

Any nut will do for Veggie Burgers: walnut, pecans, hazelnuts (the latter must be skinned—see page 217). There's no need to toast any of these; in fact, it's better if you don't. The intense flavor will override everything else. Besides, they will toast in the mixture once they're fried in the patties.

Also try cashews or peanuts. In either case, use unsalted varieties; but also in either case, use roasted versions—or toast these in a dry skillet until lightly browned. Since neither is a nut, both need a little boost to avoid becoming relentlessly dull.

As to herbs and spices, less is definitely more. Use no more than 1 teaspoon dried spice total—for instance, a combination of, say, ½ teaspoon ground cumin and ½ teaspoon ground cinnamon. Indeed, there's nothing wrong with adding ¼ teaspoon grated nutmeg and calling it quits. For fresh herbs—basil, rosemary, and such—use no more than 1 minced tablespoon.

You can also add a flavoring agent: barbecue sauce, ketchup, prepared mustard, jarred horseradish, chutney, mashed roasted garlic cloves, pesto, or minced sun-dried tomatoes—but again, less is more. Use no more than 1 teaspoon; the beans or lentils will carry the flavors extraordinarily well.

The nuts provide most of the fat and an earthy richness; the oats are the binding agent (along with the egg). Do not use quick-cooking or steel-cut oats. There's no need to go through the extra step of toasting the oats. In fact, don't. Toasted oats lose some of their adhering properties; the patties are more likely to fall apart over the heat.

Pulse in the food processor; don't process. There's no reason to turn this into a paste. Instead, you want a little of the nuts' crunchiness, a little of the beans' hulls, all mixed together into a fairly uniform mass that still has some texture. Baby food is no adult's dinner.

• **STEP 3** Shape the mixture into four patties. Heat 1 tablespoon fat in a large skillet over medium heat and fry the patties until darkly browned, even a little crunchy, turning once, about 7 minutes. The mixture can be a little sticky, thanks to the beans' starches, the oats, and the egg. It helps to refrigerate it an hour or so, but it's not necessary. Wet your hands and scoop up about ½ cup of the mixture. (But first remove that blade from the food processor!) Shape into a patty about 4 inches in diameter and about ½ inch thick, then repeat with the remaining mixture, setting the patties aside on a cutting board.

The oil you use is largely a matter of taste: unsalted butter will burn slightly and turn a little bitter. Ghee (see page 25) might be a better substitute. Or what about walnut oil? There will then be even more nutty flavor. Sesame oil? A great pair to

Asian flavorings. Almond oil? Pale and enticing. Canola oil? An effortless way to let the flavors in the patty come through. Rendered bacon fat? Probably not. Why are you making veggie burgers in the first place?

Pick up the patties with a metal spatula and slide them into the skillet. If your skillet won't hold them all, make them in batches, adding another tablespoon of fat for each batch. Veggie burgers will not freeze well; but once they've been cooked, they can be refrigerated for a day or two and crisped again in a skillet with a little oil.

Once out of the pan, it's your business to turn them into burgers. On whole wheat buns topped with carrot-and-raisin salad? In pita pockets and shredded lettuce and a buttermilk dressing? Or toasted English muffins with chutney and a thin slice of red onion? Or just the good ol' fashioned backyard way: on white buns with pickle relish.

A summertime treat: White Bean and Sage Burger

Recipes for Veggie Burgers

	Lentil Burgers	Black Bean Burgers	Moroccan Chickpea Burgers	Pinto Bean Burgers with Pine Nuts
1. Cook	1 Tbs canola oil 1 medium yellow onion, chopped	1 Tbs canola oil 4 ounces shallots, chopped	1 Tbs canola oil 1 medium yellow onion, chopped 1 minced garlic clove	1 Tbs canola oil 1 medium yellow onion, chopped 1 minced garlic clove
2. Add and process	1¾ cups cooked lentils ½ cup walnut pieces ½ cup rolled oats 1 large egg 1 tsp chili powder 1 tsp salt Ground black pepper	1¾ cups cooked or canned and drained black beans ½ cup sliced almonds ½ cup rolled oats 1 large egg ½ tsp ground cinnamon 1 tsp salt Ground black pepper	1¾ cups canned, drained chickpeas ½ cup walnut pieces ½ cup rolled oats 1 large egg ½ tsp ground cardamom ¼ tsp ground cumin ¼ tsp ground cinnamon 1 tsp salt Ground black pepper	1¾ cups cooked or canned and drained pinto beans ½ cup pine nuts ½ cup rolled oats 1 large egg ½ tsp ground cinnamon ½ tsp ground cumin 1 tsp salt Ground black pepper
3. Shape into patties; fry	1 Tbs canola oil	1 Tbs canola oil	1 Tbs olive oil	1 Tbs canola oil

	White Bean and Sage Burger	Curried Veggie Burgers	Kidney Bean Chile Burgers	Bistro Veggie Burgers
1. Cook	1 Tbs olive oil 4 ounces shallots, chopped	1 Tbs canola oil 1 medium yellow onion, chopped 1 Tbs minced peeled fresh ginger 1 garlic clove, minced	1 Tbs canola oil 1 small red onion, chopped 1 garlic clove, minced	1 Tbs unsalted butter 1 medium yellow onion, chopped
2. Add and process	1¾ cups cooked or canned and drained white beans ½ cup sliced almonds ½ cup rolled oats 1 large egg 1 Tbs minced sage 1 tsp salt Ground black pepper	1¾ cups cooked lentils ½ cup cashews ½ cup rolled oats 1 large egg 1 tsp curry powder (see page 113) 1 tsp salt Ground black pepper	1¾ cups cooked or canned and drained red kidney beans ½ cup walnut pieces ½ cup rolled oats 1 large egg 1 Tbs chili powder 1 tsp salt Ground black pepper	1¾ cups cooked or canned and drained red kidney beans ½ cup skinned chopped hazelnuts ½ cup rolled oats 1 large egg 1 Tbs minced tarragon 1 tsp Dijon mustard 1 tsp salt Ground black pepper
3. Shape into patties; fry	1 Tbs olive oil	1 Tbs mustard oil or ghee (see page 25)	1 Tbs canola oil	1 Tbs olive oil

Vindaloo

East Indian restaurants in North America notwithstanding, vindaloo is not the hottest thing on the menu. Rather, it's first and foremost aromatic, and then pleasingly spicy. Vindaloo is originally a Portuguese dish (the name is a corruption of the Portuguese for "wine and garlic") and should be a well-balanced stew, rather than a sensory overload. • MAKES 6 HEARTY SERVINGS

• **STEP 1** Heat ¼ cup ghee or oil in a large Dutch oven over medium-low heat. Ghee is the best fulcrum for the spices. (See page 25 for an explanation and even a way to make your own.) Don't use plain unsalted butter—the heat will eventually scald the milk solids before the stew has a chance to develop its aromatic appeal.

Also, don't use nut or seed oils (too strong) or olive oil (too European—the dish may be originally Portuguese, but there shouldn't be much left from back home). Rather, stick with a simple, neutral oil: canola, sunflower, corn, or the like. Peanut oil is a fine balance between the richness of ghee and the neutral canvas of canola oil.

• **STEP 2** Add 3 medium yellow onions, halved and thinly sliced, and ¼ cup chopped dried fruit; cook, stirring often, until golden and sweet, about 10 minutes. Cut the onion in half through the stem end, then turn it cut side down on your cutting board and cut down in thin slices. Separate the layers so there are lots of little half-rings.

Chop up any dried fruit you like: golden raisins or dried currants as well as dried mango, pineapple, nectarines, papaya, cherries, blueberries, or even dried strawberries. The point is to get a little sweetness in the stew without resorting to sugar—and to add the pleasant, appetizing taste of fruit to the heat. To that end, you can even use chopped, unsweetened coconut (sometimes called "desiccated coconut").

The onions should not brown. All brown coloration will come from the paste in the next step. Rather, stir them over the heat until golden and quite soft. If you notice browning, reduce the heat further.

• **STEP 3** Add 2 to 3 tablespoons prepared vindaloo paste; cook, stirring constantly, until aromatic, about 20 seconds. Now the dish takes off. If desired, use purchased vindaloo paste, available at East Indian markets and some high-end supermarkets, as well as from suppliers on the Web. Read the label carefully. Is the paste all cayenne? Is it labeled "extra hot"? Consider instead a milder variant, one more in keeping with the aromatic nature of this stew. In any event, do not use a vindaloo curry powder, too dry for this dish.

Or you can make your own vindaloo paste. Grind with a pestle in a mortar or whir together in a mini food processor or a spice grinder:

Rather than chopping the onion, cut it in half, then slice it into half-moon rings, which will not dissolve as readily as diced bits over the heat.

The onions and dried fruit should be well coated in the vindaloo paste before the meat is added.

6 garlic cloves, quartered
2 tablespoons red wine vinegar
1 tablespoon minced peeled fresh ginger
1 to 2 teaspoons cayenne
1½ teaspoons salt
1 teaspoon dry mustard
1 teaspoon ground cumin
1 teaspoon ground coriander
½ teaspoon ground cardamom
½ teaspoon ground cloves
¼ teaspoon ground mace

Of course, you can play with these ingredients, provided you keep the garlic, vinegar, ginger, and salt fairly stable. Less heat? Drop the cayenne to ½ teaspoon and add a little more cardamom to compensate. Don't like ground cloves? Try ground fenugreek instead.

In the end, you want a grainy paste, not smooth but with no garlic chunks in the mix. Scrape down the bowl of the processor or spice grinder several times—or keep working the pestle against the mortar's sides to grind everything to a grainy mush.

The paste will be aromatic in no time over the heat. Don't let it go too long or it will begin to burn and turn bitter. Stir constantly until the onions are well coated.

• **STEP 4** Raise the heat to medium-high and add 2½ pounds cubed stew meat or 4 pounds bone-in meat; cook, stirring constantly, just until it loses its raw, red color. Again, the color and depth of flavor will come from the spice paste. The meat need not brown; rather, it should simply change colors over the heat as you stir. You also don't want too much of its juice to evaporate; every last drop should get into the stew. But do trim the cuts so that there's not too much fat. No, you can't trim it all off—and shouldn't. But you can cut down a bit on what can become a greasy dish if you're not careful.

Consider any of these:

lamb—2½ pounds cubed lamb stew meat, leg of lamb, or deboned shoulder chops
beef—2½ pounds cubed top round, bottom round, chuck, shoulder, or stew meat
chicken—4 pounds skinless bone-in thighs
duck—4 pounds skinless legs
pork—2½ pounds cubed boneless loin, shoulder, or country-style boneless ribs

veal—2½ pounds cubed stew meat or shoulder

venison—2½ pounds cubed stew meat or leg

goat—2½ pounds cubed stew meat

Avoid fish, shellfish, and tofu. Yes, you can make these into vindaloo, but the spices have no time to develop complexity and the final dish is rarely satisfying.

• **STEP 5** Pour in ¾ cup broth, wine, or an enhanced version of either; bring to a simmer, cover, reduce the heat to low, and simmer slowly until tender, about 1½ to 2 hours. What liquid to use? Actually, there's a wide range. Consider the base as one of these: chicken, beef, or vegetable broth, white or red wine, or dry vermouth. Then mix it up with a combination of broth and wine. Or try ¼ cup dry vermouth or another dry fortified wine with ½ cup broth. You can also use ¼ cup cream with either ½ cup broth or wine—loads of richness in the aromatic stew. Or substitute ¼ cup coconut milk for the cream, adding another aromatic layer to the pot.

After you pour in the liquid, make sure you scrape off and dissolve any spices stuck to the pan's inner walls. After that, the only trick is to let the thing go slowly so that any collagen or connective tissue melts into the liquid and the meat gets quite tender. Although chicken thighs will be done in 40 minutes or so, they can hold up to longer stewing and should be left to braise so that the flavors permeate the meat. Other cuts—veal, lamb—will take the full time. And you'll only know by spearing a piece, cutting it, and tasting it. (And once you get some experience at this, you'll be able to tell if the meat's tender just by sticking a fork in it.) Indeed, if you've got 2 hours, let the stew simmer slowly the whole time.

If you'd rather not watch a pot for such a long time, dump the entire contents of the pan into a slow cooker, cover, set it on low, and let it go about 8 hours, an all-day treat for when you get home from work. Or make vindaloo the day before—it's quite nice after it's been refrigerated overnight. However, you may need to thin it out with a little extra broth or wine while it reheats. Freezing, however, is not recommended; the spices will be depressingly dulled.

SERVING SUGGESTIONS

Like all braises, vindaloo should be served in bowls; it also needs an aromatic rice. Basmati, white or brown, is best. Or serve it over Middle Eastern and East Indian varietals like jasmine, Texmati, Bhutanese red, wehani, or so-called "bamboo" (green) rice. Skip the rice altogether and ladle the stew over toasted stale bread rounds. Or try it over mashed potatoes, turnips, parsnips, or a combination of all three.

Vindaloo may taste very aromatic, but it can look dull in the bowl: just a brown stew. For a little color, sprinkle individual bowls with chopped cilantro, basil, or mint; perhaps diced peeled seeded mango, apple, or pears; and even dollops of plain yogurt.

Veal Vindaloo

Recipes for Vindaloos

	Lamb Vindaloo	Duck Vindaloo	Chicken Vindaloo	Goat Vindaloo
1. Heat	¼ cup canola oil	¼ cup ghee (see page 25)	¼ cup canola oil	¼ cup canola oil
2. Add and cook	3 medium yellow onions, halved and thinly sliced ¼ cup chopped dried mango	3 medium yellow onions, halved and thinly sliced ¼ cup chopped dried cherries	3 medium yellow onions, halved and thinly sliced ¼ cup chopped golden raisins	3 medium yellow onions, halved and thinly sliced ¼ cup chopped unsweetened coconut
3. Stir in	2 to 3 Tbs prepared vindaloo paste	2 to 3 Tbs prepared vindaloo paste	2 to 3 Tbs prepared vindaloo paste	2 to 3 Tbs prepared vindaloo paste
4. Add	2½ pounds lamb shoulder chop meat, deboned, trimmed, and roughly chopped	4 pounds skinless duck legs	4 pounds skinless bone-in chicken thighs	2½ pounds goat stew meat, cubed; or goat leg meat, trimmed and cubed
5. Pour in before covering and simmering	¾ chicken broth	½ cup chicken broth ¼ cup port	½ cup chicken broth ¼ cup dry white wine	½ cup dry white wine ¼ cup coconut milk

	Pork Vindaloo	Veal Vindaloo	Venison Vindaloo	Beef Vindaloo
1. Heat	¼ cup canola oil	¼ cup ghee (see page 25)	¼ cup canola oil	¼ cup ghee
2. Add and cook	3 medium yellow onions, halved and thinly sliced ¼ cup chopped dried pineapple	3 medium yellow onions, halved and thinly sliced ¼ cup chopped golden raisins	3 medium yellow onions, halved and thinly sliced ¼ cup chopped dried apricots	3 medium yellow onions, halved and thinly sliced ¼ cup chopped dried blueberries
3. Stir in	2 to 3 Tbs prepared vindaloo paste	2 to 3 Tbs prepared vindaloo paste	2 to 3 Tbs prepared vindaloo paste	2 to 3 Tbs prepared vindaloo paste
4. Add	2½ pounds pork loin, trimmed of fat and cubed	2½ pounds veal stew meat, trimmed and cubed	2½ pounds venison stew meat, trimmed and cubed	2½ pounds cubed trimmed beef bottom round
5. Pour in before covering and simmering	½ cup chicken broth ¼ coconut milk	½ cup chicken broth ¼ cup dry white wine	¾ cup red wine	¾ cup red wine

Index